T0323642

Employee Surveys and Sensing

THE SIOP PROFESSIONAL PRACTICE SERIES

Series Editor
Nancy T. Tippins

Titles in the Series
Performance Management Transformation: Lessons Learned and Next Steps
Edited by Elaine D. Pulakos and Mariangela Battista

Employee Surveys and Sensing: Challenges and Opportunities
Edited by William H. Macey and Alexis A. Fink

Employee Surveys and Sensing

Challenges and Opportunities

Edited by

WILLIAM H. MACEY

and

ALEXIS A. FINK

Published in partnership with

SOCIETY for INDUSTRIAL and ORGANIZATIONAL PSYCHOLOGY

SCIENCE FOR A SMARTER WORKPLACE

OXFORD
UNIVERSITY PRESS

OXFORD
UNIVERSITY PRESS

Oxford University Press is a department of the University of Oxford. It furthers
the University's objective of excellence in research, scholarship, and education
by publishing worldwide. Oxford is a registered trade mark of Oxford University
Press in the UK and certain other countries.

Published in the United States of America by Oxford University Press
198 Madison Avenue, New York, NY 10016, United States of America.

Library of Congress Cataloging-in-Publication Data
Names: Macey, William H., editor. | Fink, Alexis A., editor.
Title: Employee surveys and sensing : challenges and opportunities /
edited by William H. Macey and Alexis A. Fink.
Description: New York, NY : Oxford University Press, [2020] |
Series: The SIOP professional practice series |
Includes bibliographical references and index.
Identifiers: LCCN 2019044752 (print) | LCCN 2019044753 (ebook) |
ISBN 9780190939717 (hardback) | ISBN 9780190939731 (epub) |
ISBN 9780190939748 (online)
Subjects: LCSH: Employee attitude surveys. | Organizational effectiveness.
Classification: LCC HF5549.5.A83 E47 2020 (print) |
LCC HF5549.5.A83 (ebook) | DDC 658.3/140723—dc23
LC record available at https://lccn.loc.gov/2019044752
LC ebook record available at https://lccn.loc.gov/2019044753

For my grandchildren, Billy, Sarah, Brandon and Justin (WHM)

For my parents, Bill and Gerda, and my children, Kristiane, Jack and Ben (AAF)

Contents

Foreword   xi
About the Editors   xiii
Contributors   xv

1. *Surveys and Sensing: Realizing the Promise of Listening*
   to Employees   1
   William H. Macey and Alexis A. Fink

SECTION 1. SURVEYS AS A COMPONENT OF TALENT
ANALYTIC STRATEGY

2. Strategic Surveying for Driving Organizational Change:
   A Very 3M Story   23
   Karen B. Paul and Kristofer J. Fenlason

3. Improving the Design and Interpretation of Sample
   Surveys in the Workplace   38
   Paul M. Mastrangelo

4. Exploring the Universe of Pulse Surveys and Continuous
   Listening Opportunities   53
   Jeffrey A. Jolton and Cameron Klein

5. Lifecycle Surveys: Individual and Organizational Journeys   68
   Jeffrey M. Saltzman, Scott M. Brooks, and Victoria Hendrickson

6. Design and Application of Employee Engagement Surveys:
   An Evidence-Based Approach   86
   John P. Meyer

7. Focus Groups: Blending Qualitative and Quantitative
   Methodology to Improve the Survey Process   103
   Jeffrey M. Cucina and Ilene F. Gast

8. Strategic Climate Research: How What We Know Should
   Influence What We Do   121
   Benjamin Schneider

9. The Unique Role of Corporate Culture in Employee
   Listening Systems   135
   Daniel Denison, Marcus W. Dickson, Michelle W. Mullins,
   and Jessie Sanchez

10. Employee Preferences: Why They Matter and
    How to Measure Them   153
    Diane L. Daum and Jennifer A. Stoll

11. How Did We Do? Survey Benchmarking and Normative Data   171
    Elizabeth A. McCune and Sarah R. Johnson

12. Writing Organizational Survey Items That Predict
    What Matters in Organizations   186
    Daniel J. Ingels, Kathryn E. Keeton, and Christiane Spitzmueller

13. Open-Ended Questions: The Role of Natural Language
    Processing and Text Analytics   202
    Subhadra Dutta and Eric M. O'Rourke

14. Is the Engagement Survey the Only Way?
    Alternative Sources for Employee Sensing   219
    Madhura Chakrabarti and Elizabeth A. McCune

SECTION 2. ANALYZING DATA TO TELL
THE SURVEY STORY

15. Mechanics of Survey Data Analysis   239
    Melinda J. Moye and Alison L. O'Malley

16. Taking Action to Drive Change Through Survey Key
    Driver Analysis   254
    Jeff W. Johnson

17. Linkage Analysis: Tying Employee Attitudes to
    Business Outcomes   272
    Shawn M. Del Duco, Patrick K. Hyland, David W. Reeves,
    and Anthony W. Caputo

18. Optimizing Differences Between Groups Is Important:
    Examples from Applied Settings   288
    Paul D. Bliese, Eliza W. Wicher, and Dhuha Abdulsalam

19. Data Visualization   306
    Evan F. Sinar

20. Creating and Delivering the Executive Presentation: Telling the Story of the Survey   324
Sarah R. Johnson

21. Action Taking Augmented by Artificial Intelligence   338
Sara P. Weiner and Melissa McMahan

SECTION 3. CHALLENGES AND OPPORTUNITIES

22. Rediscovering the Art of Surveys for Organization Change   357
Allan H. Church and Janine Waclawski

23. Employee Survey Research: A Critical Review of Theory and Practice   374
Lewis K. Garrad and Patrick K. Hyland

24. From Identified Surveys to New Technologies: Employee Privacy and Ethical Considerations   391
Lise M. Saari and Charles A. Scherbaum

25. Managing Workplace Job Attitudes and Performance in Organizations with Labor Unions   407
James K. Harter and Denise R. McLain

SECTION 4. THE STATUS QUO AND THE CONTINUING EVOLUTION OF SURVEY RESEARCH

26. Current and Future Trends in Employee Survey Practice: A View from Employee Survey Practitioners   425
Christopher T. Rotolo, Christina R. Fleck, and Brittnie Shepherd

27. Employee Surveys Move into the Future: A Tale of Evolution, Revolution, and Speed Bumps   443
Allen I. Kraut

Name Index   461
Subject Index   473

Foreword

The Professional Practice Series plays a major role in achieving SIOP's goal to be the premier professional group advancing the science and practice of the psychology of work, and the series publisher is an important factor in the editorial board's ability to fulfill this mission. During my tenure as editor (2013–2019), SIOP identified a new publisher, Oxford University Press, for the series. To date, Oxford University Press has been an enthusiastic partner in meeting the challenges of identifying timely and appropriate topics, publishing useful and informative books, and bringing them to market.

At the same time that a new publisher for the Professional Practice Series was identified, the editorial board also made the decision to include volumes on the "basics" into its plans for new books and develop volumes focused on "core" industrial–organizational (I-O) psychology topics that include the latest research and best practices. This current volume in SIOP's Professional Practice Series, *Employee Surveys and Sensing: Challenges and Opportunities*, edited by William H. Macey and Alexis A. Fink, is the second "back to basics" effort.

Surveys remain popular tools in business today, and many I-O psychologists use them in their practice and research. Two of the bestselling volumes in the Professional Practice Series were on surveys: *Organizational Surveys* (1996) and *Getting Action from Organizational Surveys* (2006), both edited by Allen Kraut. Much in the world of surveys has changed since these volumes were published, and the editorial board felt strongly that it was time to offer a new book that updates survey research and practice. Bill and Alexis have stepped up to that challenge and coedited a book that will be a useful reference for practitioners and researchers.

Employee Surveys and Sensing: Challenges and Opportunities covers traditional survey methods and emerging methods for sensing. Older practices such as annual surveys, newer ones such as pulse surveys and continuous listening, and the advantages and disadvantages of each are addressed in the context of a workforce that has concerns about privacy and transparency and organizations that require strong business cases for all human resources initiatives. The book's chapters summarize the science of surveys as well as the lessons learned from real-world experience.

The book comprises four sections. The first discusses surveys as a component of talent analytic strategy, including the role of surveys, the constructs to be measured, sampling, and timing. The second reviews data-analysis approaches ranging from basic analyses to linkage research and multilevel analysis. This section also provides material on telling a compelling story with tools including data visualization. The third section identifies the difficult questions survey practitioners must answer and explores the challenges and opportunities in survey research. The chapters in the final section conclude the book with chapters on the current state of survey practice and the continuing evolution of survey practice.

The editors of this volume, Bill Macey and Alexis Fink, are survey experts. Both have spent many years working the field, delivering sophisticated survey programs, and researching some of the thorny questions that arise with surveys. Bill and Alexis are joined by other survey experts who have authored the 27 chapters of this book. These authors present many different ideas on survey methods and offer an array of perspectives.

Edited books like this one require an extraordinary amount of time and energy. Bill and Alexis have done a masterful job of organizing this book, selecting a team of authors, and shepherding each chapter to completion. Similarly, writing a chapter is no trivial undertaking. Moreover, the extrinsic rewards associated with contributing to a SIOP book series hardly compensate the editors and authors for the tremendous amount of time and effort spent to bring this volume to fruition. I am grateful to Bill and Alexis and all the chapter authors for their hard work, and I thank them all for their contributions to SIOP and the Professional Practice Series. I hope you will enjoy this book and find it useful in your work.

Elaine Pulakos is the new editor for the Professional Practice Series. I am confident that she and her team will continue to advance the practice and science of I-O psychology and generate books that highlight best practices as well as science.

Nancy T. Tippins
Series Editor
2013–2019
September 2019

About the Editors

William H. Macey, Ph.D., is Senior Research Fellow at CultureFactors, Inc. He was the CEO of Valtera Corporation for 35 years until the acquisition of Valtera by CEB in 2012. A SIOP past-president, he is a Fellow of SIOP, APA, and APS and was recipient of SIOP's Distinguished Professional Contributions Award in 2017. He is a member of the editorial board of the *Journal of Business and Psychology*. He received his Ph.D. from Loyola University Chicago in 1975 in Experimental Psychology. His current professional interests include organizational surveys, culture and climate, and leader assessment. Some of his more widely cited publications include "The Meaning of Employee Engagement" (Macey & Schneider, 2008); and "Employee Engagement: Tools for Analysis, Practice, and Competitive Advantage" (Macey, Schneider, Barbera, & Young, 2009).

Alexis A. Fink, Ph.D., is Vice President, People Analytics and Workforce Strategy at Facebook. She has previously held similar roles at Microsoft and Intel, as well as extensive work in organizational transformation, organizational culture, leadership assessment, and the application of advanced analytical methods to human capital problems. She is a Fellow of SIOP, and was recipient of SIOP's Distinguished Service Award in 2019, and was Chair of the IT Survey Group, an industry consortium dedicated to employee surveys. She earned her Ph.D. in Industrial/Organizational Psychology at Old Dominion University in 2000. She also serves as the Practice Editor for *Industrial and Organizational Psychology: Perspectives on Science and Practice*.

Contributors

Dhuha Abdulsalam
Department of Marketing and
Management
College of Business Administration
Kuwait University

Paul D. Bliese
Professor
Darla Moore School of Business
University of South Carolina

Scott M. Brooks
Partner and Vice President,
Consulting
OrgVitality, LLC

Anthony W. Caputo
Vice President of People Science
Remesh.ai

Madhura Chakrabarti
Global Head
People Insights & Analytics
Syngenta

Allan H. Church
Senior Vice President
Global Talent Assessment &
Development
PepsiCo

Jeffrey M. Cucina
Personnel Research Psychologist
U.S. Customs and Border Protection

Diane L. Daum
Principal Strategist
CultureIQ

Shawn M. Del Duco
Director
HR Business Insights
VMware, Inc.

Daniel Denison
Professor Emeritus
IMD Business School

Marcus W. Dickson
Professor of Psychology
Wayne State University

Subhadra Dutta
Director
People Science & Analytics
Stitch Fix

Kristofer J. Fenlason
Global Surveys Leader
HR Strategy & Culture
3M

Alexis A. Fink
Vice President
People Analytics and Workforce
Strategy
Facebook

Christina R. Fleck
Performance Analytics & Interventions
Manager
Deloitte

Lewis K. Garrad
Partner
Mercer

Ilene F. Gast
Personnel Research Psychologist
(Retired)
U.S. Customs and Border
Protection

James K. Harter
Chief Workplace Scientist
Gallup

Victoria Hendrickson
Partner & Vice President
OrgVitality, LLC

Patrick K. Hyland
Director of Research & Development
Mercer | Sirota

Daniel J. Ingels
Doctoral Candidate
University of Houston

Jeff W. Johnson
Principal Research Scientist
SHL

Sarah R. Johnson
Vice President
Enterprise Surveys and Analytics
Perceptyx, Inc.

Jeffrey A. Jolton
Managing Director
People Analytics Practice
PwC

Kathryn E. Keeton
Managing Consultant
Minerva Work Solutions

Cameron Klein
Manager
People Analtyics Practice
PwC

Allen I. Kraut
Professor Emeritus
Baruch College
City University of New York
President
Kraut Associates

William H. Macey
Senior Research Fellow
CultureFactors, Inc.

Paul M. Mastrangelo
Principal Strategist
CultureIQ

Elizabeth A. McCune
Director
Employee Listening and Culture
Measurement
Microsoft

Denise R. McLain
Senior Practice Expert & Principal
Gallup, Inc.

Melissa McMahan
Principal Consultant
Glint

John P. Meyer
Professor
Department of Psychology
The University of Western Ontario
Adjunct Professor
Curtin School of Business
Curtin University

Melinda J. Moye
Manager, Employee Engagement
Analytics & Innovation
Talent Management
Deere & Company

Michelle W. Mullins
Director of Research and
Development
Denison Consulting, LLC

Alison L. O'Malley
Senior Behavioral Scientist
BetterUp

Eric M. O'Rourke
People Analytics Manager
Facebook

Karen B. Paul
Executive Planning Leader
Human Resources
3M

David W. Reeves
Senior Consultant
Mercer | Sirota

Christopher T. Rotolo
Vice President, Global Talent
Management & Organization
Development
PepsiCo, Inc.

Lise M. Saari
Adjunct Professor
Department of Psychology
New York University and
Baruch College

Jeffrey M. Saltzman
CEO
OrgVitality, LLC

Jessie Sanchez
Graduate Student
Wayne State University

Charles A. Scherbaum
Professor
Department of Psychology
Baruch College, City University
of New York

Benjamin Schneider
Professor Emeritus
University of Maryland

Brittnie Shepherd
Leadership Specialist
Russell Reynolds Associates

Evan F. Sinar
Head of Assessments
BetterUp

Christiane Spitzmueller
Professor of Psychology
University of Houston

Jennifer A. Stoll
Principal Strategist
CultureIQ

Janine Waclawski
Senior Vice President of Human
Resources
Chief Human Resources Officer,
Latin America
PepsiCo

Sara P. Weiner
Principal Advisor, Glint
and Independent Consultant

Eliza W. Wicher
Global Head of Talent Development
Groupon

1

Surveys and Sensing

Realizing the Promise of Listening to Employees

William H. Macey and Alexis A. Fink

Talent analytics has risen to the top of the HR agenda since at least 2010 (Davenport, Harris, & Shapiro, 2010). Talent analytics helps organizations to optimize the talents and energy that employees bring to work and at the same time to create an environment and employment brand that attract and retain talented people. Increasingly, it is a business imperative to identify, collect, analyze, and act on data aligned to these priorities.

Organizational surveys have long been used to identify issues and concerns regarding employee morale and welfare and today remain a primary source of the data most useful for talent analytics. Their predominance as a source of data results from the fact that they allow for a planned, thoughtful, and comparative approach to the information-gathering process.

A good deal of what we know about survey design, administration, analysis, and follow-through had been developed and institutionalized in a number of active survey programs by the early 1970s. Indeed, much of what is considered conventional wisdom is available in a significant number of books, monographs, and, to a lesser extent, journal articles. Viewing survey practices through a historical lens can tell us more than simply what has changed. The lessons learned by those in the survey research community can and should be of particular value to those both new and old to the field. Schneider (Chapter 8) provides a thoughtful history of the evolution of engagement and climate thinking, and Kraut (Chapter 27) provides a perspective on survey practices that have evolved along with a view of what comes next.

William H. Macey and Alexis A. Fink, *Surveys and Sensing* In: *Employee Surveys and Sensing*. Edited by: William H. Macey and Alexis A. Fink, Oxford University Press (2020). © Society for Industrial and Organizational Psychology. DOI: 10.1093/oso/9780190939717.003.0001

A Changing Survey Research Landscape

Change in survey methodology is inevitable and welcome. Garrad and Hyland (Chapter 23) note that survey methodology was born in the 20th century and that some of the assumptions behind that methodology are outdated and represent significant shortcomings. Not surprisingly, some very significant differences of opinion regarding survey practices have surfaced, some from observers outside our field (Bersin, 2014) and some reflecting sources of tension within the science-practitioner model (Rotolo et al., 2018).

We, like many others who are active survey research practitioners, have the palpable sense that the context in which surveys are conducted and the manner in which they are deployed is shifting, perhaps even radically, as new methods such as always-on pulsing (Chapter 4), new data sources such as passive gathering of sentiment (Chapter 14), and new approaches to reporting and action-planning (Chapter 21) emerge. That said, the data and our perception do not entirely match. Rotolo, Fleck, and Shepherd (Chapter 26) provide a data-based description of organizational survey practices as of the time that work on this volume began; readers may note that while the landscape is indeed changing, it is perhaps evolving more slowly than some might have expected. Similarly, data reported by the HR Institute indicate that while organizations are giving consideration to using "new ways to acquire more frequent and better-focused employee feedback" (HR.com, 2019, p. 18), the majority of organizations still measure employee engagement using an annual survey.

This view—perhaps one looking more to the future than to the present—is worth deconstructing. Many champions of these evolving approaches suggest that employee feedback should be gathered more frequently and that the quality of feedback provided from the traditional annual survey is lacking in relevance or timeliness (or both), resulting in lower usefulness. This impression is in no small part a reflection of the marketing practices of the technology firms in the space as well as consultancies that leverage technology assets in their survey practice.

Several specific areas of the emerging trends are noteworthy, and readers will find multiple references to these throughout the volume. It will be no surprise that these issues are largely reflections of changes in the technology landscape, either directly or as consequences of the use of technology. As Kraut (Chapter 27) notes, it is difficult to discuss the evolution of survey methods apart from the impact of new technologies that have significantly shaped how organizations think about the advanced talent analytics.

A Push Toward Continuous Listening

Survey programs must necessarily meet stakeholder expectations. The aggregate investment of time across an organization to conduct, analyze, and share survey findings has long been considered disquieting. Not surprisingly, then, organizational surveys have become increasingly shorter, a phenomenon arguably the result of stakeholder demands. At the same time, there has also been a push toward "continuous listening."

The conversation represents a distinct turn in thinking about surveys, from an annual event to data collection in a continuous stream of information gathering and data sharing. This is variously operationalized as (1) the use of frequent "pulse" surveys (see Jolton & Klein, Chapter 4) and lifecycle surveys (see Saltzman, Brooks, & Hendrickson, Chapter 5) in addition to or in replacement of the traditional annual survey (Johnson, 2018) and/or (2) the use of several or more alternative devices for discerning employee behaviors, affect, and decisions/choices and linking those data to important talent management considerations in the areas of employee attraction, recruitment, retention, and engagement. Technology has made it simple to quickly author and deploy surveys at remarkably low cost. Indeed, some technology vendors recommend that managers should use survey technology to ramp up their personal feedback cycle. This raises concerns for survey fatigue and the integrity of the survey process from both an ethical and a psychometric standpoint. Moreover, this represents a clear risk to the strategic intent of the survey effort (see Paul & Fenlason, Chapter 2, and Church & Waclawski, Chapter 22).

Thus, there are significant pitfalls in deploying pulse strategies, including the unintended consequences of oversurveying and lower response rates that follow from a lack of necessary communication and buy-in to the survey process. Jolton and Klein (Chapter 4) provide a complete discussion of the benefits and limitations of strategies and speak specifically to considerations of cadence and survey length.

Pulse surveys are often deployed in a context where respondents are sampled from the employee population, perhaps to minimize costs, survey fatigue, and disruption. Sampling strategies pose particular problems to the interpretation of results when sampling error is not taken into consideration, a very real likelihood when survey ownership is transferred to line managers in the name of continuous feedback. Mastrangelo (Chapter 3) provides an overview of relevant sampling methods and concerns. Across Chapters 3 and 4, readers will find a balanced treatment of the pros and cons of pulse surveys as well as implementation considerations to support practitioners in thoughtfully designing their own employee research programs.

The Evolution of Data and Technology

The evolution of data and technology is likely the greatest force contributing to innovation in employee surveys and sensing. New data sources are becoming available due to the ubiquity of technology in our workplaces. New approaches to data storage, analysis, and reporting are becoming more available as computing power increases in speed and availability.

Just as consumer information can be mined to identify what is relevant to market to specific individuals, the vast amount of information available about what employees do, where they are, with whom they interact, and so on seemingly provides a fertile ground for understanding how employee opinions emerge and translate into individual and team performance. Moreover, the vast scale and continuous flow of these data are exactly what is needed to leverage the potential of artificial intelligence (AI) and machine learning algorithms to find subtle or complex patterns in the data, especially those that might not be illuminated using more traditional methods. Some of these new data sources have the benefit of bypassing employees' recollections or estimates and directly recording, for example, the nature and frequency of interactions among a group of employees. It is also within this context that the claim of relevance is made for data passively collected in the normal course of business. Chakrabarti and McCune (Chapter 14) discuss these sensing mechanisms in detail.

It is no secret that organizations are making large investments in the application of AI to resolve information-management challenges. This trend has also extended to employee-focused feedback systems. Employee survey and sensing vendors are increasingly providing options for real-time data reporting. Additionally, there are now competitive offerings in the marketplace that claim to rely on AI for delivering both more immediate and salient feedback from survey results. Weiner and McMahan (Chapter 21) provide a discussion of current practice around reporting and in particular the role that AI can play in honing action planning. There is great promise for the democratization of expert coaching to managers through these AI tools. However, there is also a good deal of work ahead of us as a field to fully deliver on that potential; applications of new technologies including AI and machine learning have disappointed early adopters (Kaur & Fink, 2017).

Historically, one of the most challenging aspects of survey interpretation has been the analysis of written comments. Larger organizations may have many tens of thousands of written comments, and while individual managers or leaders may read many or all of their comments, analysis at the enterprise level generally remains difficult and time consuming. For decades, automated analysis was limited largely to crude keyword searches. Advances in computing power and natural language processing (NLP) have dramatically improved organizations' ability to process and find themes in large amounts of unstructured data such as survey comments. Dutta and O'Rourke (Chapter 13) provide a thorough overview of methods and key considerations for deploying NLP as part of an employee research program.

New data streams and faster, more flexible reporting are important innovations. However, employee research is fundamentally a meaning-making exercise. Machine learning and AI also bring new potential to our ability to detect patterns among our data. First, "unsupervised" learning is useful for defining a sense of structure to data, as in identifying the number of distinct topics that emerge in employee comments. It should be obvious that interpretation rests with the survey researcher. Second, "supervised" learning serves to uncover relationships between important outcome measures (such as retention/attrition) and patterns of individual difference measures using a statistical algorithm. That said, the appropriate method for analyzing data is not necessarily obvious, particularly with respect to the interactions among variables. Some models fare better (i.e., are more accurate in cross-validation) in capturing complex interaction patterns that are at the heart of person-centric thinking. Person-centric analyses center on individual patterns of data from multiple measures; that is, each person is represented by a profile of measures (e.g., engagement, network centrality, tenure). Profiles may be derived from data at the same or different points of time (including trajectories). Person-centric analyses have been far less evident in the industrial–organizational (I-O) literature, although relevant notable exceptions include the work of John Meyer and his associates on commitment profiles (e.g., Meyer, Stanley, & Parfyonova, 2012) and certain aspects of the interpersonal personality literature. Particularly worth noting is that the use of *identifiable* data information (needed to create personal profiles) has very significant implications for ensuring confidentiality, much less anonymity. Further, the requirement for potentially large quantities of identifiable information raises concerns about privacy.

Meeting Concerns for Privacy and Transparency

The choice to administer an identifiable survey is simply one of the most important decisions made in survey program design. Moye and O'Malley (Chapter 15) discuss the considerations necessary for conducting identifiable yet confidential survey research. Yet, data management is often overlooked as a source of both effort and time, and this is particularly true in a world of "always-on" survey data collection. As readers consider the application of newer technologies, they may find it particularly relevant to ask how the protections of rigorous data management can be achieved as data later become aggregated through person-centric analyses, particularly in real time where the mechanisms to ensure privacy must continually look to what has been previously analyzed and reported. Thus, simple decision rules around minimum n reporting requirements do not work when data are constantly updated and queried.

Also, with broader emphasis on sensing and listening, there is a need to critically evaluate the ethics of data collection and use. For example, Waber (2013) describes the particular challenges in ensuring confidentiality using sociometric badges (anonymity is impossible). Sensing methods may also be perceived akin to electronic surveillance. To that point, Yost, Behrend, Howardson, Darrow, and Jenson (2019) suggest that people who are high on trait reactance may react negatively to electronic monitoring regardless of the purpose of that surveillance. More generally, the requirements of the General Data Protection Regulation of the European Union (European Parliament, 2016) and pending state regulations within the United States (e.g., the California Consumer Privacy Act of 2018) have significant implications for obtaining informed consent as to how personal data are both gathered and used. Saari and Scherbaum (Chapter 24) provide a critical evaluation of transparency and privacy concerns as they impact the organizational survey process.

Survey Science and Data Science

Organizational survey science is essentially about gathering intelligence from informed observers of the organization, typically employees. Survey development follows a logical progression, balancing both inductive and deductive processes. That is, the researcher gathers preliminary information, often using qualitative methods such as focus groups and interviews. These are conducted with key stakeholders to construct a pool of survey items that represent reasonable hypotheses about what is important to measure. Survey development may also benefit from what is known about key constructs (see Ingels, Keeton, & Spitzmueller, Chapter 12). Data science provides useful exploratory techniques for analyzing data and potentially for predicting important outcomes.

Three observations are worth noting when considering the marriage of survey research and data science:

- First, surveys ask questions, and the value derived from the survey effort depends completely on what is measured. Crafting good survey questions takes skill, and the amount of effort and time required is easily underestimated. Even practitioners who wish to use ambient data must carefully consider what to measure and in what way.
- Second, systems supporting action planning have long been the Achilles heel of survey efforts. AI, or any other form of data science, cannot in itself provide for a better solution than that which can be identified in the data. Survey science is thus about assembling the right information to analyze, whether acquired through traditional survey questions or by means of other methods.
- Third, it is in the end up to "management" to take action, whether directly or through shared participation with organization members. Yes, technology can assist in the effort, and Weiner and McMahan (Chapter 21) argue convincingly that AI can help to both "nudge" managers along as well as give guidance. The reality is that that successful employee listening programs have the support of strong change management and organization development (OD) expertise.

Readers should not take our comments to imply that technological shifts will fail to greatly enhance the efficiency and quality of survey processes. To the contrary, innovations driven by both commercial and academic interests (e.g., applications of text analytics for comment analysis) have become both more practical and financially viable. Most importantly, leveraging technology has the very real potential of accelerating action, both from the data-collection and the data-analytic standpoints. To emphasize our point, the benefits of leveraging technology are realized by our clients only when built upon a solid foundation of survey design and OD practices.

Yet, it is clear that employee sensing and survey practitioners will need to become conversant in the more advanced methods of data science. For example, one important issue that should be given careful consideration is the reliance on consultancies to develop the "intelligence" on which recommendations are derived; the process by which this work is accomplished can be less than transparent. Effective management of a survey program thus requires at least an understanding of how those analytics are applied.

Challenges and Opportunities in Survey Practice

Given the history of employee survey research, it might be expected that best practices—acceptable to both scientific and practice communities—might be readily identifiable. There are indeed many, but there remain considerable areas where conflicting views exist with respect to both reasonable and good practice. This volume highlights a number of the opportunities and challenges and differences of opinion that define the current employee survey landscape.

Focusing on the Right Content

Engagement
It is obvious that determining the survey focus is paramount. Yet, organizations continue to conduct surveys that are topical and based on what is on the shelf in the airport bookstore. Perhaps the most egregious example is the now ubiquitous engagement survey, which, after having been the survey focus de jour for more than a decade, has now given way to concepts such as organizational health, employee well-being, and the employee experience. This growing disaffection with engagement is in no small part due to the fact that the employee engagement construct remains loosely defined by many

practitioners and operationally defined in ways that are no different from satisfaction and commitment (Macey & Schneider, 2008). This is one area where science and practice have diverged perhaps to the detriment of ongoing survey programs. Fortunately, Meyer (Chapter 6) clarifies the effects of related attitudinal constructs (such as satisfaction, commitment, work engagement) on different behavioral engagement outcomes (such as retention, citizenship behavior) and thus integrates a long and important stream of academic research with the divergent thinking represented in some engagement survey practices.

The Employee Experience

The shelf life of popular management concepts may be limited, but the basic management problems remain. For example, recently, the popular management press has elevated the notion of managing the "employee experience" as the ultimate talent management challenge. This reflects the competition for talent, where employees know or at least believe that if their expectations are not met, they will be able to find an employer who will meet their needs. That said, the "employee experience" is not a monolithic concept, although for the present purposes it can be regarded as a composite impression characterized by specific encounters between the individual and the organization including peers, leadership, one's manager, and various work-flow systems such as technology and physical space. Over time, the pattern of these experiences can be described as a journey, with some experiences being particularly salient for how the individuals evaluate their relationship to their work and organization (Erickson & Gratton, 2007).

The Employee Lifecycle

The emphasis on the journey highlights the importance of recognizing measurement opportunities throughout the employee life cycle and stresses the role of employees' expectations and early experiences as well as their ongoing reactions to the employee value proposition (EVP). Saltzman et al. (Chapter 5) detail the considerations of applying survey research to the various phases of the employee journey from onboarding to exit. Daum and Stoll (Chapter 10) speak to the various attributes that define the EVP and reveal how those attributes can be incorporated in survey content to better understand how expectations develop and determine engagement and retention. Outside the discussion of AI applications, person-centric analyses are particularly useful for identifying patterns that define classes or groups of people who share values and expectations in common. Once these patterns are identified, organizations can build personas and design the appropriate recruitment and retention efforts (Shepherd, 2014). The kinds of survey questions appropriate for evaluating the employee experience may very likely extend beyond the traditional Likert format, particularly for measuring employee preferences and values; for example, ranking exercises and conjoint studies can be quite useful. Also of particular current interest is the use of machine learning to identify patterns within a larger body of employee data that are predictive of individual outcomes.

Well-being

With the positive psychology movement, well-being is certainly not a new area of academic interest but has gained status as a focus of talent analytics, in part because of an increasing emphasis on employee wellness (Hyland, Caputo, & Reeves, 2018), holistic well-being (VirginPulse, 2017), and the links between employee wellness, engagement, and productivity (Kaplan, DeShon, & Tetrick, 2017).

Employee Sentiment

Related to the emphasis on well-being is a renewed interest in employee sentiment, perhaps most notably represented in the response to the question, "How likely are you to recommend your organization as a place to work?" Sentiment is an evaluative construct, and the manner in which it is determined generally focuses on what people say more than on what they actually do (there may be exceptions such as in facial expression and approach or avoidance behaviors). *Sentiment* refers to the valence of a topic or object and is very different from the descriptive content that comprises behavioral engagement measures or the reporting of organizational conditions such as those captured in strategic climate surveys.

Sentiment analytics has value to the extent that it is attached to a specific topic and to the extent that insight into corrective action follows. Employee sentiment is expressed in variety of ways that are accessible to survey researchers that extend beyond the traditional survey research paradigm. One of the most notable and visible to executives is the "star rating" found on employee review sites such as Glassdoor or work-related comments found on Twitter.

Employee sentiment is also frequently captured through written comments, either as part of an organizational survey or through other channels such as comments or posts on an organization's intranet or collaboration platform. Dutta and O'Rourke (Chapter 13) address the use of NLP to analyze such text-based data.

Organization Strategy

In potential contrast to a focus on employee experiences and well-being, there is a growing emphasis on the use of surveys to support the execution of organizational strategy. While employee engagement nominally remains a focus of many surveys, many organizational survey efforts leverage the capacity of employees to report on their observations regarding climate and culture specifically as they relate to organizational goals.

Paul and Fenlason (Chapter 2) offer 11 lessons from their collective experience in designing surveys that take a long-term perspective on creating and enhancing competitive advantage. They emphasize in particular that their clients for these efforts are the top leaders in their organization. Speaking directly to this motivation, Schneider (Chapter 8) provides detailed examples of survey items that are highly useful for creating surveys that generate outcomes strongly linked to what matters most to the sponsors of survey research (i.e., organizationally relevant criteria). Creating surveys with a strategic emphasis implies the development of content that is precisely descriptive of the conditions that are relevant to producing positive organizational outcomes. Methods and criteria in linkage research at the unit level are addressed in detail by Del Duco, Hyland, Reeves, and Caputo (Chapter 17).

Determining the Appropriate Survey Population

In this context it is worth noting that not all survey questions are intended or even appropriate for organization-wide administration. In other words, the choice of survey content is relative to both the topics and the population of interest. For example, leadership surveys are often used in organizations to address specific issues focusing on strategy creation and execution (see Paul & Fenlason, Chapter 2). Onboarding, exit, and alumni surveys (see Saltzman et al., Chapter 5) represent other examples of surveys targeted at specific populations. Some contexts are sufficiently different that special consideration is due. Thus, Harter and McLain (Chapter 25) discuss the nuances of survey-based research and taking action in the unionized setting.

Meaning-Making

Benchmarking

Employee sensing is, at its core, an exercise in meaning-making. Organizations seek to understand what is working well or what their employees value. If one were to examine the surveys in the organizations with long-standing survey programs, a considerable degree of similarity would be evident. Some of this similarity among those organizations is due to the fact that many of these organizations have membership in one of the major survey consortia such as Mayflower or the Information Technology Survey Group (ITSG; see McCune & Johnson, Chapter 11, and Kraut, Chapter 27) or because many organizations rely on the proprietary survey content of their survey provider/vendor. Because survey stakeholders often require historical and/or benchmark comparisons, there is a need for identical wording and common response scale formats (see McCune & Johnson, Chapter 11) across organizations and time. Thus, there is often significant pressure to maintain the survey status quo. Nonetheless, the move toward a continuous listening paradigm has initiated the need for more frequent changes to survey content. Yet, survey real estate is typically a scarce commodity; and thus, survey development requires significant crafting of items and pilot testing prior to deployment. The push to quickly deploy surveys in a rapid feedback cycle very much works against good survey design. Survey design principles are discussed in detail by Ingels et al. (Chapter 12). Cucina and Gast (Chapter 7) discuss the use of focus groups in developing and evaluating survey content. Bliese, Wicher, and Abdulsalam (Chapter 18) provide a unique perspective on selecting items that best account for between-group variance.

Leveraging Qualitative Data

Open-ended survey comments can greatly enrich the understanding of quantitative data and can lead to otherwise unanticipated insight. As noted earlier (see "Employee Sentiment"), text-based content (Dutta & O'Rourke, Chapter 13) can be efficiently parsed into content themes and sentiment through modern NLP methods. Also, focus groups and similar methods have long been regarded as useful for understanding quantitative results and identifying next steps for taking action. Cucina and Gast (Chapter 7) provide a detailed guide to their use.

Identifying the Appropriate Level of Analysis

Organizational survey data have traditionally been interpreted at the individual level even when the items are framed at the team or organizational level. Consideration of the appropriate level of analysis is important for determining how data are analyzed, including the psychometric methods used, and has implications for taking corrective action as a result of findings. Attention to levels of analysis issues is particularly important to climate and culture surveys when the organization is the unit of analysis (see Chapter 9 by Denison, Dickson, Mullins, & Sanchez). Thus, what matters most in many applications is whether survey items capture between-group differences. Bliese et al. (Chapter 18) discuss and demonstrate the appropriate analyses and provide source code examples to facilitate their implementation.

Identifying Key Drivers

Executives often expect answers to their questions about what is most important in the survey results so that actions and responses can be focused in the most efficient and effective way. Survey practitioners have used various forms of regression-based analytics for decades to identify key drivers of survey-measured outcomes. Prototypical are analyses intended to identify the most important correlates of intent to stay, overall organizational satisfaction, organizational commitment, or an engagement index. Following Jeff Johnson's seminal article (2000), many survey practitioners adopted relative weights analysis as a preferred method of identifying key drivers and (appropriately) abandoned the practice of simply reporting correlations.

Importantly, not all practitioners agree on the best approach to survey key driver analysis (SKDA). Cucina, Walmsley, Gast, Martin, and Curtin (2017; also see Chapter 7) argue that SKDA is often inappropriately applied and that advanced analytic methods cannot fully guide the action-planning process. Kraut (2017) directly argues that SKDA is "falsely comforting" (p. 266) and suggests that survey practitioners need to rather focus on using OD methods to explore the meaning and follow-up steps to survey implementation. Jeff Johnson (Chapter 16) provides a critical review of both the methods of and the limitations on how they should be applied and interpreted.

Communicating Survey Findings and Taking Action

Real-Time Feedback

Newer survey technology now allows real-time reporting. This can be especially useful where organizations use pulsing strategies that update results frequently and for which elaborate rollout schedules are unreasonably cumbersome. In this context, the local manager is seen as the owner of the survey results who can use the data to the best advantage, typically in a fairly agile and responsive way. Proponents of this thinking argue that the traditional census survey is irrelevant, in large part because of the delays in reporting that have historically been characteristic of a top-down results dissemination process. While clearly trendsetting, if not popular, when judged by the comments of industry observers (e.g., Bersin, 2014), this shift in deployment strategy is not without accompanying challenges.

Executive Presentations

Executive buy-in is a clearly important element of a successful survey program. Paul and Fenlason (Chapter 2) provide powerful examples of gaining exposure and relevance to C-suite executives. The executive presentation is the key moment in the survey program cycle. This is a "make or break" moment for the I-O professional as executives have expectations for a succinct and compelling meeting whether delivered personally or virtually. Sarah Johnson (Chapter 20) details the need for creating a story that communicates the key findings with the appropriate level of detail. Preparation is key, and successful delivery depends heavily on knowing the audience. Visualizations (see Sinar, Chapter 19) are particularly important, so details like the room and setting are important considerations for their use. It is a fact that the skills needed to deliver an executive presentation are developed over time and through experience with senior audiences. That said, the advice provided by Johnson will greatly help both new and seasoned practitioners.

Ownership of Results

Church and Waclawski (Chapter 22) describe in detail the differences between survey programs designed to emphasize quick feedback at the local level from programs intended to foster organizational change. Readers may want to read their chapter immediately after having read Chapter 21, where Weiner and McMahan argue for the benefits that are realized from AI-augmented action taking. It is also worth noting that a focus on prodding local leaders to action may need to be made in a broader context of what is strategically relevant.

Balancing Science and Practice Considerations

The growing interest in pulse surveys illustrates what seems to some a basis for tension between scientist and practitioner. The requirement for shorter surveys often means that themes are represented by only single survey items. In the peer-reviewed literature, great emphasis is made on the development of measures that are reliable and fit in a nomological net that establishes their construct validity. In that context, it is reasonable to presume that multiple items, reflective of the underlying construct, will be written, thus comprising a scale that is internally consistent. Some (see Ingels et al., Chapter 12) argue that this is the only method of survey development that is acceptable in a science-based community. Some practitioners will plainly say their organization cannot support the use of lengthy surveys comprised of numerous multi-item scales. Consequently, in many organizational surveys each item may serve a unique focus or construct and is regarded as interpretable at that level; reliability is achieved though the aggregation of data across individuals. Also, many organization surveys measure constructs with a formative rather than a reflective model. Perhaps the most notable example is the Gallup Q^{12} (Harter & McLain, Chapter 25), where engagement is measured by the conditions which are believed to cause it. This is not dissimilar to how certain global climate (e.g., service climate; see Schneider, Chapter 8) constructs are measured. The point is that reconciliation of the views of the peer reviewer and the practitioner may seem unachievable.

Both sides of this disagreement are represented in this volume. On the one hand, it is worth noting that in many instances the use of well-constructed multi-item scales has very practical benefits. A twist on an old adage might be "there is nothing as practical as a multi-item scale." Schneider (Chapter 8) argues forcefully that surveys should include at least one "bundle" of items that measure what is important to management, that the bundle is needed precisely because a single item cannot possibly provide an unambiguous example of all that matters, and that this has implications in turn for the evaluation of climate strength. Jeff Johnson (Chapter 16) argues that key driver analyses are best conducted first at the dimension (scale) level and then secondarily at the item level separately for the key dimensions. Thus, there are also very practical reasons to recommend the development of well-formed multi-item indices. On the other hand, these arguments may nonetheless not satisfy the executive who sets the boundaries on the domains of interest as well as survey length. What we hope is that readers will find in the volume the information that will help them better understand the tradeoffs in the choices they make, even if that is sometimes disquieting.

What is critical is that survey data must be interpretable within the context of the survey objectives. In many contexts, this includes using data from individual items as part of a feedback and action-planning sequence (see Cucina & Gast, Chapter 7, and S. Johnson, Chapter 20); and in others, well-developed scales are both necessary and desirable. Readers will hopefully recognize that reconciliation among views is possible when one steps back from considering a specific survey to reflect on the potential of a family of related survey efforts. Along these lines, Church and Waclawski (Chapter 22) argue for a tier of survey efforts that meet different purposes and needs. So, we do not see evidence of a science–practice schism but rather the need for a well-articulated listening and action-oriented strategy, implemented using well-written and appropriately evaluated measures.

Using Sensing Data Wisely

Sensing approaches are varied and leverage the availability of data both passively and actively collected by a variety of talent management systems. These include those supporting time and attendance, employee sensors, and social-media analysis. They can also include the direct observation and documenting of employee behavior, such as recording how often employees smile in greeting customers (Davenport et al., 2010). These sensing methods can help one to understand what people value, their preferences, and how they engage, communicate, and organize within organizations. An important characteristic of sensing mechanisms is that they are often based on the fortuitous exploitation of data-collection opportunities in both the operating and social environments. Sensing data can be particularly helpful when phenomenon driven (Wenzel & Van Quaquebeke, 2018), leading to further inquiry and insight. They are particularly useful where survey-based methods are too expensive, burdensome, or biased. They often bear little direct cost other than the data-collection burden. Most importantly, they generally do not require the direct engagement of employees and are thus largely passive. In contrast, it is worth noting that surveys both are conversational in nature (Johnson, 2018) and directly engage employees in the data-collection effort. Thus, surveys communicate what is important in a specific context by the questions that are asked. Further, surveys invite a response and are best regarded as one step in a larger information-gathering, feedback, and change-focused process. Sensing mechanisms can have a diagnostic function and provide data for predictive analytics, but they are not conversational and may not lend themselves to a larger cycle of data gathering and feedback. Sensing is similar to hearing a conversation between others. We may be able to glean important details, but we are restricted to the transaction that occurs between the parties or systems. Thus, readers may wish to consider that sensing efforts are not a useful replacement for the traditional employee survey. Chakrabarti and McCune (Chapter 14) explore the challenges and advantages that accompany both collecting and using sensing data.

Building a Business Case

The employee survey program is but one talent management initiative and one that can be seriously questioned by executives due to both direct and indirect costs. Moreover, past failures to demonstrate change are often part of the collective executive memory. Del Duco et al. (Chapter 17) discuss in detail the value of linkage research in practical problems that such research entails. Schneider (Chapter 8) argues persuasively that survey content must itself address executives' specific interests.

Organization of This Book

The 27 remaining chapters in this book are organized into four sections:

1. **Surveys as a component of talent analytic strategy** (Chapters 2–14). Here, chapters focus on the strategic role of surveys, what constructs are best measured, who should be asked to participate, and when it is best to collect data. Topics include crafting good items including open-ended questions, assessing climate and engagement, determining survey cadence and length, survey sampling, and deploying surveys to understand the employee experience throughout the lifecycle. Special treatment is given to sensing methods that fall outside the typical survey data-collection context.

2. **Analyzing data to tell the survey story** (Chapters 15–20). Chapters in this section focus on the basic mechanics of data analysis, determining key drivers of survey outcomes including the basics of linkage research, multilevel analyses, delivering the executive presentation including the effective use of compelling visualizations, and the use of AI for guiding follow-up actions.

3. **Challenges and opportunities** (Chapters 22–25). The third section of the book tackles some of the more difficult questions faced by survey practitioners. Particularly important is answering the question implicit in many of the earlier chapters, namely, "How can surveys be used to drive change?" Issues of privacy and ethics are considered, as well as the philosophical basis for survey work. Challenges to doing professional survey work are discussed, and special attention is given to doing survey work in organizations where some or all employees are union-organized.

4. **The status quo and the continuing evolution of survey research** (Chapters 26 and 27). The last two chapters in the volume present descriptive data as to the current state of practice and a final review of that status quo as well as the continuing evolution of practice.

References

Bersin, J. (2014, April 10). It's time to rethink the employee engagement issue. *Forbes*. Retrieved from https://www.forbes.com/sites/joshbersin/2014/04/10/its-time-to-rethink-the-employee-engagement-issue/#6ef513d16cf3

Cucina, J. M., Walmsley, P. T., Gast, I. F., Martin, N. R., & Curtin, P. (2017). Survey key driver analysis: Are we driving down the right road? *Industrial and Organizational Psychology, 10*(2), 234–257.

Davenport, T. H., Harris, J., & Shapiro, J. (2010). Competing on talent analytics. *Harvard Business Review, 88*(10), 52–58.

Erickson, T. J., & Gratton, L. (2007). What it means to work here. *Harvard Business Review, 85*(3), 104.

European Parliament. (2016, April 27). Regulation (EU) 2016/679 of the European Parliament and of the Council. *Official Journal of the European Union, L119*, 1–88.

HR.com. (2019). The state of employee engagement in 2019: Leverage leadership and culture to maximize engagement. Retrieved from https://www.hr.com/en/resources/free_research_white_papers/hrcom-the-state-of-employee-engagement-may-2019_jwb9ckus.html

Hyland, P., Caputo, A. W., & Reeves, D. (2018). Understanding new era workplace relationships: Insights from employee engagement research. *Industrial and Organizational Psychology, 11*(3), 523–530.

Johnson, J. W. (2000). A heuristic method for estimating the relative weight of predictor variables in multiple regression. *Multivariate Behavioral Research, 35*(1), 1–19.

Johnson, S. R. (2018). *Engaging the workplace: Using surveys to spark change.* Alexandria, VA: ATD Press.

Kaplan, S., DeShon, R., & Tetrick, L. (2017). *SHRM-SIOP Science of HR Series. The bigger picture of employee well-being: Its role for individuals, families and societies.* Alexandria, VA: Society for Human Resource Management; Bowling Green, OH: Society for Industrial and Organizational Psychology. Retrieved from https://www.siop.org/Portals/84/docs/SIOP-SHRM%20White%20Papers/2017_02_SHRM-SIOP_Employee_Well-being.pdf.

Kaur, J., & Fink, A. A. (2017). *SHRM-SIOP Science of HR Series. Trends and practices in talent analytics.* Alexandria, VA: Society for Human Resource Management; Bowling Green, OH: Society for Industrial and Organizational Psychology. Retrieved from https://www.siop.org/Portals/84/docs/SIOP-SHRM%20White%20Papers/2017%2010_SHRM-SIOP%20Talent%20Analytics.pdf.

Kraut, A. I. (2017). Does SKDA make it too easy for survey practitioners and clients to avoid harder (OD) challenges? *Industrial and Organizational Psychology, 10*(2), 265–268.

Macey, W. H., & Schneider, B. (2008). The meaning of employee engagement. *Industrial and Organizational Psychology, 1*(1), 3–30.

Meyer, J. P., Stanley, L. J., & Parfyonova, N. M. (2012). Employee commitment in context: The nature and implications of commitment profiles. *Journal of Vocational Behavior, 80,* 1–16.

Rotolo, C. T., Church, A. H., Adler, S., Smither, J. W., Colquitt, A. L., Shull, A. C., . . . Foster, G. (2018). Putting an end to bad talent management: A call to action for the field of industrial and organizational psychology. *Industrial and Organizational Psychology, 11*(2), 176–219.

Shepherd, W. (2014). The heterogeneity of well-being: Implications for HR management practices. *Industrial and Organizational Psychology, 7*(4), 579–583.

VirginPulse. (2017). *The business of healthy employees.* Retrieved from https://www.virginpulse.com/blog-post/results-2017-business-healthy-employees-survey-report/.

Waber, B. (2013). *People analytics: How social sensing technology will transform business and what it tells us about the future of work.* Upper Saddle River, NJ: FT Press.

Wenzel, R., & Van Quaquebeke, N. (2018). The double-edged sword of big data in organizational and management research: A review of opportunities and risks. *Organizational Research Methods, 21,* 548–591.

Yost, A. B., Behrend, T. S., Howardson, G., Darrow, J. B., & Jensen, J. M. (2019). Reactance to electronic surveillance: A test of antecedents and outcomes. *Journal of Business and Psychology, 34*(1), 71–86.

SECTION 1
SURVEYS AS A COMPONENT OF TALENT ANALYTIC STRATEGY

2

Strategic Surveying for Driving Organizational Change

A Very 3M Story

Karen B. Paul and Kristofer J. Fenlason

We have learned over the years, often the hard way, about creating and implementing strategic surveys for driving organizational change. What follows are some of the significant lessons learned over our careers, working separately and together with nearly 60 years of collective experience.

We started working together in 1990 at a consulting firm, where we honed the pragmatic part of our craft. We began our careers with strong academic foundations and a raft of tools and techniques. We were, in a way, like well-trained musicians beginning to find our way in our chosen profession. But, like many things in life, you can never be fully prepared for the unique situations in which you may find yourself. In fact, we found that our "life in surveys" was less like being members of an orchestra that played scored music and more like being jazz musicians who were improvising their pieces. We believe this improvisational nature is especially true regarding the strategic use of surveys. There were no courses and few texts on this topic in our early years, and much of what we've learned has come through that year-to-year improvisation driven by the needs and constraints of our clients and organizations.

To be clear, we are not saying that our improvisation was devoid of rigor and we were "just making it up as we went along." In fact, we believe mastery of, and fluency with, the scientific underpinnings of survey research are essential to success. However, this chapter is intended not as a scientific treatise on the topic but as a review of the less often chronicled, storied lessons learned from the trenches of practice. Our intent in this chapter is to add to the body of knowledge and published literature by focusing on some practical lessons gained over time through our "improvisation." So, we have

Karen B. Paul and Kristofer J. Fenlason, *Strategic Surveying for Driving Organizational Change* In: *Employee Surveys and Sensing*. Edited by: William H. Macey and Alexis A. Fink, Oxford University Press (2020). © Society for Industrial and Organizational Psychology.
DOI: 10.1093/oso/9780190939717.003.0002

approached this chapter as a series of "lessons learned" that we have accumulated over our careers, focusing on the strategic use of surveys.

What Do We Mean by "Strategic" Surveying?

First, we have some anchoring comments to help define strategic surveying. Certainly, the word and the concept of being *strategic* get tossed around in many contexts, sometimes in specific reference to the formally articulated strategies of the organization but also just as a business-speak term meant to impart a certain undeniable importance to whatever is being proposed.

Strategy has been defined in many different ways over the years, but we believe that Michael Porter's definition is well reasoned and well regarded. In his influential *Harvard Business Review* article "What is strategy?" Porter (1996) writes about competitive strategy—essentially how one's firm wins against others in the marketplace. Porter writes that "Competitive strategy is about being different" and asserts that "the essence of strategy is in the activities—choosing to perform activities differently or to perform different activities than rivals" (p. 64). In alignment with Porter's definition, the work of both Wiley (2010) and Schiemann and Morgan (2006) helps inform our views around strategic surveying.

However, our favorite definition is from Schneider, Ashworth, Higgs, and Carr (1996): "In these surveys employees are asked about the practices and policies they experience and see happening to them and around them *with regard to specific strategic goals of the corporation*" (p. 696, italics in the original). We believe, aligned with Schneider et al. (1996), that a key element to strategic surveying is using employees as well-placed and well-informed observers. As the authors state, employees in the organization "are in an optimal position to report on the degree to which strategic initiatives are being carried out" (p. 695). The Schneider et al. (1996) framework has some important advantages. The definition directly connects surveying to the strategy of the business, ensuring relevancy. Strategy is about choice. By using the business strategy as the organizing framework for what topics should be included in the survey, the process becomes diagnostic and evaluative for business strategy and the survey itself a strategic sensing tool.

Surveys become more strategic when the efforts, content, and process focus on one or more of the following:

- A long-term perspective
- Corporate-driven issues and change
- Clients who are the top leaders in the organization (the chief executive officer [CEO], executive vice presidents, etc.)
- The articulated strategies of the organization
- Initiatives, goals, and programs that support the articulated strategies
- Maintaining or improving a competitive advantage for the corporation
- Aspects of organizational culture that support the articulated strategies and/or competitive advantage

Following is a collection of "lessons learned" for creating strategic surveys. Selection of these lessons was made with this list in mind to help differentiate what creates strategic surveys versus just good survey practices in general.

The Mechanics of Being Strategic

Lesson 1: Be Relevant

Organizational survey consulting is a very competitive field. Rival firms are full of highly motivated, intelligent people who are constantly trying to take work away from you. Those firms that do well tend to learn how to explain the science in simple terms and quickly discover how to be the most relevant to clients. In the 1990s the consulting firm we worked for had created a survey approach that assessed the organization's perceived need for change. In our opinion, a significant "hook" was that this method promised a way to quickly identify important client issues—in this case, things that needed to change. The details of the approach are unimportant, but the necessity of making surveys *relevant* to the organization is as true today as it was then.

In the case of strategic surveying, we first seek to understand client needs, within the context of company history, but with particular emphasis on understanding leadership views and company direction. We then articulate and focus efforts on the issues that would have a significant effect on the organization. The best way we know how to do this is to study the CEO's agenda in multiple ways, including interviewing as many senior executives in the organization as we can. The goal is to listen for issues and then write survey items for verification. In our opinion, the best strategic surveys we've created have clearly reflected not only the main competitive and strategic issues but also the more nuanced sides of dilemmas faced by the organization. In the end, the survey should educate survey takers on the issues of the day, and the resulting data should provide insight into what the collective believes about the strategies.

Lesson 2: Assess "Appetite for Truth"

This lesson title is intentionally provocative. In our experience, even CEOs who excel at strategically using surveys can differ massively in how they want to approach the survey and the process itself. Strategy is about decisions and choice. Yet each CEO is different in her or his approach and style, and how decisions and choices are made differs from one to another. The survey approach taken needs to mirror the information needs and style of the CEO in her or his strategic pursuit. Some CEOs want to use the survey as an in-depth diagnostic. They want to identify potential blind spots and ask the really tough questions to surface the state of the entire enterprise in which they are trying to drive their agenda. Other CEOs approach the survey as a way of confirming the organization's understanding of, and alignment around, their specific agenda. Yet other CEOs take a hybrid approach, seeking to deeply understand specific issues in areas in which they are contemplating action while also communicating other areas of importance.

The crux of this lesson is accurately assessing the context and information needs that the survey is to provide. In the first scenario, the practitioner must write really difficult, probing questions on all areas to provide the widest possible view of the corporation and the people's opinions of it. The need is for a real read of the environment in which the strategic efforts are taking place. In the second scenario, the practitioner is writing fairly easy, basic questions that are extremely targeted to the change agenda. In the third scenario, the practitioner is trying to design a survey that covers all the strategic issues but is balanced between areas of action and communication.

The Art and Opportunistic Nature of Strategy

In 1993, Karen was hired away from the consulting firm to one her clients, 3M. Kris left the consulting firm in 1994 and went on to gain additional consulting experience at two other firms before joining Karen at 3M in 2000.

Organizational surveying has a long history at 3M, beginning in 1951. By 1968 the company had already instituted a corporate policy mandating organizational surveying. The department at 3M in which we would work had been started in 1955 by industrial–organizational (I-O) psychologists and had been run by them since that time. We knew solid work when we saw it and sought to continue and to build on the successes of our predecessors. By studying the work and what had been successful by those who came before us, several other lessons emerged about how to build a successful reputation for surveying strategically—in particular, our next lesson.

Lesson 3: The Importance of History Data

When Karen arrived at 3M, surveying had already been going on for over 40 years at the corporation. One 3M survey process had panel data dating back 10 years. Cataloguing what had been done by those who had gone before and continuing to preserve this historical data helped enable several unanticipated or "opportunistic" uses in present-day surveys. For instance, 3M first measured employees' views of banning smoking on 3M property in 1986 (39% favorable). By knowing and using corporate survey historical data, when discussion on banning smoking occurred decades later there was complete confidence in how the employee base would receive the new policy in 2013. By showing current scores compared to the earlier scores, it was clear that perceptions had unmistakably shifted. 3M surveys have also tracked employee interest in balancing personal and professional demands, which led to numerous initiatives over time, including personalized work schedules, job sharing, and, more recently, 3M's FlexAbility™ program.

To some extent, you never know what will be relevant in the future. But if something was important enough for a predecessor to include a topic on the survey, then it may be key in the future. Keeping track of historical data and being aware of the topics raised in prior surveys can provide an opportunity to shed light on a current topic. Keeping a large item inventory on all past items, even if only used once, can result in a valuable payoff.

These are just a couple examples from a long line of opportunistic uses. We continued to keep our eyes open for other opportunistic uses of survey data, which in turn started to encourage other policy and decision-making situations for the survey, slowly shifting the focus to more and more strategic imperatives.

Lesson 4: Know Your Level of Analysis and Intervention

Two major corporate survey processes have been in place at 3M since the 1980s. One survey process is designed for local intervention at a country or business-unit level. The other process is a sampling survey that runs across the entire global enterprise. Both surveys are strategic in nature and carry content that supports 3M strategy. Yet, the questions vary widely due to the needs of an individual general manager/managing director versus those of the corporation and the executive management team. Keeping in mind the level of analysis when designing a survey is critical for its use. Where leaders sit in the organization determines the strategic issues facing them and the types of decisions they make to advance strategy. Our advice is to match the level of strategic content to the level of the leader intending to use the data.

Lesson 5: Shifting to Business Focus

Several years ago, Karen received some powerful feedback that she had indeed been successful in transitioning the survey business to being more strategic. During a corporate operations meeting review of survey results, a C-suite member cautioned his peers by stating "we really need to be careful and discuss the implications as this isn't just an HR thing anymore we're making business decisions here." It was clear senior leaders were paying attention to results and using them as a business tool.

Organizations are focused on business health, and their leaders are focused on maintaining and growing that health. Alignment with that focus seems obvious but is critical. Understanding the issues from the perspective of business leaders helps ensure acceptance of results and facilitates meaningful business decisions that in turn support strategy achievements.

So how was the survey process moved to that position of business focus and centrality? Again, there was no silver bullet. However, diligent work in three key areas does help. First, gain an understanding of the business concerns. This requires work on the front end of the process in terms of a lot of listening and trying to understand the concerns of the business itself. Second, translate those business concerns into survey content and into a vernacular accepted by the business. Work in this area is what makes a survey relevant to the business, from which results will drive subsequent action. Third, focus attention on critical results in subsequent reporting and develop a comprehensive view of what is occurring. A great deal of work is required to display results on the back end of the process to easily gain senior management's attention, illuminate the issues, and drive concrete actions on the results.

Developing an understanding of your business leader's perspectives in order to guide your work in all three areas can be done in many ways. In general, work on your own business acumen as a core competency. Within your company, seek out and pay attention to business presentations, attend earnings calls, constantly collect information about the business goals and initiatives in the company, network with leaders to understand their perspective, and develop good sources inside and outside of Human Resources (HR) to help you understand what drives the business. Use that understanding to craft your questions. Invite others to challenge your content for how well your focus and phrasing fit into the business perspective of the organization. Set a standard for yourself that if you get a negative or positive result in response to the questions, you personally would know what to do with the information.

Lesson 6: Don't Fear Failure, Do Be Skeptical of Success

Working at 3M means you have the freedom and support to try a lot of things. If you try something and fail, you learn from it and move on. It is part of the culture. The bigger problem can be success. Keeping things status quo and fearing failure so much that you don't innovate is in and of itself a sure path to eventual failure. We would argue, and have been given leadership feedback, that 3M has developed some great approaches to the strategic use of surveys and that those approaches have been successful. So, how do you keep innovating and pushing the organization when the program is already highly successful and the organization itself is essentially encouraging you to just repeat what has already been done? Over the years we've tried to innovate several different aspects of our strategic surveying efforts. Some were "hits," and others were "learning opportunities."

We have embraced various survey technological offerings as soon as they became available, from providing data reports on CDs in 2003 (totally bombed) to providing crowdsourcing in 2018 (big success). Yet, as in many things in life, more often important lessons are learned from failure than success, such as the following example. In 2009, we proactively conducted many complex analyses of Generation X turnover; but in the end, we basically couldn't even give away the research. In hindsight, we had been having a successful run and strayed away from our own hard-earned lessons. We had to relearn that if it isn't an issue facing the business (and it wasn't), then "theoretically interesting" is pretty much useless internally and certainly isn't strategic. However, there is a silver lining. Years later, in 2014, questions on Millennials were emerging from our businesses. We were able to take what we had learned from the Gen X work and quickly gather information, pinpoint needs, and target interventions and positioning to attract, engage, and retain Millennials. In fact, 3M emerged as an early leader around Millennial issues and in 2016 was named as the number one top dream company for Millennials by the National Society of High School Scholars (Strauss, 2016). There is value in trying to anticipate business questions even if you are wrong, and it requires much less risk in the long run than complacency, which risks total obsolescence.

Lesson 7: Helping the Business Teach Itself

Having some survey items in common across time (a.k.a. history data) has proven useful time and time again in our work. Besides the obvious benefits of being able to demonstrate real improvements or gaps, history data can also help the organization learn about itself and become a strategic teaching tool. In 1994, per corporate policy, 3M Mexico was due to take one of our surveys. At the time, Mexico as a country was experiencing a devaluation of its currency that was dramatic and impacting both organizations and their employees in a very real fashion. There were discussions about whether the subsidiary should be exempted from taking the survey, especially since the managing director was relatively new to the subsidiary. At the time, leadership there was working hard on taking tough actions to ensure survival. Executive management, of course, was both active and concerned. The decision was made to conduct the survey to see what else could be learned and with the view that, if nothing else, it would be a good baseline for the future.

Surprising everyone (including the survey professionals), employee engagement, satisfaction, commitment, and views of leadership were extraordinarily high and much higher than 3M Mexico's scores 2 years earlier in relatively good economic times. In fact, overall the survey was up across all topics. Later, after the currency stabilized, 3M Mexico had record financial results, pulling out of the financial crisis faster and ahead of its competition. An important lesson was learned by the corporation, that excellent leadership during a crisis is truly appreciated and noticed by employees and that financial results followed employee perceptions. The survey had now moved to a new level of strategic use as a leadership tool. The survey could be a tool to assess leaders in different situations and remind executives that how leaders handle the people challenges can predict future financial outcomes. The lessons and how to use the survey were mainstreamed in leadership-development programs among the executive population. By 1997 when the Asian flu financial crisis started impacting so many subsidiaries, 3M did extremely well in knowing how to manage through the crisis and how to use the survey as a feedback mechanism on how management was doing during the crisis. Of course, not all of the success can be attributed to the survey process as the organization itself was learning on multiple fronts how to handle economic events and teaching its members how to lead and succeed. Still, it is telling how much of that time period's executive conference (meeting of top 100 leaders) and leadership-development programs featured leaders discussing what they did in terms of leadership and gave evidence of such by way of pre- and post-survey scores and resulting financial results.

Lesson 8: Be Aware of Ignoring Old Wine in New Bottles

While the results of 3M's employee engagement journey have been both well documented and well received (Macey, Schneider, Barbera, & Young, 2009; Paul & Fenlason, 2014; Paul & Johnson, 2011; Schneider & Paul, 2011), what has not been heretofore discussed is the current authors' initial resistance to the construct of employee engagement. In 2005, engagement was just beginning to be discussed in 3M businesses. Much of the early emerging hype on engagement was a haphazard mishmash of existing scientific findings that the authors were reluctant to be involved in lest their more heavily researched and psychometrically sound approach be set aside. Of course, avoiding old wine in new bottles is not unique to surveying (Ones, Kaiser, Chamorro-Premuzic, & Svensson, 2017; Rotolo et al., 2018).

However, a central influence that shaped our response to the organization's questions can be traced to a story told to Karen earlier in her career by her mentor, Dr. Patricia Cain Smith. Dr. Pat recalled working for a plant manager who knew she did not believe in interviewing people for jobs (based on all of the available scientific literature, of course!) but still demanded she interview someone. His response when she declined was "given everything you know about interviewing and given everything I know about it which one of the two of us do you really think should do it?" Dr. Pat went ahead with the interview and went on to invent behaviorally anchored rating scales (Smith & Kendall, 1963). The moral of her story prevailed and led Karen and her team to a more formal investigation of the engagement construct and to make sense of the emerging research.

The team considered the research literature, assessed various consulting firms' positions on this trend, and reviewed 3M's business situation. As a result, in 2006 3M began its journey to both drive efficiency and support innovation by taking a different and more consistent global approach to employee engagement (Paul & Johnson, 2011; Schneider & Paul, 2011). Ultimately, this led to one of the largest, multiyear, global interventions in 3M's history. And the results were phenomenal. 3M both improved employee engagement scores and improved business performance (Donlon, 2009; Paul & Fenlason, 2014).

There are a couple of takeaways here. Savvy practitioners and I-O psychologists are often well ahead of trends by years. You may consider an approach/technique to be "old wine in a new bottle" (a well-established practice, construct, finding) when in fact it may not be well known or widely practiced in the organization. The "old wine" may be in a new bottle for a reason—it captures attention and enables the organization to relearn a critical lesson. Above all, we should be willing to "lean in" and embrace these opportunities and not immediately dismiss popular fads because they didn't pass a quick scientific smell test. If you decline involvement and there is sufficient organizational appetite, it is likely that others with less knowledge and skill will be asked to take charge. Being in the game is better than being out of the game, and applying prior solid approaches to new and emerging concepts (or even silly fads) can result in advancing the organization over time and in a sustainable way.

Lesson 9: Use the Right Tool for the Job

We endorse experimentation, but switching methodologies simply for the sake of change is a recipe for disaster. Recently, it has become quite trendy to bash organizational surveys in favor of pulse or crowdsourcing techniques. Much like the old parable where one blind man describes feeling an elephant's trunk and another blind man describes the tail, both accurately describe the focal characteristic but miss the larger picture. A well-run organizational survey provides insights on a variety of topics important for comprehensive diagnosis (larger picture), while crowdsourcing typically focuses tightly on one topic. Each technique has its place. A well-developed, strategic listening strategy will avoid simply abandoning one approach for another and use various tools in conjunction to meet the total information needs of the organization.

Playing the Long Game

In 2001, Kris was lured away to run the show at another consulting firm but in 2011 rejoined 3M, where he and Karen continue to work. Karen has since taken on more responsibility in a variety of roles within HR but outside of surveys. The preceding provides a look back at some of our lessons gained over those years that were applied at various points in time. However, we don't see strategic surveying as just a bundle of discrete interventions. Organizational history and strategy unwind over a long period of time, and we believe that 3M's success with surveying is also a result of developing our "long game." Consequently, this section looks back across the historical sweep of strategic surveying at 3M. We believe that it is important to develop a long-term perspective on strategic surveying to guide your own approach over time. You might even call it a "strategy for strategic surveying."

Lesson 10: Strive to Have Top Leadership as Your Client

When Karen started with 3M, the CEO was not viewed as the major client for survey work—HR was considered the client. Coming from consulting, Karen insisted on interviewing the CEO for the process and making him the primary client. This was managed as a result of raising a variety of strategic questions about the CEO's agenda while urging a discussion within HR leadership on how best to have results accepted by the business.

Today at 3M, the CEO directs the process, and there are multiple touchpoints with top leadership throughout the process. We have presented directly to CEOs, their leadership teams, and the board of directors. Each survey summary of a division or subsidiary also goes to the CEO and senior vice president of HR for review, ensuring a direct and enduring connection with that critical constituency.

Lesson 11: You Can Make a Difference to Corporate Strategy

3M has had a number of performance indicators over the years that it has shared externally with the financial and investor communities. One such metric at 3M is called the New Product Vitality Index (NPVI), which measures the percentage of new products in 3M's portfolio that were introduced in the last 5 years divided by total sales. The metric has been in place in various forms and used in a variety of ways for many years. From 2005 to 2012, the NPVI was used as a key performance metric.

In late 2012, comments were emerging from interviews for the upcoming survey that potentially indicated that the metric might no longer be as useful as originally conceived. As background, the metric focused on the number of new innovations, and over time a portion of executive compensation became directly tied to this metric.

In February of 2012, 3M had named a new CEO, and this was to be the first strategic survey of the entire global operation under this new administration. When we proposed our first draft of the survey to the CEO, approximately two-thirds of the items were new, and we sought to keep about one-third of the items to provide historical data and benchmarks on how we were doing. Included in this latter group was the item "The NPVI (New Product Vitality Index) is a useful metric for a growth company," which had scored quite favorably in the last administration. Part of the rationale for selecting this item was to gather information on the topic and use it as a soft check to see if the views expressed in the interviews were the perceptions of a few, the beginning of a trend, or already a widespread belief.

Overall, the results of the survey turned out to be some of the most positive scores of all time (as measured by common items tracking back to the 1990s). Further, when the overall survey results were compared to the previous survey, which had itself been extremely positive, they were even more positive. Likewise, the NPVI metric, in this administration of the survey, scored quite favorably but was down more than 20 percentage points in favorability among senior leaders. After reviewing the results with the CEO and leadership team, action planning began; and the CEO invited Karen to present a high-level set of survey results to the board of directors.

Included in this presentation were the NPVI results. The presentation was very well received, and the survey score on the NPVI was actively discussed. As part of the action-planning process, the CEO had decided to move the NPVI to a secondary metric and shared this with the board. To our knowledge, we are the only survey program that has witnessed such a direct and tangible change in corporate strategy due to employee opinions. Why this drop occurred and how we addressed the problem are not relevant to our story. What is pertinent is that by applying the lessons we have learned, employee thoughts, feelings, and opinions on strategic issues are at the forefront at 3M.

Lesson 12: Don't Be Complacent

We believe that we have been well served by essentially acting as if we were "starting from zero" when a new CEO comes into the role. With each CEO change we review everything, from the structure and names of the global processes to the survey items, the timing, etc. and propose changes that we believe will be of most use to the new CEO in the current marketplace and corporate culture. Danger exists for survey providers in complacency in the belief that past success means anything. All of the lessons learned need to be reapplied as if no prior credibility existed.

Change, Creativity, and Going with the Flow

Overall, the lessons articulated here represent foundational practices and principles that are likely to endure into the foreseeable future. In the same way as well-known "best practices" like leadership buy-in, public accountability, and robust communication help drive success in nearly any organizational change effort, our experience indicates that these lessons will remain staples of effective and "sticky" change for years to come (pun intended, we are from 3M after all).

If there is one "uber lesson" we would offer, it is that embracing change and creatively responding to the organization's needs, culture, and leader styles are critical to both short- and long-term success with strategic surveys. With each new leader and set of circumstances we encountered, we learned and adapted. Much of the success of strategic surveys, like any other service we provide to our organizations, rests in building on lessons and best practices from the past, adapting to the present, and creating a new future.

To return to the metaphor at the beginning of this chapter, we believe strategic surveying practice in organizations tends to be more like playing jazz than playing "paper music." You need great musical skills to play either well but are only valuable in the jazz context if you also can improvise and go with the flow. We believe survey professionals can do both, bringing solid science and practice to bear on issues that are critical for organizations to survive and thrive but also being creative enough to adapt to the ever-changing needs and circumstances of the organizations we serve.

References

Donlon, J. P. (2009, January/February). 20 best companies for leaders: How George Buckley's 3M shot to the top. *Chief Executive Magazine, 38.*

Macey, W. H., Schneider, B., Barbera, K. M., & Young, S. A. (2009). *Employee engagement: Tools for analysis, practice, and competitive advantage* (Vol. 31). Chichester, England: John Wiley & Sons.

Ones, D. S., Kaiser, R. B., Chamorro-Premuzic, T., & Svensson, C. (2017). Has industrial-organizational psychology lost its way? *The Industrial-Organizational Psychologist, 55*(2). Retrieved from http://www.siop.org/tip/april17/lostio.aspx Google Scholar

Paul, K. B., & Fenlason, K. J. (2014). Transforming a legacy culture at 3M: Teaching an elephant how to dance. In B. Schneider & K. M. Barbera (Eds.), *The Oxford handbook of organizational climate and culture* (pp. 569–583). New York, NY: Oxford University Press.

Paul, K. B., & Johnson, C. L. (2011). Engagement at 3M: A case study. In K. Oakes & P. Galagan (Eds.), *The executive guide to integrated talent management* (pp. 133–143). Alexandria, VA: American Society for Training & Development.

Porter, M. (1996, November–December). What is strategy? *Harvard Business Review, 61–78.*

Rotolo, C. T., Church, A. H., Adler S., Smither, J. W., Colquitt, A. L., Shull, A. C., . . . Foster, G. (2018). Putting an end to bad talent management: A call to action for the field of I-O psychology. *Industrial and Organizational Psychology, 11*(2), 176–219.

Schiemann, W. A., & Morgan, B. S. (2006). Strategic surveys: Linking people to business strategy. In A. Kraut (Ed.), *Getting action from organizational surveys: New concepts, technologies and applications* (pp. 76–101). San Francisco, CA: Jossey-Bass.

Schneider, B., Ashworth, S. D., Higgs, A. C., & Carr, L. (1996). Design, validity, and use of strategically focused employee attitude surveys. *Personnel Psychology, 49*(3), 695–705.

Schneider, B., & Paul, K. B. (2011, January). In the company we trust. *HR Magazine,* 40–43.

Smith, P. C., & Kendall, L. M. (1963). Retranslations of expectations: An approach to the construction of unambiguous anchors for rating scales. *Journal of Applied Psychology, 47*(2), 149–155.

Strauss, C. (2016, June 13). The 25 companies where top millennials most want to work in 2016 (Google is no longer no. 1). *Forbes*. https://www.forbes.com/sites/karstenstrauss/2016/06/13/the-25-companies-where-top-millennials-most-want-to-work-in-2016-google-is-no-longer-1/#70788f7e163f

Wiley, J. W. (2010). *Strategic employee surveys: Evidence-based guidelines for driving organizational success*. San Francisco, CA: Jossey-Bass.

3

Improving the Design and Interpretation of Sample Surveys in the Workplace

Paul M. Mastrangelo

Twenty-first-century organizations with an employee survey program increasingly want contradicting outcomes: a large amount of timely data but a process that does not oversurvey employees or overwhelm staff. Timely data are an understandable requirement given the accelerating pace of change in the business environment. The traditional approach of inviting all employees to participate in a survey once every 12, 18, or 24 months seems antiquated when social media provide global communication instantly. Customer and financial data arrive continuously. Why should employee feedback be formally collected over the course of years? Yet, the idea of inviting all employees to participate in a survey administered weekly, monthly, or just quarterly would be challenged as too burdensome. These challengers will say that employees are being surveyed so much that many will not participate thoughtfully or at all (i.e., survey fatigue: Weiner & Dalessio, 2006; Wiltse, 2008). Indeed, with inexpensive survey technology readily accessible, employees are asked for feedback not just from Human Resources (HR) but also from managers, support functions, and vendors. The resulting tension between data timeliness and survey fatigue has led some to sound the death knell of the employee survey (Bersin, 2014; Keen, 2015) and sing the praises of various newfound technological solutions, such as surreptitiously analyzing employees' electronic communications (Chiu, 2016; Rowh, 2011) or assessing employees' moods via visual interfaces on a cell phone app (Beagrie, 2015). Still, the employee survey lets leaders choose areas of inquiry and compare results to external benchmarks such that survey insights are more specific, diagnostic, and actionable than newly invented feedback mechanisms.

These business needs coupled with information age technology have brought the "pulse" survey into prominence. This chapter reviews how

Paul M. Mastrangelo, *Improving the Design and Interpretation of Sample Surveys in the Workplace* In: *Employee Surveys and Sensing*. Edited by: William H. Macey and Alexis A. Fink, Oxford University Press (2020). © Society for Industrial and Organizational Psychology.
DOI: 10.1093/oso/9780190939717.003.0003

inviting a sample of employees complicates the design and interpretation of one survey as well as a series of surveys used to take the pulse of an entire organization over time (while Chapter 4 compares and contrasts potential uses of the pulse survey). This chapter further explains the limitations of the sample survey, provides recommendations for ideal and less-than-ideal circumstances, and maximizes the usefulness of sample surveys for those who rely on the technique.

While changes in technology continuously affect the capabilities of the sample survey, the method itself has been used in the workplace for decades. Kodak may have been the first company (circa 1986) to administer monthly surveys to a random sample of its workforce, a practice that would become known as "taking the pulse" of the company (Colihan & Waclawski, 2006). What typically has distinguished the pulse survey from the traditional census survey is (a) fewer survey items, (b) more frequent administrations, and (c) invitations sent to just a portion of the full population (i.e., a *sample* survey). The purpose of the pulse survey has been to monitor for any change in work climate and employee engagement, whether such changes are anticipated because of planned organizational change (e.g., actions executed after a full census survey) or unanticipated (e.g., unknown consequences from planned or unplanned organizational changes). Thus, the scores from a pulse survey need to have enough accuracy to detect an effect that no one is expecting and to not produce an erroneous detection.

Accuracy, however, is often overlooked. Survey scores are usually treated the same whether they come from nearly all or hardly any of the relevant employees. Steady pulse scores can be interpreted as a stable climate instead of an instrument not sensitive enough to detect change, and large differences in pulse scores can be interpreted as real instead of random fluctuations due to small sample sizes. Furthermore, the precautions for using this technique are now rarely communicated to those who need accurate interpretation of sample survey results. The ability to use low-cost, easy-to-use survey software has led to unintended shifts in the profession. Whereas in the 1970s and 1980s the design, administration, and interpretation of an employee survey were usually done by someone trained in industrial and organizational psychology (or a similar social science background), now a similar project may be directed by a staff member with limited training in research design, inferential statistics, or psychological measurement. Given this trend, the process of interpreting results may be taking place with little regard to sample size considerations, sampling error, the difference between statistical significance and the margin of sampling error, the difference between sampling error and measurement error, the effects of low response rates, the limited utility of demographic "cuts" of sample data, and the necessary circumstances to judge improvements in the population score based on different sample scores over time. As a result, the efficacy of sample pulse surveys is at risk until survey practitioners and their stakeholders become better grounded in the details of the methodology.

Considerations When Using Sample Surveys

When Sampling Is a Better Option Than a Census

If all that mattered were scientific rigor such that time, cost, workload, and other practical aspects were disregarded, then every relevant employee should be invited to participate in the survey. If information is needed from salespeople, invite the entire sales team. If morale is low in the Mexico City location, invite all employees who work there. If leaders want to gauge organizational engagement, invite everyone. Inviting every employee of interest (i.e., the population) maximizes the number who will actually respond to survey items and therefore creates results that most closely resemble responses from all relevant employees. As a result, data from a census survey provide the best opportunity to examine demographic cuts within the organization. If desired, reports can be generated for all mangers, including front-line supervisors of small teams. Finally, a census is highly visible, demonstrating leaders' desire to hear from employees while also creating the expectation that the organization will react to feedback and attempt to make changes.

Yet, in reality, a census is not always the right option. Some assessment projects suffer from too much visibility or require quick turnaround. Inviting just a portion of all relevant employees makes the survey administration more manageable, reduces the number of employees who are pulled away from their job duties, and generally creates a more discreet process that keeps a survey out of the spotlight. Sampling provides a less expensive and less time-consuming method of providing more frequent assessments of engagement and climate, particularly with the development of self-service software solutions that can be licensed to organizations for unlimited use. With the increased demand for data, the simplification of collecting data, and the concern about oversurveying the population, sample surveys have never been more prevalent in the workplace.

When and How Sample Surveys Are Being Used

Organizations generally use sample surveys in one of three ways. The first approach is a *census–sample alternating pattern*, where an organization uses a sample survey in between full census administrations. Here, the desire is to evaluate post-census changes without delivering the full slate of reports, training all managers on results interpretation, and expecting extensive action-planning. Many companies began using sample surveys instead of census surveys to reduce internal and external costs (Van Rooy, Whitman, Hart, & Caleo, 2011). Not surprisingly, sample surveys often have lower response rates than do census surveys because of the reduced investment in communications. Organizations using this approach are not getting more data but simply using one sample survey as a replacement for one census. A second approach is using *supplemental pulses*. This increasingly common approach uses multiple sample surveys, often through a series of quarterly or monthly administrations, to complement the information culled from the full census. Evidence exists that an organization's survey scores vary cyclically because of regularly occurring internal events and external seasonal patterns (Colihan & Waclawski, 2006). Monitoring the fluctuation of scores over time requires multiple administrations of the same survey items, and using separate samples over time reduces survey fatigue. Still, the census survey is maintained to take advantage of the visibility and expectation of action-planning, so forthcoming pulse scores can have the highly accurate census baseline. A third approach is the *continuous listening pulse*, which describes how some companies are replacing the census survey entirely in favor of quarterly or monthly sample surveys. Thus, what distinguishes the continuous listening pulse from the supplemental pulse is that there is no census survey to use as a comparison point. The major disadvantage to eliminating the census survey is that the samples do not provide the same level of accuracy in representing the organization and major segments within. Although separate survey administrations can be aggregated to simulate a census, the responses will not come from the same point in time (e.g., some responded in January, some in October), and some segments of the company may not be pieced together accurately (because of organizational changes or sampling problems). The concern in each of these three classifications is that sample scores tend to be treated as if they are far more accurate than they are in reality (as explained in the following sections).

Perhaps the best compromise is to employ a *census plus 3 pulses* pattern. Such an approach produces survey results each quarter while (a) asking each employee to participate in a survey just twice a year (the census and one of the three pulses), (b) using the census to create a catalyst for organizational change followed by pulse monitoring to keep attention on implementation, and (c) providing statistical rigor from having the accurate census baseline as well as larger pulse samples from administering three mutually exclusive pulses rather than four quarterly or 12 monthly mutually exclusive pulses. The rationale for this recommendation comes from re-examining basic concepts in sampling and prescribed sample sizes.

Basic Concepts in Sampling

A census survey maximizes the accuracy in survey scores, not just for the entire organization (i.e., the population) but also for demographic subpopulations (e.g., the organization's female employees, its call center employees, or its newly hired employees) that may be much smaller in number but still the focus of attention. Yet even for a census survey, the degree to which data collected reflect the population(s) of interest depends on the number of employees who actually respond to the survey items. Running a census invites the full headcount (population N size), but the number of respondents (sample n size) is usually smaller, which is why response rates (n/N) need to be monitored. As the sample size n becomes substantially smaller than the population size N, there is an increased potential for sampling error, which is the difference between a sample score and the actual population score (i.e., if everyone took the survey) due to random and often unknown sources of variation. Comparing response rates across key demographic variables can help detect sample bias, which occurs when individual members of the population do not have an equal chance of being sampled, causing a misrepresentation of the population. When participants differ in meaningful ways from those who did not participate, misrepresentation is labeled *nonresponse bias* (see Borg & Mastrangelo, 2008, pp. 183–187; Rogelberg, 2006). For example, employee survey administrations that hinder participation from part-time employees might reduce the n size for women more than men. Likewise, job demands might impede call center employees from participating to a greater extent than those from other job types. In both examples, the overall company scores might not represent the population, and the demographic scores for these groups might not represent the demographic subpopulations.

Fundamental concepts like these are often overlooked when planning a sample survey, where we must distinguish the respondent sample size (n_r) from the invited sample size (n_i). If 90% of all women invited to a survey actually responded to a survey item, that score could accurately represent all of the organization's female employees if used in a census–sample alternating pattern, where say 25% of all employees were invited. However, a 90% response rate might not represent all of the organizational female employees if used in a supplemental pulse or continuous listening pulse, where say 1 in 12 employees were invited to a monthly survey (90% of one twelfth of women is a much smaller sample than 90% of one fourth of women). Furthermore, the problem is exacerbated by low response rates, which further reduce the size of the sample. Note, however, that even high response rates are not effective indicators of sampling error. Here is the first of multiple warnings in this chapter that to ensure accurate representation of a population, *the response rate is not as important as having a prescribed minimum sample size.*

Planning for a Prescribed Minimum Sample Size

The goal for a sample survey is to produce scores that represent the population(s) of interest. Even if individuals from the population have an equal chance of being included in the sample, there needs to be enough individuals in the sample to reduce sampling error. No one knows that population score (or else why conduct the survey?), but we can infer that it is the mean of all possible sample scores. Some sample scores will be errors that overestimate the population score, but an equal number will be errors that underestimate it, thus forming a normal distribution where the standard deviation represents the average error or standard error. Based on this number and other inputs specific to the situation, the minimally acceptable sample size can be calculated before a survey is administered. Borg and Mastrangelo (2008, Chapter 7) is one of many sources (cf. Colihan & Waclawski, 2006, or various websites if one searches for "sample size calculator") that can guide readers to estimate what minimally acceptable sample size fits their specific situation, but I will provide default answers based on typical conditions assuming that the measure is a proportion. Most employee survey items use a response scale with five options, and most reports show a percent favorable score (i.e., the percentage agreeing or strongly agreeing, also known as the "top two boxes").[1] Percent favorable scores depend on the specific wording of an item (e.g., the norm score for "I am willing to give extra effort to help my company meet its goals" is 84%, but the norm score for "I look forward to coming to work each day" is 53%). This matters because a 50–50 split is the maximum amount of variance when judging a dichotomous assessment, like favorable or not favorable. So, I will use this most difficult scenario—a population score of 50% favorable—to provide a conservative estimate for the minimally acceptable sample size. Further, I assume that most practitioners want to be 95% confident that the actual population score will be within ±5 points of the sample score, a minimally accepted margin of error.

Under these conditions, a sample size larger than $n_r = 385$ will never be necessary because that number accurately represents a population of 10 billion. There is no statistical reason to exceed a sample of 385 to represent a population. Of course, as stated earlier, employee surveys are often used to estimate multiple subpopulations. Does this mean that one needs the minimum sample size of 385 for every required demographic cut? Not necessarily. Table 3.1 displays the minimally acceptable sample size based on the size of the population or subpopulation. These values indicate that sample sizes can be much smaller than 385, but these samples must be an increasingly higher percentage of the population to the point where a sample from a population of 20 or fewer cannot meet the desired statistical rigor unless everyone participates in the survey. Stated differently, if a manager of 20 employees gets a report based on fewer than 20 respondents, the margin of error will exceed the standards set here. Contrary to common belief, there is no standard percentage of the population that needs to be included in a sample. The accuracy for a sample of 30 people representing a population of 50 (a 60% response rate) is actually not as high as the accuracy for a sample of 350 representing a population of 10,000 (a 3.5% response rate).

Planning how many employees to invite is dependent not just on the desired sample size but also on the expected response rate for the sample survey. Often, pulse surveys are minimally promoted with communications, leading to a typical response rate near 50%. Thus, a safe assumption for a

Table 3.1 Minimally Acceptable Sample Size Needed to Represent Various Population Sizes

For a Population (Headcount), N	Minimum Sample Size, n_r	Percentage of Population
10,000,000,000	385	<1%
20,000	377	2%
2,000	323	16%
1,000	278	28%
500	218	44%
200	132	66%
100	80	80%
50	45	90%
20	20	100%

Notes. These values assume the least optimal population score of 50% favorable and the criterion of 95% confidence that the actual population score will be within ±5 points of the sample score. n_r = respondent sample size.

first-time survey is to plan for an invited sample size n_i that is twice the minimally acceptable respondent sample size n_r. This assumption can be adjusted in subsequent administrations.

An additional complication occurs for supplemental and continuous listening pulse surveys, which likely invite one fourth of the population for a quarterly pulse or one twelfth of the population for a monthly pulse. Given that the invited sample n_i is a small fraction of the total population N, having a response rate of 50% means that even large populations will not have respondent sample sizes that meet the criteria we have established. A population of 1,000 employees that is to have a quarterly pulse survey where 25% shall be invited in each administration cannot produce sample scores within the ±5 point criterion for accuracy because the minimally acceptable sample size ($n_r = 278$) exceeds the number invited ($n_i = 250$). Rarely is this statistical "fact of life" considered in today's usage of pulse surveys: Inviting one quarter or less of the organization to a pulse survey means less than optimal accuracy for any demographic subpopulation smaller than 1,000. For example, a pulse survey can't accurately estimate the engagement score for 800 call center employees if 25% (or less) of them were invited.

In these situations where statistical guidelines are violated, the sample score remains the best guess for the population score; but the larger the difference between actual sample size and desired sample size, the less likely the guess is even close to being correct. Practitioners are then forced to answer the question of how badly one can violate statistical rules and still have useful data. Those with a limited background in research methods will ask "How small can a sample be and still be statistically significant?"[2]

Bare Minimum Sample Sizes When Statistical Rigor Must Be Sacrificed

Obviously, if one can live with less accuracy, then scores from inadequate sample sizes can still have limited use. And in organizational settings, there is no putting the cat back in the bag; leaders will not completely disregard survey data because they lack statistical rigor. Survey practitioners need to make use of the data while protecting stakeholders from overinterpreting results. Several rules of thumb follow that are admittedly arbitrary but defendable.

The first rule of thumb is to critically examine scores from samples with fewer than 100 employees. This value is more than just a memorable round number. A sample size of 100 will represent a population of 10 billion with a margin of error just under ±10 percentage points. Coincidentally, 10 percentage points happens to be the approximate difference between the 50th percentile and the 90th percentile in normative data for a single survey item (Macey & Eldridge, 2006). So, if a margin of error were to exceed this 10-point difference between interpretations of average score and top-decile score, then the survey measurement would no longer be an accurate diagnostic. Unless the sample includes at least 80% of its population, scores from a sample with fewer than 100 respondents should be ignored.

A second consideration for whether to interpret data from a small sample is to consider what consequence the interpretation will have in terms of action. A census survey usually leads to investing time and money for focus groups, goal-setting, action-planning, and change intervention; however, most pulse surveys do not create the same level of post-survey investment. If the consequence of a disconcerting score from a continuous listening pulse is that a manager will walk around and informally ask members of the team questions, then there is low risk of wasting resources over a potentially erroneous interpretation because of an inadequate sample size. In contrast, if decisions regarding a manager's promotion or a project's budget depend on a certain score from a pulse survey, then a large margin of error should invalidate the use of the data.

A final consideration for whether to interpret data from a small sample is the degree to which managers and other stakeholders understand technical jargon. Interpreting survey scores involves knowledge about sampling error as well as measurement error and comparisons of scores using significance testing. Most survey stakeholders will not know or care about each cautionary tale. Therefore, when explaining the limitations of interpreting survey results, one should create plain-talk guidelines. Table 3.2 provides example wording from a training to HR business partners who needed to instruct leaders how to interpret their continuous listening pulse scores. The response rates were well below 50%, but managers were promised reports if even 10 employees responded—a regrettable situation once they understood the sampling concepts discussed in this chapter. The interpretation guidance was based on margins of sampling error, margins of measurement error (assumed to be ±2 percentage points for each survey item), and thresholds for significant differences between two scores from the same groups (which decreases as n_r increases). The bright spot for this company was that it was soon administering a census survey, which can be used as a more accurate baseline for future sample pulse surveys. Such is the advantage of a supplemental pulse.

Table 3.2 Example Guidance for When Managers Should Conclude That Scores Have Changed from the Prior Pulse Survey

---

A report based on 350 or more can be trusted when it shows a significant improvement or decline from the prior pulse (e.g., a >5-point improvement is probably "real")

A report based on 100–300 can be trusted only when the difference between pulse scores is beyond 9 points (e.g., a 10-point improvement is likely to be "real")

A report based on 45–100 can only be trusted when the difference between pulse scores is very large (e.g., a 16-point improvement is believable as "real") and scores were based on at least 60% of the headcount

A report based on 45 or fewer respondents requires three or more survey administrations that show the same pattern of change before one can assume it is real (e.g., a 15-point improvement followed by another increase, such as 5 points, is good evidence that things have really improved)

Note. Designed for a company that had low response rates but needed to supply reports to as many managers as possible, these rough guidelines were based on margins of error and the use of chi-squared tests of independence.

Methods of Sampling

Gathering samples from an employee population should always involve a random selection procedure. Database software often have a method of randomly selecting a certain percentage or number of cases. Those employees not selected would be the only ones eligible for subsequent samples (as in a supplemental or continuous listening pulse). A quarterly pulse, for example, is often planned so that there are four mutually exclusive samples, each accounting for 25% of the population. However, employee surveys frequently oversample certain demographic subpopulations, as in the case of a company that randomly sampled 30% of its population for the pulse in the odd year of its alternating census–sample pattern but invited 100% of its corporate service function staff because there were not enough of them to accurately generate scores for the five different vice presidents who wanted pulse scores. Indeed, business units and corporate staff can be considered as subpopulations because often a leader from these groups demands a report from the sample survey. So rather than randomly selecting employees from the total organization (providing proportionate representation across the subpopulations but not necessarily enough respondents to trust that scores represent them), it is common to randomly select a sample separately from each business unit. This is an example of *stratified random sampling* in an employee survey, where the strata correspond to business units.[3] One company's pulse survey, for example, looks to invite about 600 employees from each of its largest units to achieve the minimally adequate sample size (roughly 325 employees), and this means inviting about 15% of the headcount from these units. However, the company invites all employees from units with a headcount less than 600 because the response rate has been near 50% in the past. This approach ensures adequate representation from each unit that demands a report of its survey score, but the total company scores will suffer from sampling bias because units with a smaller headcount are going to be overrepresented in the total aggregation. The HR unit, for instance, represents just under 2% of the total company headcount, but it accounts for nearly 6% of the total company sample, meaning that its scores are weighted three times higher in the sample compared to its population proportion. As HR employees often have more positive responses on employee surveys, the total company score would be artificially inflated because of the sampling methodology. To eliminate this sampling bias when estimating the total company population score, the data must be weighted so that disproportionately sampled groups are reconfigured to reflect proportions found in the population.

Weighting Scores from Disproportionately Sampled Subpopulations to Better Estimate the Population Score

In a situation where a subpopulation is over- or underrepresented in the sample, whether due to stratified random sampling or just markedly different response rates, the calculation of total company (i.e., the population) scores can be adjusted by "reversing" the incorrect proportions. This adjustment, known as *weighting*, can be done for percent favorable scores by multiplying each individual's dichotomous favorability value (1 = favorable, 0 = not favorable) by the ratio of subpopulation size N divided by respondent sample size n_r.[4] (Note that the sample sizes may vary by item if responses can be left blank or marked as not applicable.) To use an example, suppose the HR unit's headcount was $N = 260$ but the sample size was $n_r = 130$; that item's weight for all HR employees would be 260/130 or 2. That item would have a different weight for each of the subpopulations (e.g., HR, IT, Sales, Production). The sum of all the item's weights (for all sample respondents) should equal the total population N. So, while the original raw data for this item would have 1s and 0s to note favorable versus not favorable, this new calculation of those scores would be weighted by unit. Where there is a raw value of 1, there would now be a weighted value of 2 if that data point came from the HR unit or some other weighted value for the other units.

If one is only able to work with aggregated scores (not the original raw data), one can still weight these scores to improve the estimate of the total company population. Weighting aggregated scores for each unit (or other demographic subpopulations) requires multiplying each subpopulation's score by its actual proportion of the total headcount and then summing up those values across all of the groups. If the HR unit has 260 of the company's 14,500 employees, then the score from HR would be multiplied by 260/14,500; and similarly, the other units' scores would be multiplied by their actual proportion so that the sum of all of the weighted aggregated scores would equal the estimated company score.

In practice, weighting sample scores typically does not alter the estimated population score by that much unless the disproportionate sampling comes from demographic groups with vastly different scores (Mandell, 1974). For example, weighting scores by country would be warranted even if just India were oversampled because survey scores from India tend to be markedly more favorable than other countries' scores. Left uncorrected, the estimated company score would be artificially inflated. Yet, if only the United States were oversampled, weighting by country might not matter as much because scores from the United States are near the global average. Lastly, weighting will never fix poor sampling techniques; if some of the sample sizes are so small that they result in large margins of error, weighting the scores will not suddenly produce accurate population scores—the old adage "garbage in, garbage out" applies here.

A Summary of Practical Recommendations for Various Uses of Sample Surveys

Ideally, a person designing a pulse survey should use a respondent sample of 385 employees to create a ±5-point margin of error when estimating a very large population. To represent smaller populations, one can use a smaller sample and still reach this margin of error, but the minimum sample size must be 100 respondents (or over 80% of the population). Any company unit or demographic that needs its own set of scores should be treated as a subpopulation, where these same sampling recommendations apply (unless subsequent decisions about taking action will have little consequence or little risk of wasting resources). Given the likelihood of having low response rates, one should consider inviting twice as many employees as needed to reach an adequate sample size. Employees should be selected at random, but if the survey must produce scores for small subpopulations (e.g., business units, countries), then the sample should be selected from each of the subpopulations at whatever proportion is necessary to reach the ±5 margin of error. If some subpopulations are oversampled to reach this criterion, the total company scores can be more accurately estimated using weighted scores to reduce potential sample biases.

Finally, consider again the conflicting need for more data without oversurveying. Given the increasing desire for ongoing accurate data from as many segments of the company as possible while minimizing the number invited to any given survey, this review of sampling guidelines suggests this compromise: Administer a census survey in one quarter, followed by a pulse survey that invites one third of employees in each of the next three quarters—the census plus 3 pulses. To allay fears of survey fatigue from the pulses, consider blending census items with ones that ask how changes are progressing in order to demonstrate a concern over making progress rather than a love of repetitive surveying (Jolton, Barnett, Fink, Mastrangelo, & Weiner, 2017). In the hands of a thoughtful survey practitioner, the employee survey can meet the demands of 21st-century organizations as well as the demands from our research methods professors.

Notes

1. To estimate sampling error for mean scores instead of percent favorable scores, one can create a 95% confidence interval where the actual population score is 95% likely to be between $\bar{x} - 1.96(S_e) \leq \mu \leq \bar{x} + 1.96(S_e)$, where $Se = \sqrt{\left(\dfrac{\sigma^2}{n}\right)\left(1 - \dfrac{n}{N}\right)}$ and σ is estimated to be the standard deviation of the item, which for 5-point survey items is typically near 1 (Borg & Mastrangelo, 2008). Increasing the sample size n would produce a more accurate estimate of the population score. The prescribed minimum sample sizes provided in this chapter are nonetheless applicable for mean scores.

2. Of course, the term *statistically significant* is completely misused here. One might respond that accurate survey interpretation is affected by the sample size in two ways. First, we want to reduce sampling error so that estimates of scores based on everyone (respondents and nonrespondents) are ideally within ±5 percentage points of the survey scores from respondents; and obviously, the more respondents sampled, the better. Then, when we compare two different scores, we will test for significant differences based on the sizes of the groups being compared because the scores from larger groups are more accurate.

3. Although some would use the term *cluster sampling*, this is not technically correct. Cluster sampling is typically used to randomly select geographical areas in order to reduce the time it takes to have interviews or in-person data collection. This is not usually a concern for employee surveys. However, one potential use of cluster sampling would be inviting all employees from some retail stores rather than some employees throughout all stores. There may be some tactical advantage in only disrupting the workflow in some stores rather than all stores. Cluster sampling would also let the survey practitioner estimate the variation of scores within a complete unit of analysis—a common practice when assessing the strength of the climate and more accurate when all members in the unit are invited to the survey.

4. Mean scores also can be weighted by multiplying the original numeric response (5, 4, 3, 2, or 1) by the ratio of subpopulation N divided by respondent sample size n_r. Weighted scores can then be summed to create the estimated total company score.

References

Beagrie, S. (2015, July 30). Next generation employee engagement tools. *HR Magazine*. Retrieved from http://www.hrmagazine.co.uk/article-details/next-generation-employee-engagement-tools

Bersin, J. (2014, April 10). It's time to rethink the "employee engagement" issue. *Forbes*. Retrieved from https://www.forbes.com/sites/joshbersin/2014/04/10/its-time-to-rethink-the-employee-engagement-issue/#9ebfd246cf36

Borg, I., & Mastrangelo, P. M. (2008). *Employee surveys in management: Theories, tools, and practical applications*. Cambridge, MA: Hogrefe & Huber.

Chiu, M. (2016, October 13). What HR needs to know about sentiment analysis. *CEB Talent Daily*. Retrieved from https://www.cebglobal.com/talentdaily/hr-needs-to-know-sentiment-analysis/

Colihan, J., & Waclawski, J. (2006). Pulse surveys: A limited approach with some unique advantages. In A. Kraut (Ed.), *Getting action from organizational surveys: New concepts, technologies, and applications* (pp. 264–293). San Francisco, CA: Jossey-Bass.

Jolton, J. A., Barnett, G., Fink, A., Mastrangelo, P. M., & Weiner, S. (2017, April). *Breaking from the norm: Argument for new survey best practices*. Alternative session format at the 32nd Annual Conference of the Society for Industrial and Organizational Psychology, Orlando, FL.

Keen, L. (2015, August 11). Is it time to sack the annual employee engagement survey? *Financial Review*. Retrieved from http://www.afr.com/leadership/company-culture/is-it-time-to-sack-the-annual-employee-engagement-survey-20150810-givd0r

Macey, W. H., & Eldridge, L. D. (2006). National norms versus consortium data: What do they tell us? In A. Kraut (Ed.), *Getting action from organizational surveys: New concepts, technologies, and applications* (pp. 352–376). San Francisco, CA: Jossey-Bass.

Mandell, L. M. (1974). When to weight: Determining nonresponse bias in survey data. *Public Opinion Quarterly*, *38*, 247–252.

Rogelberg, S. G. (2006). Understanding nonresponse and facilitating response to organizational surveys. In A. Kraut (Ed.), *Getting action from organizational surveys: New concepts, technologies, and applications* (pp. 312–325). San Francisco, CA: Jossey-Bass.

Rowh, M. (2011, November 9). How to find out what employees really think. *CIO*. Retrieved from https://www.cio.com/article/2402428/enterprise-software/how-to-find-out-what-employees-really-think.html

Van Rooy, D. L., Whitman, D. S., Hart, D., & Caleo, S. (2011). Measuring employee engagement during a financial downturn: Business imperative or nuisance? *Journal of Business & Psychology*, *26*, 147–152.

Weiner, S. P., & Dalessio, A. T. (2006). Oversurveying: Causes, consequences, and cures. In A. Kraut (Ed.), *Getting action from organizational surveys: New concepts, technologies, and applications* (pp. 294–311). San Francisco, CA: Jossey-Bass.

Wiltse, D. (2008, October). The employee survey: What's in it for me? *Certification Magazine*, *10*(10), 50, 51, 56.

4

Exploring the Universe of Pulse Surveys and Continuous Listening Opportunities

Jeffrey A. Jolton and Cameron Klein

Since 2010 there has been an increased interest and urgency within organizations to create more opportunities to hear and learn from employees. Getting timely people insights has become a critical tool to help organizations shape and inform actions and decisions. This chapter is designed to help organizations better understand what it means to have continuous listening and pulsing programs, outline different approaches to these programs, and define a strategy that will work best for them.

The increased interest in pulsing and continuous listening stems from a multitude of factors, with technology being one of the most notable. Technological advances now allow for more frequent and diverse ways to assess employee perceptions and preferences. These advances have increased the speed with which data from employees, whether direct (e.g., via surveys and polls) or indirect (e.g., tracking badge in and out activities or e-mail patterns), can be leveraged to help in making human capital decisions. Technology has also helped to reduce the cost of employee listening initiatives, as well as create greater independence from vendors to run the listening programs, which in turn makes increased frequency more feasible.

A second key factor is ever-growing evidence that has tied employee perceptions (e.g., engagement) to business outcomes (Gong, Law, Chang, & Xin, 2009; Harter, Schmidt, & Hayes, 2002; Heskett, Sasser, & Schlesinger, 1997; Hogreve, Iseke, Derfuss, & Eller, 2017; Piening, Baluch, & Salge, 2013). These studies have helped organizational leaders to better understand how shifts in employee attitudes and behaviors can have a notable impact on a variety of business outcomes (e.g., turnover, individual performance, customer satisfaction, and financial performance; see Chapter 17 for more details on

Jeffrey A. Jolton and Cameron Klein, *Exploring the Universe of Pulse Surveys and Continuous Listening Opportunities* In: *Employee Surveys and Sensing*. Edited by: William H. Macey and Alexis A. Fink, Oxford University Press (2020).
© Society for Industrial and Organizational Psychology.
DOI: 10.1093/oso/9780190939717.003.0004

linkage research). As the linkage between employee perceptions and business outcomes has become clear, leaders have exhibited greater interest in understanding these perceptions. The result has been an increased desire to measure and track on the same frequency as other key business metrics.

Related to this leadership interest, the increased use of human capital analytics to help drive organization decisions and actions has also influenced the increased use of pulsing. There is a growing desire for more data points to help feed and support a variety of analytics and to help keep these metrics up to date (e.g., statistical models that predict the likelihood of voluntary turnover often rely on employee survey results). When the surveys are limited to annual census measures, the utility of the models becomes limited by the infrequent, annual collection method. More frequent surveying on key items in the predictive model enables the model to maintain viability and utility over time.

Although interest in conducting more frequent pulsing or continuous listening efforts has grown, many organizations struggle to figure out what exactly pulsing or continuous listening means for them. They are unsure how it should best be applied to help them reach their strategic goals. As a result, many pulsing programs fail to take hold appropriately or provide the insight and directions being sought.

Surveys may make up some or all of the activities as part of a continuous listening program, but it is important to recognize that the definition also allows the inclusion of a growing range of overt and unobtrusive measures that organizations may use for employee listening (see Chapter 14 for more details on these measures). Furthermore, pulsing and continuous listening programs are not limited to measuring just attitudes and perceptions; they also can directly measure specific behaviors and actions within the organization being taken by employees, leaders, or the organization as a whole.

Pulsing and continuous listening also suggest that the surveys are tracking employee perceptions and experiences. *Tracking* underscores that there is a longitudinal element to continuous listening—that we are looking at these perceptions and experiences not just at one point in time but across multiple points. This does not mean, however, that the measure is the same at each point in time. Continuous listening programs can track a topic or issue in different ways across the time period. For example, we may find in one survey that employees are frustrated with leadership transparency. A follow-up survey may allow employees a way to express preferences for how they would like leaders to communicate or on what topics.

Finally, the design of any continuous listening effort needs to be purposeful and to drive decisions, action, and change. Although technology and curiosity make it easier to reach out to employees more often, doing so without a clear purpose or connective tissue across the various surveys and measures can seriously undermine the long-term effectiveness of the program. Effective programs should be relevant and tied to clear organizational goals and interest, and feedback should have a clear direction for how the information will be used. When these elements are lacking, we are likely to see decreases in participation in the surveys as well as loss of credibility with leadership in the value of these programs.

Keeping Opportunities and Risks in Mind

As you design your pulsing or continuous listening program, it is important that organizations understand the opportunities and risks inherent in these efforts. Among the opportunities continuous listening surveys offer are the following:

- *Providing organizations a greater source of information from employees.* Instead of a longer one-time survey, organizations can conduct a variety of surveys to understand trends on key initiatives, information on hot topics, or reactions to recent organizational events.
- *Increased leadership involvement and ownership.* As leaders themselves are among the drivers of increased listening efforts, our experience has indicated greater involvement and ownership by leaders in what is being asked and how the results are to be used.
- *Experience shaped by feedback, increased connectivity to experience.* Ultimately, employees benefit from providing feedback that actively influences their work experiences and processes. Furthermore, by creating changes that take employee feedback and concerns into account, there is the potential of increased acceptance of changes that occur (through greater ownership) (e.g., Erez & Arad, 1986; Locke & Latham, 1990). This positive outcome requires, obviously, that survey feedback is actively used to make decisions or shape actions and, equally as important, that participants in the process see the connection between their feedback and these outcomes.

These benefits can be outweighed or mitigated by a number of risks inherent in these efforts. The more common to keep in mind include the following:

- *Oversurveying and survey fatigue.* Perhaps the most commonly discussed risk to enhanced continuous listening concerns the experience of *survey fatigue*, which refers to the belief that the more surveys people are invited to, the less likely they will be to continue to engage in the survey process (e.g., Porter, Whitcomb, & Weitzer, 2004). There are a number of factors that influence survey participation, but feeling that results are being used for actual action and change has been shown to be the biggest predictor of participation (e.g., our research across 220 firms and locations within organizations showed a correlation of .70, $p < .01$, between response rates and perceptions that action is being taken because of the survey; Jolton & Tate, 2017). Allen Kraut (2006) discusses in his book that the worst thing to do in employee surveys is to share results but not take action. Mastrangelo (Jolton, Barnett, Fink, Mastrangelo, & Weiner, 2017) discusses that people are less weary of multiple surveys than of lack of action on surveys (lack-of-action fatigue more than survey fatigue). Thus, although oversurveying can be a risk and sensitivity to this is warranted, it is more likely that lack of action on feedback is going to drive down participation than the frequency of surveys alone.
- *Focus on tracking versus action and change.* Related to fatigue is the perception that continuous listening is more about tracking scores and performance than it is about creating action and change. Although tracking progress on actions and change is useful and can often be a valid purpose for a continuous listening effort, when it is the only focus, the power and benefit of more frequent surveys lose value. Tracking can be a strategy when scores are dipping or falling flat, but there should still be a plan for action when the expected patterns are not where they should be. If not, the focus becomes tracking numbers for the sake of tracking rather than creating a meaningful work experience.
- *Leader- and manager-created surveys may not include useful content and could even create legal vulnerabilities.* As survey technologies become more prevalent, leaders, managers, and others can readily create their own pulses. The risk here is that the questions that they are asking may not necessarily be appropriate and useful (e.g., double-barreled, not able to get to the issue they are trying to resolve) or create legal risks (e.g.,

asking questions about how work affects family time, items that can be perceived as discriminatory, or content not being truly job-relevant). Organizations promoting more frequent surveys will need to have defined policies and governance in place to help override these risks, alongside other efforts to protect employee privacy and data security (see Chapter 24 for more on this topic).

- *Accountability is not always clear.* Unlike many annual survey programs, continuous listening activities do not always have clear accountability as to who is taking action on the survey. Global census surveys have the benefit of broad communications that reach everyone with plans that allow managers to cascade messaging and Human Resources (HR) being aligned to provide support where needed. Pulsing and frequent listening programs often rely on sampling versus census surveys and likewise don't incorporate broad communication campaigns. As a result, awareness of the survey being in field and the purpose of the survey may be limited, which can affect participation and increase misperceptions of what the results are being used for. Similarly, more frequent surveys do not have the same broad level of reporting as an annual program. Greater effort is required to help participants understand what their feedback will be used for and who is owning the results and follow-up.

These risks and opportunities point to the obvious conclusion that a good continuous listening survey program requires a strong overarching strategy for each event that is launched as a part of the program. In short, focus not just on what you are surveying about but also on the purpose you are surveying for. Having a strong strategic orientation allows your organization to capitalize on the opportunities while mitigating the risks.

Creating Your Pulsing and Continuous Listening Universe

Up to this point we have outlined what should be considered for a successful listening program. But what are the different types of surveys that can make up your listening universe? There are, of course, an endless number of variations of what the survey design can be. We propose the following taxonomy to help define the surveys that may be used. This not only helps pinpoint the action, purpose, and strategy of each element but also helps ensure that there is a balance to your program.

As seen in Figure 4.1 there are two continua for the taxonomy: action focus and formality. Action focus, along the *x*-axis, indicates whether the ultimate purpose of the measure is to be action-tracking or action-driving.

Action-driving indicates that the measure is designed to help inspire and generate new action, change, or behaviors in the organization. Many annual census surveys are action-driving in that there is an expectation that managers and leaders use the results to create action plans and drive change.

Action-tracking indicates that the measure is more for the purpose of trending or following on progress of defined actions or initiatives than for defining new directions for action. Many pulse survey programs traditionally fall toward action-tracking, with the goal to check in on how actions from a census survey are taking hold. Action-tracking surveys are also those that are collecting data for dashboards and analytics—the results in of themselves are not for direct action but to be used to keep measures up to date. Although some action could come from action-tracking based on the trending feedback, action is not the primary goal.

Formality, along the *y*-axis, reflects the degree of organizational support and resources, breadth of data usage, and depth of reporting.

Formal surveys tend to be more top-down-driven, with more communication, in-depth reporting, and widespread actions. The data may be applied to a number of applications. Formal programs are typically heavily supported with a variety of organizational resources.

Informal surveys tend to be more locally driven (e.g., business division) or have less broad involvement in terms of ownership, reporting, and action.

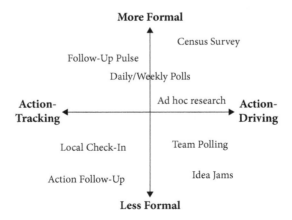

Figure 4.1. Taxonomy for defining pulse and continuous listening surveys.

They are usually more specific in what they measure and how the data will be used and not as reliant on broader organizational resources.

Using this taxonomy, we can define the more commonly used surveys in a continuous listening program. There is obviously a wide variation even within each of these survey programs that may shift where the survey falls in the taxonomy. However, the taxonomy helps focus how to define each element of your program and how the pieces can interact to fit within your broader listening strategy.

Census Surveys (Action-Driving/More Formal)

Although not typically thought of as part of a pulsing or continuous listening program, a census survey is often the keystone of an organization's listening strategy and should be considered as you design your pulse programs. Census surveys remain among the most common forms of employee surveys, with many organizations running them on an annual basis, surveying all employees (Jolton & Tate, 2017; see also Chapter 26 for more detail on survey frequency and audience).

The scope of content for the census survey is often broad, usually with a focus on employee engagement and covering a range of work experience elements (manager effectiveness, vision/strategy, communication, recognition, customer/quality focus, etc.). These surveys typically range from about 30 to 60 items.

Census surveys are more formal in that they are usually run centrally (often by the HR function), with high visibility across the organization to drive participation. The results are typically widely distributed, often provided at the manager or department level. Senior leadership is invested in the results, and training is generally provided to managers or to "survey champions" (or similar others assigned to support the process).

The action-driving element comes from the expectation that the census survey creates new initiatives and actions at all levels of the organization (or at least by those receiving reports). In many cases, leaders will take organization-wide action or cascade an area of priority for all levels of the organization to focus on.

Census surveys are not without their criticism—criticism that has helped fuel the demand for other kinds of listening. In our experience common charges levied against census surveys include (a) that results only come once a year; (b) that content and process are often driven top-down, missing issues or needs at the local level; and (c) that they focus on so many elements at once that they may miss opportunities to improve a broader range of areas (e.g., many companies end up focusing on the same two or three topics each year). However, census surveys still provide immense value in creating momentum across the entire organization. There is clearly something powerful in having everyone focused on the same thing at the same time. When truly focused, our experience suggests that most organizations are able to make progress in those areas where attention is placed. Beyond momentum and having a shared purpose, census surveys provide a large, complete data source to work from for research (i.e., linkage to turnover and business metrics). An increase in listening frequency doesn't necessarily mean that census surveys are obsolete, but their focus and frequency may shift over time (e.g., shorter and every 18–24 months).

Census-Based Pulsing (Action-Tracking/More Formal)

This class of measurement represents a more traditional way in which frequent surveying was done. Historically, these pulse surveys were used to track on actions initiated by the census survey—either by focusing on items from the census survey that were selected or identified as priorities for action and/or the key performance indicator (typically engagement index). These pulses differ from other kinds of pulses, in short, because they build directly on content and actions taken from the census survey itself.

Typically, census-based pulses are conducted one to three times between annual or biannual census surveys (e.g., either at the midpoint or quarterly). The survey is administered as either a census or a sample survey depending on how deep reporting needs to go in the organization, with sampling used more often when the focus is on tracking key performance indicators or global actions (see Chapter 3). Depending on the overall goal of the pulse (global tracking or local tracking), there may be supplemental items for each major business unit or territory to allow them to track specific topics being worked on at that level.

Census-based pulses are beneficial in that they help keep survey actions "top of mind" for leaders and managers and can help make actions from the census survey visible to employees and action that is based directly on their feedback. They can also identify opportunities to adjust actions taken where results are not moving the needle as expected. However, these programs also run the risk of focusing on just driving the numbers rather than on true change in work experience. A related risk in using the same items as the census is that the pulse is monitoring scores rather than a process that provides unique insights suggestive of change. Other programs, such as deep-dive and action pulsing, used in conjunction with census-based pulsing help counter some of these risks.

Deep-Dive Pulsing (Action-Driving/More Formal)

Deep-dive pulsing is like census-based pulsing in that it is somewhat tied to key issues that emerge from the census surveys but differs in that it is comprised of new items that provide additional insights and understanding to the issue. Organizations often use deep-dive pulsing to gather more information from employees, in either seeking more specific clarity on responses from the census or testing out specific actions that might help address the issue. For example, if the census survey revealed that career development was a problem area for the company, the follow-up pulse might look to determine what specific elements of career development were in the most need of attention (e.g., online training, coaching from managers, promotion opportunities) or if having more conversations or more career development resources would be most welcomed.

Deep-dive pulse surveys are typically administered less often than other approaches—most often conducted in just one or two administrations as a follow-up to the census. In addition, deep-dive pulse surveys typically only require a sample of employees as the need for localized reporting is lower. Content may also be unique by business unit, function, or territory, with each conducting its own pulse rather than one global pulse to capture all issues.

Benefits of deep-dive pulse surveys include providing more specific direction for action and buy-in from employees on those actions. These types of pulse surveys also help keep the focus on the changes to the work experience rather than just tracking on a number. Moreover, they can facilitate more immediate action on the issue being exposed on the census survey but are sometimes used as a substitute for a meaningful discussion with employees (i.e., doing another survey rather than talking with the teams). However, if the issue is widespread and requires a more formal initiative to create change, the deep-dive pulse survey can help ensure that the company or division is on the right track.

Action Pulsing (Action-Tracking/Less Formal)

Pulsing on actions initiated helps to address one of the key drawbacks to census-based pulsing, in that it is designed to measure specific actions being taken (including those inspired by the census or from elsewhere) rather than repeat the item used in the census to track change. For example, a business may have seen "open and honest two-way communication" as an issue on the census and, in response, decided to make sure at least 10 minutes of any team meeting was dedicated to an open discussion with attendees as an action. The action pulse would then ask an item like "I am given an opportunity to ask or share opinions in my team meetings."

Action-tracking pulses tend to be run one to two times between census survey administrations, but the reality is they can be run at any sensible point in follow-up to any key actions. They are often done at more local levels (even down to specific teams) rather than as a more centralized program in order to capture the specific actions. This makes it a more informal kind of listening. There is a greater challenge here to design items for the pulse as they need to be a direct reflection of the actions being taken. They do have the benefit, however, of focusing on precise actions and, therefore, may provide a more realistic assessment of impact and change than the original census item. These also tend to be very short, easy-to-answer surveys and are not necessarily restricted to just census-driven actions.

Ad Hoc Surveys (Action-Driving/Less Formal)

These surveys typically diverge from actions or items that are reflective in the census survey. They often focus on "hot topics" or key initiatives of importance to leaders. These programs are sometimes thought of as "research surveys" and can range broadly from program evaluation–type surveys (e.g., evaluating benefits, communications) to information required for analytic studies (e.g., commute-to-work challenges, life changes) to reaction (e.g., "What do you think of the cafeteria redesign?").

These programs typically are limited in how broadly results are reported. They are often conducted as sample surveys and can be run with any frequency. The survey contents/topics are usually asked just once (although in some cases the research is tracking impressions over time). Ad hoc surveys also tend to be more stakeholder-owned (e.g., diversity team) rather than manager-owned in terms of decisions and actions, making them less centralized (less formal) even if the survey administration itself is managed centrally. Finally, some companies run "omnibus" surveys that help capture results on a wide variety of topics that are not otherwise part of a census as a way of consolidating and minimizing the number of ad hoc surveys being run.

A key benefit of the ad hoc survey is that it helps to keep other surveys more "pure" in terms of content and focus. Too often, a census survey becomes a catch-all measure, representing a wide range of topics that are not actionable at the level of census reporting and can create a distraction from the main purpose (e.g., enriching employee work experience). Ad hoc surveys typically don't need to be conducted multiple times or tracked and can still provide rich information for decisions, actions, and research. One notable drawback here is that ad hoc surveys generally do not come with built-in mechanisms (or even the need) to provide clear feedback to participants. In such cases, a potential result is a decrease in participation in other surveys. Care is needed to make sure that results are shared and an action path is articulated to participants.

Always-On Polling (Action-Tracking or Action-Driving/More Formal)

This category covers a range of newer listening measures where employees are asked a single question or two each day or week. The question(s) could be the same each day or pulled from a small curated list (e.g., related to key priorities for that quarter). This approach is considered to be on the more formal side because these programs are usually centrally driven and require a fair amount of coordination/planning by the organization to effectively manage. These planning efforts may include the design of an ongoing library bank of questions and topics aligned to appropriate stakeholders. In addition, the methodology can vary greatly—for example, from a census that mandates employees complete the survey to unlock their workstations (e.g., Kim, 2018) to carefully crafted sampling approaches that accurately represent the population while also minimizing survey fatigue. In addition, one must consider how the results will be used (which can range from just getting a "health check" on morale to getting reactions to specific events or materials to helping define specific programs).

Always-on polling can also include somewhat less structured programs. As an example, some organizations have created programs where people can opt in to participate in short surveys that range from opinions about different programs to making naming suggestions for initiatives and tools. As well, we know of other organizations with voluntary daily polls that may not always be program-related (e.g., "Are you traveling for Thanksgiving this year?"). However, care should be taken with always-on programs to make sure there is a real purpose. It should not only bring value to your organization but also ensure that the program won't be harmful to other survey efforts (e.g., create mistrust in how data are being used). Time should be taken, as with any other listening program, to determine where it fits into the overall strategy, what kinds of insights will come from the program, and who is accountable for action and communicating results.

Always-on polling is beneficial in creating a constant exchange with employees across a variety of topics. They can bring an element of fun into the listening efforts, as well as quick insights on critical-to-employee topics (e.g., commute times) that might not readily be picked up by other listening programs. Sampling design is critical with these programs, and one of the common missteps is to assume the population is accurately represented (when there is potentially a high self-selection bias at play) or cutting results to levels that are inappropriate for the sample or response rate (see Chapter 3).

Manager-Driven Polling (Action-Tracking or Action-Driving/Less Formal)

This method takes advantage of the myriad of evolving technologies that allow managers to set up and launch short surveys for their teams. These programs are more informal as they are in the hands of the manager to define what to measure and when to launch the survey. Survey content typically is fairly limited, one to five items, covering any variety of topics and without a defined cadence. Some managers have used polling to evaluate the effectiveness of most every meeting they lead, while others initiate a once-a-month poll to determine what support the team needs to be effective on a given project. It is also common for managers to use polling once or twice a year to support a specific initiative or decision. Involvement is usually voluntary and can include the entire team, but managers have used polling to ask questions of clients, other colleagues, or subsets of employees when they have a larger team (e.g., division manager).

The biggest challenge with manager-driven polling is around governance and risk mitigation. As previously mentioned, managers are not always skilled at good survey item design or avoiding legally sensitive topics. These programs always require an increased sensitivity to confidentiality of results as well as maintaining trust with those invited to participate. One best practice to help mitigate these concerns is to have the managers choose items from a preset library rather than have the freedom to ask whatever they would like.

Centralizing polling tools, where the company provides the app or technology for the polling, also can allow governance and tracking to ensure that people are not being oversurveyed and can limit when or how many polls are released. Furthermore, centralized tools allow the organization insight in to what is being measured and can consider that as direction for other listening efforts as well.

It is recommended that manager-driven polling be packaged with training or guidance to ensure that the managers help them use polling appropriately. The more structure and guidance the organization can provide around manager-driven polling, the more likely the program can avoid any pitfalls.

Manager-driven polling provides a great degree of democratization that was difficult to achieve prior to various advances in surveying technology. Managers can get direct input on key topics of interest to them, in a way that is confidential or anonymous, from employees who might not otherwise share their feedback. It also allows them to track behaviors changes they are working on and get more immediate feedback to help reinforce these changes. There are risks in managers using the poll as a substitute for a more meaningful and direct conversation with employees. The hope is that the polling should help encourage and augment these discussions.

Other Surveys in the Universe (Mixed Methods)

The list presented in this chapter reflects, in general, various surveys in the continuous listening universe but is not by any stretch an exhaustive list of what can comprise the system. For example, we did not incorporate exit and onboarding or other lifecycle measures (e.g., anniversary or alumni surveys), which likely would fall on the more formal end of the spectrum but have a unique purpose in understanding specific events and programs (e.g., onboarding training or recruiter effectiveness) (see Chapter 5 for more on lifecycle measures).

Reaction measures, such as responses to town halls or training events, can be covered to some extent by polling but are often part of other more specific assessment efforts (e.g., training evaluations in learning management systems) or use alternative approaches (e.g., real-time polling using smart phone apps).

Other emerging areas of employee input are "idea jams" and virtual focus groups, which leverage technology that can solicit real-time brainstorming and evaluation by individuals or teams. Idea jams capitalize on some of the same tools we use in evaluating surveys (e.g., natural language processing, ranking, or rating), but ultimately the focus is on the final set of solutions or ideas rather than the full wealth of information collected along the way.

Make the Most of Your Universe

Ever-evolving technologies and understanding of pulsing and continuous listening methodologies means that organizations will not be short on options when seeking to enhance their listening programs. With increased options will come a desire to try everything, but we encourage you to think through your pulsing and continuous listening holistically—how various surveys interact and support one another and how they fit into broader HR analytics, talent, and business strategies. Break away from thinking just about the "next survey," and think about the program across the next 3 or 5 years, rather than one piece at a time.

There is no one-size-fits-all approach here. Be considerate of your organization's culture and approach to employee feedback. Better to slowly introduce different elements of continuous listening that are right for your organization than flood your employees with surveys that end up hurting your program as a whole.

Finally, don't be afraid to have some fun with your listening programs. This is a great opportunity to engage and interact with your employees. Use surveys more expansively to get ideas and input, to let employees know they are active influencers in their work environment. Use the freedom to measure more often to expand your HR analytics and be more creative in the stories you tell. The taxonomy of continuous listening provides a universe of options. Be courageous, explore, and make the right discoveries for your organization.

References

Erez, M., & Arad, R. (1986). Participative goal-setting: Social, motivational, and cognitive factors. *Journal of Applied Psychology, 71*(4), 591–597.

Gong, Y., Law, K. S., Chang, S., & Xin, K. R. (2009). Human resources management and firm performance: The differential role of managerial affective and continuance commitment. *Journal of Applied Psychology, 94*, 263–275. doi:10.1037/a0013116

Harter, J. K., Schmidt, F. L., & Hayes, T. L. (2002). Business-unit-level relationship between employee satisfaction, employee engagement, and business outcomes: A meta-analysis. *Journal of Applied Psychology, 87*, 268–279. doi:10.1037//0021-9010.87.2.268

Heskett, J., Sasser, W. E., & Schlesinger, L. (1997). *The service profit chain: How leading companies link profit and growth to loyalty, satisfaction, and value.* New York, NY: Free Press.

Hogreve, J., Iseke, A., Derfuss, K., & Eller, T. (2017). The Service–Profit Chain: A Meta-Analytic Test of a Comprehensive Theoretical Framework. *Journal of Marketing, 81*(3), 41–61.

Jolton, J., Barnett, G., Fink, A., Mastrangelo, P., & Weiner, S. (2017, April). *Breaking from the norm: Argument for new survey best practices.* Debate presented at the 32nd Annual Conference of the Society for Industrial and Organizational Psychology, Orlando, FL.

Jolton, J., & Tate, R. (2017, December). *PwC people analytics employee landscape study.* Unpublished raw data.

Kim, E. (2018, March 30). Amazon employees start their day by answering a simple question about work. CNBC.com. Retrieved from https://www.cnbc.com/2018/03/30/amazon-employee-reaction-to-hr-programs-connections-forte.html

Kraut, A. I. (Ed.). (2006). *Getting action from organizational surveys: New concepts, technologies, and applications.* San Francisco, CA: John Wiley & Sons.

Locke, E. A., & Latham, G. P. (1990). *A theory of goal setting & task performance.* Englewood Cliffs, NJ: Prentice-Hall.

Piening, E. P., Baluch, A. M., & Salge, T. O. (2013). The relationship between employees' perceptions of human resource systems and organizational performance: Examining mediating mechanisms and temporal dynamics. *Journal of Applied Psychology, 98*, 926–947.

Porter, S. R., Whitcomb, M. E., & Weitzer, W. H. (2004). Multiple surveys of students and survey fatigue. *New Directions for Institutional Research, 2004*(121), 63–73.

5

Lifecycle Surveys

Individual and Organizational Journeys

Jeffrey M. Saltzman, Scott M. Brooks, and Victoria Hendrickson

There's an old proverb that says, "Journeys start by putting one foot in front of the other." An employee's experience with an organization, from initial attraction, selection, and contribution to ultimate exit, can be thought of as a journey as well. What caused the individual to consider an employer? What makes someone choose one over the other? Once hired, how long did it take to get his or her bearings straight, and when did the employee begin to contribute meaningfully? What made the employee consider leaving the organization? Would the employee ever consider returning, or if entering retirement, does he or she feel prepared?

Clearly, many questions can be asked, many more than any one organization has the resources to pursue. But understanding which ones are worth pursuing—and how far back on the employee's journey you travel—depends on why an organization is undertaking such research in the first place. What's often missed in designing a lifecycle approach is a very simply question— "What are the organization's goals and needs?"—that often has a more complicated answer. A simple answer focuses on the tools, with the project team thinking "We need an exit survey" or "We need an engagement survey." What is lost with a focus on the tools is a direct line of sight to what the organization needs to accomplish.

Consider this example: One large healthcare provider was losing a whopping 15,000 nurses per year. It was such a large number that it was affecting the organization's ability to deliver services to its patients. A postemployment survey of the 15,000 who left in the previous year asked if there was anything that could have been done to get them to stay. The number one answer? "Someone should have asked me to stay." While unhappiness about work schedules was also an issue, many of these nurses could have been convinced to stay if only someone had reached out, ensured them of their importance,

Jeffrey M. Saltzman, Scott M. Brooks, and Victoria Hendrickson, *Lifecycle Surveys* In: *Employee Surveys and Sensing*. Edited by: William H. Macey and Alexis A. Fink, Oxford University Press (2020). © Society for Industrial and Organizational Psychology.
DOI: 10.1093/oso/9780190939717.003.0005

and asked them to stay. Unfortunately, what happened instead was an organizational assumption that it was the end of that employee's journey, which triggered a standard exit survey and the loss of these nurses. About 30% of those who left indicated in a boomerang survey that they would return if only someone would ask.

As happened with the healthcare company, the practitioner needs to determine the pain points as well as the talent and staffing needs that the research is trying to resolve. That is where you begin, and some of those answers may depend on where the organization is in its own life cycle. Everyone's journey—and every organization's journey—is going to be somewhat unique.

Today, certain advances in technology—such as the ability to look across vast volumes of information in a "big data" fashion—better enable organizations to meet these complementary needs. These advances have created new tools that represent both opportunity and risk for the practitioner. The opportunity is obvious: such tools provide the ability to gain new insight into how to maximize organizational performance and what drives employees during the course of their pre-employment, employment, and postemployment. The risk may not be as clear, but it occurs when the tool is confused with the goals or the objectives of the research. New technology might be attractive and cool, but it must be adequately evaluated, both psychometrically and against the goals and objectives of what the organization and the practitioner are attempting to accomplish.

Planning Lifecycle Programs

Traditional Human Resources (HR) outlets frequently recommend lifecycle surveys such as onboarding surveys to help organizations gauge how welcomed employees feel as they join an organization or exit surveys to tell them why individuals want to quit. These types of surveys reflect the building and maintaining of a discipline of listening and responding to employees and helping to improve the experience of individuals' roles, but the common advice often reflects two of the most common limitations or mistakes made with lifecycle surveys:

1. *Focusing on the individual experience at the expense of the organizational system's performance.* Understanding how welcomed new employees feel can be very important, but often an equal or even more important

organizational need is to manage the overall flow of employees into, through, and out of the organization.

2. *Confusing the tool with the objective.* For example, exit surveys help organizations understand part of the story of why employees choose to quit but are not the only—or arguably not the best—way to predict or to mitigate turnover.

Regarding the first pitfall, there are two main ways to look at the design and deployment of these surveys: through the employee's journey or through the perspectives and needs of the organization. This is illustrated by the following case.

A technology company has emerged from its entrepreneurial roots into being a major corporation. Growth is fast, acquisitions are constant, and scalability is a primary concern.

If that were the context, a lifecycle survey program built to support those needs might pursue the following objectives:

- How the organization can better manage the constant flow of new employees across the whole organization to keep teams—not simply individuals—at maximum performance. Beyond helping new employees become and stay engaged, there needs to be a focus on performance of teams or larger groups.
- How systems and processes can be designed to enable scalability, making it easier to integrate new employees, not just as evaluated by those new employees but by their more veteran teammates.
- How to manage institutional knowledge so that the constant churn of employees into, around, and out of the organization is appropriately maintained.
- How the organization itself can properly manage the evolution of its competencies to strengthen its uniqueness in the marketplace.

These issues are clearly related to, yet different from, those more traditional HR concerns about how individuals progress through their cycle of joining, working within, and departing organizations. There are some implications of this kind of thinking:

1. Any single organization will have its own unique objectives for lifecycle surveys to address. Organizational strategies should maximize uniqueness and differentiation in the marketplace. They should not be simply a jumble of best practices executed elsewhere. The combination of unique individual talents contributes to the cultures and systems that differentiate organizations not only in terms of the employment experience but the way work is done and the resulting differentiation in the market (Ployhart & Hale, 2014). Similarly, managing the flow of employees, talents, and competencies will have different emphases to support those strategies (see Brooks & Saltzman, 2016, for a discussion of how being strategic requires being unique).

2. The kinds of objectives and needs to manage the flow of employees will not always be addressed by just one survey. Instead, a lifecycle survey program should be "criterion-focused" and not "predictor-focused"— once the objectives/criteria are assembled, integrating several different kinds of data will likely be required.

The main point here is that, as survey designers, we can and often do focus on the life cycle of any single employee, as many programs do. But we should also absolutely focus on the constant flow of employees through an organization and how flow is managed to help that organization succeed.

Alongside this comes the second pitfall in the list. There are automatic assumptions that we should critically evaluate. If you want to know how effectively new employees become solid performers, asking the new employees themselves may not be the more predictive approach (hint: asking their more veteran teammates can be more effective). If you want to know why people quit, asking them in exit surveys is not necessarily the best approach.

It is a critical point: The questions these surveys address are more important than the surveys themselves. Accept/decline surveys, onboarding surveys, traditional opinion surveys, or exit surveys can all be important and useful. But the more important focus are the questions we ask to manage issues like candidate experience, likelihood of acceptance, bringing new employees up to speed, ongoing engagement, what employees see in the business, or why they may decide to quit, no matter how we gather the evidence.

It is important for those engaged in organizational survey programs to focus on the strategic organizational goals and then match the mechanics, events, employee roles, and more to organizational needs. The aim is to provide direction on how to design these systems so that they yield meaningful data that the organization can act upon. And as the survey landscape grows more complex, we need to ensure that our measurements are grounded in science and clear methodological thinking.

To set the stage, first let's look at the most common types of lifecycle surveys:

1. *Prehire survey*: Measures attitudes and opinions of job applicants.
2. *Accept/decline survey*: Measures differences in attitudes between individuals who chose to either accept or decline a job offer.
3. *Onboarding/new hire survey*: Measures attitudes and situations of new employees during their first 2 weeks or so on the job. These surveys can cover two main areas:
   i. Transactions (e.g., "When you showed up on the first day did you have an e-mail address and computer?")
   ii. The environment (e.g., "Did you feel welcomed; was anyone orienting you to the environment?")
4. *Assimilation survey*: Measures attitudes of employees after their first 90 days on the job.
5. *Employee opinion surveys (ongoing)*: Typically the most commonly used survey, measures employee attitudes throughout their tenure at an organization, ability to help the organization achieve its goals or some common concepts such as employee engagement.
6. *Confidence surveys*: Gathers information from the employee perspective, can be useful in predicting an outcome or event, such as success of a new product launch.
7. *Exit survey/interview*: Measures attitudes of individuals upon their notice of intent to leave the organization.
8. *Attrition/boomerang survey*: Measures attitudes of individuals 4–6 weeks after departure (also assesses willingness to return to the organization).
9. *Preparation for retirement*: Measures employee readiness to exit from the organization by retirement.

In 2018, OrgVitality conducted an industry-wide survey to evaluate how organizations are implementing and acting upon and what they are hoping to achieve with lifecycle surveys. The survey was sent to internal survey practitioners at organizations with a strong history of employee surveys. The resulting sample describes the practices of 43 organizations, representing the Fortune 500, government agencies, quickly growing technology startups, and not-for-profits. Of the organizations participating, 81% have 10,000+ employees, 10% have 5,000–10,000, and the remaining 9% have 1,000–5,000. Industries include high-tech, consumer goods, and manufacturing. This sample provides insight into large-scale survey programs across a variety of contexts.

So how common are various types of lifecycle surveys? Discussions with survey practitioners, conference programs, and other measures of industry trends would suggest that each of the different touchpoints are quite common. Actual usage varies quite a bit. As shown in Table 5.1, general employee opinion surveys, exit surveys, and, to a lesser extent, onboarding surveys are most common, with a smattering usage of other kinds of survey work.

Utilization of Lifecycle Surveys

Within each of these survey types, there are the lifecycle events themselves. As referenced in Table 5.1, the most common types of lifecycle surveys are those that align with commonly defined lifecycle events—joining an organization, ongoing experience, and leaving the organization. We review onboarding, employee opinion, and exit surveys in this section. Notably, however, we will not simply be providing an overview of these kinds of surveys themselves but will focus mainly on the kinds of questions they are designed to answer.

Onboarding

If an organization already has an annual employee survey, it may be able to glean important insights about onboarding even before launching a new effort to collect information via a specialized onboarding survey.

As an example, consider any organization experiencing fast growth, high turnover, or other conditions where it is particularly important for new employees to quickly become proficient performers. In those cases, an employee opinion survey may have an item such as, "New employees get the

Table 5.1 Types of Lifecycle Surveys and Their Frequency (by Percent of Respondents)

	Not at all	Completely different unit to unit	Depends on unit/use varies somewhat	Enterprise-wide solution-managed, deployed locally as needed	Enterprise-wide solution-managed, deployed centrally in consistent way
Prehire	67	2	0	12	16
Accept/decline	70	7	9	2	12
Onboarding/new hire	23	9	21	9	37
Assimilation	37	7	19	7	30
Employee opinion	0	0	0	2	98
Confidence	58	7	7	0	26
Exit	7	19	21	9	44
Attrition	79	12	7	0	2
Retirement prep	84	12	2	2	0

training they need to quickly become high performers." Consider the sample results to that item as presented in Figure 5.1.

It is a very common pattern for the newest employees to rate this kind of item more favorably than more experienced tenure groups. If all an organization had was the evaluation of the newbies, it might not fully understand the gravity of the issue. In these cases, it is the more experienced employees who feel the burden of low-performing newbies, taking time away from their own jobs to supplement training, double-check quality, clean up problems, and so forth. It is not the new employees themselves who are the best informants regarding this issue. When looking at results across units of an organization, questions like this can help prioritize which areas need more support to prepare for expected growth. This illustration highlights that even without a companion onboarding survey, the more traditional or annual employee surveys can absolutely provide insight into the onboarding process.

Yet onboarding surveys, sometimes called "new hire surveys," are the third most common lifecycle event survey (after general employee opinion surveys and exit surveys)—76% of organizations that do lifecycle surveys conduct onboarding surveys. Generally, onboarding surveys are administered within the first 3 months of employment. The overall goal is to assess how an employee is acclimating to the organization—the specifics of the survey itself can vary widely. The process of getting an employee up to speed includes a range of activities from the tactical, such as getting e-mail set up, to the strategic, including learning how their work fits into the bigger picture, and everything in between. Many onboarding surveys focus heavily on the tactical to get a sense of whether immediate needs have been met. Results can be used to change the cadence of how these needs are met. While these

Survey Item: New employees get training they need.

	Favorable	Neutral	Unfavorable
Newbies (up to 1 year)	49	23	27
Experienced (1–3 years)	35	30	35
Seasoned (4–6 years)	32	32	36
Veterans (7 or more years)	33	34	33

Figure 5.1. Case study results: New employee training evaluation by tenure.

tactical topics often cover the most immediate needs, focusing solely on logistics risks ignoring other issues.

To optimize the use of onboarding surveys, they should be used to gather critical information about an employee's early experiences that can predict later outcomes (Gundry & Rousseau, 1994). Research shows that 22% of turnover happens within the first 45 days of hire (Farren, 2007) and that 52% of turnover occurs in the first year (Hay Group, 2014). Clearly, this is a critical point in an employee's life cycle, and many needs are not met in this time. The first few weeks and months are critical for employees to build relationships, get to know the company culture, learn specifics for their job, and generally get what they need to be successful. Topics often include the following:

- Company culture and values, including ethics policy and safety measures
- Leadership introductions and values
- Manager relationships
- Team relationships
- Job role goals and expectations
- Performance evaluation to be expected

A good onboarding survey should address each of these components for multiple reasons, both short and long term. In the short term, learning where new employees need more support is useful in running these programs. In the long term, results from these onboarding surveys can be connected to other measures, like annual employee opinion surveys, performance data, turnover data, and exit surveys. By connecting these measures, it's possible to identify what experiences in the first 90 days predict successful outcomes (assuming that surveys are identified—see Chapter 15 for further detail). While the nuances of the survey questions and exact mechanics differ across organizations, the overarching principles are consistent:

- *Be strategic with your content.* Focus on the turning-point experiences that impact whether an employee gets what he or she needs to be successful. Typically, this is focused around relationships and the work itself.
- *Time it right.* Generally, the best time to do a survey is when you do it well. That said, you want to make sure you get people early, while they have a newcomer's perspective, yet allow enough time for them to have had some training, introduction, and onboarding experiences

in order to provide meaningful feedback. Often, this is within the first 30–60 days.

- *Act on aggregated data.* Resist the urge to act on individual cases. Like most other surveys, the most intelligence will come from group-level patterns such as comparisons across employee segments and changes over time.
- *Be clear on who owns what.* All too often, lifecycle event surveys are kept at a local level and only pieces are fed back to centralized groups or vice versa. Assign clear ownership for guiding the survey program including survey development, results analysis and cascade, and, most importantly, action.
- *Connect the data.* For a lifecycle survey program to be effective, the data should be integrated. Onboarding surveys provide particularly actionable intelligence on what early experiences lead to success. This is actionable for programmatic support and ongoing refinement of questionnaires.

If how an employee onboards is important, an equally important event is how that employee leaves the organization. This is covered in the next section.

Terminations

Understanding and managing employee turnover are the challenges that most inspire lifecycle surveys. We want to know why people quit. And it feels like the most natural approach is to ask them. But a more refined question is to ask what can be done months ahead of time to prevent regrettable talent loss. While subtle, reframing the question in this way points us to a more useful way to leverage surveys to address this organizational need.

First, we will set the stage with a useful model of employee termination, adapted from customer turnover. In essence, the decision to leave a job is a combination of three forces (Figure 5.2):

1. The "push": dissatisfaction with aspects of the current organization or job
2. The "pull": attraction to an alternative, whether another job or occupation of one's time (e.g., back to school or family life)

Push:
Dissatisfaction

Friction:
Switching Costs

Pull:
Alternative

Figure 5.2. The three forces of turnover.

3. The "friction": difficulty in making a change, whether logistical concerns (like commutes or relocations) or other ties to a particular organization that work to keep one in the job regardless of pushes or pulls (like on-site childcare or deferred compensation)

The literature on employee turnover is vast (e.g., Hom, Mitchell, Lee, & Griffeth, 2012), and a review of it is beyond the scope of this chapter. That said, efforts to locally measure and understand turnover tend to categorize into efforts to track each of these forces.

Evaluating the Push to Exit with Employee Opinion Surveys

Employee opinion surveys are well suited to evaluating the push, which commonly evaluate engagement, intentions to quit, career progress, recognition and respect, and a myriad of other topics often associated with voluntary terminations. Most critically, surveys can easily set up research projects that are designed to predict the future. It is of particular value to organizations to not simply track why people have already quit but to be able to identify and act upon the forces that might lead to future quitting.

If retention is a focus, it is easy to use an existing employee opinion survey to predict turnover. Most simply, you can evaluate and track turnover risk within the organization. Often, the best single-item predictor of actual turnover is an "intention-to-quit" survey item. In Figure 5.3, those who intend to quit can be tracked over time and across important groups or demographics

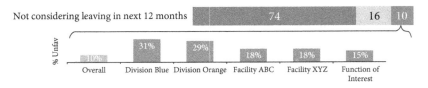

Figure 5.3. Tracking turnover risk with intentions to leave.

Drivers of Intent to Stay	% Fav
Able to fulfill my career goals	66
Trust decisions by leadership	75
Manager eliminates barriers	63
Schedules for high workload periods clear enough to plan around them	60

Intent to Stay

Figure 5.4. Key drivers of intentions to leave.

within the organization. In this case example, if stability in Division Blue or Orange is particularly important, then the organization knows it has a problem to address.

With the next level of analysis, key drivers of intentions to quit can be determined to identify the levers to pull and the "story" of what separates those who intend to quit versus those who do not (see Figure 5.4). In this case, the drivers are ranked by potency. Thus, the factors that most prevent quitting include ability to meet career goals, a faith in senior leadership's decisions, an immediate manager who is effective at helping get the work done, and the ability to manage those inevitable periods of high workload. These illustrate typical "push" forces.

While each of these approaches help tell the story of exiting employees, the question of turnover can be better addressed with actual turnover as a criterion. Assuming that a survey is confidential and not anonymous, an employee survey data set collected at one point in time can be augmented with termination information from the subsequent 6 months or year. These analyses can become very involved, depending on the heterogeneity of the organization, the N sizes of terminations available to work with, and the sophistication of the audience. In one simple case, shown in Table 5.2, logistic regression identified the survey items that most differentiated the voluntary departures from those who stayed.

Evaluating Terminations with Exit Surveys

While employee opinion surveys have the methodological advantage of representing opinions collected before the decision to quit, exit surveys uniquely are suited to provide information about the exit decision explicitly. Some key examples include the following:

Table 5.2 Survey Items That Most Differentiate Stayers Versus Leavers, Ranked by Gap in Favorable

Survey Item (Abbreviated)	Percent Favorable		
	Current Employees	Left Voluntarily	Gap
Promising future for me	69	49	−20
Job makes good use of skills, abilities	80	60	−20
Can meet career goals	66	47	−19
Feeling of accomplishment	78	59	−19
Opportunities to develop professionally	59	43	−15
Confidence in company ability to succeed, grow	84	70	−13

- Known drivers of retention, such as those listed in Figure 5.4 or Table 5.2. When these items matched to an annual employee survey and the scores can be compared, these issues can be tracked better across time and employee segments.
- Characteristics of the decision to quit itself, such as
  - Whether the employee would have continued to work at the organization if a couple of issues were resolved
  - Whether the employee would work for the organization again
  - Whether it was hard for the employee to decide to leave the organization
- Information about the pull forces (which cannot easily be gathered elsewhere), such as
  - Active job search
  - Whether a new job was (or will be) easy to find
  - What kind of job/role the employee is moving into (e.g., similar job with a competitor, significant career move, completely different role such as back to school)

When this type of information is woven into the data landscape along with information from other sources, notably a more traditional employee opinion survey, more complete characterization of the push and the pull (and friction, to a lesser extent) can be developed.

Employee Opinion/Engagement/Strategic Surveys

Beyond providing insights into onboarding and exit experiences, employee opinion surveys certainly provide information about other touchpoints in the employee life cycle. Since opinion surveys are well covered throughout this book, the goal of this section is how to consider these measurements in the context of a full employee life cycle.

Employee opinion surveys are what people generally think of in terms of organizational surveys, and they are popular. Within those we surveyed, 100% of organizations that conduct lifecycle surveys use opinion surveys, whether annual census surveys or variations. These surveys gather opinions simultaneously from all employees regardless of life stage, offering an opportunity to compare how employees at different stages experience various topics.

The goal of these surveys is to understand the employee experience on the topics that most impact organizational effectiveness, with the intention that findings are used to create action plans that improve the areas that are both critical for organizational effectiveness and underperforming in some way. These points can't be fleshed out from off-the-shelf engagement models (e.g., see Brooks & Saltzman, 2012, 2016). Organizational strategies and their corresponding tactics require uniqueness—you cannot copy your way to competitive differentiation. Thus, the best approaches are often developed by interviewing leaders or conducting employee focus groups to understand the company's unique secret sauce. Once these constructs are articulated in a way that feels like that company, life cycle can help describe how different segments of employees experience these goals differently.

A valuable connection of data streams is employee opinion surveys and exit surveys. If a piece of the business is experiencing high turnover, it's valuable to take the set of employees who quit and look at how their employee survey scores rated before they quit (and how they compare to those who stayed). Were there frustrations on getting the work done? Were relationships with other members of the leadership negative? How do these experiences align with exit survey results? In short, what experiences highlighted on the employee opinion survey could have predicted they would leave? This allows the company to address these experiences and to identify employees who may be at risk for turnover.

Challenges

Implementing an effective lifecycle survey program can be an exercise in cross-functional collaboration and organizational influence. With many choices on how to execute a lifecycle survey program come a variety of challenges in their execution. As we gather more data from across organizations, this brings in the complexity of a holistic strategy, ownership, and requirements around using the data, not to mention the mechanics of actually bringing multiple data streams together. In increasing level of granularity, some considerations to keep in mind when beginning a lifecycle journey include the following:

- *Overarching lifecycle strategy.* Typically, different components of the employee life cycle are owned by various groups. Often, an analytics group is responsible for overall employee engagement and census surveys, whereas a talent-management group is responsible for onboarding programs and surveys as well as exit surveys. No one group or role owns the life cycle–measurement strategy. Creating a holistic strategy of how to measure and support the entire employee life cycle will require cross-functional collaboration.
- *Ownership of data and actions.* As a lifecycle program rolls out, there will be decisions to make around how to gather, report, and act on data for each event. While an overarching strategy is critical, each lifecycle event is slightly different from others and will require an owner to make a call on how to best frame the data and drive action.
- *Mechanics.* Gathering data files from across the organization is an effort not to be underestimated. Often, different measures are administered on asynchronous schedules, in different formats from different vendors. Depending on the measure, results may be stored at different levels of aggregation. The key is to identify what measures will be integrated and ensure that there are unique identifiers (such as a common employee ID) to join data sources together.

The overarching point is to begin by creating an overall lifecycle strategy that will enable the right collaborations and guidelines to prioritize research questions that have the most impact and make mechanical decisions that support those questions.

Beyond data ownership and cross-functional implications, data privacy is another challenge that has become more intricate in recent years with the advent of the European Union's General Data Protection Regulation and other social, legal, and ethical standards to meet. "Big data" are often at odds with privacy, and managing an increasingly complex survey landscape is no exception (see Chapter 24 for more on data privacy and security). For example, consider the fundamental issue of "minimum N," the minimum number of individuals to be combined before reporting survey results. In many onboarding and exit programs, it is possible to view individual-level data. What are the employee's rights to privacy and confidentiality if they can now be tracked and measured, in an identified fashion, at each step of the journey? What are the implications of using the resulting analyses for individual-level decisions, such as promotion or training assignments versus more global (and anonymous) decisions, such as designing a more effective training program for salespeople?

It is tempting to view onboarding and exit survey responses individually, to understand what any one employee is looking for and simply try to provide it. While this is often a good intent, any view of individual-level data should be carefully thought through. There can be good reasons to view responses individually and follow up with employees. For example, if employees raise uncertainty on an onboarding survey, safety or ethical concerns in a census survey, or a possible way to reconcile differences on an exit survey, these data are most actionable at the individual level and can only be resolved by clarifying with that individual directly. The key is to retain the ability to view individual-level data while ensuring that employees feel comfortable with the confidentiality of the survey program. The best analysis plan is useless if few employees respond due to a lack of trust in the program. Guidelines for striking this balance include the following:

- Only specific, event-based surveys allow for individual-level responses to be viewed. This includes onboarding, exit, new manager, etc., which are managed by HR or other centralized groups, rather than a census or pulse where managers receive results.
- Communicate clearly with employees. Clarify in survey invitations and frequently asked questions who has access to the data. By sharing this with employees, you can ease the concerns of managers viewing their direct reports' responses and retaliating for negative results.

- Give employees choice. Rather than providing all individual results for review, it is possible to give employees a choice if they would like to be contacted about their survey responses.

Conclusion

Lifecycle survey programs can be overwhelming. It takes a great deal of effort to chart out an overall strategy, collaborate across the organization to get the right data, and ultimately pull all the pieces together in a way that yields meaningful data. In our discussions with practitioners, few disagree that these are the steps that lead to a valuable program, yet none are completely satisfied with their programs. In our industry survey, 100% of respondents saw value in connecting lifecycle touchpoints, while only one in five actually do so. If you are starting your lifecycle journey or want to review what you have in place, here are our top considerations for a robust lifecycle program:

1. Start with the right questions of the data; technology/mechanics will follow.
2. Work on personal and organizational questions.
3. Start with census survey or other existing data—lifecycle "nuggets" can come from there.
4. Move to exit survey, perhaps then onboarding.
5. Don't underestimate the challenge of organizational navigation and collaboration.
6. Integrate data sources, such as employee surveys, actual turnover, and workforce stats.
7. Data mechanics vary widely—adapt to your own situation and workforce requirements.
8. Finally, consider a systemic lifecycle point of view. The individual and organizational experiences are intertwined, and understanding each level of aggregation leads to valuable insight.

Over time, you will learn to navigate the nuances of your organization's sharing of data and perfect the mechanics of synthesizing data to gain greater insights and focus on the most actionable takeaways for various stakeholder groups. As these tangible aspects become more streamlined, the key to a valuable lifecycle program is to ensure that the overall strategy remains aligned with current business needs. Over time, different business challenges and market conditions and broader social context will change priorities. Like all measurement programs, your lifecycle program should flex to best inform the current business needs and do so at the most critical components of the employee life cycle.

Acknowledgment

The authors acknowledge Amanda Dundas for her invaluable support in the construction and editing of this chapter.

References

Brooks, S. M., & Saltzman, J. M. (2016). *Creating the vital organization: Balancing short-term profits with long-term success.* New York, NY: Palgrave Macmillan.

Brooks, S. M., & Saltzman, J. M. (2012). Why employee engagement is not strategic. *HR People & Strategy, 35*(4), 4–5.

Farren, C. (2007). Help new hires succeed: Beat the statistics. Retrieved November, 28, 2018, from http://thewynhurstgroup.com/wp-content/uploads/2014/07/Help-New-Hires-Succeed.pdf

Gundry, L. K., & Rousseau, D. N. (1994). Critical incidents in communicating culture to newcomers: The meaning is the message. *Human Relations, 47*(9), 1063–1088.

Hay Group. (2014). *Trends in employee engagement.* White paper. Retrieved from www.haygroup.com.

Hom, P. W., Mitchell, T. R., Lee, T. W., & Griffeth, R. W. (2012). Reviewing employee turnover: Focusing on proximal withdrawal states and an expanded criterion. *Psychological Bulletin, 138,* 831–858.

Ployhart, R. E., & Hale, D., Jr. (2014). The fascinating psychological microfoundations of strategy and competitive advantage. *Annual Review Organizational Psychology & Organizational Behavior, 1*(1), 145–172.

6

Design and Application of Employee Engagement Surveys

An Evidence-Based Approach

John P. Meyer

Since the turn of the millennium, engagement surveys have become extremely popular in organizations, and a major product for human resources consulting firms. The expectation is that an engaged workforce will provide the organization with competitive advantage, and there is indeed evidence linking engagement to superior individual (Christian, Garza, & Slaughter, 2011) and organizational (Schneider, Yost, Knopp, Kind, & Lam, 2017) performance. Engagement surveys are one tool that organizations can use to evaluate where their employees are on the disengagement–engagement continuum and where to address their attention if engagement levels are below optimal. But to be of value, engagement surveys must be carefully designed, and the information generated must be put to good use.

My objective in this chapter is to provide an evidence-based guide to the design and application of engagement surveys. In doing so, I build on the theoretical model proposed by Macey and Schneider (2008) in their insightful critique of the academic and practitioner literatures. The framework guiding this chapter is depicted in Figure 6.1. At the center of the figure is what Macey and Schneider referred to as *state engagement*. Here, I address the issue of what we mean by *engagement* and how it relates to similar concepts such as job satisfaction and organizational commitment. I also address the question "engagement with what?" Employees might be highly engaged in the tasks they perform, but is that enough? Are they also engaged and willing to work toward the success of their teams and/or the fulfillment of the broader mission of the organization? The answers to these questions have important implications for survey design because, as Macey and Schneider (2008, p. 4)

John P. Meyer, *Design and Application of Employee Engagement Surveys* In: *Employee Surveys and Sensing.* Edited by: William H. Macey and Alexis A. Fink, Oxford University Press (2020). © Society for Industrial and Organizational Psychology. DOI: 10.1093/oso/9780190939717.003.0006

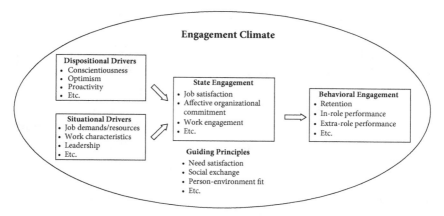

Figure 6.1. The engagement process and underlying principles.

point out, "end users of these products expect interpretations of the results to be cast in terms of actionable implications. Yet, if one does not know what one is measuring, the action implications will be, at best, vague and, at worst, a leap of faith."

On the right side of Figure 6.1 are the behavioral manifestations of state engagement, or what Macey and Schneider (2008) described as *behavioral engagement*. These are behaviors that organizations hope to encourage on the belief that they will contribute to enhanced performance and organizational success. On the left are the antecedents, or *drivers*, of state engagement. These fall into two categories, one reflecting dispositional characteristics, described by Macey and Schneider as *trait engagement*, and the other involving conditions of work and the workplace. Both are important, but I focus on the latter because it is these conditions, as seen through the eyes of employees, that are the primary focus of engagement surveys.

The final element included in Figure 6.1 reflects what I refer to as *guiding principles*. These principles are based on decades of scientific research and help to explain the linkages between the drivers and both state and behavioral engagement. More importantly, they can be particularly useful in the design of post-survey intervention strategies. Together, the drivers of engagement, particularly the situational drivers, along with state and behavioral engagement with their potential for contagion effects (Bakker, van Emmeri, & Euwema, 2006), contribute to the overall *engagement climate* within the organization.

Defining and Measuring State Engagement

William Kahn (1990) is credited with coining the term *engagement*. In his seminal article, he defined engagement as "the harnessing of organizational members' selves to their work roles; in engagement, people employ and express themselves physically, cognitively, and emotionally during role performances" (p. 694). More recently, Wilmar Schaufeli and his colleagues defined engagement as "a positive, fulfilling, work-related state of mind that is characterized by vigor, dedication, and absorption" (Schaufeli, Salanova, Gonzalez-Roma, & Bakker, 2002, p. 74). There have been many other attempts at definition (see Saks, 2017), but these are among the most popular. Both definitions describe what Macey and Schneider (2008) referred to as state engagement. Various measures of this state have been developed (e.g., May, Gilson, & Harter, 2004; Rich, LePine, & Crawford, 2010), but the most widely used measure in the scientific literature is the Utrecht Work Engagement Scale (UWES) (Schaufeli et al., 2002). The UWES includes items measuring vigor ("At work, I am bursting with energy"), dedication ("My job inspires me"), and absorption ("When at work, I forget everything else around me") as facets of engagement.

At first glance, the measurement of state engagement might appear "academic," with questionable practical value. Indeed, one of the most widely used measures in the consulting world, the Gallup Workplace Audit (see Harter, Schmidt, & Hayes, 2002), takes a much different approach by focusing on specific conditions believed to contribute to engagement (e.g., knowing what to expect, having the necessary equipment and materials). This is an important issue that I return to below. First, I want to address what might be considered an even more "academic" question: How is "engagement" different from many of the other employee attitudes (e.g., job satisfaction, organizational commitment) that companies used to measure before *engagement* became the new buzzword. Some critics have argued that this is another case of "old wine in new bottles"—only the label has changed. There is no clear consensus on this issue, and it is not one that can be resolved here. However, thinking more carefully about the similarities and differences between engagement and related concepts can have practical implications. There are many concepts with potential overlap with engagement, but for the present purpose I focus on job satisfaction and affective organizational commitment.

In his seminal article, Locke (1976, p. 1300) defined job satisfaction as "a pleasurable or positive emotional state resulting from the appraisal of one's job or job experiences." Measures of satisfaction typically focus on the job in general or specific facets (e.g., pay, supervision, work). A sample item from the Job Diagnostic Survey (Hackman & Oldham, 1980) is "Generally speaking, I am very satisfied with this job." Like engagement, job satisfaction reflects a positive emotional state but one that is arguably muted in comparison with the high level of positive activation (e.g., vigor, dedication, absorption) associated with engagement (Macey & Schneider, 2008). Employees who are satisfied may be complacent, whereas those who are engaged are more likely to be energized.

Commitment has been defined in various ways, but one of the best-established definitions is that offered by Meyer (2009, p. 40): "an internal force [mindset] that binds an individual to a target (social or non-social) and/or to a course of action of relevance to that target." As a binding force, commitment is arguably a more stable state than satisfaction or engagement, with potentially longer-term implications. Perhaps not surprisingly, theory and research pertaining to commitment became popular when organizations were particularly concerned about employee retention (Mowday, Porter, & Steers, 1982). It has since been used in other contexts where there is concern about predictability of future behavior (e.g., employees' commitment to support a change through the implementation process and beyond) (Herscovitch & Meyer, 2002). According to Meyer and Allen (1997), commitments can be characterized by different psychological states, but the one that has been studied most frequently is *affective commitment*. Affective organizational commitment reflects an emotional attachment to, involvement in, and desire to remain with the organization. A sample item from the affective commitment scale is "This organization has a great deal of personal meaning for me."

Despite the differences in definitions and measures, meta-analytic studies generally report moderate to strong correlations between work engagement, job satisfaction, and affective organizational commitment (e.g., Christian et al., 2011; Harrison, Newman & Roth, 2006; Meyer, Stanley, Herscovitch, & Topolnytsky, 2002; Newman, Joseph, & Hulin, 2010). Newman and his colleagues proposed that underlying the measures of the three concepts is a general positive attitude, or an "A factor." These findings make it clear that there are similarities among the concepts, but they are not identical. Correlations generally range in the neighborhood of .5 to .7 (with 0 indicating no relation and 1.0 indicating perfect correspondence). Therefore, it is important to consider more carefully whether the differences matter.

At a conceptual level, work engagement, job satisfaction, and affective organizational commitment differ in at least two important ways. The first has to do with focus. In common practice, engagement is measured as it pertains to one's work (tasks), satisfaction as it pertains to the job in general, and commitment as it pertains to the organization. It is not unreasonable to expect that employees who are engaged in their work will be relatively satisfied with their jobs and committed to their organizations—hence the relatively strong correlations reported. However, the relations are not perfect, suggesting that it is possible for employees to be engaged in their work and/ or satisfied with their jobs without being committed to their organization. Therefore, focus is an important consideration when comparing the three concepts. Keep in mind, however, that we are talking about applications of the measures in common practice. It is possible to shift the focus for all three concepts, as when one measures engagement in the organization (Saks, 2006), satisfaction with specific job facets such as work (Smith, Kendall, & Hulin, 1969), or commitment to goal attainment (Klein, Wesson, Hollenbeck, & Alge, 1999).

As noted, a second conceptual distinction has to do with relative stability. Mowday et al. (1982) argued that satisfaction with one's job can ebb and flow, but commitment implies the continuation of a relationship or course of action over time. Consequently, commitment was expected to be a better predictor of long-term retention than was job satisfaction. Engagement can also fluctuate, as has been demonstrated in recent diary studies (e.g., van Woerkom, Oerlemans, & Bakker, 2016), although it might do so around a relatively stable baseline (Schaufeli et al., 2002).

Despite these conceptual distinctions, one might question whether the differences have practical implications. Newman et al. (2010) demonstrated that the A factor presumed to underlie work engagement, job satisfaction, and affective organizational commitment is a good predictor of an E factor that reflects what is common among various indicators of behavioral engagement (e.g., retention and performance). These findings suggest that work engagement, job satisfaction, and affective organizational commitment can all serve as reasonable indicators of state engagement. However, a closer look at some of the other meta-analytic evidence available (e.g., Christian et al., 2011; Meyer et al., 2002) reveals that work engagement is a better predictor of job performance than is affective commitment and that the latter is a better predictor of turnover intention and turnover. This is consistent with the conceptual distinctions I have described and suggests that organizations might benefit from matching the way in which they conceptualize engagement in their surveys with the outcomes of greatest importance. I have focused here on engagement in one's work and commitment to the organization, but the argument extends to other potential targets of engagement/commitment, including teams, projects, customer service, and the like. The way in which engagement is conceptualized, and the target of the measure(s), should be aligned with the outcomes one hopes to achieve.

I have raised the question of why an organization might want to measure "state engagement" (or commitment) at all. Knowing the strength of employees' engagement or commitment tells us little about what actions to take should levels be weaker than desired. This is true, but these states are relatively easy to measure and can serve as a "dashboard" indicator of how well the organization is functioning. High scores indicate that things are running smoothly, whereas low scores are analogous to a "check engine light"; they do not point to the specific problem but do indicate the need to do a more careful investigation. More direct indicators of organizational functioning (e.g., turnover rates, financial performance) might not show signs of problems until much later, and perhaps too late.

Engagement surveys typically measure more than the state of engagement, often including questions pertaining to various aspects of work and the work environment (i.e., drivers of engagement). The answers can be very informative but can also be a bit daunting, especially when they reflect different opinions about what needs to be fixed. The issue then becomes where to address one's attention in making improvements. This is another reason why including state measures (e.g., engagement, commitment) can be important. Some conditions may have a greater bearing on engagement or commitment than others. If the sample is sufficiently large and reasonably representative, there are several statistical techniques that one can use to determine which conditions have the greatest impact on engagement/commitment and should be given greatest priority in subsequent intervention. I cannot do justice to the complexities of conducting statistical analyses with survey data, but one of the most useful is relative importance analysis (see Chapter 16 for more detail). Under proper conditions, this analysis helps to identify the conditions that contribute most to understanding variability in state engagement or commitment.

Measuring the Drivers of Engagement

Again, the drivers of engagement can be both dispositional and situational, but I focus here on the latter, with emphasis on conditions most likely to be under the control of the organization, its agents (e.g., managers), or employees themselves. There is no universal taxonomy of work conditions, so organizations need to find a way to identify those they consider sufficiently important to include in an engagement survey. There are several ways this can be achieved, each with its benefits and limitations. One is to rely on the recommendations of a reputable consulting firm experienced in administering engagement surveys in similar organizations. In addition to benefiting from the expertise of the professionals, it is often possible to use accumulated data from other clients to serve as benchmarks to facilitate interpretation of one's own data. However, not all the questions included in "stock" surveys may be relevant, and there may be conditions unique to the organization that could be missed. An alternative, or complementary, strategy is to conduct initial interviews and/or focus groups with key stakeholders to identify conditions that are important to them. This is likely to surface some of the unique conditions absent in stock surveys but can create its own problems including a "laundry list" of idiosyncratic concerns, often ill-defined, that can become unwieldy when incorporated into a survey.

A third possibility is to take an evidence-based approach by drawing on the scientific literature to identify conditions that have been found to predict employee engagement, job satisfaction, organizational commitment, or any other "state" of interest. This is admittedly a challenging task given the large body of research that has cumulated over the last several decades. Even restricting the search to meta-analyses of the "antecedents" (potential drivers) of engagement, satisfaction, or commitment yields an extensive list of conditions that one could measure. To simplify the task, I focus here on a few existing taxonomies that help to sort the myriad variables into categories. The first is the job demands–resources (JD-R) model (Demerouti, Bakker, Nachreiner, & Schaufeli, 2001) that has served to guide much of the research on work engagement. The second is the job characteristics model (JCM) developed initially by Hackman and Oldham (1980) and recently expanded by Humphrey, Nahrgang, and Morgeson (2007). The third is Bass and Avolio's (1997) full-range model of leadership styles.

Job Demands and Resources

According to the JD-R model, *demands* refer to those aspects of the job that require sustained physical and mental effort. *Resources* refer to conditions that help to meet demands, facilitate goal attainment, and/or stimulate personal growth (Demerouti et al., 2001). Job demands can be further classified into two categories, hindrance and challenge demands (Crawford, LePine, & Rich, 2010). In their meta-analysis, Crawford et al. found that hindrance demands (e.g., administrative hassles, role conflict) relate negatively with work engagement, whereas challenge demands (e.g., job responsibility, time urgency) relate positively. Job resources (e.g., feedback, opportunity for development, support) also relate positively. The list of potential demands and resources is extensive, but the taxonomy provided by the JD-R framework is relatively easy to apply as one attempts to extract information from the research literature or sort through the issues raised in pre-survey focus groups.

Job/Work Characteristics

The JCM (Hackman & Oldham, 1980) was developed initially as a guide to job design. The objective was to identify those qualities characterizing what Herzberg, Mausner, and Snyderman (1959) referred to as *enriched* jobs. Employees with enriched jobs are expected to be more intrinsically motivated, satisfied, and productive. Hackman and Oldham proposed that jobs can be enriched by increasing the variety of skills required, the identity and meaningfulness of the tasks, the level of responsibility afforded, and the amount of feedback provided. Importantly, they proposed that the effects of these job characteristics are mediated by three critical psychological states: perceived meaningfulness, felt responsibility, and knowledge of results. That is, employees performing enriched jobs are energized and perform at a higher level because they understand how their personal efforts contribute meaningfully to the success of the organization and/or the satisfaction of its customers/clients. Although it predates the notion of employee engagement by a few decades, this combination of critical psychological states is remarkably similar.

Over the years, theory and research on job design have continued to evolve. Humphrey et al. (2007) developed and provided meta-analytic evidence pertaining to an elaborated work-design model incorporating many of the new developments. The revised model included additional motivational characteristics (e.g., task variety, information processing) as well as characteristics of the social environment (e.g., interdependence, social support) and work context (e.g., physical demands, ergonomics). It also expanded the list of outcomes, including affective organizational commitment. In addition to demonstrating empirical links between the various work characteristics and engagement-related outcomes, Humphrey et al. demonstrated the mediating effects of the critical psychological states, most notably the perceived meaningfulness of the work. Interestingly, Christian et al. (2011) computed meta-analytic correlations using work engagement as an outcome and reported correlations with work characteristics of similar magnitude to those obtained by Humphrey et al. for job satisfaction and affective organizational commitment. Both meta-analyses provide a list of potential drivers of engagement with empirical evidence to support their inclusion in engagement surveys.

Leadership

Theory and research on leadership in organizations have a long history and are far more complex than can be dealt with here. For the present purposes, I focus on the full-range theory of leadership advanced by Bass and Avolio (1997). One major distinction made by the full-range theory is between transactional and transformational leadership. *Transactional* leaders use reward (contingent reward leadership) or sanctions (management-by-exception) to encourage employees to do what is required of them. In contrast, *transformational* leaders inspire followers (e.g., provide a compelling vision), serve as role models, encourage innovation and creativity, and show concern for the needs of followers. Although both transactional (especially contingent reward) and transformational styles of leadership are expected to contribute to effective performance, Bass (1985) proposed that transformational leadership would encourage "performance beyond expectation." Consequently, transformational leadership can be expected to relate most strongly to state and behavioral engagement.

As expected, transformation leadership has been shown to have a strong positive correlation with followers' work engagement, job satisfaction, and affective organizational commitment (i.e., state engagement) as well as various indices of behavioral engagement (Christian et al., 2011; Jackson, Meyer,

& Wang, 2013; Judge & Piccolo, 2004). Contingent reward leadership has also been found to relate positively, whereas correlations with management by exception are considerably weaker and sometimes negative. Although the full-range model does not capture all the different leadership styles that have been studied within an organizational context (e.g., authentic, ethical, servant), it makes distinctions that are relevant to both state and behavioral engagement and should be candidates for inclusion in engagement surveys.

Summary

Each of the foregoing taxonomies helps to categorize a set of potential drivers of employee engagement. Not surprisingly, given their strong relationships, many of these drivers have been found to relate similarly with work engagement, job satisfaction, and affective organizational commitment. However, there are likely to be benefits to tailoring the measurement of these drivers to the engagement target(s) of greatest relevance. For example, support from one's peers or immediate supervisor can be expected to have stronger implications for job satisfaction or work engagement, whereas perceived support from the organization or senior management team can be of greater importance in shaping affective commitment to the organization. A similar case can be made for measuring the leadership style of front-line managers versus senior leadership. Each of the drivers discussed here can be considered a target for intervention.

Designing Interventions

Providing feedback from engagement surveys is an important first step in designing interventions to foster higher levels of engagement. First, it communicates the fact that the organization is listening and takes the results seriously. This information should be shared as widely as possible, with due concerns for privacy (e.g., data should be aggregated to a level that protects the anonymity of individual respondents). Second, it serves as the basis for discussion of areas of strength and weakness. Strengths should be duly acknowledged and celebrated, but weaknesses need to be prioritized and addressed. Priorities can be set through consultation with leaders and informed by survey results. Identifying those areas where scores are lowest might seem like an obvious place to start, but there are other factors to consider. For example, if benchmarking data are available, relative as well as absolute performance can be considered (see Chapter 11). If relatively low scores are the norm, it might suggest that the focal issue (e.g., time pressure) is not readily amenable to change. If numbers are sufficiently large, statistical analyses (e.g., relative importance analysis) can be used to identify those factors likely to have the greatest impact on engagement. Alternatively, the research literature can be consulted to identify those factors that have the strongest and most consistent links to engagement. Ideally, all three sources of information will be available and used to guide an evidence-based approach to designing an intervention.

A "driver analysis" such as that described above (also see Chapter 16) can help to identify issues that should be given the highest priority for change. However, they do not necessarily produce obvious solutions. Further consultation with affected parties might generate viable options. However, it may also be necessary to look externally for strategies that have worked elsewhere. These "best practices" might indeed be the solution to the current problem. However, what works effectively in one context might be less effective, or even counterproductive, in another. Another approach is to consider "best principles" (Meyer, 2013) that help to explain why a particular practice worked elsewhere. These best principles derive from decades of scientific research in the behavioral and organizational sciences and are too numerous to be listed, let alone discussed, here. Therefore, I consider only a few of particular relevance: need satisfaction, social exchange, and person–environment fit (see Meyer, 2013, for more detail).

Need Satisfaction

The notion that employees seek to satisfy their needs at work is not new (e.g., Maslow, 1954). However, our notion of what constitutes a need and how our psychological needs are satisfied has been greatly refined in recent years (Baumeister & Leary, 1995). One of the leading theories in this regard is self-determination theory (SDT) (Gagné, 2014; Ryan & Deci, 2000). According to SDT, all human beings seek to satisfy three innate psychological needs: autonomy (volition and self-endorsement of behavior), competence (self-efficacy and self-control), and relatedness (social significance and connection). Satisfaction of these needs is essential for psychological health but also has implications for work engagement and affective organizational commitment.

The principle of need satisfaction can explain the effects of many of the drivers I have discussed. For example, several aspects of work design (e.g., increased responsibility) help to satisfy the need for autonomy. Resources such as constructive feedback and training can help to satisfy the need for competence. Social support and individualized consideration provided by transformational leadership can satisfy the need for relatedness. Importantly, therefore, knowing that employees seek to satisfy their psychological needs at work, organizations might be able to better understand why a "best practice" worked elsewhere (i.e., as a source of satisfaction of one or more needs) and whether it might work equally well for them. Indeed, the potential effectiveness of any planned intervention can be evaluated by asking "Will this change serve to satisfy or thwart employees' basic psychological needs"?

Social Exchange

The notion of social exchange as a basic underpinning of human relationships has a long history (Blau, 1964; Gouldner, 1960). Admittedly, the social exchange process is complex, and there are gaps in our understanding of how these processes play out in exchanges between organizations and their employees (Cropanzano & Mitchell, 2005). Nevertheless, the principle of social exchange is sufficiently well established to serve as the basis for several theories relevant to the development and maintenance of engagement, including theories of perceived organizational support (Eisenberger, Huntington, Hutchison, & Sowa, 1986), organizational justice (Greenberg, 1987), trust (Mayer, Davis, & Schoorman, 1995), leader–member exchange (Liden, Sparrowe, & Wayne, 1997), and psychological contracts (Rousseau, 1995). Perceived organizational support, or the belief that the organization values employees' contributions and is concerned about their well-being, has been found to be one of the best predictors of employees' affective organizational commitment (Meyer et al., 2002) and to relate positively to several other indicators of state and behavioral engagement (Kurtessis et al., 2017). Similarly, fairness in the distribution of resources (distributive justice), in the policies and procedures guiding distribution (procedural justice), and in the treatment of employees (interactional justice) has been shown to have moderate to strong relations with indices of both state and behavioral engagement

(Meyer et al., 2002; Colquitt, Conlon, Wesson, Porter & Ng, 2001). The same is true for perceptions of trust in management (Colquitt, Scott & LePine, 2007), quality of leader–member exchange (Dulebohn, Bommer, Liden, Brouer, & Ferris, 2012), and the organization's fulfillment/violation of the psychological contract with employees (Zhao, Wayne, Glibkowski, & Bravo, 2007). In short, we have learned a great deal about the formation of employer–employee relationships and their implications for engagement.

Like the principle of need satisfaction, the basic principle of social exchange and related theories can be used to explain the effects of many of the drivers of engagement. For example, transformational leadership and efforts to enrich jobs might be perceived as evidence of organizational support and can instill a sense of trust and justice. Such treatment should lead employees to reciprocate with increased commitment to organizational goals and exertion of discretionary effort toward their attainment. When contemplating any intervention, managers can ask, "Will it be perceived by employees as evidence of the organization's support?" "Will employees consider it to be fair?" "Is this decision consistent with or a violation of the psychological contract?" "Will it help to build or undermine trust?" If the answers are not immediately obvious to managers, they might be obtained in interviews or focus groups with employees.

Person–Environment Fit

The notion that people adjust better to environments where they fit than to those where they do not also has a long history—indeed, this is arguably a central tenet in psychology (Schneider, 2001). Of course, both people and environments are complex, so there are many ways that fit can be conceptualized and measured. Even within a work context, fit can be conceptualized in terms of abilities, personality traits, values, goals, and other human qualities and can be operationalized in terms of similarity, complementarity, or compatibility with the characteristics of other individuals, collectives, careers, jobs, and so on. Despite this complexity, however, there is strong evidence to suggest that fit matters (Kristof-Brown, Zimmerman & Johnson, 2005).

Kristof-Brown et al. (2005) conducted an extensive meta-analytic review of research relating to person–environment fit within a work context. Although they examined other operationalizations (e.g., fit with group and supervisor), the greatest number of studies and the strongest findings were obtained for person–organization and person–job fit. Both forms of fit were found to have moderate to strong relations with indices of state engagement (job satisfaction and affective organizational commitment) and weak to moderate relations with indices of behavioral engagement (e.g., intention to remain, job performance). Not surprisingly, person–organization fit is a better predictor of affective organizational commitment and turnover intention than is person–job fit, whereas the latter is a better predictor of job performance. Fit is obviously an important consideration in the hiring process, but it can also be a factor to consider when interventions are being considered. Therefore, it is another general principle that can be applied by asking, "Will this change enhance or undermine employees' perceptions of fit with their jobs and/or the organization (or any other target of interest, such as team, unit, or clientele)"?

Recommendations

1. As a first step in designing an "engagement" survey, it is important to consider one's ultimate objectives. This will aid in deciding what target(s) of engagement is most relevant. For example, affective organizational commitment will be relevant to organizations concerned with long-term retention, whereas work engagement will be of relevance when task performance is of particular concern. If engagement in, or commitment to, teamwork, customer service, sustainability, or any other target is of importance, the focus of the engagement index(es) should change accordingly.

2. Measuring state engagement can serve as a dashboard indicator of the level of engagement overall or within specific units. Measures of behavioral engagement (e.g., turnover intention, willingness to exert effort) can also be included, but it is difficult to capture the full set of behaviors that will be relevant across jobs. State engagement is easier to measure and has been shown to predict many of the behavioral outcomes of interest. Finally, measures of state engagement can be used as criteria in driver analyses to aid in setting priorities for intervention.

3. Deciding what drivers to measure should be based on a combination of professional consultations, interviews, focus groups, and the scientific literature. Measurement should be restricted to those conditions that the organization has the ability and willingness to change.

4. Survey results should be disseminated widely, with due consideration to protection of anonymity. Leaders at various levels throughout the organization should discuss the results with their staff, celebrate their strengths, and develop an action plan to address weaknesses.

5. Interventions should be designed in consultation with professionals, affected parties, and the scientific literature. Prior to adopting "best practices" used elsewhere or designing new ones, it can be helpful to apply "best principles" by asking, among other things, "Will this intervention serve to satisfy employees' needs; help to build a supportive, fair, and trusting relationship; and/or improve perceptions of fit?"

6. Actions taken in response to the survey, as well as the results of these actions, should be communicated broadly. Doing so can help to ensure strong response rates to the subsequent surveys required to monitor progress.

References

Bakker, A. B., van Emmeri, H., & Euwema, M. C. (2006). Crossover of burnout and engagement in work teams. *Work and Occupations, 33*(4), 464–489.

Bass, B. M. (1985). *Leadership beyond expectations.* New York, NY: Free Press.

Bass, B. M., & Avolio, B. J. (1997). *Full range leadership development: Manual for the multifactor leadership questionnaire.* Palo Alto, CA: Mindgarden.

Baumeister, R. F., & Leary, M. R. (1995). The need to belong: Desire for interpersonal attachments as a fundamental human motivation. *Psychological Bulletin, 117,* 497–529.

Blau, P. M. (1964). *Exchange and power in social life.* New York, NY: Free Press.

Christian, M. S., Garza, A. S., & Slaughter, J. E. (2011). Work engagement: A quantitative review and test of its relations with task and contextual performance. *Personnel Psychology, 64,* 89–136.

Colquitt, J. A., Conlon, D. E., Wesson, M. J., Porter, C. O. L. H., & Ng, K. Y. (2001). Justice at the millennium: A meta-analytic review of 25 years of organizational justice research. *Journal of Applied Psychology, 86,* 425–445.

Colquitt, J. A., Scott, B. A., & LePine, J. A. (2007). Trust, trustworthiness, and trust propensity: A meta-analytic test of their unique relationships with risk taking and job performance. *Journal of Applied Psychology, 92,* 909–927.

Crawford, E. R., LePine, J. A., & Rich, B. L. (2010). Linking job demands and resources to employee engagement and burnout: A theoretical extension and meta-analytic test. *Journal of Applied Psychology, 95*(5), 834–848.

Cropanzano, R., & Mitchell, M. S. (2005). Social exchange theory: An interdisciplinary review. *Journal of Management, 31,* 874–900.

Demerouti, E., Bakker, A. B., Nachreiner, F., & Schaufeli, W. B. (2001). The job demands–resources model of burnout. *Journal of Applied Psychology, 86,* 499–512.

Dulebohn, J. H., Bommer, W. H., Liden, R. C., Brouer, R. C., & Ferris, G. R. (2012). A meta-analysis of antecedents and consequences of leader-member exchange: Integrating the past with an eye toward the future. *Journal of Management, 38*(6), 1715–1759.

Eisenberger, R., Huntington, R., Hutchison, S., & Sowa, D. (1986). Perceived organizational support. *Journal of Applied Psychology, 71*, 500–507.

Gagné, M. (Ed.). (2014). *The Oxford handbook of work engagement, motivation, and self-determination theory*. New York, NY: Oxford University Press.

Gouldner, A. W. (1960). The norm of reciprocity: A preliminary statement. *American Sociological Review, 25*, 161–178.

Greenberg, J. (1987). A taxonomy of justice theories. *Academy of Management Review, 12*, 9–22.

Hackman, J. R., & Oldham, G. R. (1980). *Work redesign*. Reading, MA: Addison-Wesley.

Harrison, D. A., Newman, D. A., & Roth, P. L. (2006). How important are job attitudes? Meta-analytic comparisons of integrative behavioral outcomes and time sequences. *Academy of Management Journal, 49*, 305–325.

Harter, J. K., Schmidt, F. L., & Hayes, T. L. (2002). Business-unit-level relationship between employee satisfaction, employee engagement, and business outcomes: A meta-analysis. *Journal of Applied Psychology, 87*, 268–279.

Herscovitch, L., & Meyer, J. P. (2002). Commitment to organizational change: Extension of a three-component model. *Journal of Applied Psychology, 87*, 474–487.

Herzberg, F., Mausner, B., & Snyderman, B. B. (1959). *The motivation to work*. New York, NY: Wiley.

Humphrey, S. E., Nahrgang, J. D., & Morgeson, F. P. (2007). Integrating motivational, social, and contextual work design feature: A meta-analytic summary and theoretical extension of the work design literature. *Journal of Applied Psychology, 92*, 1332–1356.

Jackson, T. A., Meyer, J. P., & Wang, X. H. (2013). Leadership, commitment, and culture: A meta-analysis. *Journal of Leadership and Organizational Studies, 20*, 84–106.

Judge, T. A., & Piccolo, R. F. (2004). Transformational and transactional leadership: A meta-analytic test of their relative validity. *Journal of Applied Psychology, 89*, 755–768.

Kahn, W. A. (1990). Psychological conditions of personal engagement and disengagement at work. *Academy of Management Journal, 33*, 692–724.

Klein, H. J., Wesson, M. J., Hollenbeck, J. R., & Alge, B. J. (1999). Goal commitment and the goal-setting process: Conceptual clarification and empirical synthesis. *Journal of Applied Psychology, 84*(6), 885–896.

Kristof-Brown, A. L., Zimmerman, R. D., & Johnson, E. C. (2005). Consequences of individuals' fit at work: A meta-analysis of person–job, person–organization, person–group, and person–supervisor fit. *Personnel Psychology, 58*, 281–342.

Kurtessis, J., Eisenberger, R., Ford, M. T., Buffardi, L. C., Stewart, K. A., & Adis, C. S. (2017). Perceived organizational support: A meta-analytic evaluation of organizational support theory. *Journal of Management, 43*(6), 1854–1884.

Liden, R. C., Sparrowe, R. T., & Wayne, S. J. (1997). Leader–member exchange theory: The past and potential for the future. In G. R. Ferris (Ed.), *Research in personnel and human resources management* (Vol. 15, pp. 47–119). New York, NY: Elsevier Science/JAI Press.

Locke, E. A. (1976). The nature and causes of job satisfaction. In M. D. Dunnette (Ed.), *Handbook of industrial and organizational psychology* (pp. 1297–1349). Chicago, IL: Rand McNally.

Macey, W. H., & Schneider, B. (2008). The meaning of employee engagement. *Industrial and Organizational Psychology, 1*, 3–30.

Maslow, A. H. (1954). *Motivation and personality.* New York, NY: Harper & Row.

May, D. R., Gilson, R. L., & Harter, L. M. (2004). The psychological conditions of meaningfulness, safety, availability and the engagement of human spirit at work. *Journal of Occupational and Organizational Psychology, 77,* 11–37.

Mayer, R. C., Davis, J. H., & Schoorman, F. D. (1995). An integrative model of organizational trust. *Academy of Management Review, 20,* 709–734.

Meyer, J. P. (2009). Commitment in a changing world of work. In H. J. Klein, T. E., Becker, & J. P. Meyer (Eds.), *Commitment in organizations: Accumulated wisdom and new directions* (pp. 37–68). New York, NY, and London, England: Routledge.

Meyer, J. P. (2013). The science-practice gap and employee engagement: It's a matter of principle. *Canadian Psychology, 54,* 235–245.

Meyer, J. P., & Allen, N. J. (1997). *Commitment in the workplace: Theory, research, and application.* Thousand Oaks, CA: Sage Publications.

Meyer, J. P., Stanley, D. J., Herscovitch, L., & Topolnytsky, L. (2002). Affective, continuance, and normative commitment to the organization: A meta-analysis of antecedents, correlates, and consequences. *Journal of Vocational Behavior, 61,* 20–52.

Mowday, R. T., Porter, L. W., & Steers, R. (1982). *Organizational linkages: The psychology of commitment, absenteeism, and turnover.* San Diego, CA: Academic Press.

Newman, D. A., Joseph, D. L., & Hulin, C. L. (2010). Job attitudes and employee engagement: Considering the attitude "A-factor." In S. L. Albrecht (Ed.), *Handbook of employee engagement: Perspectives, issues, research, and practice* (pp. 43–61). Cheltenham, England: Edward Elgar.

Rich, B. L., LePine, J. A., & Crawford, E. R. (2010). Job engagement: Antecedents and effects of job performance. *Academy of Management Journal, 53,* 617–635.

Rousseau, D. M. (1995). *Psychological contracts in organizations: Understanding written and unwritten agreements.* Thousand Oaks, CA: Sage.

Ryan, R. M., & Deci, E. L. (2000). Self-determination theory and the facilitation of intrinsic motivation, social development, and well-being. *American Psychologist, 55,* 68–78.

Saks, A. M. (2006). Antecedents and consequences of employee engagement. *Journal of Managerial Psychology, 21,* 600–619.

Saks, A. M. (2017). Translating employee engagement research into practice. *Organizational Dynamics, 46,* 76–86.

Schaufeli, W. B., Salanova, M., Gonzalez-Roma, V., & Bakker, A. B. (2002). The measurement of engagement and burnout: A two sample confirmatory factor analytic approach. *Journal of Happiness Studies, 3,* 71–92.

Schneider, B. (2001). Fits about fit. *Applied Psychology: An International Review, 50,* 141–152.

Schneider, B., Yost, A. B., Knopp, A., Kind, C., & Lam, H. (2017). Workforce engagement: What is it, what drives it, and why it matters. *Journal of Organizational Behavior, 39*(4), 462–480.

Smith, P. C., Kendall, L., & Hulin, C. L. (1969). *The measurement of satisfaction in work and retirement.* Chicago, IL: Rand McNally.

van Woerkom, M., Oerlemans, W., & Bakker, A. B. (2016). Strengths use and work engagement: A weekly diary study. *European Journal of Work and Organizational Psychology, 25*(3), 384–397.

Zhao, H., Wayne, S., Glibkowski, B. C., & Bravo, J. (2007). The impact of psychological contract breach on work-related outcomes: A meta-analysis. *Personnel Psychology, 60*(3), 647–680.

7

Focus Groups

Blending Qualitative and Quantitative Methodology to Improve the Survey Process

Jeffrey M. Cucina and Ilene F. Gast*

Recently, there has been a growing recognition of the value that qualitative research provides to industrial–organizational (I-O) psychology. Examples include Pratt and Bonaccio's (2016) focal article in *Industrial and Organizational Psychology* and a special issue of *Organizational Research Methods* (Easterby-Smith, Golden-Biddle, & Locke, 2008). There is movement within I-O psychology to better embrace qualitative research methodology. One such qualitative method, focus groups, has much to offer the survey process.

Focus Groups as Qualitative Research in I-O Psychology Practice

In a focus group, a skilled facilitator poses open-ended topical questions to a group of individuals who are alike in important respects. From discussion, analysts extract a set of themes, which are supported by notes from, or transcriptions of, group dialogue. Focus groups have been used in organizational research, as early as the Hawthorne studies (Mayo, 1933), which included 21,000 employee interviews examining work conditions and attitudes. The researchers found that when compared to closed-ended questioning, open-ended questioning produced more informative results.

* Both authors contributed equally. Ilene F. Gast is retired from U.S. Customs and Border Protection. The views expressed in this chapter are those of the authors and do not necessarily reflect the views of U.S. Customs and Border Protection or the U.S. federal government. A portion of this chapter was presented at the 34th meeting of the Society for Industrial and Organizational Psychology, National Harbor, MD.

Jeffrey M. Cucina and Ilene F. Gast, *Focus Groups* In: *Employee Surveys and Sensing.* Edited by: William H. Macey and Alexis A. Fink, Oxford University Press (2020). © Society for Industrial and Organizational Psychology.
DOI: 10.1093/oso/9780190939717.003.0007

Practitioners still employ focus groups during the survey process. For example, Gallup recommends that managers conduct focus groups with their team's employees to discuss the survey results, gather additional information, and brainstorm action plans (Gallup, 2013). Gallup (2012) has developed a guide that provides focus group talking points and potential action plans for each Q12 survey item. Each year, the U.S. Office of Personnel Management surveys federal employees and recommends conducting focus groups to address the results (Berry, 2012).

Potential Uses of Focus Groups

Focus groups provide valuable input prior to survey development, during survey development, and after survey administration. Each of these uses is described.

Using Focus Groups Prior to Survey Development

Focus groups can provide a starting point for generating survey content. Focus groups can help in adapting or updating an existing generic survey (e.g., job satisfaction, employee engagement) to the specific needs of an organization by identifying more salient topics, adding familiar terminology, fine-tuning response scales, and otherwise aligning content more closely with the organization's mission. Focus groups also provide in-depth knowledge about organization-specific topics, programs, or policies. Group members are an excellent source of the specialized knowledge and terminology needed for generating credible survey items. Finally, through focus groups, practitioners can learn about an organization's culture, knowledge that can be used to generate hypotheses about underlying issues that may be affecting organizational effectiveness.

Survey Development

Focus groups can assist in developing surveys. Group members can write survey items in much the same way that subject matter expert panels develop job-knowledge tests. Practitioners also can use focus groups to evaluate items for inclusion in surveys. The cognitive interview/verbal protocol procedure of Willis, Royston, and Bercini (1991) can be used in focus groups to determine whether respondents will perceive survey items in the manner intended, thereby reducing construct-irrelevant variance.

Focus groups can also be used to review the content of a draft survey. Focus groups can help refine surveys by narrowing content to the most important issues. Additionally, focus groups can assess whether survey items are appropriate for all employees and whether different employee groups (e.g., clerical, technical, and managerial) perceive items similarly. Focus groups can also be used to conduct usability testing; Fenlason and Suckow-Zimberg (2006, p. 195) used focus groups to test online survey platforms.

Post-Survey Administration and Analysis

After survey administration, focus groups can provide information about the issues measured by the survey items when more detailed, in-depth data are desired. Focus groups can assist in explaining unanticipated/counterintuitive/perplexing survey results (e.g., radical shifts in attitudes, increases in the percentage of neutral or "do not know" responses).

In our opinion, focus groups provide a better method of collecting information on potential root causes for survey results than survey key driver analysis (SKDA). Cucina, Walmsley, Gast, Martin, and Curtin (2017) identified statistical and methodological issues with SKDA and recommended beginning a direct dialogue with employees on organizational issues using focus groups. Additionally, many organizational survey items are too general or too broad in scope to provide sufficient information on the sources of employee satisfaction and organizational functioning. Here, focus groups provide diagnostic information on the underlying causes and can suggest potential actions/interventions.

Also, after survey administration, focus groups can be used to provide feedback to employees and management. During focus groups, participants can be given an item-by-item review of the survey results and presented with the overall interpretations of the findings. Group participants can respond to and comment on the findings and then indicate whether they concur with the interpretations.

Designing Effective Focus Groups

The focus group process can be divided into six phases: (1) planning, (2) establishing procedures, (3) attending to logistics, (4) conducting the groups, (5) analyzing the data, and (6) reporting findings. In this section we provide guidance for each.

Planning the Focus Groups

Assess the Appropriateness and Practicality of Focus Groups

In this step, critically examine the goals of the project or study and decide whether focus groups will yield the data necessary for decision-making. In addition, evaluate available resources, including availability of personnel with the skills necessary to organize, deploy, and administer focus groups and to analyze data and prepare reports for the intended audiences. Also consider the feasibility and likelihood of success in carrying out focus groups in one's research or organizational setting. If focus groups are deemed appropriate and practical, develop a project timeline and budget.

Design the Study

Develop research questions and specify the methodology for investigating them. Determine whether other sources of data are required. Describe the potential pool of research participants.

Deciding Who Should Be Included in the Groups

Decide how many focus groups and focus group members are needed. Project goals and scope also dictate how many groups are required. A single group may be sufficient when obtaining input for designing a new training course or implementing a new procedure within a centralized branch of the organization. A special topic such as localized turnover may only require a few groups. However, an organization-wide intervention will require widespread use at multiple sites.

The recommended group size is 6–12 participants. Smaller groups will not yield a diversity of ideas, and larger groups become difficult to manage and hamper participation. Determine which demographic characteristics are desirable for study and which will cause unnecessary conflict. Consider organizational level, occupation, geographic location, ethnicity, and organizational tenure. It may be beneficial to hold separate focus groups for different demographics. Finally, determine how participants will be selected and invited. We encourage the use of random sampling.

A Note on Focus Group Composition

Focus groups consist of small numbers of demographically diverse individuals who are (a) alike in important respects, (b) able and willing to provide the desired information, and (c) representative of the population of interest. Personal experience with the focus group's topic enables participants to provide meaningful feedback. In addition, try to balance diversity and homogeneity. A good balance enables participants to establish a common ground during group discussions. Too much similarity of attitudes and opinions creates obstacles to generating novel ideas and alternative solutions to problems.

Preexisting relationships can curtail the range of attitudes and opinions that participants express. Such relationships can potentially induce conformity within focus groups (Morgan & Krueger, 1993) and cause participants to be reluctant to speak candidly. Similarly, groups of coworkers may tend to focus on narrowly defined issues particular to their situation. To alleviate these effects, consider expanding the number of groups and using skilled facilitators.

Participants may be reluctant to express their views in groups that mix organizational levels (e.g., first- and second-line supervisors). Holding separate groups for each level is ideal but becomes impractical when organizations have multiple locations, each with too few participants at each level. When the authors encountered this situation, they resolved it by allowing participants to confidentially share additional responses with the facilitator by phone/e-mail after the session.

Establishing Procedures for Conducting the Focus Groups and Preparing Focus Group Materials

Develop the Questions That Will Be Asked During the Focus Group

These questions stem directly from the underlying research questions. They should address topics that will enable decision-making. Open-ended questions form the backbone of focus groups, but they differ from open-ended questions used to spur discussion in working groups and to evaluate candidates in selection interviews. Focus group questions place greater emphasis on feelings and impressions and differ in their degree of structure and their sequencing. Regardless of how open-ended questions are used, the same general principles apply to their development.

Degree of Structure

The questions should allow the facilitator considerable latitude to ask follow-up questions and probe for additional information. As in more structured situations, the facilitator may begin by asking "how" or "what" but might then pose a follow-up question asking how the group felt about an issue or event or what it meant to group members.

The amount of standardization in how the questions are asked depends on the number of groups in the study. Standardization ensures comparability of data across groups and simplifies data analysis. Standardization also simplifies facilitator training and ensures consistent administration.

Terminology

Focus group questions address the quality of participants' experiences. Participants are asked to describe the quality of their experience; discover, generate, explore, and identify ideas or approaches; and describe their feelings and opinions. The result is deeper and richer insight into the issues or events under investigation.

Question Sequencing

Questioning within focus groups follows a specific sequence (Krueger & Casey, 2015). Questioning begins after the facilitator welcomes the group, provides an overview of the topic, and establishes the ground rules for discussion (see Table 7.1.) It helps to summarize key points during transitions between types of questions.

The *opening question* kicks off discussion and is not research-related. Rather, it serves to acquaint group members with each other and to establish their trust. Typically, participants are asked about something personal yet appropriate for the group (e.g., where participants work, how long they have been there).

Introductory questions are broad questions that introduce the topic and begin to direct the group's attention to the central topic. Responses help the facilitator gauge participants' feelings about the topic and speculate where

Table 7.1 Sample Ground Rules

- Participation in the focus group is voluntary.
- Silence/turn off cell phones.
- Protect others' privacy by not discussing details outside the group.
- No one will be able to link statements to individuals.
- Speak in a clear voice, loud enough for everyone to hear.
- There are no right or wrong answers.
- istening is as important as talking.
- Disagreement and differences of opinion are good.
- Common courtesy is exhibited at all times.
- Only one person speaks at a time.
- Treat other participants with respect.
- Refrain from interrupting others. However, the facilitator can interrupt to keep everyone on task.
- No one is permitted to attack anyone else.
- Please respect the opinions of others, even if you do not agree.

the discussion might head. For example, the introductory question could ask about participants' reactions to a new program.

Transition questions create a link between the introductory questions and the key questions. They set the stage for the key questions by asking participants for greater depth on the topics raised by the introductory questions. For example, participants may be asked to think about their early impressions of a new program.

Key or core questions take the majority of the time and move participants to the heart of the discussion. Participants discuss five or six questions that focus on the major areas of concern such as how they feel about a new program and what might preclude their participation in the program.

Closing questions allow participants to reflect on the discussion and provide a sense of closure to the session. The facilitator might ask what was most important or if participants would like to add anything. The facilitator might also provide a summary of the session and ask participants about its accuracy.

Prepare the Facilitator Guide

This guide outlines the details for conducting the focus group session. It summarizes the purpose of the project or program and explains how participants were selected. Other components of the guide include the following:

- A sample demographic form for collecting participants' tenure, occupational group, job grade, organizational unit, geographic location, etc. The form should be anonymous, and it is best to make a policy (and inform participants) that only summary data will be reported.
- A sample informed consent form that identifies the sponsors and purpose of the project, ensures that participation is voluntary, and indicates whether any recording devices will be used.
- A schedule for the focus group meeting indicating the time allotted to the introduction, to each question, and to the wrap-up.
- A script for beginning the session, in which the facilitators welcome the group and thank them for participating, introduce themselves and any other on-site personnel, explain the purpose of the focus group, and establish the ground rules (see Table 7.1).
- The focus group questions and suggested follow-up questions and probes.

Select and Train Facilitators and Note Takers

Facilitators and note takers must be able to fulfill the roles as described in this section. Prior group leadership experience (e.g., conducting focus groups, leading subject matter expert panels) is desirable for facilitators. A brief review of the project goals and the facilitator guide should be sufficient for experienced facilitators. Less skilled facilitators require more extensive training. Role-playing exercises provide experience in managing challenging participants and serve to screen out individuals who would make poor facilitators. Similarly, when training inexperienced note takers, use observational exercises during which they make observations, take notes, and receive constructive feedback. If qualified in-house personnel are not available, consider hiring outside personnel.

The Facilitator

Facilitation requires knowledge about the overall program's purpose or goals and finely honed interpersonal skills. Skillful facilitators can keep the group focused, maintain momentum, and get closure on key questions or tasks. They must accomplish these goals without inadvertently biasing the direction of the conversation through physical cues and verbal comments.

Table 7.2 Guidelines for Asking Questions in Focus Groups

- Avoid asking "why." Ask "how" or "what" instead.
  - Why questions can make participants defensive or may elicit socially desirable responses.
- Probe to clarify responses or to get additional detail.
  - Use neutral probes, such as
    - "Can you explain further?"
    - "Can you give me an example of what you mean?"
    - "Is there anything else you would like to add?"
    - "What do you mean by_____?"
- Use nonverbal cues
  - Use hand signals to acknowledge those who want to speak.
  - Signal interrupters to wait.
  - Use eye contact to encourage reticent participants to speak.
- Limit the number of principal questions to five or six.
- Avoid questions that might be divisive:
  - Questions that establish distinctions in status
  - Questions that are likely to polarize the group

Facilitators must also be able to handle responses to qualitative questions, which are likely to evoke strong feelings and opinions, which, in turn, affect group interactions. Essential skills include active listening, maintaining a neutral demeanor, dispute resolution, and unobtrusive leadership. Facilitators should be prepared to manage challenging participants: the person(s) who seeks to dominate the conversation or influence the group, the reticent participant who rarely speaks up, the interrupter, and those who are overly negative or aggressive. (See Table 7.2 for guidance on asking focus group questions.)

Note Takers and Assistants

Focus groups can yield deep, rich data; but taking advantage of such data requires attentively monitoring who is talking and what thoughts they are expressing. Note takers should identify and track individual speakers using a pre-established coding system; however, the process is difficult and likely to be inaccurate. Note takers should be able to take accurate notes, record body language or other subtle but relevant cues, and operate any equipment. The ideal note taker is able to quickly and accurately take notes without disrupting the flow of conversation. An editor for this book noted that individuals with experience as court recorders are often excellent note takers.

In addition, note takers should observe and record the following:

- The words participants use to describe issues and events. Are these words being used consistently? Do they have new or unusual meanings?
- The context in which comments are made and the tone and intensity of comments.
- The extent of group member agreement and whether agreement has been influenced by group pressure.

Determine the Feasibility of Additional Means of Data Collection

A digital record is helpful when reviewing notes or when searching for meaty quotes to include in the final report. Video recording is the easiest and most reliable way to identify contributors, and online meeting software, which yields automatic recording, is becoming increasingly common. Audio recording is also helpful but only if speakers remember to identify themselves. Older literature sources assume that data will be transcribed (Pokela, Steblea, Steblea, Shea, & Denny, 2007). However, transcription is labor-intensive and costly and becomes more so with increasing numbers of groups.

If recordings are planned, establish clear policies and procedures governing their storage and use. Participants need reassurance that their comments will remain confidential. They may be reluctant to respond candidly if they believe organizational leaders can access session recordings.

Preparing to Conduct the Focus Groups

Select the Focus Group Location(s) and Schedule the Venue(s)

The optimal room is private, quiet, and free from interruptions. It should allow participants to be arranged in a loose circle so that they are able to see and hear what is going on. Note takers can sit outside the circle, situated so that they can comfortably hear and observe the group. Space for refreshments should be available. The location should be convenient to all participants. For shorter focus groups (1–2 hours), the organization's site may be most convenient. On-site focus groups avoid transportation and parking issues. When focus groups last a full day or longer, off-site locations can prevent participants from returning to their workstations.

Invite Participants

After identifying the participants, assign them to groups and issue invitations. In the invitation, explain the purpose of the group, describe any applicable reimbursement or honorarium, and ensure anonymity and confidentiality. In addition, provide the date, time, and location of the group and directions to the facility. Also include a contact phone number and e-mail address. Send reminder and follow-up messages at appropriate intervals.

Conducting the Focus Groups

Before each focus group, the facilitator should allow enough time to

- Set up the room and arrange seating and refreshment areas
- Distribute forms and handouts and set up tent cards and markers
- Test equipment (audio recorder, microphones, computers)

Once participants arrive, the facilitator

- Welcomes participants, covering the material included in the facilitator guide
- Covers administrative details (reimbursement, location of restrooms and emergency exits)
- Collects forms (informed consent, demographic information)
- Conducts the focus group discussion following the instructions in the facilitator guide
- Ends the session by thanking participants

After the session, the facilitator and note taker meet for debriefing and discuss what transpired during the session.

Conducting Virtual Focus Groups

When faced with an organization that has multiple, widely dispersed field locations, we found facilitated in-person focus groups at all locations to be neither practical nor cost-effective. Virtual focus groups offered a potential solution.

We conducted virtual focus groups in parallel with facilitated, on-site focus groups. Both sets of groups received the same questions. However, virtual focus group participants typed their responses into an online survey tool. Although the virtual format precluded interactions among focus group members and the opportunity for follow-up questioning, it yielded themes and findings similar to the on-site focus groups and, more importantly, permitted us to get input from employees whose location prevented participation in the on-site focus groups.

Focus groups also can be led remotely through teleconferencing or videoconferencing. Technological limitations (bandwidth limitations, connectivity issues, video resolution issues) can be problematic. We have seen that group facilitation is more difficult when using video cameras in remote locations. Interaction suffers from loss of direct eye contact and inadequate microphone coverage. Also, without the physical presence of a facilitator, participants tend to be less talkative.

Alternately, focus groups can be conducted via chat rooms, message boards, GoToMeeting, Zoom, or Skype/Lync group conversations. However, these technologies tend to increase the typing burden on note takers and place more cognitive demands on participants and facilitators than an in-person panel. Nevertheless, when trying to reach geographically dispersed individuals, remote and virtual focus groups are preferable to sacrificing potentially valuable input.

Analyzing the Data

Primarily, analysis of focus group data relies on content analysis; however, quantitative analyses can summarize trends. Triangulation helps integrate the findings of qualitative data analysis and those from other sources.

Content Analysis

In this section, we outline the steps for content analysis, a systematic method for summarizing the notes and other data from focus groups, which enables data to be coded, analyzed, and interpreted. Dutta and O'Rourke (Chapter 13) discuss how natural language processing might reduce the burden inherent this process.

Define Recording Units and Categories Based on Themes in the Data

Examine the data, and determine what to use as the basic unit of text to be analyzed. Weber (1990) suggests using words, phrases or idioms, complete sentences, and independent themes within sentences, paragraphs, or whole texts.

Define Preliminary Categories

Review the data to identify meaningful categories based on themes. Here, too, automated text analytic methods may be useful in determining topics. Think carefully about how broad or narrow these categories should be before defining the categories.

Test the Preliminary Categories

We recommend engaging two experienced analysts to code a representative subset of the data using the preliminary categories. If the coders' responses agree, the categories are working reasonably well. Disagreement on the categories can be indicative of coder problems or unclear categories. If the coders find the categories to be unclear or difficult to apply, make necessary revisions. We also recommend determining whether subcategories are needed; subcategories can provide richer data.

Refine or Revise the Categories

Use the revised categories to recode the data, and again evaluate how well the categories are working.

Develop a Code Book

Once the content categories are working satisfactorily, establish numerical codes for each category and any subcategories. Provide a brief explanation and examples for each category.

Establish Procedures for Coding

Decide whether to allow a single comment to be coded into multiple categories. If possible, have two analysts independently code the data; if not, have one code the data and a second verify.

Quantitative Analysis

Summarizing participants through descriptive statistics documents the size and composition of the focus groups for reporting purposes (e.g., "We conducted 10 focus groups with a total of 200 participants"). Often, leaders are skeptical of focus group and survey findings, especially negative findings. A presentation of participant demographics, without revealing group membership, can prevent skeptical leaders from discounting findings from the qualitative data.

Quantitative analyses can be used to evaluate the importance of topics presented in the key questions. Take, for example, employee development. The facilitator might poll group members on the importance of providing work time for personal development. Tallies from polls repeated across groups can help to support the survey results.

A multirater version of Cohen's (1960) kappa statistic can be used to assess the agreement of themes identified by different focus groups. It is possible to compute and report the percentage of focus groups that generated each identified theme. Statistical tests can be used to examine differential rates of theme generation by different employee groups (e.g., non-supervisory vs. supervisory focus groups).

Statistical tests can create a false illusion of quantitative rigor. Focus group discussions are fluid and social situations. Group pressures might prevent a group from endorsing a particular theme, or a facilitator's probes and follow-up questions might result in the introduction of a unique but important theme. Similarly, a group might veer off topic completely and raise concerns that are unrelated to the goals of the study. Therefore, it is important not to overemphasize quantitative findings based on what are essentially qualitative data.

Combining Analyses from Focus Groups with Other Data

Perhaps the simplest, most straightforward way of combining the two data sources (i.e., survey and focus group results) is to use appropriate focus group themes to illustrate content categories derived from the other data source (i.e., the survey). For example, when examining employee satisfaction, one might match a survey result (e.g., "Only 35% of employees are satisfied with their benefits") to topical quotes from the focus groups (e.g., "Lack of communication hampered employee awareness of recent changes in the benefits program," "Employees desire more educational benefits," "Employees in field locations wanted childcare benefits").

A more robust approach to mixing qualitative and quantitative data is triangulation. Marshall and Rossman (1999) describe data triangulation as "the act of bringing more than one source of data to bear on a single point." It has its roots in Campbell and Fiske's (1959) multitrait, multimethod procedure. Triangulation has been used to verify findings by showing that the findings resulting from independent measures agree or at least do not contradict.

When focus group findings and survey results agree, they permit corroboration, elaboration, or elucidation of findings. When findings fail to converge, further investigation can determine whether either method of data collection might be biased or whether the different methods truly assess divergent constructs.

Reporting Findings

A written technical report provides background information on the organization and its issues. It includes detailed information on research questions and design, focus group methodology and procedures, and the materials. It provides enough information for another individual to replicate the study. Next, the report describes the themes, qualitative findings, and any relevant quantitative information.

The report concludes with recommendations from the focus groups. We like to include recommendations generated by the focus group participants and best practices contributed by the facilitators. A representative sample (or the entire population) of anonymized verbatim comments can be included as supporting material. Senior leaders in our client organizations frequently have reported reading each comment verbatim. If transcripts or other information was prepared or collected, these should be organized and stored for future retrieval.

We also provide an oral presentation with slides and handouts. When we have conducted focus groups as a follow-up to a quantitative survey, we include relevant highlights of the survey results and tie those to the focus group findings. We typically begin with an overview of the issues facing the organization, then follow with a brief description of the focus group methodology and the main findings. We then turn to detailed findings, first describing a quantitative survey result (if available), followed by related focus group themes. We include verbatim comments, which help convince audience members that the themes are valid and genuine. This format works well for the organization's senior leaders, its employees, and other stakeholders. Webinars can be an effective means for reaching employees.

Additional communications can include periodic progress reports published on the organization's intranet, in employee newsletters, or in mass e-mails. Video-recorded messages and town hall presentations are also valuable. Findings become more salient when we can report actions that organizational leaders are taking to address the issues or, if not possible, a sincere acknowledgment and explanation for issues that cannot be addressed.

Conclusion

Focus groups are a useful qualitative tool for gathering valuable information that supplements organizational survey results. Focus groups provide rich, insightful information that can be used to identify potential root causes of the survey results and potential solutions. We close by providing additional resources for readers interested in conducting focus groups in Appendix A.

References

Berry, J. (2012). *Guide for interpreting and action on Federal Employee Viewpoint Survey results*. Washington, DC: U.S. Office of Personnel Management. Retrieved from http://www.chcoc.gov/transmittals/TransmittalDetails.aspx?TransmittalID=5175

Campbell, D. T., & Fiske, D. W. (1959). Convergent and discriminant validation by the multitrait-multimethod matrix. *Psychological Bulletin, 56*(2), 81–105.

Centers for Disease Control and Prevention. (2008, July). *Data collection methods for program evaluation: Focus groups*. Atlanta, GA: Department of Health and Human Services. Retrieved November 27, 2018, from https://www.cdc.gov/healthyyouth/evaluation/pdf/brief13.pdf

Cohen, J. (1960). A coefficient of agreement for nominal scales. *Educational and Psychological Measurement, 20*, 37–46.

Cucina, J. M., Walmsley, P. T., Gast, I. F., Martin, N. R., & Curtin, P. (2017). Survey key driver analysis: Are we driving down the right road? *Industrial and Organizational Psychology, 10*(2), 234–257.

Easterby-Smith, M., Golden-Biddle, K., & Locke, K. (2008). Working with pluralism: Determining quality in qualitative research. *Organizational Research Methods, 11*(3), 419–429.

Fenlason, K. J., & Suckow-Zimberg, K. (2006). Online surveys: Critical issues in using the web to conduct surveys. In A. I. Kraut (Ed.), *Getting action from organizational surveys: New concepts, technologies, and applications* (pp. 183–212). San Francisco, CA: Josey-Bass.

Gallup. (2012). *Employee engagement action guide*. Omaha, NE: Author.

Gallup. (2013). *Q12* survey implementation guide*. Omaha, NE: Author. Retrieved November 13, 2018, from https://q12.gallup.com/Content/pdf/Q12SurveyResourceGuide_FULL.pdf

Krueger, R. A., & Casey, M. A. (2015). *Focus groups: A practical guide for applied research* (5th ed.). Thousand Oaks, CA: Sage Publications.

Mack, N., Woodsong, C., MacQueen, K. M., Guest, G., & Namey, E. (2005). *Qualitative methods: A data collector's field guide*. Research Triangle Park, NC: Family Health

International. Retrieved November 26, 2018 from https://www.fhi360.org/resource/qualitative-research-methods-data-collectors-field-guide

Marshall, C., & Rossman, G. B. (1999). *Designing qualitative research* (3rd ed.). Thousand Oaks, CA: Sage Publications.

Mayo, E. (1933). *The human problems of an industrial civilization* (Vol. 6). New York, NY: Macmillan.

Morgan, D. L., & Krueger, R. A. (1993). When to use focus groups and why. In D. L. Morgan (Ed.), *Sage focus editions. Successful focus groups: Advancing the state of the art* (Vol. 156, pp. 3–19). Thousand Oaks, CA: Sage Publications.

Nagle, B., & Williams, N. (2013). *Methodology brief: Introduction to focus groups.* Retrieved November 27, 2018, from http://www.uncfsp.org/projects/userfiles/File/FocusGroupBrief.pdf

Pokela, J., Steblea, I., Steblea, J., Shea, L., & Denny, E. (2007). *Getting started with market research for out-of-school-time planning: A resource guide for communities. Workbook D—Conducting focus groups: Appendix and prototype materials.* Northampton, MA: Market Street Research. Retrieved November 27, 2018, from https://www.wallacefoundation.org/knowledge-center/Documents/Workbook-D-Focus-Groups.pdf

Pratt, M. G., & Bonaccio, S. (2016). Qualitative research in IO psychology: Maps, myths, and moving forward. *Industrial and Organizational Psychology, 9*(4), 693–715.

Stewart, D. W., & Shamdasani, P. N. (2014). *Applied Social Research Methods. Focus groups: Theory and practice* (Book 20, 3rd ed., Kindle ed.). Thousand Oaks, CA: Sage Publications.

U.S. General Accounting Office. (1996, September). *Content analysis: A methodology for structuring and analyzing written material* (PEMD-10.3.1). Retrieved November 27, 2018, from https://www.gao.gov/products/PEMD-10.3.1

Weber, R. P. (1990). *Quantitative applications in the social sciences. Basic content analysis* (07-049, 2nd ed.). Thousand Oaks, CA: Sage Publications.

Willis, G. B., Royston, P., & Bercini, D. (1991). The use of verbal report methods in the development and testing of survey questionnaires. *Applied Cognitive Psychology, 5*(3), 251–267.

Appendix A

Additional Resources

This appendix describes additional resources for readers who are conducting focus groups.

Brief Summaries

- The Centers for Disease Control and Prevention (2008) has a useful two-page management brief summarizing the focus group process.
- Nagle and Williams (2013) describe a five-stage process for conducting focus groups and reporting the results. They include materials such as a project timeline, facilitation tips, a consent form, and a facilitator's script.

Comprehensive Guidance

- Mack, Woodsong, MacQueen, Guest, and Namey (2005) prepared a series of "modules" for training public-health personnel in qualitative data collection. Descriptions of data-collection procedures are supplemented by case studies, summary tables, and sample materials. Module 4, Focus Groups, is a concise but thorough presentation of focus group methodology. Module 5 covers the steps involved in transcribing and organizing qualitative data.
- Krueger and Casey's (2015) practical guide addresses problems likely to arise when conducting focus groups. It provides guidance for all phases of designing and implementing focus groups and gives copious examples of materials. The book features an exceptionally detailed chapter devoted to developing questions.
- Pokela et al.'s (2007) *Workbook D* is an excellent source of information on focus groups. It provides in-depth coverage of each step of the process and outlines the decisions that must be made during each step. Appendix A provides example forms and correspondence that could be adapted to an organization's specific needs.
- Stewart and Shamdasani's (2014) book blends focus group theory, historical perspective, and practice. The authors guide readers through focus group development and data analysis. They provide an informative discussion of leadership, group dynamics, and how these factors shape the role of the facilitator. The final chapter describes how to adapt procedures designed for face-to-face focus groups to virtual focus groups.

Content Analysis

- Weber (1990) describes techniques for content analysis and discusses issues in interpreting the data.
- The U.S. General Accounting Office (1996) explains how to (1) select textual material for analysis, (2) develop an analysis plan, (3) code textual material, (4) ensure data reliability, and (5) analyze the data.

8

Strategic Climate Research

How What We Know Should Influence What We Do

Benjamin Schneider

There I was at Bar-Ilan University (Israel) on a Fulbright, and the 1973 Yom Kippur War had begun and classes were canceled. I was not prepared for the war, but neither, unfortunately, was Israel; that story is for another time. With classes canceled, I decided it was an opportunity to do some writing. I had an itch to pursue the topic I had worried about ever since I had entered the Ph.D. program at Maryland: context effects on people. Unlike my classmates in industrial psychology (there was no "O" then) at Maryland, I had taken my second specialty in social psychology, not measurement, and had become interested in the social psychology of organizations à la Katz and Kahn's (1966) then-recent book by that title.

By 1973 I had already been doing some research on what I called *climate* (Schneider & Bartlett, 1968, 1970; Schneider & Hall, 1973) but was not feeling good about what I had done. The climate construct was not very clear at that point in time (it was often called "environmental variation" [Campbell, Dunnette, Lawler & Weick, 1970]), the validity of it against important outcomes was inconsistent at best, there was debate over whether we needed such a construct (some claiming it was old satisfaction in a new climate bottle [Guion, 1973]), and there was essentially no discussion of the level of analysis at which research on it should be done. In fact, essentially all of the research then (and up through the early 2000s for sure [Carr, Schmidt, Ford, & DeShon, 2003]) was conceptualized and done at the individual level of analysis while using the "climate" label. As we know, inadequately/poorly conceptualized constructs, varying foci for research, different levels of analysis for studies, and inconsistent findings lead to confusion over what is being studied. I set out to resolve some of these issues about the climate construct as the Yom Kippur War unfolded and as classes continued to be delayed. The result was my "Organizational Climates: An Essay" (Schneider, 1975).

Benjamin Schneider, *Strategic Climate Research* In: *Employee Surveys and Sensing.* Edited by: William H. Macey and Alexis A. Fink, Oxford University Press (2020). © Society for Industrial and Organizational Psychology. DOI: 10.1093/oso/9780190939717.003.0008

The essay had four central themes: (1) climate is a perception and follows the rules of gestalt psychology; (2) climate is a description of a setting and not an affective evaluation of it or outcomes from it; (3) research can be done at different levels of analysis, but the level must be made explicit and both the climate being assessed and the measures of it must be at the same level of analysis; and (4) the climate being assessed should be focused on specific outcomes (I called this idea "the climate for something" then and have called it "strategic climate" since). I go into some detail here with regard to these themes because, although climate research has made considerable progress (Schneider, González-Romá, Ostroff, & West, 2017), practitioners (a) frequently ignore the basics of the gestalt nature of the construct, (b) generalize from data collected at the individual level of analysis to organizational consequences, and (c) create surveys that have no strategic focus.

Climate Is a Perception

Early research on "environmental variation" focused on perceptions of settings along a set of between 5 and 10 dimensions or facets of social/organizational psychological conditions (see Campbell et al., 1970, for a review). Measures of those conditions covered topics then popular in the literature: leadership, conflict, support, rewards, structure, job characteristics, and so forth. Explicit consideration of what was being assessed was rarely addressed, the implicit idea being that "the situation" in which people worked was important to and for them and that they somehow processed those perceptions into some higher-order meaning or sense of what the setting was. It is important to note that the higher-order meaning was rarely labeled and not assessed; there was just this implicit belief that the more positively people viewed their settings across these context facets, the better off they—and, of course, the organization—would be.

Because this work was perception-based research, there was some concern that there was "no there there" in the study of organizational climate, that is, that research was being done from a perceptual vantage point. Payne and Pugh (1976), James and Jones (1974), and Guion (1973) took the position that the only way one could place credence on the measurement of climate was to tie perception-based measures to measures of organizational structure (size, number of levels in the hierarchy, and so forth). In their opinion, climate required some tangible assets to which it was linked, or it would remain vague and not useful.

I argued in my essay that climate was perception and summarized the gestalt school of psychology so that it was clear where I stood on the issue. I proposed that incumbents in organizations perceive bundles of experiences and assign meaning to those that they perceive as being connected; that the meaning attached to the bundles is the climate. That is, a table is not just pieces of wood (or metal or whatever) but a bundle of attributes that, because of the connections among the elements, connotes a specific object. Decision makers in organizations can easily fail to understand that climate is a summary perception of a bundle of perceptions of attributes and not the perceptions of just one thing. I recently worked with a company and showed them that the climate of interest—a feedback climate—was the result of a bundle of six practices and procedures employees perceived to be happening vis-à-vis feedback. They, of course, asked me the following: "Well, if we were going to take action to improve the climate for feedback, on which of the six should we focus?" That is like asking "Which one stick should I use to build a table?"

In the 1975 essay I also summarized the functionalism school of psychology (p. 451): "While Gestalt psychologists hypothesized that people apprehend and create order because they have no choice, Functionalists proposed that order is apprehended and created so people can function adaptively in their world." In short, the perceptions of climate serve to help people to know the kinds of behaviors—and the focus of those behaviors—that are appropriate in their (work) setting. The work I will describe on the strategic focus of climate is based on this idea that people perceive what happens in their settings and attach meaning to those perceptions because the meaning attached to the perceptions yields cues to the focus of the behaviors most useful in the setting.

Climate Is a Description, Not an Evaluation

At the time the 1975 essay was written, an argument was being made by some (Guion, 1973; Johannesson, 1973) that measures of climate and measures of job satisfaction contained overlapping items and, therefore, that climate was an unnecessary addition to the quiver of useful constructs and measures. However, I presented considerable evidence that it was the measures of job satisfaction that inappropriately overlapped with measures of climate and not the reverse. That is, the most prominent measure of satisfaction at the time was the Job Descriptive Index[1] (Smith, Kendall, & Hulin, 1969), and I showed that the items comprising, for example, satisfaction with work were both descriptive and evaluative, that the descriptive and the evaluative items were poorly intercorrelated, and that, as Payne and Mansfield (1973) had shown, the descriptive items correlated poorly with measures of pure job satisfaction.

Theory and research have subsequently revealed findings showing a clear conceptual and statistical separation between climate and job satisfaction when items in each measure are appropriately written. That is, when items are descriptive of policies, practices, and procedures, they may correlate with but are clearly distinguishable from items that are evaluative in content (LaFollette & Sims, 1975; Schneider & Snyder, 1975). Contemporary evidence suggesting that all employee surveys are assessing the same A factor—A for Attitude (Newman & Harrison, 2008)—is really a function of the fact that measures of constructs with different labels reveal extensive overlap in items used to assess them (e.g., commitment, satisfaction, and engagement), so it is not surprising that they are highly (.70) intercorrelated.

My conclusion from such evidence is that if the concept being assessed is not matched by the appropriate item content, then what is being assessed is unknowable and items will correlate highly with each other. The use of the same employee opinion/attitude/culture/climate/engagement/experience surveys in business and industry for the last 50 years or so, regardless of what the survey has been called, yields information about unknown constructs; and, thus, the usefulness of such data is questionable. One startling example is the Gallup Q-12 survey, promoted as a measure of work engagement, wherein none of the 12 (or 13 in some cases) items in the measure are conceptually related to the engagement construct that exists in the academic research literature (Bakker & Leiter, 2010). As Gallup researchers themselves have noted (Harter, Schmidt, Asplund, Killham, & Agrawal, 2010, p. 378) in describing the Q-12, "The instrument is composed of 12 items . . . measuring antecedents to (causes of) personal job satisfaction and other affective constructs (measured on a 1–5 agreement scale), and one overall satisfaction item (satisfaction with the overall organization, measured on a 1–5 satisfaction scale)." The point is that if the items do not refer to facets of the engagement construct and are seemingly random examples of things that happen to and around people at work, then what has been assessed is not known. So, vaguely conceptualized and unfocused employee surveys, regardless of what they are called, cannot predict important organizational outcomes; and because the surveys are typically more evaluative than descriptive, they yield little of use as a basis for making changes with likely known consequences. In short, confounding evaluative with descriptive items in surveys, and further confounding issues of frames of reference (levels of analysis) in items and then doing all analyses at the individual level of analysis against a proxy for important organizational outcomes (e.g., against engagement), is not a good use of employee surveys. I turn to the issue of levels of analysis next.

Levels of Analysis Issues

Survey data analyzed at the individual level of analysis are not usually useful in companies because it is aggregate (unit, team) performance that is the typical target of interest.[2] Also, items in employee surveys to be aggregated beyond the individual level of analysis must be written to describe practices and procedures occurring at the level of analysis to which the data will be aggregated (Chan, 1998). The items must therefore address practices and procedures that characterize the unit of interest (as well as the strategic outcome of interest; more on that in the section on Focus in Climate Assessment), not those that are evaluations of personal experiences. For example, a leadership item that says "I am supported by my supervisor for my work effort" is a psychological climate item, but if it said "Our work group supervisor is supportive of us in our work efforts," then it would be a work-group climate item. Of course, if it said "Senior leadership in this company is supportive of employees' work efforts," then it is obviously written to be aggregated to the company level of analysis.[3] I have more to say about how to write climate survey items in the next section, where we dig deeper into the issue of focus in strategic climate surveys.

In 1974 Larry James and Alan Jones wrote what is probably the most significant paper on climate research. It is significant because it clarified for all time the difference between climate assessed as an individual variable (they called this "psychological climate") and climate assessed at the unit and organizational levels of analysis (they called this "organizational climate"). Indeed, by 1975 I was already able to show, based on the scant evidence at the time, that aggregate data to depict "organizational" climate were reliable and, further, that individual-level data that were sometimes being used to characterize a setting were not reliable: "In short, these data suggest that *aggregate* reports of practices and procedures can be reliable. They also suggest that *an* individual's report will not be a very reliable report of what is happening in the situation" (italics in the original; Schneider, 1975, p. 469).

The issue of levels of analysis bedraggled climate research for almost two decades, finally being somewhat resolved in the Klein and Kozlowski (2000) book on levels issues, especially in the chapter by Bliese (2000). I shan't go into detail on this issue (because it pains me so much!) and shall simply state that aggregates of individuals' perceptions of practices and procedures vis-à-vis focused or strategic climates are reliable (Klein & Kozlowski, 2000; Ehrhart, Schneider, & Macey, 2014), and we have good answers to almost any question about how to calculate the reliability of aggregated data (LeBreton & Senter, 2008).

Focus in Climate Assessment

I summarized the issue of focus in the original paper this way: "the indiscriminate use of the term 'organizational climate' should be supplanted by reference to a climate for something" (Schneider, 1975, p. 472). Most climate research of the time, as I indicated earlier, had no focus; and my review of the then-existing literature revealed that this was a problem in two ways. First, measures of climate in use then had upward of 20 facets or dimensions being assessed (House & Rizzo, 1972), and it would be difficult to study the effects of each on some outcome or outcomes of interest. The second problem was that the chances for validity against important outcomes were diminished because the item content did not tap into the social psychological construct directly tied to an outcome of interest.

It is not that there were no existing examples of climate surveys that were designed to help understand specific outcomes. For example, Fleishman (1953) designed a leadership climate measure to assess the conditions under which some trainees transferred their learning back to their job situation and others did not, and Taylor (1972) focused on a climate for creativity. But these were exceptions, and they went unnoticed as being different from the usual or typical measures being used. This was all quite strange given that industrial psychologists were doing this work, and they had (hypothetically) been thoroughly trained in measurement for personnel selection where it was pounded into their/our heads to be sure to select tests that had some conceptual—bandwidth—relevance for the criterion of interest. In essence, all I did was propose that climate researchers pay attention when designing survey items that had conceptual overlap with the outcome of interest.

I note here and will note again later that all employee surveys (regardless of what those surveys are said to measure) that are in use today should have at least one set of six to eight items that cover practices and procedures with direct relevance for a specific outcome of interest, or the measure will likely not be reflected in the outcome. I have no doubt, as I have said before and will keep repeating, that a reason why employee surveys of all kinds are not seen by management to be valuable and useful is because they do not focus on something that is important to them. What a focused climate measure does is assess how employees perceive the priority given to a specific outcome: safety, service, creativity, and so forth. This is accomplished by having items on a survey that assess the policies, practices, and procedures and the behaviors that get rewarded, supported, and expected with regard to the outcome of interest (Ehrhart et al., 2014; Zohar, 2014). Focused items in strategic climate surveys must have the outcome of interest in the item.

Here are two examples of valid strategic safety climate items, the first set for items to be aggregated to the company level of analysis and the second set for items to be aggregated to the supervisory level of analysis (from Zohar & Luria, 2005, p. 628)[4]:

Top management in this plant/company

1. Reacts quickly to solve the problem when told about safety hazards.
2. Insists on thorough and regular safety audits and inspections.

My direct supervisor

1. Makes sure we receive all the equipment needed to do the job safely.
2. Frequently checks to see if we are all obeying the safety rules.

The first set of items reveals that it is not just that senior management reacts quickly but that it reacts quickly to solve safety problems and that top management is not just insistent on doing audits but is insistent on doing safety audits. The set of items focusing on what supervisors do reveals that supervisors provide the tools and technology needed not only to do the work but also to behave safely and that they check to see if people are not just following the rules but following the safety rules. I have unfortunately seen too many so-called climate surveys that not only failed to focus on a strategic outcome but also failed to have items written to the level of analysis to which the items will be aggregated. Why is this important? This is important because (1) these kinds of focused strategic surveys have validity (to be detailed in the section on Evidence for Strategically Focused Climate Surveys) and (2) that Zohar and Luria (2005) showed that there is a significant effect of top management focus on safety with regard to accidents in the workplace over and above the effects from the supervisory level of analysis! Multilevel strategically focused surveys are beginning, fortunately, to characterize climate research in general (Schneider, González-Romá, et al., 2017), and the Zohar and Luria findings make it imperative to understand the multilevel effects on strategically important outcomes.

Recalling the discussion of gestalt psychology, measures of safety climate (like the Zohar and Luria measure) and service climate focus not on only one or two facets of practices and procedures related to these foci but on a bundle of issues that reveal the priority given to them. For example, in just seven items, Schneider, White, and Paul (1998) were able to capture a bundle of issues to characterize what they called "global service climate." The seven items they used are rated by employees on a five-point scale (Poor, Fair, Good, Very Good, Excellent) and are shown below (see Schneider et al., 1998, p. 154)[5]:

- How would you rate the job knowledge and skills of employees in your business to deliver superior quality work and service?
- How would you rate efforts to measure and track the quality of the work and service in your business?
- How would you rate the recognition and rewards employees receive for the delivery of superior work and service?
- How would you rate the overall quality of service provided by your business?
- How would you rate the leadership shown by management in your business in supporting the service quality effort?
- How would you rate the effectiveness of our communications efforts to both employees and customers?
- How would you rate the tools, technology, and other resources provided to employees to support the delivery of superior quality work and service?

In recent research with this scale, we have added an eighth item that captures the meaning of the seven service climate items: "How do you rate the atmosphere in your work unit for promoting superior quality work and service?"

One might ask, "Why do such focused climate measures have to focus on a bundle of issues?" The answer is that there must be numerous exemplars of the focus of interest assessed to ensure that the climate is not ambiguous for those who experience it (Zohar, 2014). That is, if a relatively comprehensive set of similarly focused items is not assessed, then there will be ambiguity; and ambiguity yields unreliability and weak climate strength (González-Romá & Peiró, 2014). Unless the focused climate is established through numerous practices and procedures, it will be ambiguous, yielding unreliability (weak climate strength) in the way it is perceived and thus likely to not be correlated significantly with the outcome of interest.

Climate strength is a relatively recent construct in climate research (Schneider, Salvaggio, & Subirats, 2002), and it refers to the dispersion of respondents in a unit or organization when aggregating individuals' perceptions (usually just a simple standard deviation). This is, of course, not an issue when all analyses are done at the individual level of analysis; but when aggregating such data to unit and/or organizational levels of analysis, it is good to have a reliable indicator—and the evidence indicates that the more reliable the indicator, the more strongly it will correlate with the outcome of interest.

Evidence for Strategically Focused Climate Surveys

Research began to appear many years ago that this focused approach to climate research has validity. The earliest studies were of accidents—safety climate (Zohar, 1980)—and customer satisfaction—service climate (Schneider, Parkington, & Buxton, 1980). Meta-analyses of the safety climate literature reveal that it is a robust predictor of various indicators of safety (injuries as well as accidents) at the individual (Clarke, 2006) and unit and organizational (Beus, Payne, Bergman, & Arthur, 2010; Christian, Bradley, Wallace, & Burke, 2009) levels of analysis across industries and countries (Zohar, 2014). And the validity is true across various operationalizations of safety climate (they can differ somewhat by industry and by the level of analysis on which the items focus) and for definitions of safety ranging from injuries to Occupational Safety and Health Administration–reportable accidents.

With regard to service climate, there are several extensive reviews of the literature (Bowen & Schneider, 2014; Dean, 2004; Yagil, 2008) and one technical meta-analysis (Hong, Liao, Hu & Jiang, 2013), all of which reveal that the link between service climate and customer experiences/customer satisfaction appears robust and reliable at both unit (bank branches; Schneider et al., 1998) and company (Schneider, Macey, Lee, & Young, 2009) levels of analysis. This is true for various operationalizations of the service climate construct including the measure shown in the section on Focus in Climate Assessment.

Following up on Guion's (1973) comment on climate being satisfaction in a new bottle, it is worth noting that in 1980 (Schneider et al., 1980) and more recently (Way, Sturman, & Rabb, 2010) there is evidence that service climate is a stronger correlate of customer experiences and customer satisfaction than is job satisfaction. What is likely true is that conditions in an organization that employees find to be positive and that facilitate their work efforts (they are engaged?) provide a receptive foundation on which a service climate can be built. Indeed, there is evidence to indicate that such a mediated model—work engagement > service climate > customer satisfaction—exists (Salanova, Agut, & Peiro, 2005; Schneider et al., 1998). It is very important to note that it is not work engagement that leads to or causes service climate but that work engagement provides a foundation on which a service climate can be built. In this line of thinking, service climate—or any focused strategic climate—is a mediator between an engaged workforce and the outcomes of interest, so it is not surprising that workforce engagement itself (or a climate for well-being or a positive work culture or aggregate positive employee experiences—and so forth) is not that strongly related to outcomes of interest (Schneider, Yost, Kropp, Kind, & Lam, 2017). In short, focused strategic climate survey items appropriately operationalized with regard to bandwidth and content vis-à-vis an outcome of interest have validity for important strategic outcomes at various levels of analysis.

I am convinced that the major reason senior management continuously (like every 5 years or so) changes what it wishes Human Resources to assess in employee surveys (opinion, satisfaction, climate, culture, engagement, experience) is that the surveys are not useful as a basis for change because they (a) are not descriptive of what actually happens and (b) do not relate significantly to important organizational consequences—like accidents and customer satisfaction. All of the relative weights analysis (Cucina, Walmsley, Gast, Martin, & Curtin, 2017) in the world showing linkages among evaluations and opinions—what are the strongest item correlates of overall engagement/satisfaction—is not the way to show the usefulness of employee survey data and contributes little that is useful for an evidence-based management (Rynes & Bartunek, 2017). In other words, employee engagement indices are very poor proxies for real organizational outcomes, so knowing their correlates ("drivers") is not useful for improving organizational effectiveness on specific strategic outcomes. This is particularly true when essentially all engagement survey practice and research is at the individual level of analysis. What does it tell an organization when the items in a survey are evaluations/feelings and analyses are done at the individual level of analysis against an engagement index? Moreover, what does it tell an organization when the items in a survey are written about different levels of analysis focused on random content and then explored at the individual level of analysis?

Summary and Conclusion

Strategically focused climate surveys are valid. Such surveys have specific characteristics: (1) the items in such surveys seek the perceptions of workers about specific strategic foci of the practices and procedures they experience; (2) following gestalt thinking, perceptions of a bundle of such practices and procedures are assessed because climate is a summary perception based on numerous instances of a similar focus and there are no silver bullets; (3) the survey items must be written to capture perceptions at the level of analysis to which the data will be aggregated. Research suggests that strategically focused climate surveys are significantly different from job satisfaction surveys and surveys that focus on the generic, unfocused aspects of organizational functioning. Research also suggests that survey data of the sort reviewed here can be reliably aggregated to yield unit and organizational data that relate consistently and significantly to the outcomes that are the focus of such surveys. In the present case the focus was on accidents/injuries for safety climate and on customer satisfaction for service climate, but there is no reason why strategically focused surveys of a similar sort cannot be designed around any outcome of interest. Practitioners would do well to have outcome foci in their surveys because the results from such surveys attract management's attention precisely due to the fact that they are valid and have direct implications for action.

Notes

1. Need I comment on the paradox that it was called the Job *Descriptive* Index?
2. Obviously, there are situations where individual scientists, programmers, architects, or what have you are the focus of interest; but that is rare.
3. If the item said "I have a good working relationship with my supervisor" or "I am satisfied with the support I receive from my supervisor," then it would be not a description but an evaluation.
4. Copyright by the American Psychological Association and used by permission.
5. Copyright by the American Psychological Association and used by permission.

References

Bakker, A. B., & Leiter, M. P. (Eds.). (2010). *Work engagement: A handbook of essential theory and research*. New York, NY: Psychology Press.

Beus, J. M., Payne, S. C., Bergman, M. E., & Arthur, W., Jr. (2010). Safety climate and injuries: An examination of theoretical and empirical relationships. *Journal of Applied Psychology, 95,* 713–727.

Bliese, P. D. (2000). Within-group agreement, non-independence, and reliability: Implications for data aggregation and analyses. In K. J. Klein & S. W. J. Kozlowski (Eds.), *Multilevel theory, research and methods in organizations: Foundations, extensions, and new directions* (pp. 349–381). San Francisco, CA: Jossey-Bass.

Bowen, D. E., & Schneider, B. (2014). A service climate synthesis and future research agenda. *Journal of Service Research, 17,* 5–22.

Campbell, J. P., Dunnette, M. D., Lawler, E. E., III, & Weick, K. E. (1970). *Managerial behavior, performance, and effectiveness*. New York, NY: McGraw-Hill.

Carr, J. Z., Schmidt, A. M., Ford, J. K., & DeShon, R. P. (2003). Climate perceptions matter: A meta-analytic path analysis relating molar climate, cognitive and affective states and individual level work outcomes. *Journal of Applied Psychology, 88,* 605–619.

Chan, D. (1998). Functional relations among constructs in the same content domain at different levels of analysis: A typology of composition models. *Journal of Applied Psychology, 83,* 234–246.

Christian, M. S., Bradley, J. C., Wallace, J. C., & Burke, M. J. (2009). Workplace safety: A meta-analysis of the roles of person and situation factors. *Journal of Applied Psychology, 94,* 1103–1127.

Clarke, S. (2006). The relationship between safety climate and safety performance: A meta-analytic review. *Journal of Occupational Health Psychology, 11,* 315–327.

Cucina, J. M., Walmsley, P. T., Gast, I. F., Martin, N. R., & Curtin, P. (2017). Survey key driver analysis: Are we driving down the wrong road? *Industrial and Organizational Psychology, 10,* 234–257.

Dean, A. (2004). Links between organizational and customer variables in service delivery: Evidence, contradictions, and challenges. *International Journal of Service Industry Management, 15,* 332–350.

Ehrhart, M. G., Schneider, B., & Macey, W. H. (2014). *Organizational climate and culture: An introduction to theory, research, and practice.* New York, NY: Routledge.

Fleishman, E. A. (1953). Leadership climate, human relations training and supervisory behavior. *Personnel Psychology, 6,* 205–222.

González-Romá, V., & Peiró, J. M. (2014). Climate and culture strength. In B. Schneider & K. M. Barbera (Eds.), *The Oxford handbook of organizational climate and culture* (pp. 496–531). New York, NY: Oxford University Press.

Guion, R. M. (1973). A note on organizational climate. *Organizational Behavior and Human Performance, 9,* 120–125.

Harter, J. K., Schmidt, F. L., Asplund, J. W., Killham, E. A., & Agrawal, S. (2010). Causal impact of employee work perceptions on the bottom line of organizations. *Perspectives on Psychological Science, 5,* 378–389.

Hong, Y., Liao, H., Hu, J., & Jiang, K. (2013). Missing link in the service profit chain: A meta-analytic review of the antecedents, consequences, and moderators of service climate. *Journal of Applied Psychology, 98,* 237–267.

House, R. J., & Rizzo, J. R. (1972). Toward the measurement of organizational practices: Scale development and validation. *Journal of Applied Psychology, 56,* 388–396.

James, L. R., & Jones, A. P. (1974). Organizational climate: A review of theory and research. *Psychological Bulletin, 81,* 1096–1112.

Johannesson, R. (1973). Some problems in the measurement of organizational climate. *Organizational Behavior and Human Performance, 10,* 118–145.

Katz, D., & Kahn, R. L. (1966). *The social psychology of organizations.* New York, NY: Wiley.

Klein, K. J., & Kozlowski, S. W. J. (Eds.). (2000). *Multilevel theory, research and methods in organizations: Foundations, extensions, and new directions.* San Francisco, CA: Jossey-Bass.

LaFollette, W. R., & Sims, H. P., Jr. (1975). Is satisfaction redundant with climate? *Organizational Behavior and Human Performance, 10,* 118–144.

LeBreton, J. M., & Senter, J. L. (2008). Answers to twenty questions about interrater reliability and interrater agreement. *Organizational Research Methods, 11,* 815–852.

Newman, D. A., & Harrison, D. A. (2008). Been there, bottled that: Are state and behavioral work engagement new and useful construct 'wines'? *Industrial and Organizational Psychology, 1,* 31–35.

Payne, R. L., & Mansfield, R. (1973). Relationships of perceptions of organizational climate to organizational structure, context, and hierarchical position. *Administrative Science Quarterly, 18,* 515–526.

Payne, R. L., & Pugh, D. S. (1976). Organizational structure and climate. In M. D. Dunnette (Ed.), *Handbook of industrial and organizational psychology* (pp. 1125–1173). Chicago, IL: Rand McNally.

Rynes, S. L., & Bartunek, J. M. (2017). Evidence-based management: Foundations, development, controversies and future. *Annual Review of Organizational Psychology and Organizational Behavior, 4,* 235–261.

Salanova, M., Agut, S., & Peiro, J. M. (2005). Linking organizational resources and work engagement to employee performance and customer loyalty: The mediation of service climate. *Journal of Applied Psychology, 90,* 1217–1227.

Schneider, B. (1975). Organizational climates: An essay. *Personnel Psychology, 28,* 447–479.

Schneider, B., & Bartlett, C. J. (1968). Individual differences and organizational climate, I: The research plan and questionnaire development. *Personnel Psychology, 21*, 323–333.

Schneider, B., & Bartlett, C. J. (1970). Individual differences and organizational climate, II: Measurement of organizational climate by the multitrait–multirater matrix. *Personnel Psychology, 23*, 493–512.

Schneider, B., González-Romá, V., Ostroff, C., & West, M. (2017). Organizational climate and culture: Reflections on the history of the constructs in *Journal of Applied Psychology*. *Journal of Applied Psychology, 102*, 468–482.

Schneider, B., & Hall, D. T. (1973). Towards specifying the concept of work climate: A study of Roman Catholic diocesan priests. *Journal of Applied Psychology, 56*, 447–455.

Schneider, B., Macey, W. H., Lee, W., & Young, S. A. (2009). Organizational service climate drivers of the American Customer Satisfaction Index (ACSI) and financial and market performance. *Journal of Service Research, 12*, 3–14.

Schneider, B., Parkington, J. P., & Buxton, V. M. (1980). Employee and customer perceptions of service in banks. *Administrative Science Quarterly, 25*, 252–267.

Schneider, B., Salvaggio, A. N., & Subirats, M. (2002). Climate strength: A new direction for climate research. *Journal of Applied Psychology, 87*, 220–229.

Schneider, B., & Snyder, R. A. (1975). Some relationships between job satisfaction and organizational climate. *Journal of Applied Psychology, 60*, 318–328.

Schneider, B., White, S. S., & Paul, M. C. (1998). Linking service climate and customer perceptions of service quality: Test of a causal model. *Journal of Applied Psychology, 83*, 150–163.

Schneider, B., Yost, A. B., Kropp, A., Kind, C., & Lam, H. (2017). Workforce engagement: What it is, what drives it, and why it matters for organizational performance. *Journal of Organizational Behavior, 39*, 462–480.

Smith, P. C., Kendall, L. M., & Hulin, C. L. (1969). *The measurement of satisfaction in work and retirement*. Chicago, IL: Rand-McNally.

Taylor, C. W. (Ed.). (1972). *Climate for creativity*. New York, NY: Pergamon.

Way, S. A., Sturman, M. C., & Raab, C. (2010). What matters more? Contrasting the effects of job satisfaction and service climate on hotel food and beverage managers' job performance. *Cornell Hotel Quarterly, 51*, 379–397.

Yagil, D. (2008). *The service providers*. New York, NY: Palgrave Macmillan.

Zohar, D. (1980). Safety climate in industrial organizations: Theoretical and applied implications. *Journal of Applied Psychology, 65*, 96–102.

Zohar, D. (2014). Safety climate: Conceptualization, measurement, and improvement. In B. Schneider and K. M. Barbera (Eds.), *The Oxford handbook of organizational climate and culture* (pp. 317–334). New York, NY: Oxford University Press.

Zohar, D., & Luria, G. (2005). A multi-level model of safety climate: Cross-level relationships between organization and group-level climates. *Journal of Applied Psychology, 90*, 616–628.

9

The Unique Role of Corporate Culture in Employee Listening Systems

Daniel Denison, Marcus W. Dickson, Michelle W. Mullins, and Jessie Sanchez

Employee listening systems (ELSs) can be highly useful for tracking the evolution of an organization's culture. In contrast to many employee engagement surveys that focus primarily on the reactions of individuals to the workplace culture, the focus of the culture perspective is on the character of the workplace itself. This focus on the system is the most unique contribution offered by the culture perspective (Katz & Kahn, 1978). Every organization creates a unique work environment that provides the context in which work gets performed. To understand an individual's reaction to the context, we must first understand the context itself.

Despite the common assumption that a highly engaged and committed workforce is the most effective, there are many examples to the contrary. Is an intense level of engagement in a highly stable, inwardly focused culture the best strategy for coping with a dynamic, fast-moving business environment? Probably not (Kotrba et al., 2012). Is a high level of commitment to an organization still rooted in fossil fuel–based energy sources a key asset in adopting a strategy of sustainability? Not exactly. Does a high level of satisfaction in a "bricks and mortar" retail environment help prepare for an online business model designed to compete with Amazon? Don't bet on it. Each organization's culture is rooted in its history, and the organization continuously evolves in reaction to its environment. Engagement must be viewed in that context.

In this chapter, we focus on the unique role that measures of organization culture can play in the creation of an ELS. We begin by tracing the evolution of the culture perspective, as it has moved from the periphery of the field to the center stage. Next, we highlight the unique contributions that the culture perspective has made and give an overview of some of the dominant

Daniel Denison, Marcus W. Dickson, Michelle W. Mullins, and Jessie Sanchez, *The Unique Role of Corporate Culture in Employee Listening Systems* In: *Employee Surveys and Sensing.* Edited by: William H. Macey and Alexis A. Fink, Oxford University Press (2020). © Society for Industrial and Organizational Psychology. DOI: 10.1093/oso/9780190939717.003.0009 frameworks. Finally, we focus on the implications of our discussion for the design of an ELS.

From the Edge to the Center Stage

The earliest mention of the culture perspective in organizational studies comes from Eliot Jacques' (1951) classic *The Changing Culture of a Factory*. This case study captures many of the essential elements that helped shape the culture perspective: a focus on the evolving character of the organization itself and the creative way in which the culture served as both a cause and an effect of individual behavior. That same year, Trist and Bamforth (1951) presented their classic representation of the close link between organizational systems, job design, and work behaviors. While they did not frame their work as "organizational culture," their approach showed that an organization designed with a higher degree of interdependence created a more resilient workforce. The workforce was organized to manage a broader team task, rather than a narrower individual task; and this created an environment that was safer, more satisfying, and more effective.

This central influence of underlying values and assumptions on organizational systems moved much closer to the mainstream in the 1960s with the work of iconic scholars such as Rensis Likert (1961) and Douglas McGregor (1960). Both of these authors articulated the central tenet of culture research: Values and assumptions lie at the heart of an organizational system, and leadership behavior brings these values to life. Likert's "System 4" and MacGregor's "Theory X and Theory Y" both describe the profound impact that core assumptions about managing people can have on the evolution of an organizational system. These authors also highlighted the tremendous inertia that is created by an organization's culture. Changes in one part of an organization often meet with tremendous resistance from the other parts.

Lawrence and Lorsch (1967) added to this legacy by describing the connection between the internal dynamics of an organization and the external business environment. Their study of the manufacturing, sales, and research and development subcultures of six organizations showed how a differentiated approach to time perspective, hierarchical control, and level of involvement characterized the most effective organizations. The highest performers were both highly differentiated and highly integrated. This classic study also used a mix of quantitative and qualitative methods that would influence culture researchers over the coming years: They made their points by comparing a small number of in-depth case studies.

The topic of corporate culture took another major step toward the mainstream with the first management bestseller, *In Search of Excellence* (Peters & Waterman, 1982). They described the cultures of excellent companies and positioned culture as a powerful driver of success. Other authors writing for a popular business audience responded to a challenging period of American economic decline by emphasizing the central importance of corporate culture and leadership (Collins & Porras, 1994; Deal & Kennedy, 1982; Ouchi, 1981).

Academic colleagues emphasized the importance of qualitative, ethnographic research, building from the concept's anthropological roots. Paradigm wars over method and epistemology dominated the culture literature (Denison, 1996). Qualitative research, they argued, provided an in-depth understanding of the unique nature of each organization that could never be captured through quantitative methods alone (Frost, Moore, Louis, Lundberg, & Martin, 1991; Schein, 1985). Research based on stories captured the meaning in each organization's context and provided greater depth of understanding (Martin, 1992; Van Maanen, 1979).

This debate helped culture researchers move forward with a multimethod approach. Kotter and Heskett (1992) created a framework stressing the importance of adaptability. Cameron and Quinn (1999) developed an approach based upon Quinn's competing values model (Quinn & Rohrbaugh, 1983). O'Reilly, Chatman, and Caldwell (1991) created a values-based organizational fit framework. House and his colleagues created the GLOBE framework that was used to study cross-cultural differences in organizations (House et al., 1999). Hofstede adapted his well-known model of differences in national culture to develop a set of organization-level measures (Hofstede & Peterson, 2000). Schneider, White, and Paul (1998) created a set of comparative measures of customer service climate that they found were closely correlated with customer satisfaction. Denison and Neale (1996) created an organizational culture model based on research linking four culture traits to key indicators of organizational performance (Denison, Nieminen, & Kotrba, 2014). Cooke and Rousseau (1988) adapted Human Synergistics' leadership framework to create an organization-level assessment of culture. These frameworks helped establish culture as a mainstay of the organizational assessment world.

In 2000 and 2001, two handbooks appeared that summarized the research on culture and climate (Ashkanasy, Wilderom, & Peterson, 2000; Cooper,

Cartwright, & Earley, 2001). They showed a wide range of common interests that transcended the methodological debates. The handbooks included contributions from nearly all of the leading voices in the field and helped move past the paradigm wars to integrate a diverse set of perspectives on how work environments are formed (Denison, 2003). A later review by Sackmann (2011) presented an integrative review of all of the 55 published culture–performance linkage studies.

This introduction has traced the evolution of the culture perspective from the edge of our field to the center stage. Organizational culture has become a mainstream topic in both the academic and the applied worlds. Next, we take a look at some of the trends that have appeared since 2015.

Recent Developments

In recent years, interest in organizational culture has expanded dramatically in the business world. The accelerated rate of change has required leaders to engage in a virtually continuous level of transformation in order to remain successful. New technologies such as pulse surveys (see Chapter 4) and Web-based analytics have also influenced culture assessments. In contrast to a broader-based, enterprise-wide culture assessment, pulse surveys are designed to provide real-time information on very targeted issues and to build momentum for action. While they have perhaps been oversold on occasion—"Pulse surveys are different. They're faster, smarter, better, and infinitely cooler than your average survey. They can increase and measure engagement in a split second. They're sleek, exciting, and relevant" (Sims, 2017)—they do provide a useful component of a state-of-the-art ELS.

But these new developments have had little impact on the academic literature. We searched peer-reviewed English-language articles since 2015 and identified over 10,000 articles. But a careful review identified only about 100 articles relevant to this chapter. Several interesting themes emerged from our review.

Organizational Type

A number of recent studies around the world have used Cameron and Quinn's (1999) Organizational Culture Assessment Instrument (OCAI) to "type" organizations. This model categorizes organizations into one of four types: clans, bureaucracies, adhocracies, and market-oriented. Jaeger, Yu, and Adair (2017) looked at the impact of type in a sample of Chinese-owned construction companies located in Kuwait. Teräväinen, Junnonen, and Ali-Löytty (2018) identified culture type in Finnish construction companies. Pilch and Turska (2015) found that bullying was more likely in a hierarchy culture and less likely in a clan culture.

Influence on Attitudes and Behaviors

Recent studies have also focused on the impact that the work environment has on employee attitudes and behavior. Factors ranging from office layout to leadership style have an influence on employee attitudes and behaviors. Zerella, von Treuer, and Albrecht (2017) found that office layout features such as privacy and proximity were related to job satisfaction in clan cultures. Cronley and Kim (2017) found that job satisfaction mediated the relationship between organizational culture and turnover intentions. New forms of leadership, such as authentic and transformational leadership, were shown to influence satisfaction, primarily through the mechanism of culture (Azanza, Moriano, & Molero, 2013; Belias & Koustelios, 2015; Lee, Idris, & Delfabbro, 2017). Other researchers have linked organizational culture to trust among coworkers engaging in counterproductive work behaviors and relational conflict (Terzi, 2016; Zoghbi-Manrique-de-Lara & Ting-Ding, 2016).

Diversity and Inclusion

Creating a unified culture that respects and nurtures the range of social identities present in contemporary organizations has also received a lot of attention since 2015 (Paolillo, Silva & Pasini, 2016). Creating an inclusive work environment, free of unconscious bias and attractive to organizational members from all backgrounds with respect to race, gender, ethnicity, nationality, expertise, and sexual orientation, has become an imperative (Cunningham, 2015). Creating a supportive institution that allows a firm to attract talent in all its forms has become a critical element of talent strategy and diversity, and inclusion issues have become visible in many leadership competency models, especially in the public sector. Culture is an important component in the institutionalization of organizational values and an important place to intervene to drive change. Nonetheless, scholarly research on the importance of building an inclusive culture has, unfortunately, lagged well behind practice.

"Facets" of Culture

The trend toward examining "facets" of an organization's culture and climate, rather than just overall culture, has also continued. Innovation culture, lean culture, agile culture, safety culture, ethical culture, risk culture, customer service culture, and culture for diversity are all examples of approaches to culture that have focused on specific organizational outcomes and the work contexts that support them (Huhtala, Tolvanen, Mauno & Feldt, 2015; Jiang, Hu, Hong, Liao, & Liu, 2016; Mor Barak et al., 2016; Naranjo-Valencia, Jimenez-Jimenez, & Sanz-Valle, 2017; Nielsen, 2014; Paro & Gerolamo, 2017). There are many commonalities across these "facets" of culture that parallel the key dimensions appearing in the general frameworks. But these approaches also add specific content, designed to fit these more focused contexts.

The Unique Contributions of Culture Research

The Organization Is the Unit of Analysis

The most distinct feature of the culture perspective is the viewpoint that each organization has a unique character and style. The organization is the unit of analysis. Understanding the impact that an organization's work environment has on individual members often means that the first step is to understand the nature of that work environment itself.

The People Make the Place

This catchy phrase was coined by Benjamin Schneider (1987) in his Society for Industrial and Organizational Psychology presidential address. This captures another important contribution: Cultures are created by the interactions of the people within them. Over time, the routine day-to-day behaviors of an organization's people create an enduring context that long outlives the daily interactions that created it. The culture perspective has at its base the recognition that the people ultimately create the environment that they work in. In principle, at least, this insight is fundamentally empowering and inclusive. In contrast to the typical employee engagement survey that leaves us waiting for the next Human Resources initiative designed to improve employee engagement, the culture perspective is far more often an initiative designed to engage the entire organization in an effort to create the work environment of the future.

Qualitative and Quantitative Methods

A qualitative approach provides a deep understanding of an organization's culture. But it can be time-consuming, subjective, and difficult to compare across organizations. A quantitative approach allows for cross-organizational comparisons and defines a common set of dimensions for comparison. But the questions and dimensions, established independently of the organization's context, may miss important features. The history of paradigm wars has left most contemporary culture researchers with a relatively eclectic approach, giving practitioners lots of complementary choices. Surveys, focus groups, interviews, observations, ethnographies, case studies, pulse surveys, crowdsourcing, verbatims, text analytics, and social media analyses are all good options that offer a much wider range of choices than typical engagement surveys.

Prescriptive or Descriptive?

Culture frameworks encompass both prescriptive and descriptive approaches. Prescriptive frameworks include Denison's work on culture and performance (Denison, Hooijberg, Lane, & Leif, 2012) and Keller and Price's (2011) work on organizational health. These frameworks are very useful because they provide a set of measures that help a client organization track its progress toward a desired future state. A well-researched normative model can help provide an organization with a compelling map of the desired future state that it is trying to achieve.

More descriptive frameworks, such as the Organizational Culture Inventory (OCI) (Cooke & Lafferty, 1989), offer valid measures of organizational culture rooted in a conceptual model. Or, like O'Reilly's model, their inventory of value dimensions came from an exhaustive review of the values literature (O'Reilly et al., 1991). Their framework describes a set of values, and the benefit comes from managing the fit between the individual's values and the organization's values.

Driving Outcomes

The literature presents a wide range of studies linking culture with organizational performance (Sackmann, 2011). Sackmann cites 55 studies but notes that linkage studies are at a relatively early stage of maturity. The research evidence is often weak and inconclusive, and important issues remain unresolved. Is culture a leading indicator or a lagging indicator? Recent research has shown that culture is a leading indicator in one of the first time-series studies of culture and customer satisfaction (Boyce, Nieminen, Gillespie, Ryan, & Denison, 2015). By way of contrast, linkage research on engagement has focused primarily on individual-level performance (Saks, 2006; Schneider, Ehrhart & Macey, 2013; Schneider, Yost, Kropp, Kind, & Lam, 2018).

As noted, linkage studies have addressed a range of organizational outcomes. Is there a specific culture for safety? Quality? Innovation? Customer satisfaction? Growth? Profitability? Market value? A number of outcome-specific culture measures have been developed, but the literature says very little about when to use facet-specific measures and when to use more general measures.

Making Meaning

Culture research has also placed a unique emphasis on meaning and sense-making. From the very beginning, researchers have focused on the social construction of meaning in the workplace (Weick, 1979). Organizations resist change, in part because the old ways of doing things have a lot of meaning for people. Creating change involves creating new practices, but it must also involve creating new meanings so that those new practices convey a sense of purpose. This perspective sometimes clashes with more rational perspectives that emphasize an economic or mechanistic rationale for organizing. But the continued emphasis on the importance of mindset underscores the importance of meaning to strategic change.

Dominant Frameworks

The set of useful, well-researched culture frameworks is an important asset for those who are designing an ELS. There is little consensus around a specific set of dimensions (Reichers & Schneider, 1990), but the frameworks present different measurement strategies for different purposes. In the next part of our chapter, we present a brief overview of several of the leading frameworks discussed in this chapter.

Hofstede's Model of Organizational Culture

In addition to his well-known model of the four dimensions differentiating national work cultures, Hofstede and his colleagues developed a framework for assessing organizational cultures (Hofstede, 1980: Hofstede & Peterson, 2000). The core of this approach is that culture and strategy are interdependent and require close alignment to achieve successful implementation.

Hofstede's model of organizational culture identifies six dimensions:

- Means-oriented versus goal-oriented
- Internally driven versus externally driven
- Easygoing work discipline versus strict work discipline
- Local orientation versus professional orientation
- Open system versus closed system
- Employee-oriented versus work-oriented

This model was developed through research conducted by Hofstede Insights, with a focus on organizational practices, which they argue is the appropriate focus for measures of organizational culture (https://www. hofstede-insights.com/).

Project GLOBE

Project GLOBE, established by Robert J. House, was a large-scale study of leadership and culture involving several hundred researchers around the world and several thousand cases from over 60 countries in 37 languages. Project GLOBE was established to assess the extent to which the effectiveness of different leadership styles was moderated by national culture (House, Hanges, Javidan, Dorfman, & Gupta, 2004). The project team recognized that organizational culture could also moderate those relationships, so it included organizational measures as well.

GLOBE assesses culture at both the societal and organizational levels in terms of "practices"—the "as is" assessment—and "values"—the "should be" assessment. Building on the work of Hofstede (1980), Triandis (1995), and McClelland (1985), GLOBE developed a nine-dimensional model of organizational culture. Unfortunately, there has been little research using these measures (Bajdo & Dickson, 2001; Dickson, Resick, & Hanges, 2006), even though they remain publicly available (https://globeproject.com/).

Human Synergistics' Organizational Culture Inventory

Human Synergistics built its culture assessment around its leadership assessment, the Lifestyles Inventory (Cooke & Rousseau, 1988). The model identifies constructive, aggressive/defensive, and passive/defensive styles at the individual, team, and organizational levels. The broad research base ranges from the leader's role (Gaucher & Kratochwill, 1993) to service delivery (Agbényiga, 2011) to how culture can provide a source of competitive advantage (Klein, 2011).

Organizational Culture Assessment Instrument

The OCAI assessment was developed by Cameron and Quinn (1999), building on Quinn and Rorhbaugh's (1983) competing values model. Like the OCI, this model was developed as an extension of a leadership model and offers the possibility of looking at organizations from both levels, using the same underlying model. The OCAI is based on a typology that categorizes organizations into four types: clan, market, adhocracy, and bureaucracy.

The OCAI continues to be the foundation for a number of studies that examine the impact of organizational "type" on employee attitudes and behaviors. The OCAI framework is also supported by extensive validation research and several studies showing the impact that culture has on organizational effectiveness. The authors make no claim that one type is more effective than the others, but they do show that each specific type does tend to be linked to its own distinct set of organizational outcomes.

Denison Organizational Culture Survey

Denison's model focuses on managerial behavior and values and developed from research on four cultural traits—involvement, consistency, adaptability, and mission—that predict business performance (Denison et al. 2014). These four traits are measured through a set of 12 indexes that are benchmarked against a global sample of firms and offered in over 50 languages. Denison's model is supported by extensive research and a long-standing focus on business performance, including a recent time-series study that helps address the direction of causality in the culture and performance studies (Boyce et al., 2015; Denison et al., 2012).

Organizational Health Index

Another relevant framework, the Organizational Health Index (OHI), has developed outside of the academic research literature but has many similarities to the frameworks introduced here. Building on the work of Keller and Price (2011), McKinsey & Company developed this framework and built its organizational transformation practice around it. It describes "organizational health" as the capacity of an organization and its management practices for effective functioning. Although none of the OHI research is published in peer-reviewed journals, McKinsey & Company does present a range of proprietary studies supporting the connection to performance.

The OHI measures nine traits that define the health of an organization:

- Direction
- Leadership
- Work environment

- Accountability
- Coordination and control
- Capabilities
- Motivation
- Innovation and learning
- External orientation

Although this work in not well grounded in the research literature, it still has a lot in common with the other frameworks reviewed in this chapter. It also adds to the breadth of this review because of the way that this assessment is positioned as a key driver of the transformation process.

Organizational Culture Profile

Building on the research of O'Reilly, Chatman, and Caldwell (1991), the Organizational Culture Profile represents the best framework for measuring person–organizational culture fit. These researchers defined 40 values that are characteristics of both individuals and organizations and asked individuals to rank these characteristics according to their own values. They then compared those rankings with the rankings of those same values for the organization. The gap between the two profile defines the fit between the individual and the organization. Their research shows that person–organization fit is a good predictor of job satisfaction, commitment, and actual turnover.

This work stands apart from most of the rest of the frameworks that we have reviewed in this chapter because it is perhaps the least prescriptive culture framework in the literature. There is no intent to define the characteristics of an effective organization, but there is a very clear focus on how individuals fit into different work environments. Thus, it stands as a useful and well-researched framework for those who want to understand how to strengthen the link between individuals and their organizations.

Recommendations for ELSs

This chapter has focused on ways in which the culture perspective can be used to enhance a multifaceted ELS. An ELS should certainly include a core of questions focused on individual engagement, but this review suggests that there is a lot of value in incorporating a broader perspective. We complete our chapter with some recommendations for incorporating culture insights in an ELS.

Tracking Progress

The rich set of frameworks described here offers a range of organization-level measures that can be drawn upon to track an organization's progress. The prescriptive approaches we reviewed allow organizations to track their progress against a normative model of positive organizational characteristics that can help guide them to a desired future state. Incorporating a set of measures that characterize the work environment of the organization itself can also make the results regarding individuals' reactions to the workplace culture far easier to interpret and act upon.

Qualitative and Quantitative

The long debate over qualitative and quantitative methodology in the culture and climate literature offers a simple recommendation for practitioners: Use both! In-depth interviews, focus groups, open-ended survey questions, text analytics, and crowdsourcing can all be useful complements to quantitative survey results. Using qualitative insights to support quantitative conclusions is always an advantage over using either approach on its own. Incorporating qualitative insights can also help create a more "high-touch" feel to an ELS that is designed to amplify employee voice.

Real Time + Long Term

A contemporary ELS should take advantage of both the power of an enterprise-wide approach and the real-time targeted approach of single-item pulse surveys. Pulsing with "fast and frequent snapshots" is an excellent way to identify immediate reactions to specific events, but it is no substitute for a more strategic, enterprise-level ELS. But the combination of the two can be very powerful. Pulse technology can also be highly useful for crowdsourcing ideas from the workforce and can greatly amplify the kind of qualitative understanding of the culture on a scale that was impossible to realize in the past.

Crowdsourcing can identify an agenda for culture change that can complement and inform all of the other elements of an ELS.

Mobilizing People

An ELS is an important way to mobilize an organization's people to implement strategic change and to create the culture upon which future success can be built. The culture perspective is an important asset in this effort because of the emphasis on the role of the workforce in creating the work environment. Using all of the insights produced by an ELS to create a set of honest, inclusive conversations that lead to action planning and implementation is the path to follow. Extensive feedback and targeted discussions are key ways to build the level of involvement necessary to drive a change process. They build on the tradition that the human character of the organization is created not by managerial action alone but by managerial action that mobilizes people to create a shared future.

Performance

Our final recommendation for incorporating the insights of the culture perspective into an ELS is to take advantage of the tradition of linkage research in culture studies. Although most of the academic research on the topic involves comparing performance across organizations, some of the highest-impact studies have actually been comparisons of operating units within organizations. Internal comparisons across stores, business units, sales regions, or locations can help build an understanding of the patterns of performance that exist throughout the organization and how leadership and culture issues can drive those internal differences. This approach also helps build support for an ELS and its related activities among the line management and business leaders in the organization.

Conclusion

This chapter has provided an overview of the organizational culture perspective, with an eye to understanding the contributions that this approach can make to the design of an ELS. The uniqueness of the system's mindset that lies at the heart of the culture perspective is an invaluable complement to the individual orientation of traditional engagement surveys as practitioners and researchers alike endeavor to help create workplaces that are both effective organizations and good places to work.

References

Agbényiga, D. (2011). Organizational culture–performance link in the human services setting. *Administration in Social Work*, *35*(5), 532–547.

Ashkanasy, N., Wilderom, C., & Peterson, M. (Eds). (2000). *The handbook of organizational culture and climate*. Thousand Oaks, CA: Sage.

Azanza, G., Moriano, J., & Molero, F. (2013). Authentic leadership and organizational culture as drivers of employees' job satisfaction. *Journal of Work and Organizational Psychology*, *29*(2), 45–50.

Bajdo, L., & Dickson, M. (2001). Perceptions of organizational culture and women's advancement in organizations: A cross-cultural examination. *Sex Roles*, *45*, 399–414.

Belias, D., & Koustelios, A. (2015). Leadership style, job satisfaction and organizational culture in the Greek banking organization. *Journal of Management Research*, *15*(2), 101–110.

Boyce, A., Nieminen, L., Gillespie, M., Ryan, A., & Denison, D. (2015). Which comes first, organizational culture or performance? A longitudinal study of causal priority with automobile dealerships. *Journal of Organizational Behavior*, *36*(3), 339–359.

Cameron, K., & Quinn, R. (1999). *Diagnosing and changing organizational culture*. Reading, MA: Addison-Wesley.

Collins, J., & Porras, J. (1994). *Built to last: Successful habits of visionary companies*. New York, NY: HarperBusiness.

Cooke, R., & Lafferty, C. (1989). *Organizational culture inventory*. Plymouth, MI: Human Synergistics.

Cooke, R., & Rousseau, D. (1988). Behavioral norms and expectations: A quantitative approach to the assessment of organizational culture. *Group & Organization Studies*, *13*, 245–273.

Cooper, C., Cartwright, S., & Earley, C. (2001). *The international handbook of organizational culture and climate*. New York, NY: Wiley.

Cronley, C., & Kim, Y. (2017). Intentions to turnover: Testing the moderated effects of organizational culture, as mediated by job satisfaction, within the Salvation Army. *Leadership & Organization Development Journal*, *38*(2), 194–209.

Cunningham, G. (2015). Creating and sustaining workplace cultures supportive of LGBT employee in college athletics. *Journal of Sport Management*, *29*(4), 426–442.

Deal, T., & Kennedy, A. (1982). *Corporate cultures: The rites and rituals of corporate life*. Reading, MA: Addison-Wesley.

Denison, D. (2003). The handbook of organizational culture and climate. The international handbook of organizational culture and climate. *Administrative Science Quarterly*, *48*(1), 119–127.

Denison, D. (1996). What is the difference between organizational culture and organizational climate? A native's point of view on a decade of paradigm wars. *Academy of Management Review, 21*(3), 619–654.

Denison, D., Hooijberg, R., Lane, N., & Leif, C. (2012). *Leading culture change in global organizations: Aligning culture and strategy.* San Francisco, CA: Jossey-Bass.

Denison, D., & Neale, W. (1996). *Denison organization culture survey.* Ann Arbor, MI: Aviat.

Denison, D., Nieminen, L., & Kotrba, L. (2014). Diagnosing organizational cultures: A conceptual and empirical review of culture effectiveness surveys. *European Journal of Work & Organizational Psychology, 23*(1), 145–161.

Dickson, M., Resick, C., & Hanges, J. (2006). When organizational climate is unambiguous, it is also strong. *Journal of Applied Psychology, 91*(2), 351–364.

Frost, P., Moore, L., Louis, M., Lundberg, C., & Martin, J. (1991). *Reframing organizational culture.* Newbury Park, CA: Sage Publications.

Gaucher, E., & Kratochwill, E. (1993). The leader's role in implementing total quality management. *Quality Management in Health Care, 1*(3), 10–18.

Hofstede, G. (1980). *Culture's consequences: International differences in work-related values.* Beverly Hills, CA: Sage.

Hofstede, G., & Peterson, M. (2000). National values and organizational practices. In N. Ashkanasy, C. Wilderom, & M. Peterson (Eds.), *Handbook of organizational culture and climate* (pp. 401–405). London, England: Sage.

House, R. J., Hanges, P. J., Javidan, M., Dorfman, P. W., & Gupta, V. (Eds.). (2004). *Culture, leadership and organization: The GLOBE study of 62 societies.* Thousand Oaks, CA: Sage.

House, R., Hanges, P., Ruiz-Quintanilla, S., Dorfman, P., Javidan, M., Dickson, M., & Gupta, V. (1999). Cultural influences on leadership and organizations: Project GLOBE. In W. H. Mobley (Ed.), *Advances in global leadership* (Vol. 1, pp. 171–233). New York, NY: Elsevier Science/JAI Press.

Huhtala, M., Tolvanen, A., Mauno, S., & Feldt, T. (2015). The associations between ethical organizational culture, burnout, and engagement: A multilevel study. *Journal of Business & Psychology, 30*(2), 399–414.

Jacques, E. (1951). *The changing culture of a factory.* Oxford, England: Tavistock.

Jaeger, M., Yu, G., & Adair, D. (2017). Organisational culture of Chinese construction organisations in Kuwait. *Engineering Construction & Architectural Management, 24*(6), 1051–1066.

Jiang, K., Hu, J., Hong, Y., Liao, H., & Liu, S. (2016). Do it well and do it right: The impact of service climate and ethical climate on business performance and the boundary conditions. *Journal of Applied Psychology, 101*(11), 1553–1568.

Katz, D., & Kahn, R. L. (1978). *The social psychology of organizations* (2nd ed.). New York, NY: Wiley.

Keller, S., & Price, C. (2011). *Beyond performance.* Hoboken, NJ: Wiley.

Klein, A. (2011). Corporate culture: Its value as a resource for competitive advantage. *Journal of Business Strategy, 32*(2), 21–28.

Kotrba, L., Gillespie, M., Schmidt, A., Smerek, R., Ritchie, S., & Denison, D. (2012). Do consistent corporate cultures have better business performance? Exploring the interaction effects. *Human Relations, 65*, 241–262.

Kotter, J. P., & Heskett, J. L. (1992). *Corporate culture and performance.* New York, NY: Free Press.

Lawrence, P. R., & Lorsch, J. W. (1967). *Organizations and environment: Managing differentiation and integration.* Boston, MA: Harvard University Press.

Lee, M., Idris, M., & Delfabbro, P. (2017). The linkages between hierarchical culture and empowering leadership and their effects on employees' work engagement: Work meaningfulness as a mediator. *International Journal of Stress Management, 24*(4), 392–415.

Likert, R. (1961). *New patterns of management.* New York, NY: McGraw-Hill.

Martin, J. (1992). *Cultures in organizations: Three perspectives.* Oxford, England: Oxford University Press.

McClelland, D. (1985). *Human motivation.* Glenview, IL: Scott, Foresman.

McGregor, D. (1960). The human side of enterprise. *Harvard Business Review, 38*(5), 102.

Mor Barak, M., Lizano, E., Kim, A., Duan, L., Rhee, M., Hsiao, H., & Brimhall, K. (2016). The promise of diversity management for climate of inclusion: A state-of-the-art review and meta-analysis. *Human Service Organizations: Management, Leadership & Governance, 40*(4), 305–333.

Naranjo-Valencia, J., Jimenez-Jimenez, D., & Sanz-Valle, R. (2017). Organizational culture and radical innovation: Does innovative behavior mediate this relationship? *Creativity and Innovation Management, 26*, 407–417.

Nielsen, K. (2014). Improving safety culture through the health and safety organization: A case study. *Journal of Safety Research, 48*, 7–17.

O'Reilly, C., Chatman, J., & Caldwell, D. (1991). People and organizational culture: A profile comparison approach to assessing person–organizational fit. *Academy of Management Journal, 3*, 487–516.

Ouchi, W. G. (1981). *Theory Z: How American business can meet the Japanese challenge.* New York, NY: Addison-Wesley.

Paolillo, A., Silva, S., & Pasini, M. (2016). Promoting safety participation through diversity and inclusion climates. *International Journal of Workplace Health Management, 9*(3), 308–327.

Paro, P., & Gerolamo, M. (2017). Organizational culture for lean programs. *Journal of Organizational Change Management, 30*(4), 584–598.

Peters, T., & Waterman, R. (1982). *In search of excellence.* New York, NY: Harper and Row.

Pilch, I., & Turska, E. (2015). Relationships between Machiavellianism, organizational culture, and workplace bullying: Emotional abuse from the target's and the perpetrator's perspective. *Journal of Business Ethics, 128*, 83–93.

Quinn, R., & Rohrbaugh, J. (1983). A spatial model of effectiveness criteria: Towards a competing values approach to organizational analysis. *Management Science, 29*, 363–377.

Reichers, A., & Schneider, B. (1990). Climate and culture: An evolution of constructs. In B. Schneider (Ed.), *Organizational climate and culture* (pp. 5–39). San Francisco, CA: Jossey-Bass.

Sackmann, S. (2011). Culture and performance. In N. Ashkanasy, C. Wilderom, & M. Peterson (Eds.), *The handbook of organizational culture and climate* (2nd ed., pp. 188–224). Thousand Oaks, CA: Sage Publications.

Saks, A. (2006). Antecedents and consequences of employee engagement. *Journal of Managerial Psychology, 21*(7), 600–619.

Schein, E. (1985). *Organizational culture and leadership.* San Francisco, CA: Jossey-Bass.

Schneider, B. (1987). The people make the place. *Personnel Psychology, 40*(3), 437–453.

Schneider, B., Ehrhart, M., & Macey, W. (2013). Organizational climate and culture. *Annual Review of Psychology, 64*, 361–388.

Schneider, B., White, S. S., & Paul, M. C. (1998). Linking service climate and customer perceptions of service quality: Test of a causal model. *Journal of Applied Psychology, 83*(2), 150–163.

Schneider, B., Yost, A., Kropp, A., Kind, C., & Lam, H. (2018). Workforce engagement: What it is, what drives it, and why it matters for organizational performance. *Journal of Organizational Behavior, 39*, 462–480.

Sims, K. (2017, September 21). Why pulse surveys are an internal communicator's best friend [Web log post]. Retrieved from https://blog.bananatag.com/internal-comms/employee-pulse-surveys-internal-communications-best-friend

Teräväinen, V., Junnonen, J., & Ali-Löytty, S. (2018). Organizational culture: Case of the Finnish construction industry. *Construction Economics & Building, 18*(1), 48–69.

Terzi, A. (2016). Teachers' perception of organizational culture and trust relation. *International Journal of Organizational Leadership, 5*(4), 338–347.

Triandis, H. (1995). *Individualism & collectivism.* Boulder, CO: Westview Press.

Trist, E., & Bamforth, K. (1951). Some social and psychological consequences of the Longwall method of coal-getting. *Human Relations, 4*, 3–38.

Van Maanen, J. (1979). The fact of fiction in organizational ethnography. *Administrative Science Quarterly, 24*(4), 539–550.

Weick, K. (1979). *The social psychology of organizing.* New York, NY: McGraw-Hill.

Zerella, S., von Treuer, K., & Albrecht, S. (2017). The influence of office layout features on employee perception of organizational culture. *Journal of Environmental Psychology, 54*, 1–10.

Zoghbi-Manrique-de-Lara, P., & Ting-Ding, J. (2016). The influence of corporate culture and workplace relationship quality on the outsourcing success in hotel firms. *International Journal of Hospitality Management, 56*, 66–77.

10

Employee Preferences

Why They Matter and How to Measure Them

Diane L. Daum and Jennifer A. Stoll

Imagine a student graduating with an information technology degree. She might be drawn to a consulting career where she may build strong customer relationships and be mentored by more senior consultants. Or she might work in the IT department of a children's hospital, where she would have fewer growth opportunities but meaningful work and family-friendly policies that afford her time to pursue other interests. Another possibility is a high-tech innovator who offers challenging assignments in a fun, informal atmosphere.

She could find engaging work in any of these settings, but the opportunities she seeks will depend on her preferences. We use *employee preferences* to describe attributes that job seekers and current employees want most in their employment relationships, including job characteristics, the organization itself, manager and co-worker relationships, compensation and benefits, and working conditions, such as flexible work schedules.

These attributes, in aggregate, also define what employers refer to as the *employee value proposition* (EVP)—what the organization offers to employees in experiences and rewards in exchange for what employees bring in talent and dedication (Minchington, 2012). However, it is important to note that an employee's preferences may or may not match the EVP of a given organization. Many organizations actively manage and package their EVPs to appeal to prospective employees and communicate offerings to current employees. This is referred to as *employer branding* (Minchington, 2011). In the popular press, *EVP* and *employer brand* are often used interchangeably.

The measurement paradigm for employee preferences is different from other employee attitudes in that preferences are evidenced in "trade-offs" individuals make. That is, given distinctive experiences from which to choose,

Diane L. Daum and Jennifer A. Stoll, *Employee Preferences* In: *Employee Surveys and Sensing*. Edited by: William H. Macey and Alexis A. Fink, Oxford University Press (2020). © Society for Industrial and Organizational Psychology. DOI: 10.1093/oso/9780190939717.003.0010 what aspects of the employment relationship are most important, and what would employees be willing to forgo to have their top preferences met?

Why Should Organizations Care About Employee Preferences?

Every Employer Has an EVP

Every organization has an EVP whether or not it is actively managed. Individuals form impressions of organizations based on their interactions as customers, information from current or former employees, and media reports. As illustrated here, research has shown that people, both inside and outside of organizations, form impressions about what different organizations are like and that there is a fair amount of consensus in those opinions.

Slaughter, Zickar, Highhouse, and Mohr (2004) measured organizational personality traits and found that organizations had distinct personalities. In addition, subjects had shared perceptions of organizations that related to their assessments of organizations' overall reputations and whether they would pursue employment there. Davies (2008) also noted distinct organizational personality profiles that related to satisfaction with and affinity for organizations, as well as employees' assessments of how differentiated their employer was from others.

Lievens and Highhouse (2003) found that both instrumental traits (e.g., tangible characteristics, such as pay and benefits) and symbolic traits (e.g., less tangible characteristics, such as sincerity and innovativeness) were related to perceptions of organizations but that ratings of symbolic traits were more differentiated across organizations. Thus, to stand out, organizations must convey their symbolic as well as their instrumental traits.

These notions of attractiveness mirror observations in the marketing literature about brand. Marin and Ruiz (2006) explored the concept of company identity attractiveness and found that an organization's attractiveness was influenced by congruence between the consumer's values and the organization's and was amplified when the organization's corporate social responsibility efforts were targeted toward areas the consumer valued most. Similarly, we would expect that if a candidate identified with the employer brand, this would expand the relationship beyond the "instrumental" characteristics of the job or organization.

The implication of these studies is that both employees and more passive observers form impressions of organizations that influence their opinions toward them as consumers, employees, or candidates.

Individuals Make Judgments About Fit

The attributions that individuals make about the traits or values of organizations are important because they evaluate them in relation to their assessments of their own traits and values to determine where they would best fit. O'Reilly, Chatman, and Caldwell (1991) asked job incumbents to describe themselves and correlated their ratings to descriptions of their organizations derived from a separate sample. Those with higher levels of "fit" (evidenced by strong correlations between their characteristics and the organization's characteristics) reported higher levels of job satisfaction and commitment and had lower turnover in the subsequent 2 years.

Cable and Edwards (2004) joined two separate threads in the person–environment fit literature to describe circumstances under which individuals best "fit" within organizations. The complementary fit literature emphasized the needs of one party being offset by strengths or resources of the other (i.e., employees looking to have their needs fulfilled by desired organizational attributes). The supplementary fit literature emphasized that for "fit" to occur, the organization and individual should share similar characteristics (i.e., *value congruence*). These authors found that both need fulfillment and value congruence were important predictors of attitudes including job satisfaction, engagement, intent to stay, and identification with the organization. It follows that in measuring their EVPs, organizations should assess both what attributes are important (i.e., what is most valued) and how they are doing on them (i.e., "Are we meeting the needs associated with each valued attribute?").

More recently, Wood, Lowman, Harms, and Roberts (2019) argued that the degree of person–organization fit is largely a function of "normative" preferences. In other words, most of us are looking for the same characteristics in organizations, while idiosyncratic preferences account for little variance in fit and need not be a focus for organizations. We agree that there are a wide variety of attributes on which organizations need to meet some minimum standards of acceptability and that there is a great deal of consensus on these (for example, few people would want to work in an organization where they weren't treated with respect). However, when comparing offers that meet basic standards, we believe that individuals will still make choices based on idiosyncratic preferences, maximizing attributes that are most important to them. For example, some of us might choose a job with minimally acceptable pay to do stimulating work, while others might seek to maximize pay even if it meant doing less interesting work. In both of these cases, once the "minimum" requirement of pay is met, the individual's idiosyncratic preferences drive the decision. Thus, we believe that measurements of "fit" should consider whether top preferences are optimized and that organizations should attend to idiosyncratic preferences.

The Talent Strategy Must Support the Business Strategy

Organizations that manage their EVPs and associated brands reap benefits in their ability to attract and retain employees who support their strategies. Erickson and Gratton (2007) note that it is impossible for organizations to be attractive to everyone. Instead, they should strive to articulate a "signature experience" by describing what is unique about working there to attract people whose preferences align with their EVP and allow others to self-select out.

That signature experience should incorporate crucial elements of the talent strategy. For example, if the growth strategy depends upon current employees "upskilling" for newly created jobs, it must have employees for whom professional development is important.

Given that some EVPs are likely to attract broader pools of applicants than others, it is tempting for organizations to describe themselves in ways that appeal to the most candidates—or to those they most want to attract. However, Erickson and Gratton (2007) note the importance of accurately representing the organization's EVP. Otherwise, you risk attracting people who don't fit and feel misled, leading to turnover. This idea is substantiated by the literatures on realistic job previews (Wanous, 1973) and psychological contracts (Rousseau, Hansen, & Tomprou, 2018). Delivery of the value proposition impacts perceptions of both the instrumental and symbolic traits described earlier; just as you cannot be recognized as providing competitive pay (an instrumental attribute) when you offer less than others, you cannot be recognized as innovative (a symbolic attribute) if leaders squash new ideas and don't invest in new technology.

To the extent that the EVP matches the business strategy (and the employer brand mirrors the consumer brand), employees will be more likely to deliver customer experiences that are "on brand." As noted by Mosley (2007),

> If the brand values on which the service experience is founded are not experienced by the employees in their interactions with the organisation, the desired behaviours will ultimately feel superficial, a "show put on for customers" rather than the natural extension of a deeply rooted brand ethos. (p. 128)

Thus, it is important for organizations to close the gaps on "aspirational" characteristics before communicating them in their EVP.

Making Best Use of Organizational Resources

Meeting employee preferences can be expensive for organizations. Preference studies allow for the optimization of offerings such as compensation and benefits, such that the organization can offer programs that have value to employees that is at least commensurate to their costs. For example, flexible work arrangements might be extremely valuable but cost the organization little. This type of knowledge is useful not just for retaining and recruiting employees but also as a way to use the total rewards offering as further evidence of the brand promise.

Whose Preferences Matter?

In thinking about your EVP, there are several stakeholders whose preferences should be considered.

Executive Leadership

If the organization is to create an EVP that ultimately supports its strategy, it is important to know what that strategy is. How does the organization intend to win in the marketplace? What segments of the workforce are most critical for growth? What does the organization most want to be known for? Talking to members of the executive leadership team will get to the heart of these issues.

Current Employees

Employees are valuable information sources for several reasons. First, to retain them, it is important to know whether the current EVP appeals to them. Second, they can describe what is unique about the organization, both good and bad. Third, they are the best source of information on whether leadership's stated values are effectively communicated and acted upon. While it is often instructive to gather data from employees across the full organization, some groups are especially important.

New Hires

Because new hires were recently candidates, they can provide information regarding what other organizations candidates are talking to, how the communicated EVPs of talent competitors differ, and what was compelling about your offer. In addition, they are in the best position to comment on disconnects in how the job or organization was described to them and what they have actually experienced. These are particularly important as we noted that mismatches often lead to turnover.

In one organization we worked with, recruiters emphasized work–life balance and schedule flexibility for call center jobs. Focus groups revealed that employees were actually being asked to work overtime with rigid schedules to ensure coverage, leading to unmet expectations and dissatisfaction. Recruiters were counseled to emphasize other positive aspects of the job and to paint a more realistic picture of the work schedule.

Employees Experiencing Major Change

It can be important to understand how major changes (e.g., reorganization, implementation of new technology) influence employees' characterizations of what it is like to work for the organization. Follmer, Talbot, Kristof-Brown, Astrove, and Billsberry (2018) note that a major change can impact an individual's sense of fit and lead to negative individual and organizational outcomes. Changes can also signal shifts in organizational values, leading employees to feel that the EVP has changed (e.g., "I used to think this organization stood for innovation, but recent shifts suggest our main focus is cost").

Employees Most Critical to Retain

It is important to measure the preferences of critical talent groups (such as high performers or jobs key to delivering on the strategy) to ensure that the EVP remains compelling for them. For example, one organization's preferences study revealed that though most employees felt their preferences were met, the product design group was unfavorable regarding the degree of innovation and empowerment in the organization. The creative energy needed to drive the organization forward was being thwarted by micromanagement. This key group became a focus of action-planning efforts to increase autonomy and loosen management control to better support the creative process.

Customer-Facing Employees

Customer-facing employees often represent one of the largest segments of an organization, accounting for an outsize proportion of organizational re-sources such as pay, benefits, and time spent recruiting and training. Being an attractive employer for individuals in this segment is thus likely to save money.

In addition, they are the face of the organization to customers, and for them to deliver "on brand," their experience as employees must be consistent with the brand you portray to customers. They will notice inconsistencies and make inferences about what the organization truly values that, in turn, guide their behavior. For example, many organizations judge call center employees' performance on call handle time, encouraging reps to get off the phone quickly rather than fully resolving customer issues. This contradicts a stated value of exceptional service and rewards the wrong behavior.

Candidates/General Labor Market

In addition to current employees, it is important to know what candidates value, how talent competitors are trying to win them over, and what the "word on the street" is about an organization. However, these data can be difficult to obtain from candidates who do not receive or accept an offer. Though some information can be learned from new hires, those who accepted your offer could have different perceptions from those who went elsewhere. Another strategy is to review postings from candidates on sites such as GlassDoor, Indeed, and Blind. Though these may not represent all candidates, you are likely to uncover major themes related to your organization's reputation in the labor market and gain a better understanding of the uniqueness (or lack thereof) of your EVP. A third strategy is to conduct a study of the labor market using a provider of research panels. However, unless it is widely known to the general public what it is like to work for your organization or you are able to specifically target respondents with knowledge of your industry, these studies may not yield detailed information.

What to Measure

Your choice of measures should depend on your goals. Are you making decisions for the upcoming benefits cycle? Trying to determine your organization's EVP? A preferences study can be narrowly focused—for example, limited solely to health insurance coverage—or quite broad, looking at a wide range of attributes of the job and the organization. Examples of attributes include the following:

- Job-related: Career advancement opportunities, flexible work arrangements, training
- Rewards-related: Pay, benefits, time off
- Social: Manager quality, access to senior leadership, morale events
- Organizational: Inclusion, recognition, support for innovation
- Physical: Office space, cafeteria options, company shuttle

Many of the studies referenced so far include attribute lists that could be used to generate ideas (see Cable & Edwards, 2004; Cable & Judge 1997; Lievens & Highhouse, 2003; O'Reilly et al., 1991).

You might also consider attributes that are not currently being emphasized or even offered but which might be important to employees (or future employees). This is especially important in the total rewards space, where offerings may require periodic adjustment to meet the needs of an ever-evolving workforce.

How to Measure

Another major decision point in a preferences study is how to measure. The answer is usually a combination of methods, with quantitative measures giving a broad overview of preferences and qualitative measures providing rich context to the numeric observations.

Regardless of the type(s) of measurement used, there are some common questions to keep in mind:

- Do employee subpopulations have different preferences?
- Do employees' values align with executives' values?
- Does the organization do a good job of delivering the attributes that are most valued?

Qualitative Feedback

Qualitative data provide context and can be useful for testing hypotheses but are time-consuming to collect and analyze.

Interviews

One-on-one meetings can provoke insightful, in-depth, and personal commentary that's difficult to collect through other means but may not be practical due to the time involved. Therefore, it is good practice to pair senior leader interviews with another data-collection method; this allows you to get personal feedback from key stakeholders but also capture the opinions of a larger number of employees.

Focus Groups

Focus groups are particularly helpful when testing a new idea or program where immediate feedback is necessary or to learn more about a specific issue (e.g., "Why did employees indicate career development as a concern?"). Focus groups are covered in more detail in Chapter 7.

Open-Ended Survey Questions

If employees are already taking a survey, the burden to them is low relative to other means of collecting qualitative feedback; and this can be a quick and simple way to gain more in-depth feedback from a large number of respondents. Dutta and O'Rourke detail the use of text data in Chapter 13.

Publicly Available Data Sources

Websites such as Indeed, LinkedIn, and GlassDoor are additional sources of qualitative data. For more about publicly available data sources, please see Chapter 14.

Direct Preference Measurement

Survey questions that directly ask employee preferences with structured response options are relatively easy to collect, interpret, and evaluate. Regardless of the types of questions you ask, a best practice is to restrict questions to changes you would consider implementing; for example, if you wouldn't consider a 20% pay increase, don't put it on the survey and create the hope (or expectation) that you would. Another consideration is the number and types of analyses you want to do, particularly if you are using a sample rather than the entire population. This is important to consider up front because the smaller the sample, the less ability you will have to cut the data and still provide reliable results. For additional detail on sampling, please see Chapter 3.

As noted, preferences should be measured in ways that require respondents to make trade-offs. Otherwise, respondents will rate nearly everything as valuable, and it will be difficult to choose what the organization should focus on. Three effective ways to measure trade-offs include ranking exercises, allocation exercises, and conjoint surveys.

Ranking Exercises

Ranking exercises are particularly useful for evaluating elements of an EVP (i.e., "Which of these elements is most important to you in a potential employer?"). It's important that all the options are described at the same level of specificity; for example, you wouldn't want five attributes related to elements of leadership and one about benefits overall. Ranking is most helpful when a comparison of the attributes overall is desired; to compare more specific levels within each attribute, conjoint analysis may be more appropriate (see "Conjoint Surveys" below). In addition, a long list of attributes can be unwieldy, and research suggests that ranking becomes less reliable with too many items (Louviere, Hensher, & Swait, 2010, p. 29). To mitigate this, limit the rankings to the top and bottom several choices, rather than the entire list. This simplifies the task while still providing feedback on the attributes that employees value most (and least). An example is provided in Figure 10.1.

Allocation Exercises

In these exercises, respondents allocate a fixed number of points (usually 100) across attributes. For example, I might feel that technical skills training is the most important option to me and assign it 30 points; I might assign my second choice just 10 points, leaving 60 points to allocate between the

Below is a list of organization and job characteristics that you may or may not consider to be important in an employment relationship. Please review the full list and then rank the top 6 that are most important to you with 1 being the most important.

⠿	1 ⌃⌄	Access to Cutting Edge Technology
⠿	2 ⌃⌄	Authority to Make Decisions
⠿	3 ⌃⌄	Challenging Work
⠿	4 ⌃⌄	Commitment to Local Community
⠿	5 ⌃⌄	Competent Manager
⠿	6 ⌃⌄	Competitive Base Pay
⠿	NR ⌃⌄	Concern for the Environment
⠿	NR ⌃⌄	Friendly Coworkers
⠿	NR ⌃⌄	Health Benefits
⠿	NR ⌃⌄	Inclusive Work Environment
⠿	NR ⌃⌄	Job Security
⠿	NR ⌃⌄	Opportunities for Advancement
⠿	NR ⌃⌄	Opportunities to Earn Bonuses
⠿	NR ⌃⌄	Paid Time Off
⠿	NR ⌃⌄	Recognition for Good Work
⠿	NR ⌃⌄	Retirement Benefits

Figure 10.1. Sample partial ranking exercise.

remaining options. These exercises provide more detail than ranking because they allow more differentiation (in this example, my first choice is three times as important to me as my second choice, a distinction that wouldn't be clear in a ranking exercise). Allocation exercises allow respondents to assign the same number of points to multiple items, permitting ties if attributes are equally meaningful, and to assign a value of 0 points to something they truly do not value, whereas ranking doesn't provide a way to assign "no value" to an item. An example is provided in Figure 10.2. However, like ranking, allocation exercises can be difficult and time-consuming if the list of attributes is long.

Please allocate 100 points across the options below to indicate which new benefits would be most valuable to you. If a single option is far more important to you than others, you can allocate most or all of your points to it. If several options appeal equally to you, you may spread your points equally across them. If an option has no value to you, you may assign it 0 points.

⁝ [10 ⌄] On-Site Fitness Center

⁝ [30 ⌄] On-Site Day Care

⁝ [20 ⌄] Dental Coverage

⁝ [30 ⌄] Life Insurance Coverage

⁝ [5 ⌄] Commuter Benefits

⁝ [5 ⌄] Half-Day Fridays

⁝ [0 ⌄] On-Site Dining Options

Figure 10.2. Sample allocation exercise.

One organization we worked with had been losing employees to talent competitors and investigated cutting-edge benefits they thought would better attract and retain employees. An allocation exercise showed that employees assigned very little value to proposed new benefits but assigned more points toward additional time off. Rather than spending on expensive perks, this organization decided to review its paid time off policies and investigate telecommuting options and flexible schedules.

Conjoint Surveys
Originally implemented in the marketing sciences, conjoint surveys present a series of choice tasks to respondents. As can be seen in Figure 10.3, each

Please indicate which rewards portfolio you would prefer:

XYZ **increases** annual PTO by 5 days

401(k) match **decreases** by 1%

No change to annual incentive pay target

○

No change to annual PTO

401(k) match **increases** by 1%

Annual incentive pay target **increases** by 5% of base pay

○

Figure 10.3. Sample conjoint scenario. PTO = paid time off.

choice involves the comparison of two or more "packages" of attributes at differing levels. From their choices (and the trade-offs they are inherently making), employees' preferences are extrapolated. There are a number of types of conjoint analysis, the most common being choice-based conjoint. Others include adaptive conjoint analysis, which adapts each choice task based on previous choices, and MaxDiff, which asks respondents to choose their most and least preferred options.

Conjoint analysis allows greater specificity in measuring the impact of incremental changes to a program, as opposed to sentiment about the overall program itself; for example, at what point does an increase in vacation time offset a decrease in bonus? Conjoint exercises also require participants to make trade-offs in ways that more closely simulate real-life decision-making. A unique element of conjoint analysis is the ability to quantify and compare perceived values (how much do employees actually value something) versus actual cost, to determine where savings and investment opportunities lie.

However, it can be difficult to create conjoint surveys that are relevant to all employees (i.e., if program eligibility differs across an employee population); in these cases, you might need different survey versions for different subpopulations or to write attributes in more universally applicable ways (e.g., expressing changes in pay as a percentage change from the current state, rather than an actual dollar value). It is also necessary to do "prework" to define the exact levels and cost of each attribute, so conjoint surveys are not good choices for simply exploring possibilities. Conjoint surveys require specialized software to conduct and analyze (Sawtooth Software being the industry leader in this space). Rather than typical survey output such as means or percentages, conjoint surveys produce "utility scores" that indicate the relative importance of each attribute and level within the study, which require more specialized expertise to interpret. A more detailed treatment of conjoint methodology is beyond the scope of this chapter, but we recommend Orme (2010) as a basic primer and Louviere et al. (2010) for a deeper dive. Finally, sample size is more of a consideration with conjoint surveys because of how options are typically presented to respondents (no one participant sees all combinations of attributes); results therefore require a larger number of respondents to be considered reliable than that generally needed for ranking or allocation exercises. A comparison of direct preference measurement techniques including their relative advantages and disadvantages is provided in Table 10.1.

Table 10.1 Summary of Direct Preference Measurement Techniques

Method	Description	Advantages	Disadvantages	Bottom Line
Ranking exercises	Respondents rank options in order of preference. Options are usually stated in general terms.	Easy-to-write and implement items applicable to a wide range of employees. Does not require extensive prework to determine specific levels and costs of attributes.	Difficult to rank long lists of items, though this can be solved by ranking only top and bottom several choices. No way to assign "no value" to an item.	A relatively easy way to explore employee preferences at a general level.
Allocation exercise	Respondents allocate a fixed number of points across options to indicate preferences. Options are usually stated in general terms.	Advantages of ranking also apply here. Provides greater differentiation between attributes than ranking. Respondents can assign the same number of points to attributes that are equally meaningful or zero points to something they do not value.	Difficult and time-consuming if the list of attributes is long.	Provides more information than ranking but is most appropriate when the number of options compared is relatively small.

| Conjoint Surveys | Respondents view sets of "packages" combining different levels of the attributes and choose their preferred "package" from each set. Specific levels of each attribute are defined. Preferences are inferred by choices made. | Allows more precise measurement of the impact of incremental changes to a program, as opposed to sentiment about the overall program itself. Participants make trade-offs that closely simulate real-life decision-making. Ability to quantify and compare how much employees actually value something versus the actual cost to determine where savings and investment opportunities may lie. | Can be difficult to design in a way that is relevant to all employees. "Prework" is needed to define exact levels and costs of attributes. Requires specialized software to conduct and analyze. Surveys yield "utility scores" which are less intuitive to interpret. Generally requires larger sample sizes than ranking or allocation exercises | More complex to design and administer, but provides more specific information. Best when the organization is choosing among specific programs with different cost implications. |

Segmentation

In most organizations, it is useful to distinguish between patterns of preferences to communicate about the EVP in ways that resonate with distinctly identifiable groups. Analyzing data with an eye toward segmentation of the organization will help you to make optimal use of it.

Often, differences in preferences are related to demographic variables. Analyzing data by major job families, locations, or levels may show how offerings could be tailored for different groups. For example, in a pharmaceutical company, research scientists exploring new drugs will likely have different preferences from those manufacturing or marketing them.

Another way to characterize organizational segments is to use cluster or latent class modeling to identify profiles that emerge from the data. Just as consumers in a marketing scenario have profiles such as "luxury shopper" or "tech-savvy," employees may be grouped into profiles based on their patterns of values. For example, we worked with a retail organization to create employee preference profiles for recruiting purposes. One profile was family breadwinners concerned about maintaining enough hours to meet their financial needs. Another segment worked for supplemental income and was attracted by the social aspects of the working environment. A third profile worked at the store while pursuing an education and valued scheduling flexibility around their schoolwork. Understanding the distinct needs of each profile allowed the organization to consider all of them in their recruiting messaging. Shepherd (2014) provides an additional detailed example.

Personas representing each profile can then be created. *Personas* are short back stories of fictitious individuals that provide a "face" for each profile that conveys important context (Dion & Arnould, 2016). Recruiters, communications professionals, and others can use personas as reminders of the types of individuals in each segment and what they value so that they can tailor communications appropriately.

Assessing Satisfaction with Attributes

In defining the EVP, it is also important to know how well the organization currently delivers on attributes that employees most value. One way to find out is to follow preferences questions with more traditional Likert-type items that assess satisfaction with the attributes.

Attributes that are both "preferred" and currently being offered at satisfactory levels (e.g., are viewed as credible by current employees) can be used to form the basis of an EVP that can portray to employees and candidates what is unique and compelling about the organization. Attributes that are "preferred" but not currently credible may be worthy of action planning to credibly provide them. Or if there are enough other credible attributes to create a compelling EVP that supports the strategy, organizations may choose not to address them.

Revealed Choices

Aside from survey data, another source of quantitative preference data in organizations is *revealed choices*, or choices that employees have made in the past. For example, knowing which benefits were most popular during the previous enrollment period can guide what should be offered this year. While this represents "real-life" decision-making rather than a "stated preference," there are some drawbacks. One is that this doesn't provide the same level of trade-off information that you could get through conjoint scenarios (e.g., would employees be willing to pay a higher insurance premium to have a lower deductible"). Another drawback is that it only measures preferences for attributes that have been offered and doesn't allow for the testing of new scenarios.

Summary

Though no organization can meet all employees' preferences, a better "fit" between employee and organizational values benefits not just the employees and the organization but customers as well. By using the techniques discussed in this chapter, organizations can gain a better understanding of what matters most to their employees and assess how well they currently meet those needs. Studying preferences also allows organizations to understand their employee population better—what motivates and drives them—while recognizing that even the best-aligned organizations contain segments of individuals with different preferences. Ultimately, understanding and delivering on employees' most valued attributes will result in real business outcomes, including more effective hiring, decreased attrition, and stronger customer service.

References

Cable, D. M., & Edwards, J. R. (2004). Complementary and supplementary fit: A theoretical and empirical integration. *Journal of Applied Psychology, 89*, 822–834.

Cable, D. M., & Judge, T. (1997). Interviewers' perceptions of person–organization fit and organizational selection decisions. *Journal of Applied Psychology, 82*, 546–561.

Davies, G. (2008). Employer branding and its influence on managers. *European Journal of Marketing, 42*, 667–681.

Dion, D., & Arnould, E. (2016). Persona-fied brands: Managing branded persons through persona. *Journal of Marketing Management, 32*, 121–148.

Erickson, T. J., & Gratton, L. (2007). What it means to work here. *Harvard Business Review, 2007*, 104–112.

Follmer, E. H., Talbot, D. L., Kristof-Brown, A. L., Astrove, S. L., & Billsberry, J. (2018). Resolution, relief, and resignation: A qualitative study of responses to misfit at work. *Academy of Management Journal, 61*, 440–465.

Lievens, F., & Highhouse, S. (2003). The relation of instrumental and symbolic attributes to a company's attractiveness as an employer. *Personnel Psychology, 56*, 75–102.

Louviere, J. J., Hensher, D. A., & Swait, J. D. (2010). *Stated choice methods: Analysis and application*. Cambridge, England: Cambridge University Press.

Marin, L., & Ruiz, S. (2006). "I need you too!": Corporate identity attractiveness for consumers and the role of social responsibility. *Journal of Business Ethics, 71*, 245–260.

Minchington, B. (2011). Where to next for employer branding? *Human Resources Magazine, 16*(4), 22.

Minchington, B. (2012). Your most important employer brand asset—Your EVP! *Human Resources Magazine, 17*(4), 18–33.

Mosley, R. (2007). Customer experience, organizational culture and the employer brand. *Journal of Brand Management, 15*, 123–134.

O'Reilly, C. E., Chatman, J., & Caldwell, D. F. (1991). People and organizational culture: A profile comparison approach to assessing person-organizational fit. *Academy of Management Journal, 34*, 487–516.

Orme, B. K. (2010). *Getting started with conjoint analysis: Strategies for product design and pricing research*. Madison, WI: Research Publishers.

Rousseau, D. M., Hansen, S. D., & Tomprou, M. (2018). A dynamic phase model of psychological contract processes. *Journal of Organizational Behavior, 39*, 1081–1098.

Shepherd, W. (2014). The heterogeneity of well-being: Implications for HR management practices. *Industrial and Organizational Psychology, 7*(4), 579–583.

Slaughter, J. E., Zickar, M. J., Highhouse, S., & Mohr, D. C. (2004). Personality trait inferences about organizations: Development of a measure and assessment of construct validity. *Journal of Applied Psychology, 89*, 85–103.

Wanous, J. P. (1973). Effects of a realistic job preview on job acceptance, job attitudes, and job survival. *Journal of Applied Psychology, 58*, 327–332.

Wood, D., Lowman, G. H., Harms, P. D., & Roberts, B. W. (2019). Exploring the relative importance of normative and distinctive organizational preferences as predictors of work attitudes. *Journal of Applied Psychology, 104*(2), 270–292.

11

How Did We Do?

Survey Benchmarking and Normative Data

Elizabeth A. McCune and Sarah R. Johnson

One of the most commonly asked questions among consumers of survey data is "How did we do?" There are several ways in which organizations may address this question, but a typical approach is through the use of benchmarks. Used appropriately, benchmarks can serve as important tools in interpreting survey results and prioritizing actions. The purpose of this chapter is to provide an overview of survey benchmark data, including where and how to access external survey benchmarks, what to consider when evaluating survey benchmarks, and a glimpse into the future of survey benchmarks.

The term *benchmark* can be simply defined as standards by which others can be compared (Benchmark, n.d.). However, underneath this deceptively simple definition there are a number of different applications and contexts (Boxwell, 1994). In this chapter, when we use the term *benchmark* we refer to a quantitative data point generated from a single survey item, such as the mean or percent favorable score, that has been aggregated across some number of organizations to serve as a point of comparison to one organization's result on the same or a similar survey item. We will also refer to *normative data* and *normative databases*, which are the aggregated grouping of data across multiple organizations from which benchmarks are generated. We will also use the term *survey best-practice sharing*, which is the process of sharing information, typically across organizations, about the survey process. Best-practice sharing is in fact a form of benchmarking, and we will use the term to differentiate it from quantitative benchmark data, which is the primary focus of this chapter.

It is important to distinguish between internal and external benchmarks. Much of this chapter will discuss external benchmarks, which can be somewhat complex and difficult to navigate. But internal benchmarks can also help to answer the question "How did we do?" Internal benchmarks can take one of two forms: comparison of one part of the organization to another and

Elizabeth A. McCune and Sarah R. Johnson, *How Did We Do?* In: *Employee Surveys and Sensing*. Edited by: William H. Macey and Alexis A. Fink, Oxford University Press (2020). © Society for Industrial and Organizational Psychology. DOI: 10.1093/oso/9780190939717.003.0011 comparison of the same part of the organization to itself at an earlier time. Internal benchmarks of either kind often provide a more relevant, direct comparison than can be provided by external benchmarks and may serve as a stronger call to action than an external benchmark that is less precise and subject to caveats and qualifications in interpretation.

There are several benefits to external benchmark data for surveys. The primary benefit is in being able to compare an organization's results to the results of other organizations to determine whether the organization is doing better, about the same, or worse than other organizations. In many cases there is the opportunity to compare survey results across different topics (e.g., work–life balance, collaboration, and engagement). Particularly for C-suite executives, external comparisons are often necessary for putting survey results into context. When the question of how an organization's survey results compare to other organizations is left unanswered, discussions about survey results and action planning can stall. For this reason, external benchmarks for survey results are sometimes referred to as *table stakes*, that is, a minimum requirement to have a meaningful executive-level conversation about survey results.

However, while external benchmarks may indeed be necessary, decisions about actions to take in response to survey results should be based on additional considerations. Brooks and Hendrickson (2016) provide examples of how critical external benchmarks were in enabling survey practitioners to have a meaningful dialogue and generate actions based on survey results, but in no instance was the external benchmark the deciding factor in planning or taking action. No single data point will make the case for the investment of resources. Rather, the organization must triangulate all available data to determine an appropriate course of action. Also, there are several limitations that restrict the usefulness of external benchmarks, such as whether the companies in the benchmark are comparable, the ability of the benchmark to provide meaningful demographic cuts, and the opportunity to choose meaningful survey questions. Throughout the rest of this chapter we will further explore the benefits of external benchmarks and their limitations, including options for mitigating these concerns.

Sources of External Benchmark Data

We use two dimensions to help compare/contrast sources of benchmark data: *level of effort/investment* required to obtain access to the benchmarks and *opportunity for customization* of benchmark data. The level of effort/ investment reflects money, time, and other resources. The opportunity for customization reflects the extent to which the benchmark provider offers data on a predetermined or fixed item set or whether the provider collects benchmark data to meet the needs of the purchasing organization. Both approaches have their place in balancing concerns for cost, timing, and the extent to which the benchmark data were collected on identical items or perhaps only similar items. The latter is a question of comparability and thus relevance. Similar trade-offs can be framed for the fit between the organization's workforce characteristics and that from which the benchmark data were collected, or the question of generalizability. In what follows, we focus on the most common sources that practitioners tend to leverage and those that seem to provide the greatest value.

General Benchmarking Studies and White Papers

Several research organizations (e.g., Gartner, i4cp, and Gallup) produce studies and white papers that contain survey-based benchmarks. An external benchmark of this kind is an opportunity for a practitioner to get some sense of an external metric for a construct of interest in a way that requires little effort or investment beyond reading the study. However, there is typically also little to no opportunity for customization of the metric. Strong benchmarking studies will provide information on the demographics comprising the benchmark data they provide, and that gives the practitioner at least some information about how generalizable and relevant the benchmark might be to the organization. While we encourage practitioners to leverage benchmarking studies to build their knowledge base, we generally do not recommend directly comparing results from surveys within the organization to these broad benchmarks unless the information needed to determine that the comparison is relevant and meaningful is available.

Survey Vendor Benchmarks

Many vendors that offer employee survey administration and reporting tools and services have a set of benchmarks that are drawn from client data, and these typically represent low-medium investment, medium-high customization benchmarks. In order to receive these benchmarks, organizations typically must agree to use one or more of the same or similar survey items that exist in the database. The organization then administers that item as part of its survey, the organization's data are added to the normative database, and then the organization receives external benchmarks alongside its own organizational survey results. Generally, benchmarks can be obtained by industry, geography, and other large demographics, though availability will be dependent on the robustness of the survey vendor's database. Survey vendors may also charge a fee for the use of benchmarks. While the details of the process will vary across survey vendors, this represents the general approach.

External benchmarks provided by survey vendors are characterized as low-medium investment because the effort required to obtain the benchmark data is low since the organization will be leveraging its business relationship with the vendor and the benchmarks can often be built into survey reporting. Nonetheless, some investment may be required of the organization to determine which items to benchmark. There are two challenges related to selecting benchmark items: (1) the relevance and comparability of the available benchmark items to the organization and (2) the generalizability of the benchmarks of interest. In selecting items that are available for benchmarking to include in an organization's survey, compromise may be necessary in the design of the survey; it is advisable to address these concerns proactively rather than face questions of interpretation later.

Benchmarking Consortia

In the medium-high investment, medium-high customization category are the benchmarks available through dedicated survey benchmarking consortia. The two primary examples in this small category are the Mayflower Group and the Information Technology Survey Group (ITSG) (Johnson, 1996; Macey & Eldridge, 2006). Mayflower is a survey benchmarking group comprised of 40–50 Fortune 500 companies, and ITSG is a group of about 25 organizations in the technology industry. Both consortia require nontrivial investments, including submitting benchmark item data as well as dues and meeting attendance.

However, there is a high return on this investment in that members of these groups have access to high-quality, generalizable benchmarks that can be customized in several ways. The organizations represented in these benchmarks represent the companies with which the other member organizations most want to benchmark. In addition to a cultivated group of members, the normative databases maintained by these organizations provide several key demographics for which benchmarks can be obtained (e.g., job function, geography, gender). While the level of investment required to obtain these benchmarks may be high, members of these groups have the benefit of highly relevant, quality benchmarks.

Data Gathered Through Panels and Crowdsourcing Technology

In the high-investment, high-customization category are benchmarks created through market research panels. Indeed, some consulting firms create their benchmarks precisely in this manner. These firms maintain panels primarily for consumer research, but they are defined in terms of very specific demographics which can include industry and employer. This approach can be expensive yet can provide benchmarks that are highly generalizable and comparable. Given the opportunities for customization, this approach may be particularly useful for generating benchmarks for topic-specific, point-in-time surveys that organizations leverage to research a particular issue in depth (e.g., flexible work options).

Also in the high-investment, high-customization category are crowdsourcing technologies, with the best example being Amazon's Mechanical Turk (MTurk). Since 2009, MTurk has gained popularity as a tool for gathering data for social science research, and it may hold potential for gathering benchmark data as well. MTurk allows users to choose the desired number of respondents and to specify respondent criteria on a variety of demographics, such as employment status, industry, job function, location, age, and gender. Despite being recognized as a relatively low-cost resource, the learning curve for new MTurk users is noteworthy and should be considered among the investments for this approach. For additional cost, TurkPrime (www.cloudresearch.com) can be leveraged to increase the ease of data collection and may also provide access to a broader range of demographics through Prime Panels. Practitioners may, however, experience hesitancy or reservations within their organizations toward using MTurk for the purpose of generating benchmark data, perhaps due to lack of familiarity. As of the time of this writing, the authors are not aware of any examples of organizations using MTurk to generate benchmarks for organizational survey data, and we encourage those who are considering this approach to review the thoughtful work by Landers and Behrend (2015) for additional perspective.

Considerations in Evaluating the Quality of External Benchmark Data

The goal of this section is to equip the survey practitioner with an understanding of the elements that comprise normative databases from which external benchmarks are generated. Normative data vary on a number of evaluative dimensions, and understanding how to characterize a given normative database based on these dimensions will enable practitioners to objectively determine the utility of the external benchmarks for their particular circumstances.

Generalizability

The first question any practitioner should ask when evaluating external benchmarks is, "Are these data generalizable to my organization?" There are several criteria that inform generalizability, but some primary factors to consider when it comes to external benchmarks are typically industry, job functions, and geography. Industry is key because organizations operating in the same industry often face similar external pressures and market factors, which can influence their organizational operations and subsequently their survey results. Beyond generalizability, having benchmark data from the industry in which an organization operates often lends a degree of face validity or perceived credibility of the benchmarks in the eyes of executives.

The job functions represented in the normative database are another important element to consider. Existing normative databases often show substantial differences in results across job functions (Brooks et al., 2017), and many organizations experience this internally as well. Due to these known differences in results across job functions, practitioners will want to determine the extent to which job functions that are prominent within their organization are well represented in external benchmarks.

Geography is another important component of generalizability, as demonstrated by two studies conducted by the ITSG benchmarking consortium (Hendrickson, 2017). In these studies, researchers analyzed data submitted by 22 participating organizations across 15 items and showed that variance in survey responses were more attributable to the organization the respondent belonged to rather than the country in which the respondent resided. Still, practitioners should ensure that, at a minimum, the primary geographies in which their employees reside are represented in external benchmarks.

It is worth noting that comparisons are often sought against specific competitors within an industry or in related industries. The point of reference is not similarity to the organization but, rather, one based on reputation for specific business practices such as in the area of innovation or talent management. What is more important in these cases is being able to compare against specific companies or groups of companies. Being able to do so may not be a realistic goal given the current structure of most benchmarking groups, but understanding that the desire to have certain companies represented in external benchmarks may help the practitioner to make a more informed decision about which benchmarks to pursue and leverage.

Item Comparability

Another key consideration in the use of external benchmarks is the items for which benchmarks are available. To ensure the greatest comparability between an organization's result and an external benchmark, the items being compared should be identical or extremely similar. There are several considerations in determining whether items are similar enough to be compared, but three are especially important. First, the subject of the items needs to be identical. For example, it would not be advisable for an organization to compare results for the item "My manager inspires me" to an external benchmark for the item "The CEO of my company inspires me." Changing the subject of a question can have a demonstrable effect on the results, even within an organization. Second, the strength of the language used in the items should be similar for an appropriate comparison. For example, while the following items seem similar, we would not advise direct comparison: "I am extremely happy with the job I have today" and "I like the job I have today." While these items are certainly similar with respect to the construct they intend to measure, the difference between the descriptors "extremely happy" and "like" will likely generate different responses to the items, making them difficult to compare. While it can be difficult to objectively assess the strength of language, potential differences in this area should be taken into consideration when determining whether an external benchmark is a relevant comparison. A third important consideration is similarity in response scales. While most benchmarks will leverage some form of a Likert response scale, several variations can affect comparability: the number of response options, the anchors associated with the response options, and the presence or absence of a "not applicable" or "prefer not to respond" option. Response scales should be identical for maximum comparability.

Data Protection

Normative databases retain their viability and relevance through either the contributions of data by participating organizations (e.g., consortium members, clients). As such, organizations that are seeking out external benchmarks through consortium membership or via vendors are often asked to provide their data in return. In addition to evaluating the generalizability of normative data, practitioners need to consider how the data they provide will be protected. A full examination of data privacy and protection is beyond the scope of this chapter but is well covered in Chapter 24 of this book, but it should be noted that relevant here is the concern for the protection of organizational privacy. Two of the key considerations specific to normative databases on this topic are (1) whether the organization has the ability to remain anonymous within the database (or whether the provider reserves the right to disclose that a specific organization's data are part of the benchmark) and (2) in cases where organization membership is not anonymous, ensuring that the appropriate parties (e.g., chief human resources officer, legal) are comfortable with any policies that determine where the organization's name might be surfaced. For example, the database may provide the names of the highest scoring companies for survey items as part of the benchmarks.

Demographic Reporting

Most organizations have key employee demographics for which it would be important to have external benchmarks. One such example would be women holding technical roles (e.g., engineer, software developer) in the technology industry. Virtually all normative databases will have demographic cuts available; however, the specific demographics available will vary by and even within databases. Depending on how robust the database is and how often it is refreshed, there may be some periods for which benchmarks are not available for a particular demographic group. Informed practitioners will want to determine not only which demographics are of primary interest to their organization, but will also want to determine how well-represented those demographics are in the normative database and whether benchmark data for these demographics are typically available.

Methodological Considerations

Methodological considerations are another component of evaluating the generalizability of a normative database to a specific organization's survey results. While no study has systematically identified, measured, and explained the precise impact of every methodological variable involved in employee surveys, one primary consideration is sampling strategy. Because the number of organizations considering or implementing non-census-based surveying (Brooks et al., 2017; Johnson, Kamen, Lewis, McCune, & Skinner, 2017) and given the observed differences in survey results when using different sampling methods, knowing whether a normative database contains data gathered via a census or sampling approach is a basic but critical piece of information. Ideally, survey practitioners would seek out external benchmarks that mirror their organization's approach to sampling. However, in cases where a sampling approach is used, several questions need to be addressed, including whether employees are invited randomly or via a convenience sample and whether the responses received are representative of the organization as a whole.

There are many other methodological factors that likely contribute to the generalizability of external benchmarks (e.g., time of year, either fiscal or calendar, in which survey data are gathered; whether the survey is voluntary or mandatory; what is communicated to employees about the confidentiality of survey responses). In the authors' experience, most normative databases will only take into consideration basic methodological considerations, and they will typically do this via minimum requirements (e.g., the database only allows census-based results). We have not often seen the option for filtering benchmarks based on methodological differences (e.g., generating a benchmark for census-based and sampling approaches separately).

Changes in the Role and Utility of Benchmarks over Time

While the interest in using benchmark data to interpret survey results has been part of survey analysis since early days, the interest in normative data and best practice benchmarking heightened in the mid- to late 1980s. Inspired by books such as *In Search of Excellence* (Peters & Waterman, 1982) and *Good to Great* (Collins, 2001), best practice sharing was embraced by many organizations as a useful process that enabled them to determine which company does a specific activity the best among their peers, with the intent to emulate what they were doing in order to improve performance. As a result, benchmark data became not only the source of comparative data used to provide context when interpreting survey results but also a path to identifying leading companies in the areas of job satisfaction, employee engagement, or other considerations measurable via survey methodology. As the best practice sharing movement evolved, it became more defined and specialized and best practice sharing groups were created for specific topics and within specific industries. The logic behind such activities was clear and compelling: Insights and best practices were most useful when they were specific to an industry and/or employee group. As a result, many companies implemented policies and practices that had proven successful in other organizations.

Benchmarking had thus evolved from providing statistical context to establishing a roadmap for action and changes to policies and practices, and the interest in learning from other companies had produced an industry all its own. Over time, though, many companies recognized that what worked in one context may not be as successful in another context. This growing realization that processes and programs cannot simply be lifted from one organization and transplanted to another with identical success led many organizations away from detailed program or process benchmarking. There continued to be interest in learning from other companies, but most organizations recognized that their unique history, employee population, industry, culture, and degree of organizational maturity (or lack thereof) made them unique enough that programs and practices could not be directly transferable and produce the same results. Further, many organizations recognized that there could be a competitive disadvantage to sharing best practices. Many of these practices may have been differentiators for the organization, in their ability either to attract and retain key talent or to enhance organization functioning.

Benchmarking eventually shifted back to being more of a statistical exercise, allowing companies the opportunity to determine if their survey results are the same or different from a general industry norm or an industry group norm. However, several trends in organization survey design and administration have resulted in a reduced emphasis on benchmark comparisons.

Future of Normative Data

Interest in creating survey content that is customized to an organization's specific strategies, culture, practices, and research interests continues to rise. While the annual census survey continues to be the norm for most companies, major design changes are taking hold in many organizations. There is growing interest in dramatically reducing the number of questions in surveys, with some organizations fielding surveys with as few as 10 questions. Topics or constructs that were once measured with multiple questions now may be represented by a single question. Indeed, Harter, Schmidt, and Kraut's (2006) chapter in an earlier edition of this book speaks to the logic of using single-item measures when the group is the unit of analysis. In this situation, survey designers may opt to create a customized question to optimize the limited space available on the survey. As a result, more companies are including fewer benchmarked questions in their employee surveys focusing on a small number of key metrics.

Modern surveys continue to address the traditional topics, such as performance management, manager relationship, confidence in the future of the organization, and, of course, employee engagement. However, more organizations are expanding survey content to include questions on innovation, corporate philanthropy, changes in the marketplace, environmental consciousness, and diversity and inclusion, to name just a few. The evolution of survey topics within organization surveys demands that benchmark databases keep pace by identifying emerging topics, establishing standard survey questions, and collecting and compiling data on the new questions. This is a very challenging task as these new topics are often highly specific and uniquely defined in different companies across different industries. In fact, some companies that are members of benchmarking consortia have struggled to contribute data for traditional normative questions as their survey content is shifting more toward new and unique topics.

Improvements in the usability and quality of text analysis tools have enabled organizations to get more insight out of employees' responses to open-ended questions. Given the ability to use text analysis technology to identify survey themes and the positive or negative nature of the comments, there is growing interest in establishing benchmarks for standard text open-ended questions. However, methodological issues, such as the format of the open-ended question and the lack of consistency in the lexicons used for text analysis will be a challenge to valid comparisons. As yet, no such benchmark database exists, but as text analysis becomes more commonly used, the idea of benchmarking comments may become more realistic.

Organizations now have access to an ongoing flow of data from customers and the market, and many leaders are also looking for an ongoing flow of data from employees. These continuous listening programs can include "always on" pulse surveys available on a daily, weekly, or monthly basis to a sample of current employees, as well as onboarding and exit surveys that are continuously administered to employees who are joining or leaving the organization. There are few benchmarking resources today to address continuous listening programs or onboarding or exit surveys, but as these become more widespread, normative databases may emerge. "Always on" surveys provide a unique challenge, reflecting the ongoing flow of data. Daily, weekly, or monthly surveys produce results daily, weekly, or monthly. Normative databases are generally composed of results from many different surveys conducted at various times of the year and are summarized into a single set of results for a given year. Does it make sense to compare data collected on a dynamic basis to a static benchmark? A potential evolution could be the establishment of benchmarks that are created on a continuous basis, reflecting specific time periods. This would enable organizations to determine if fluctuations in results over time reflect meaningful change or merely seasonal fluctuations.

Insightful analysis and interpretation of survey data is, in large part, a function of providing context to the results. Context may come from recent changes in the organization or the marketplace, shifts in demographics, or an uptick or downturn in business results. Context often comes from a comparison, however limited, to external benchmark data. Consequently, it is hard to imagine a time when some level of external comparison is not of value in interpreting survey data. Benchmark data and processes will need to evolve in order to continue to provide useful insights.

Guidance and Recommendations for Survey Practitioners

In this final section we pose a few key questions relevant for survey practitioners, whether they are considering external benchmarks for the first time or are longtime users. We hope that contemplation of these questions will lead to more meaningful and intentional use of benchmark data to help drive actions.

How Can You Best Leverage Benchmarks to Drive Action?

External benchmarks can and should be an important input in identifying areas for improvement and prioritizing actions. Identify the items for which the organization's scores are lower than the benchmarks as a starting point, and then explore relevant internal benchmarks such as comparisons of groups within the organization and year-over-year comparisons to help determine areas of strengths and opportunities. In cases where organizations are running an employee survey for the first time or introducing new survey items, external benchmarks may be especially helpful given the lack of historical trend data within the organization. However, some leaders may be prone to overpivot and overvalue the gap to the benchmark. The survey practitioner must provide the appropriate context and expectation-setting around external benchmarks and their intended use.

Where Will Benchmarks Be Especially Useful for Providing Context?

In most cases, having an external benchmark for every item in the employee survey is not necessary. Practitioners can review the items available for benchmarking from their preferred source, determine which ones are likely to be of greatest value to the organizations, and then seek approval from relevant internal stakeholders to include these items in the organization's survey.

Working with stakeholders should increase the likelihood of selecting the most relevant and valuable items.

What Compromises Are You Willing to Make for External Benchmarks?

Compromises in item wording and survey administration may be required to yield the most directly comparable benchmarks. This could require weeks of internal discussion and debate, so the decision to change item wording to obtain a benchmark should not be taken lightly. Obtaining the most comparable benchmarks may require an organization to adhere to a particular administration approach (e.g., running a census-based survey). Given the changing landscape of survey administration and a move toward more continuous listening systems, this requirement may prove too great a compromise for those organizations that find value in a non-census-based survey approach. Practitioners will want to be well informed about the requirements and compromises involved in meeting benchmark requirements and whether they are acceptable trade-offs for the benchmarks received in exchange. No set of external benchmarks is going to solve all of the issues. Practitioners will need to determine which factors are the most critical based on the needs of the organization they support.

Conclusion

We end this chapter with a call to survey practitioners to be informed consumers of benchmark data by taking into account the extent to which those data can be reasonably generalized to the organization. We encourage practitioners to leverage external benchmarks for the purpose of context-setting and prioritization within the organization and to be conscious of both the benefits and the limitations that benchmarks provide.

References

Benchmark. (n.d.). In *Merriam-Webster's online dictionary* (11th ed.). Retrieved from https://www.merriam-webster.com/dictionary/benchmark

Boxwell, R. J. (1994). *Benchmarking for competitive advantage.* Columbus, OH: McGraw-Hill.

Brooks, S., DeBar, B., Harris, M. J., Lowery, M. R., McCune, E. A., & Scott, K. (2017, April). *Collected survey wisdom from Mayflower and ITSG: Lessons and advice.* Panel discussion at the 32nd Annual Conference of the Society for Industrial and Organizational Psychology, Orlando, FL.

Brooks, S., & Hendrickson, V. (October 2016). *Value and use of ITSG norms data.* Paper presented at the Fall 2016 Meeting of the Information Technology Survey Group, San Jose, CA.

Collins, J. (2001). *Good to great: Why some companies make the leap . . . and others don't.* New York, NY: Harper Collins.

Harter, J. K., Schmidt, F. L., & Kraut, A. I. (2006). Connecting employee satisfaction to business unit performance. In A. I. Kraut (Ed.), *Organizational surveys: Tools for assessment and change* (pp. 33–52). San Francisco, CA: Jossey-Bass.

Hendrickson, V. (April 2017). *Company and country effects on ITSG normative data.* Paper presented at the Spring 2017 Meeting of the Information Technology Survey Group, Orlando, FL.

Johnson, R. H. (1996). Life in the consortium: The Mayflower Group. In A. I. Kraut (Ed.), *Organizational surveys: Tools for assessment and change* (pp. 285–309). San Francisco, CA: Jossey-Bass.

Johnson, S., Kamen, A. M., Lewis, R. L., McCune, E. A., & Skinner, J. L. (2017, April). *Yearly, quarterly, monthly, daily: Choosing the best survey cadence.* Panel discussion at the 32nd Annual Conference of the Society for Industrial and Organizational Psychology, Orlando, FL.

Landers, R. N., & Behrend, T. S. (2015). An inconvenient truth: Arbitrary distinctions between organizational, Mechanical Turk, and other convenience samples. *Industrial and Organizational Psychology*, 8, 142–164.

Macey, W. H., & Eldridge, L. D. (2006). National norms versus consortium data: What do they tell us? In A. I. Kraut (Ed.), *Getting action from organizational surveys: New concepts, technologies, and applications* (pp. 352–376). San Francisco, CA: Jossey-Bass.

Peters, T. J., & Waterman, R. H. (1982). *In search of excellence.* New York, NY: Harper & Row.

12

Writing Organizational Survey Items That Predict What Matters in Organizations

Daniel J. Ingels, Kathryn E. Keeton, and Christiane Spitzmueller

The purpose of this chapter is to provide a foundation of knowledge, strategies, and tools that survey practitioners can consider when developing survey items to measure employee attitudes. First, it provides a set of guidelines that survey practitioners can utilize as they develop questions/items that work for their specific and unique organizational context. These guidelines generally pertain to content development, item language, response methods, item testing, as well as the use of single items that can be predictive of organizational outcomes if designed correctly. Second, it provides a practical overview of the theory of measurement by addressing important topics, such as test theory, reliability, validity, and item response theory, and their practical relevance for survey practitioners.

The current chapter provides a practitioner-oriented introduction to generating organizational survey items. A lot of the recommendations in this chapter are, strictly viewed from the perspective of achieving maximal scientific rigor and developing items and scales that will pass scrutiny in peer-review processes, not viable pathways. However, in developing this chapter and through conversations with experienced practitioners, they reflect practices that maximize input from multiple stakeholders, while maintaining as much rigor as possible in organizational settings where executives often demand very short surveys and are weary of the financial and opportunity costs that coincide with long employee surveys.

Daniel J. Ingels, Kathryn E. Keeton, and Christiane Spitzmueller, *Writing Organizational Survey Items That Predict What Matters in Organizations* In: *Employee Surveys and Sensing*. Edited by: William H. Macey and Alexis A. Fink, Oxford University Press (2020). © Society for Industrial and Organizational Psychology.
DOI: 10.1093/oso/9780190939717.003.0012

Deciding on Survey Content Domains—Creating Value Through Survey Content

Survey content design begins with carefully defining the survey project goals, which need to ultimately map closely onto survey sections and item content. Survey content can serve several functions—items can be used to measure employee preferences (e.g., regarding benefits) but also determine predictors of outcomes (e.g., safety outcomes, unit-level performance/productivity, career progression). In other cases, items can be used to inform employees about upcoming organizational development interventions and start a conversation. For instance, asking employees to agree or disagree with the statement "I am in favor of team performance based compensation" in an organization where all current compensation decisions are based on individual performance can be used to spark initial discussions and gather preliminary support for a potential future intervention. For survey content to be useful to the organization, stakeholders across the organization should be involved in articulating survey project goals in writing. For example, if the goal of an organizational survey is to address 50% annual employee turnover in an organization, the implications for survey content are relatively clear and can be guided by extant research on antecedents of employee turnover. In the case of other goals, such as determining internal service quality, the translation of overall survey goals into items is less straightforward. If there is limited prior research on an issue, creating survey items can be (and often is) the only way to meet survey design goals. In these cases, survey content development can be aided by conducting interviews or focus groups with stakeholders. These interviews and focus groups should be documented through notes, and categories derived from those notes can then be used by a survey team to develop items that map directly onto the desired survey content domain. Although labor-intensive to start with, this approach is likely to yield good returns on the survey project.

Notably (and fortunately), most challenges and goals an organization may want to address through an organizational survey have been faced by other organizations in the past and are hence reflected in published item pools. Among the most useful resources in this domain is the Mayflower Group item pool (Johnson, 1996), consulting firm repositories of survey items, and public domain items published in research journals.

Key Recommendations for Survey Practice

1. Decide on response scale format. Although items that utilize a response scale that allows respondents to agree or disagree are the most commonly used, respondents can also be asked to rank order choices based on priorities or delineate the top reasons for the decisions they make. However, for subsequent statistical analysis, the use of items that utilize an agreement/disagreement scale from "strongly disagree" to "strongly agree" is often preferable.

2. Design items and pilot test extensively.

   We recommend several iterations of item design and pilot testing. First, once subject matter experts (SMEs) have provided input to the core survey project team with regard to content, item design can take place. This requires the subject matter expert team to develop a shared mental model of the survey content domains, which precedes the writing of actionable items. Items have to be actionable—if they are not actionable or if it is clear at the outset that the organization lacks resources to take action on an item, the item should not be used. Oftentimes, text provided by SMEs can be used as a starting point for creating items. Initially, it often makes sense to utilize a slightly larger set of items than what is ultimately desirable for survey administration— not all items function appropriately during pilot testing, with some resulting in no variability in responses and other items not being consistently interpretable across groups. In organizations that routinely use pulse surveys, pilot items can be added as an optional component to a pulse survey.

   For actual item writing, we recommend that the core survey project team individually generate items that capture each of the content domains based on SME data. Further, as the core project team decides on which items to retain, a discussion of statistical item properties and planned analyses should also feature prominently. Generally, there are advantages to using items with continuous response scales over dichotomous response scales. Power to conduct statistical tests is further reduced if dichotomous items rather than continuous items are used. Before subjecting items to pilot testing, they should also be run through online tools that determine an item's respective reading level and translatability into other languages—in organizations that hire entry-level employees without requiring university or graduate degrees, average reading levels of field personnel, in particular, are easily overestimated by survey project teams. In such organizations, sticking to a sixth-grade reading level is recommended. For multinational organizations, using items that contain minimal jargon yields better translation results.

After narrowing the item pool, several groups of pilot test participants should be recruited. In identifying pilot testing participants, it is critical that they resemble the actual survey population—we recommend randomly selecting pilot testers. From a practical perspective, it often makes sense to go through two iterations of pilot testing. In a first round, participants can be asked to go through a "talk aloud protocol," basically sharing their thoughts on survey items, content, and goals in assessing them as they go through the item set. The survey team should ideally record the pilot participants' comments and further alter item content to reduce ambiguity, fine-tuning the link between survey content and survey goals. After suggestions derived from this first round of pilot testing are addressed, we recommend that a second, independent group of pilot test participants complete the survey tool in a close-to-final version and in an administration mode that is close to how the actual survey will be administered ultimately. Ideally, a sufficient number of respondents will be included so that preliminary tests of the predictive validity of the item set can be conducted and major demographic cuts of interest can be examined. Again, we recommend interviewing a subset of the phase II pilot participants to glean information from them on any remaining issues with regard to the readability and interpretability of survey items.

3. Determine the total number of necessary items and items per concept.

Survey project teams often wonder how many items they can ultimately include in a final item set without jeopardizing high response rates and data quality. Recommendations from survey practitioners suggest that many organizations utilize survey tools with a total length of approximately 30 items, with some surveys being as short as 10 items. Short surveys are easier to achieve when organizations can already rely on a large amount of data from prior data collections, informing them of the psychometric properties of items and the linkage between items and relevant organizational outcomes. Many organizations have made significant progress in reducing the number of items on organizational surveys, in some cases to a total of 10 survey items. However, utilizing a small number of survey items and single-item measures for many constructs requires validity data (e.g., information on organizational outcomes, such as turnover, employee performance, unit-level metrics, customer satisfaction) and substantial pilot testing to ascertain whether the items used maximize what information can be gathered. Research on abridging scales and on constructs that can be measured with single items provides further information on what constructs can and cannot be meaningfully addressed through single-item measures (see Fisher, Matthews, & Gibbons, 2016).

Nowadays, many organizations prefer using single-item measures over multi-item measures to minimize survey content and maximize the number of constructs captured in a single-survey data collection.

There is no universal number of items that are appropriate for a concept of interest. Having too few items could result in failure to adequately capture the construct of interest, while having too many items risks diminishing returns for additional items. Survey practitioners should test how long survey participants may take to complete the entire survey.

It is important to point out that multi-item scales can be particularly difficult to administer, especially if an entire survey is already lengthy. Fisher et al. (2016) demonstrate that, in some cases, single-item measures can be as strong as multi-item measures of the same construct. Survey practitioners should consider both strategies but be aware that any scale should *adequately* cover the content domain of interest. Use single-item measures when possible.

4. Create actionable items.

Some survey items can create significant problems at the back end. For instance, asking employees whether they are "satisfied with their pay" often results in large numbers of employees expressing dissatisfaction (who, ultimately, is happy with their pay?). In the absence of infinite budgets, very little can be done about low satisfaction with pay. More actionable questions geared toward compensation can ask whether employees perceive a clear link between performance and compensation or whether they consider the process of administering performance appraisal and compensation decisions fair and transparent. In contrast to the item that addresses satisfaction with pay, data collected on the more actionable items tend to be more likely to be usable for intervention design.

5. Take item difficulty levels into account.

   An item's difficulty considers what level of a variable will result in an individual indicating agreement with the item, as opposed to not agreeing with that item. Consider two hypothetical items for a diversity climate perception scale: "Diverse views are actively sought" and "Diverse views are accepted." Both of these items measure diversity climate perceptions, but they both indicate substantially different degrees of the underlying construct. The first item indicates very positive levels of diversity climate perceptions, while the second indicates more moderate levels. One could consider that fewer people should indicate agreement with the first item but that many people would likely indicate agreement with the second. This example should not simply serve as an encouragement to never use items with high difficulty levels. Both difficult and easy items may be useful, so we suggest that survey practitioners consider items with varying difficulty and choose item difficulties that are most appropriate for the variable of interest and the goals of the organization.

6. Consider evidence regarding an item's predictive validity the most important indicator of item quality.

   Through organizational surveys, we conduct *organizational sensing*, with the ultimate goal of predicting organizationally relevant outcomes (see Chapter 17 for a detailed, practitioner-oriented discussion of linkage analyses). These outcomes can vary widely and range from the prediction of branch or store performance or product quality to predicting employee turnover, participation in voluntary committees and activities, employee safety behaviors, and accidents and injuries. These myriad examples highlight that many organizational phenomena are, at least partially, driven by organizational climate and can hence be predicted through well-designed organizational survey items. In other words, concepts measured through surveys are measured because they are likely linked to relevant business outcomes. For instance, employee engagement and job satisfaction could be measured as part of a survey if an organization is interested in better understanding why certain organizational units experience high levels of employee turnover while others are relatively turnover-free. Often, the goal of measuring survey concepts is to predict business outcomes. Or perceptions of the quality of mentoring received should relate to employees' likelihood to want to continue to be employed by their current organization

(Spitzmüller et al., 2008). However, because organizational surveys should be conducted with the intention of encouraging action, it is critical to use validated items. An in-depth discussion of the particularly critical concept of predictive validity goes beyond the scope of this chapter. However, to achieve predictive validity for relevant business outcomes, it is critical that SME input be solicited in item design and that the relevant outcomes are comprehensively measured at the individual and/or unit level. Without outcome data in the right format and relevant survey expertise, linkage analyses between survey data and outcomes become impossible, severely shortselling what organizations can achieve through survey data in comprehensive data analytics and linkage solutions. For a technical description of validation, we encourage survey practitioners to consider methods presented in *Principles for the Validation and Use of Personnel Selection Procedures* (Society for Industrial and Organizational Psychology, 2018).

7. Shorter, simpler items are preferable to longer, ambiguous items.

For the sake of clarity and reading level, shorter items are generally preferable to longer items. For a further description of readability issues, refer to our section on this topic in "Ethical and Cultural Considerations" later in this chapter. Although shorter items can make the survey response process easier for participants, long items may be necessary if modifying clauses are required to fully capture the content domain of the construct of interest.

Keep in mind that longer items are more likely to serve as double-barreled items that require that individuals make agreement judgments about two or more concepts. Short questions that require one judgment are much more appropriate. In some cases, a more appropriate solution may be to create two items to disentangle an initial, double-barreled item or to identify which of the multiple concepts are most critical.

8. Consider the format of participants' responses.

A response scale is required to indicate one's agreement or disagreement with an item prompt. A response scale can take many forms, but the most common of these is the Likert-type scale (Likert, 1932). The response options with a Likert-type scale have the following characteristics: (a) an ordered continuum of response categories, (b) an equal number of positive and negative options, (c) descriptive labels for each category, and (d) numeric values assigned to each response category. Following is an example of a survey item with a Likert-type scale format:

	Strongly Disagree	Disagree	Neither Agree nor Disagree	Agree	Strongly Agree
I am satisfied with my job.	1	2	3	4	5

Likert-type scales are useful because they provide two characteristics for responses: direction and intensity. In terms of direction, Likert-type scales allow participants to indicate their agreement or disagreement with an item. In terms of intensity, Likert-type scales allow participants to indicate the degree to which they either agree or disagree with an item. Intensity is usually indicated with the presence of an adverb (e.g., *strongly, slightly, neither*) (Allison, 1963; Cliff, 1959; Jones & Thurstone, 1955). In most cases, 5-point or 7-point scales are sufficient and recommended over scales with more points as these allow participants to indicate intensity of agreement or disagreement without requiring them to engage too many cognitive resources into differentiating between subtle differences in agreement.

Variations of Likert scales that represent an ordinal scale format can be used to measure other types of responses, such as frequency of events. When used in this context, response categories typically range from "almost never" to "almost always," providing an indication of how often a certain situation or behavior occurs. Following is an example of a survey item with a Likert-type scale format, used to measure the frequency of an event:

	Almost Never	Rarely	Occasionally	Frequently	Almost Always
How often do errors go unreported to management?	1	2	3	4	5

Survey practitioners may consider using scales that have descriptive anchors (e.g., behaviorally anchored rating scales) that provide example behaviors for each response option to which participants can compare their own behaviors or their colleagues' or supervisors' behaviors. For instance, rating responses could be "exceeds requirements" or "fails to complete basic requirements."

An additional consideration is whether or not to use a neutral category for response options (i.e., "Neither Agree nor Disagree") and force participants to choose a direction for response. Research on omission of the neutral category has shown that there are no distortions to survey results through either method (Armstrong, 1987; Guy & Norvell, 1977). Thus, survey practitioners should consider both options and determine if forced-direction responses or neutral responses are most appropriate for their specific survey efforts. Generally, allowing for a neutral response has advantages—if it is possible that employees do not have an attitude in either direction, the lack of a neutral response forces them to choose agreement or disagreement, adding error variance to scores.

Lastly, nominal response scales that represent preferences or choices can also be used in organizational surveys—examples are lists of possible interventions and requests for employees to select a single choice or multiple choices that they consider desirable. Ordinal rankings, where individuals are asked to sort their preferences, are popular item response versions with many practitioners. However, their use in linkage analyses is often more cumbersome than items with continuous response scales. Still, creating basic descriptive information about preferences can be well accomplished using ordinal scales.

We generally recommend allowing respondents to skip items, to avoid negative reactions to items being "required" to complete, which can agitate respondents and result in them completing items that they feel they have insufficient experience to respond to. In other cases, requiring item completion can result in employees closing their browser window or survey altogether.

Recently, given the technological advances in commercial survey tools, the use of infinity sliders as response scales has become more common, allowing respondents, for example, to rate an item on a scale of 1–100. This produces highly nuanced and variable responses. However, the verdict on whether these infinity sliders make up for the incremental survey response time through decreased measurement error is yet to be seen. Further considerations regarding the use of infinity sliders are around inclusiveness—for individuals with limited tech proficiency or with disabilities like vision impairments, the use of infinity sliders may discourage survey completion or continuation.

Some items may require instructions for completion, especially when using less common response options or providing definitions of key terms. Such instructions should be succinct and clear, requiring only a small amount of the participant's focus while being easily readable. In many cases, respondents are likely to move directly to the items rather than reading through lengthy instructions, so keeping instructions short and to the point is of the essence.

Building on Item Pools

In a host of organizational circumstances, custom-designed, in-house surveys can be useful thermometers of an organization's temperature. In these cases, creating new items is necessary to meet organizational development goals and to provide relevant data to decision makers. At the same time, some goals of organizational surveys can only be met if existing items are adopted or adjusted to the current context. For instance, if it is important to benchmark survey results against other organizations, the use of common items is essential. Similarly, many situations and organizational challenges are not as unique or esoteric as one might think and indeed overlap with challenges experienced by other practitioners in other organizations. Reaching out to colleagues and networking with survey practitioners in other organizations may prove fruitful in identifying items that demonstrated desirable properties and significant predictive validity in other organizations. Similarly, scales published in scientific journals can often be used as a starting point in generating an item pool for a survey. Some strategies for procuring existing scales include conducting Internet database searches through Google Scholar, ResearchGate, PsycTESTS, etc. and referencing items from survey platforms, such as SurveyMonkey or partnering with industrial–organizational psychologists working in research settings such as universities (which provide them with access to library resources and item banks). Survey items can also be identified through survey consortium groups that publish their item lists on consortium websites. Note that many survey consulting firms utilize copyrighted items and are highly protective of their intellectual property.

Ethical and Cultural Considerations

The following section focuses on cultural and ethical issues that survey practitioners should consider when developing items. Although not an exhaustive list of ethical and cultural issues in the survey design process, these are particularly relevant concepts to consider when creating a scale.

Sensitive Items

One issue that can be particularly difficult in the use of organizational surveys can be the usage of sensitive items, which are items that contain content for which individuals may be encouraged to provide a socially desirable response (Tourangeau & Yan, 2007). Consider a hypothetical safety climate item: "I sometimes do not wear my appropriate safety clothing and equipment on the job." Even if an organizational survey is anonymous, an individual may feel that an indication of disagreement with that item is most appropriate as the individual just wants to appear to be a safe worker. Sensitive questions can lead to nonresponse on those items (Juster & Smith, 1997; Moore, Stinson, & Welniak, 1999) as well as nonresponse to entire surveys (Catania, Gibson, Chitwood, & Coates, 1990). Thus, survey practitioners should be thoughtful about using sensitive items in an organizational survey and recognize that responses to sensitive items are likely affected by social desirability and employee concerns about anonymity. Considering this example, a less sensitive item may be "I often wear my appropriate safety clothing equipment on the job." Alternatively, items about coworkers' behavior may reveal what respondents usually do themselves without requiring respondents to admit to socially undesirable behavior. For instance, research has demonstrated that individuals in developing countries who bribe others are more likely to report that their colleagues and friends use bribes than individuals who are unlikely to use bribes to further their business outcomes.

Cultural Differences in Interpretation of Questions

Considering the continuing and rapid globalization of the workforce, organizations may be interested in evaluating subsets of employees in different parts of the world. Using the same questions, even when translated, for employees within different cultures may lead to faulty conclusions. This is due to a concept termed *cross-cultural equivalence* (Hui & Triandis, 1985; Ryan, Chan,

Ployhart, & Slade, 1999; Ryan, Ployhart, Schmitt, & Slade, 2000). This concept considers that construct meanings, item interpretations, and response choices may or may not be equivalent across cultures.

To appropriately use newly created survey items across cultures, it is important to evaluate whether they are equally effective in different languages when completed by people from different cultural backgrounds. We will recommend the most straightforward method to do this: a back-translation process. This method, detailed by Brislin (1970), involves translating the original scale into the desired language and then translating it back into the original language. First, survey practitioners should convene a panel of appropriately informed translators, instead of just one translator, to agree upon the best translation of the scale that loses no fidelity in item content or item difficulty. Second, a different panel of translators should then attempt to translate the scale back into the original language. While the scale may not translate to the original language perfectly, it should still reflect the content and difficulty of the original scale items. After translation and backtranslation has occurred, it is critical for employees in the target country to again serve as pilot participants. Some items can be correctly translated and back-translated and still lose their original meaning entirely. For instance, the personality assessment item "I seldom feel blue" in English evidences a state of sadness and depression. Translated into German (and even though back-translation would work and result in *blue* again) the term *blue* would indicate that an individual is severely intoxicated rather than sad or depressed.

Summary Steps for Survey Item Creation

As a final point of this chapter, we provide a summary of steps that a survey practitioner may want to tackle to develop items for organizational surveys. These steps draw from guidelines by Spector (1992) that provide a practitioner-friendly approach to survey development.

Define the Construct or Concept of Interest

Item construction requires that the nature of the construct be clearly defined. To provide a universally understood definition of the phenomenon to be measured, survey practitioners should first review the scientific literature on the topic of interest to understand the nuances of the phenomenon. Second, practitioners should use SMEs and focus groups to determine the relevance of the definition and parameters of the variable to be measured as SMEs should be more familiar with the target audience and can provide feedback on item development.

Design the Item(s)

Once the construct of interest has been defined, a survey practitioner must, ideally as a member of a larger team, develop scale items that fit the entire scope of that construct. One should create as large a pool of items as is feasible that evaluate the breadth of the construct's definition and parameters. The items should be of varying difficulty and should adhere to the recommendations for item length and positivity/negativity.

Additionally, one must develop the response options and instructions to be used with the respective items. One should refer to our discussion of response categories, previously in this chapter, for guidelines on how to construct the response methods (e.g., Likert-type scales).

Pilot-Test the Scale

Once a pool of scale items, their response options, and any instructions are drafted, the survey practitioner should pilot-test the scale with an additional focus group and/or SMEs. Focus groups and SMEs are incredibly useful at this stage of scale development as they can provide feedback in a number of different ways. First, they can test whether the item content matches the definitions of the phenomenon of interest in the way that such a phenomenon would occur in the work context of the target audience. Second, think-aloud methods (e.g., van Someren, Barnard, & Sandberg, 1994) can be used to ascertain how such individuals think when presented with the scale items. Once pilot-testing of the scale is complete, survey practitioners should consider any alterations to the scale items, as is necessary, and retest the items before continuing to full analysis of the scale with a larger body of participants.

Extensively Pilot-Test and Analyze the Scale

Once pilot-testing and development of scales is completed, survey practitioners should administer the survey to a large, representative body of participants to statistically test item properties. To conduct proper item analyses, a sample of 100–200 employees is generally required. Survey practitioners should thoughtfully evaluate the statistical output to determine which items should be retained and which should be deleted.

Validate and Norm the Scale

The scale should then be validated against other organizational variables of interest and normed to the characteristics of the organization. This final step is one that survey practitioners often miss or neglect due to the difficulty and investment required, but it is arguably the most important step as it determines how useful the scale is for an organization. One should first develop hypotheses as to which other organizational variables may be related to the variable of interest. Using a sample of members of the organization, individual results for the newly created scale can be compared with data on such other organizational variables to empirically determine if the variables are related.

Items should be baselined within the organization to determine how the variable of interest manifests within the organization. Baselining can be useful because it provides a frame of reference for how all ratings within the organization are distributed, against which individual ratings can be compared to determine if they rate higher or lower than others in the organization. This process is done by calculating the mean, standard deviation, shape of the distribution of the variable ratings, possible restriction of range in ratings, and any other relevant descriptive statistics, along with percent favorable/neutral/unfavorable information. As well, these statistics can be calculated for various subgroups within the organization to determine intradepartmental norms or any other group norms that may be relevant to the variable of interest.

Conclusion

The goal of this chapter is to provide a basis of knowledge to allow organizational survey practitioners to construct their own surveys. We began by demonstrating that observed measures of individual characteristics are affected by measurement error, defining the theoretical concepts of classical test theory, reliability, validity, and item response theory. We then provided a series of recommendations for various steps in the item-creation process, including content coverage, item design, response methods, and item testing.

Lastly, we considered three important ethical issues that can plague the process of survey item creation: the usage of sensitive items, readability of survey items, and cross-cultural equivalency of survey items.

References

Allison, R. B., Jr. (1963). Using adverbs as multipliers in semantic differentials. *Journal of Psychology*, *56*, 115–117.

Armstrong, R. L. (1987). The midpoint on a five-point Likert-type scale. *Perceptual and Motor Skills*, *64*, 359–362.

Brislin, R. W. (1970). Back-translation for cross-cultural research. *Journal of Cross-Cultural Psychology*, *1*, 185–216.

Catania, J. A., Gibson, D. R., Chitwood, D. D., & Coates, T. J. (1990). Methodological problems in AIDS behavioral research: Influences on measurement error and participation bias in studies of sexual behavior. *Psychological Bulletin*, *108*, 339–362.

Cliff, N. (1959). Adverbs as multipliers. *Psychological Review*, *66*, 27–44.

Fisher, G. G., Matthews, R. A., & Gibbons, A. M. (2016). Developing and investigating the use of single-item measures in organizational research. *Journal of Occupational Health Psychology*, *21*(1), 3.

Guy, R. F., & Norvell, M. (1977). The neutral point on a Likert scale. *Journal of Psychology*, *95*, 199–204.

Hui, C. H., & Triandis, H. C. (1985). Measurement in cross-cultural psychology: A review and comparison of strategies. *Journal of Cross-Cultural Psychology*, *16*, 131–152.

Johnson, R. H. (1996). Life in the consortium: The Mayflower Group. In A. I. Kraut (Ed.), *Organizational surveys: Tools for assessment and change* (pp. 285–309). San Francisco, CA: Jossey-Bass.

Jones, L. V., & Thurstone, L. L. (1955). The psychophysics of semantics: An experimental investigation. *Journal of Applied Psychology*, *39*, 31–36.

Juster, F. T., & Smith, J. P. (1997). Improving the quality of economic data: Lessons from the HRS and AHEAD. *Journal of the American Statistical Association*, *92*, 1268–1278.

Likert, R. (1932). A technique for the measurement of attitudes. *Archives of Psychology*, *140*, 1–55.

Moore, J. C., Stinson, L. L., & Welniak, E. (1999). Income reporting in surveys: Cognitive issues and measurement error. In M. G. Sirken, D. J. Herrmann, S. Schechter, N. Schwarz, J. M. Tanur, & R. Tourangeau (Eds.), *Cognition and survey research* (pp. 155–173). New York, NY: Wiley.

Ryan, A. M., Chan, D., Ployhart, R. E., & Slade, L. A. (1999). Employee attitude surveys in a multinational organization: Considering language and culture in assessing measurement equivalence. *Personnel Psychology*, *52*, 37–58.

Ryan, A. M., Ployhart, R. E., Schmitt, N., & Slade, L. A. (2000). Hypothesizing differential item functioning in global employee opinion surveys. *Personnel Psychology*, *53*(3), 531–562.

Society for Industrial and Organizational Psychology. (2018). *Principles for the validation and use of personnel selection procedures* (5th ed.). Bowling Green, OH: Author.

Spector, P. E. (1992). *Summated rating scale construction: An introduction.* Newbury Park, CA: Sage Publications.

Spitzmüller, C., Neumann, E., Spitzmüller, M., Rubino, C., Keeton, K. E., Sutton, M. T., & Manzey, D. (2008). Assessing the influence of psychosocial and career mentoring on organizational attractiveness. *International Journal of Selection and Assessment, 16,* 403–415.

Tourangeau, R., & Yan, T. (2007). Sensitive questions in surveys. *Psychological Bulletin, 133,* 859–883.

van Someren, M. W., Barnard, Y. F., & Sandberg, J. A. C. (1994). *The think aloud method: A practical approach to modelling cognitive processes.* San Diego, CA: Academic Press.

13

Open-Ended Questions

The Role of Natural Language Processing and Text Analytics

Subhadra Dutta and Eric M. O'Rourke

Open-ended questions have traditionally elicited mixed reactions among academicians and practitioners. Some experiments came to extreme conclusions that "open questions should be eliminated from full-scale surveys wherever possible" (Payne, 1965). Over time, studies started bridging the gap between qualitative and quantitative survey data (Looker, Denton, & Davis, 1989) to the current state where hybrid survey usage increases study validity (Altintzoglou, Sone, Voldnes, Nøstvold, Sogn-Grundvåg, 2018), but intensive nonautomated coding procedures and their lack of scalability have contributed to lower popularity and underutilization of qualitative questions in employee surveys.

Traditional qualitative data-analysis techniques are of limited value in handling large data sets, and there have been consistent calls for industrial–organizational (I-O) psychology to become increasingly interdisciplinary (Afflerbach et al., 2014). Advancements in the text analytics field itself, increasing variety and volume of open-ended data being collected in organizations outside of surveys (internal blogs, intranets, etc.), and the need to provide scalable real-time insights have resulted in exploration into the computational linguistics discipline for machine learning–based methods.

This chapter discusses some computational text analytic methods for analyzing employee survey data, their evolution, the trade-offs of growing such capabilities internally versus externally, resources, and future directions.

Subhadra Dutta and Eric M. O'Rourke, *Open-Ended Questions* In: *Employee Surveys and Sensing.* Edited by: William H. Macey and Alexis A. Fink, Oxford University Press (2020). © Society for Industrial and Organizational Psychology. DOI: 10.1093/oso/9780190939717.003.0013

Text Analytics Evolution in I-O Psychology

Open-ended response analysis dates back to the earliest days of psychology. Known as *content analysis*, it involves breaking down text into smaller units to form logical analytical clusters, or themes, which can subsequently be used to code more similar textual data (inductively or deductively). An early example of this approach is when trained raters read and tagged transcripts in response to drawings to infer McClelland's theories of power, achievement, and affiliation and other subsequent theories.

More free-form content analysis techniques emerged in the 1960s via the grounded theory approach (Glaser & Strauss, 1967) that developed within sociology. The approach focuses on theory development using text analysis and coding at three levels—open, axial, and selective. Open coding requires line-by-line reading to elicit subthemes that integrate into themes at the axial level, leading to story/theory emergence through selective coding. Overall, traditional text analytic techniques were primarily categorized as thematic/content, network, or semantic (Roberts, 1997) but are manual, demanding effort and time.

The first computer-assisted content analysis program, the General Inquirer (Stone, Bales, Namenwirth, & Ogilvie, 1962), was created using a mainframe computer and an algorithm to adapt McClelland's dimensions to any open-ended text. The next milestone was the Linguistic Inquiry and Word Count program (LIWC) (Pennebaker & Francis, 1996). The program has two key components—a dictionary consisting of words in defined domains and a processor that runs text files through the dictionary to output percentage belongingness to categories. "For example, if LIWC analyzed a single speech that was 2,000 words and compared them to the built-in LIWC 2015 dictionary, it might find that there were 150 pronouns and 84 positive emotion words used. It would convert these numbers to percentages, 7.5% pronouns and 4.2% positive emotion words" (Pennebaker, Boyd, Jordan, & Blackburn, 2015). The dictionary has evolved from two categories in the first version to 80 in the 2015 version and has categories for stylistic words such as pronouns, verbs, and psychological states and traits.

Simultaneously, simpler computer-assisted programs emerged, called text mapping or cognitive mapping (Carley, 1993). These programs enhanced coding reliability, but words were stripped out of context, requiring human interpretation. Concept mapping addressed some of those limitations by sorting text based on conceptual similarity to create matrices and visualizing the clusters into coordinates to create maps (Jackson & Trochim, 2002). Distance between ideas is used to cluster those that are more proximally located. This concept is now actively used in advanced text analytics algorithms to identify distance between vectors in text and documents. In the 2010s, machines and algorithms have become progressively more effective at understanding and predicting linguistics as they continue to train on wider language rules and structures.

Machine Learning–Based Approaches: Natural Language Processing

Artificial intelligence (AI) is the field of building smart machines to accomplish tasks that generally require human intelligence. Machine learning (ML), a subset of AI, involves shallow supervised or unsupervised architectures to teach a computer to carry out tasks with the goal of making accurate predictions. Natural language processing (NLP) and ML are both subsets of AI (Figure 13.1). NLP has emerged from AI, showing promise for analyzing large unstructured data sets meaningfully.

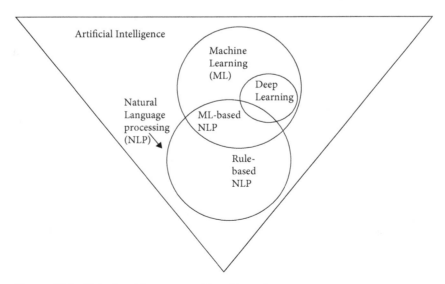

Figure 13.1. Relationships among AI and its subsets.

The goal of NLP is to decode human written language. It incorporates algorithms that apply certain rules of language for analysis. These complex algorithms are further trained on more data sets to create additional rules to parse language, with the objective of accurately identifying nuances in text that go beyond counting word frequencies or generating word clouds. NLP probabilistic models generate quantitative data from qualitative data. NLP has evolved from an empiricist approach in the 1950s to current unsupervised learning models that adapt to complex settings (Bitter, Elizondo, & Yang, 2010). One part of this evolution is the move from broader to fine-grained analysis methods such as subdocument-level emotion analysis and latent Dirichlet allocation (LDA) (Blei, Ng, & Jordan, 2003) as well as moving from classification at the document level to the subdocument level.

Such advances have resulted in various-use cases of analyzing open-ended data and providing real-time insights. The techniques discussed in this chapter are applicable not just for survey open-ended responses but also for other text data such as performance reviews or employee reviews on Glassdoor.

Preprocessing Techniques for ML-Based Text Analytics

Just like every other data set, a text-based data set has to be cleaned and prepared for analysis. The goal is to convert the text stream to a sequence of lexical items for meaningful processing. Some common preprocessing techniques (Kumar & Paul, 2016) include the following:

Tokenization. Tokenization is the process of segmenting text into words, phrases, symbols, punctuations, etc., called *tokens*, which become input for further processing. In the document, "Mr. Abuela hasn't given this company the right direction," the tokenization output will separate "has" and "n't" or "not" as two separate tokens. Similarly, we can distinguish end-of-sentence periods from those that are used for abbreviations. Tokenization is language-specific and in some languages can include detection of word boundaries (e.g., Asian and German languages where words are conjugated).

White space elimination and lowercase conversion. Two additional common preprocessing steps are white space removal and the conversion to lowercase. There are readily available commands that can do these jobs in software tools discussed later in the chapter. R is among the most popular software tools. Following are sample R commands:

```
> df <- tm_map(df, stripWhitespace)
> df <- tm_map(df, content_transformer(tolower))
```

Stop word removal. This removes common words that have little information value or low entropy. Most programming toolkits have pre-existing stop word lists, or a stop word list can be first created:

```
R> mystopwords <- c("and", "in", "is", "it", "not", "the", "to")
```

Stemming and lemmatization. Stemming is the process of removing and replacing word suffixes to arrive at a common word root. Lemmas differ from stems in that a *lemma* is a canonical form of the word, while a stem may not be a real word. For example, from *produced,* the lemma is *produce,* but the stem is *produc-.* This is because there are words such as *production.*

Other text normalization processes include removing numbers, misspellings, and HTML tags. These normalization steps, though time-consuming, are critical to create a cleaner data set which impacts outcome quality.

NLP Techniques

NLP techniques use unique terminology (Table 13.1) and can be ML-based or non-ML-based. Non-ML-based methods are rule-based, requiring humans to provide the rules, whereas in ML-based methods, the computer derives the rules from the data. The method choice and its effectiveness, rule-based or ML-based or a hybrid approach, are dependent on the research question at hand. Rule-based approaches, such as part-of-speech tagging or named entity recognition, have already been well documented (Kumar & Paul, 2016). In this chapter, we focus on relevant ML-based techniques for analyzing survey data.

ML-based NLP techniques can be classified into supervised and unsupervised models. The most straightforward method to differentiate between them is to ask, "Is there a dependent variable?"

Table 13.1 Basic ML-Based Text Analytics Concepts

Concept	Definition
Corpus	Collection of related documents or texts. In a survey context, all open-ended responses to a question asked in an employee engagement survey, "Share thoughts about your experience."
Document	A single unit from a corpus. One employee's response to a survey question.
Term	A word or word group that is of interest. In "My manager makes my work rewarding," *rewarding* is a term that is used to classify other documents.
Entity	A real-world distinct item referenced in a known object (location, product, organization, e-mail, etc.). In "I live in California," *California* is an entity, more so, a named entity, since it is known.
Vector	The numerical representation of a term/document. Each term/document exists in a vector space, making it unique.
Document-term matrix	To identify relatedness between documents, in the vector space, the corpus is expressed as a document-term matrix. The matrix rows represent each document, columns represent terms, and each cell is the term frequency count in the document. Document similarity can be inferred by calculating distance between two document points using Euclidean distance.
n-gram	Word sequence used to capture language structure for predicting the probability of the next word sequence. Combinations of adjacent words of n length. A one-word n-gram is called a *unigram*, two words are called *bigrams*, three words are *trigrams*, and so on. In "I am proud to work here," the bigrams are "I am," "am proud," "proud to," "to work," and "work here." n-grams should be optimized as longer ones can make it challenging to predict the likelihood of subsequent terms and smaller ones can miss nuance.

All NLP supervised models have known dependent variables, which the researcher tries to predict using an input text document. Common statistical methods like regression and random forest modeling are supervised models. In NLP, researchers using supervised models are likely trying to assign a "label" to an unlabeled term or document which can apply to both preprocessing and algorithmic steps. Sentiment analysis is an example of supervised machine learning (see below, "Sentiment Analysis").

Unsupervised models are generally exploratory in nature and do not make use of a dependent variable a priori. In traditional statistical analysis, both exploratory factor analysis and cluster analysis are unsupervised models. These techniques are a form of "dustbowl empiricism"; no theory drives analyses, and the data themselves determine outcomes. A frequently used unsupervised NLP model in employee surveys is topic modeling (see below, "Topic Modeling").

Although this is a common way of classifying ML-based techniques in general, for text data the techniques blur the lines between the two methods. We next discuss commonly used techniques categorized by functionality or outcomes.

Word Relatedness

These techniques attempt to identify representative terms within documents or analyze relationships between terms in the text.

Tf-idf

A researcher may desire to understand which terms in a corpus are most representative of a document or topic. An initial step to accomplish this is to calculate the term frequency, or *tf*. Although this metric will result in a term list ordered by prevalence within a document, very common, uninformative words will generally emerge as the most frequently used terms, even after stop word removal. In the employee survey context, for example, *improve* may appear often but contain little information about the topic or document content, other than potentially being an indicator of a prescriptive comment.

The inverse document frequency, or *idf*, is a measure of the number of documents which contain a given term. A term which appears in every document does not distinguish any unique features of the document; therefore, rather than calculating the document frequency of a given term, the inverse document frequency provides an indication of which terms are uniquely mentioned in a given document. However, solely relying on this metric would identify very rare terms as important, which is rarely the case. Rare terms, especially as the corpus size increases, are generally proper nouns or misspellings (which can be addressed in preprocessing) and are not very informative about a given topic.

The product of these two metrics, *tf-idf*, is a measure of the discriminating power of a given term. A term which appears often in few documents would result in a large *tf-idf* and likely indicates a term which is representative of a given topic. Terms which occur in both a few documents and on few occasions in those documents have a relatively low *tf-idf* score, and terms which appear in most documents also have a very low *tf-idf* score.

Researchers can retrieve terms which have the largest *tf-idf* to best understand the topic which a given document represents.

Principal Components Analysis and Latent Semantic Analysis

Two similar techniques are used to reduce the sparsity of a document-term matrix and cluster together similar terms: principal components analysis (PCA) and latent semantic analysis (LSA). Both techniques use a mathematical process called *singular value decomposition* to reduce the feature space of a term-document matrix (or covariance matrix) into a more manageable and likely more informative structure. PCA is employed on the covariance matrix, and LSA is employed on the term-document matrix.

A document-term matrix consists of columns of 0s and 1s, in which documents containing a given word contain a 1 and those without have a 0. In the context of employee surveys, preprocessed text data are high-dimensional and sparse; the columns will largely consist of 0s, as for any one document (each response) the likelihood of using any term is very low. This sparseness is a relatively accurate representation of the data, but it requires large storage space as it treats similar words as completely different concepts (e.g., *good* is treated as different from *great*) and is unable to distinguish between homonyms (e.g., *wind*).

LSA will likely be of most use to employee survey researchers. LSA is applied directly to the term-document matrix (which can consist of *tf-idf* weights) and reduces sparsity. What results is a low-dimensional matrix which clusters together terms of similar context. Researchers can now use this new clustered data set to better understand the corpus topics or continue to use this new structure to further process the data.

Word2vec

Whereas the aforementioned techniques highlight the relationship between terms, word2vec is a technique that sheds light on linguistic context. It groups vectors of similar words together in vector space and over large amounts of data and iterations and allows the researcher to predict a word's meaning and its association with other words. The two common models used are as follows:

(1) Cluster bag of words, where surrounding similar words and vectors are used to predict a target word
(2) Skip-gram, where a word is used to predict the surrounding words/context

Text Classification Algorithms

These techniques move beyond identifying representative terms or word associations to analyzing the themes, topics, or sentiment emerging from text data. Since these are classification methods, they are best applied at the document level rather than the sentence level.

Sentiment Analysis

Sentiment analysis (or opinion mining) is a technique which classifies terms, sentences, and documents into their emotional valence (Pang & Lee, 2008). Basic sentiment analysis is rule-based and generally groups words into one of three categorizations: *positive, neutral,* or *negative.* But more complex ML-based emotion models have emerged. Furthermore, sentiment analysis is able to take various parts of speech, such as negators, into account to modify the valence of a given term. For example, *love* has a positive valence; however, the n-gram *I don't love* is classified as having a negative valence.

Sentiment analysis uses glossaries of words and phrases, called *lexicons,* that have already been classified into sentiment or subjectivity (Ignatow & Mihalcea, 2017). There are numerous lexicons available in the public domain, including AFINN (Nielsen, 2011), which classifies words from −5 (very negative) to +5 (very positive). The tidytext package in R is a commonly used package to conduct sentiment analysis, which contains AFINN as well as other lexicons.

Sentiment analysis can be a quick, relatively simple, and accurate approach to generate insights from open-ended survey comment data, particularly when stemming from a question which has a neutral tone. Negatively loaded survey questions (e.g., "What do you like the least about working at Company X?") will result in negative responses by default, and sentiment analysis will be of less value. A common question on many employee engagement surveys asks employees to "Tell us what is on your mind" as an effort to allow the employee to communicate openly but without leading the employee into positive or negative sentiment.

Sentiment analysis allows the researcher to understand overall (or group-level) employee sentiment and can be useful for trending over time. It is important to note that sentiment analysis can be nearly as accurate as human-judged sentiment as automated sentiment analysis accuracy can range from 67% to 75% (Abbasi, Hassan, & Dhar, 2014), whereas the interrater agreement of human-judged sentiment was identified as 82% in one study

(Wilson, Wiebe, & Hoffman, 2005). Organizations typically have their own unique dialects and jargon terms; it is important to adjust the lexicon used in sentiment analysis for individual organizations. For example, the term *kill* has a negative valence in most standard lexicons. However, a comment of "My manager is killing it these days" is clearly intending to convey positivity.

Sentiment analysis can also validate responses to rating items by comparing them to sentiment derived from a similarly worded open-ended follow-up question (e.g., can employees accurately provide a single rating which aligns with sentiment from open-ended text?) or to understand areas that require more attention not covered by the rating items. It can also be used to validate with other internal social networking data.

Topic Modeling

Topic modeling refers to a class of unsupervised modeling techniques designed to determine the underlying themes (or *topics*) in a text collection by examining the co-occurrence of terms within documents. Topic modeling is similar to cluster analysis, but unlike cluster analysis, topic models group single passages of text into multiple topics. This is particularly useful in a survey setting as employees generally touch on multiple topics concurrently, and the topics themselves are often interrelated. We discuss two common forms of topic modeling in this section: LDA and correlated topic models (CTMs).

Latent Dirichlet Allocation

LDA is the most widely used method of topic modeling (Banks, Woznyj, Wesslen, & Ross, 2018). LDA has been used to identify topics in text across diverse fields, from detecting insurance fraud (Wang & Xu, 2018) to predicting personality from social network data (Liu, Wang, & Jiang, 2016). In LDA, each document is assumed to be a mixture of discrete topics, and each topic has a unique probability distribution, which is defined by the likelihood of each term appearing in it. These term-level probabilities are then aggregated, and a probability is assigned to each document for each topic. Topics can then also be defined by the most common words that are present within them. LDA is an unsupervised method, so the number of topics will need to be selected a priori (but can be done iteratively), and the generated topics will need to be labeled by the researcher. This is accomplished by (1) reading several documents that are representative of a topic or (2) reading a list of representative terms for each topic.

Table 13.2 Bag-of-Words Model

The bag-of-words model parses documents into individual terms and ignores order, grammar, and semantics. Note how *like* has a different meaning in the documents but is treated similarly by the algorithm.

1   "I like my manager."
2   "My manager is like my friend."

Document	Term					
	I	like	my	manager	is	friend
1	1	1	1	1	0	0
2	0	1	2	1	1	1

LDA uses a "bag-of-words" approach to modeling the documents in question, ignoring the order and structure of the document. Each word is either present or not in the document, and the only other information captured is the frequency of the word in the document (see Table 13.2). This approach ignores key document features like word order and grammar, but this concise representation both expedites the analysis and can be used in other types of analysis, like regression. Documents can be parsed into n-grams to make use of LDA.

Typically, parsing documents into unigrams or bigrams is sufficient to conduct LDA, but there can be situations where trigrams or more are appropriate. The text preprocessing steps (such as stop word removal) are notably important in LDA as these common words are generally not indicative of any specific topic. That being said, if the researcher has any a priori assumption about a certain common stop word, it is important to keep said word in the corpus. For example, words like *put* and *call* are typical stop words, but these words are indicative of a stock trading topic.

Correlated Topic Model

A CTM is an extension of LDA which allows for estimates of correlations between the generated topics (Blei & Lafferty, 2007). One of the main drawbacks of LDA is the assumption that the final topics are not interrelated. In the employee survey space, employees will generally touch on several themes in the same open-ended response. Thus, in many situations, conducting a CTM may often result in the best underlying data representation and will allow for a hierarchical representation of the topics. Additionally, CTM does not ignore word order.

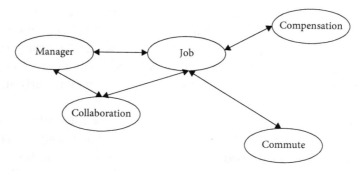

Figure 13.2. A sample CTM map. Circles indicate topics, and arrows indicate topics that co-occur in the same comment.

One useful output of a CTM is a "map" of topics. This map can visually display the interrelationships between topics, helping the end user quickly digest the common patterns between the topics (Figure 13.2).

Topic modeling can be applied to employee surveys to help classify open-ended comments. It supplements (or replaces) manual thematic analysis when enough data are present and saves time while maintaining the richness of employees' full thoughts. In addition to understanding basic topics, topic modeling can help identify comments that require further investigation because of potential harassment or company policy violations.

Conveniently, after conducting preprocessing, the input document-term matrix is the same regardless of whether the method of interest is LDA or CTM. Although other forms of topic modeling exist and continue to be developed (e.g., structural topic models), LDA and CTM cover a wide range of employee survey applications.

Text Data Visualization

Graphical representation of the output allows for meaningful interpretation. Examples of text data visualization techniques include word clouds, word trees, and matrices and maps.

Word clouds reflect word occurrences to diagrammatically represent text spatially. Advancements in this area include the Word Cloud Explorer (Heimerl, Lohmann, Lange, & Ertl, 2014), which provides interactive features, or ConcentriCloud, that compare word clouds across multiple text documents (Lohmann, Heimerl, Bopp, Burch, & Ertl, 2015). Word maps visualize word usage in a sentence or phrase and display connections between a word and other words in the corpus using a branching system (Wattenberg & Viégas, 2008). Matrices and maps, such as mind maps or cluster maps, can be used for visualizing themes or patterns arising from text analysis.

A combination of visualization techniques can be innovatively used to represent the outcomes of ML-based approaches of text analytics. For example, word trees can be used to categorize themes, and visual cluster maps can be used for CTMs to display the correlation between generated topics/themes. Interactive features can be added for visual representations (e.g., context and sentiment). Please refer to Chapter 19 on data visualization for more insights.

Internal Capability versus External Vendors

A common question facing practitioners desiring strong text analytics is whether to hire external vendors versus building internal capability. Decision points include cost, time, flexibility/customization of models, resources, and organizational size, with pros and cons to both approaches.

Outsourcing/buying vendor services makes the process easy with low ramp-up time because they already have existing algorithms and lexicons. Some considerations when hiring an external vendor are as follows:

(1) How accurate are their tagging/categorization models (accuracy percentage)?
(2) Has accuracy been improving over time?
(3) Do they conduct local validation? Training on a data set which may not generalize to internal data sets can create biases. It is highly recommended to conduct one internally where manually assigned themes to survey comments are cross-checked with algorithm-suggested themes.
(4) What data set are their models built on? If the intended use is employee survey comments, were the models built on similar employee survey documents versus customer surveys?
(5) Will they be able to eventually build models customized to your internal datasets?

High-quality vendor models are trained on multiple data sets across companies, exposing the algorithm to a wider language base, for example, using text analytics for gender/ethnicity bias detection in survey comments or performance reviews. Models trained over a variety of corpora have a larger universe of possible biased words, leading to better bias detection versus being limited to the language of one organization. However, this approach limits customization of models to an organization's linguistics. Vendors typically serve many customers, potentially making it difficult to build customized models for specific needs.

Conversely, building internal capability can lead to better control over the algorithms and interpretation of the findings. Customized models can be built for different information sources including performance reviews and interview feedback, giving the ability to tweak the models when needed. There is also more control over the insights from these analyses, leading to more innovative visualizations and integration into already existing internal tools. The consideration points for internal capability are resources, time, and organizational/leadership support to build a strong analytics practice. NLP data scientists and data visualization experts need to be hired, the number of whom depends on the size and resources of the organization. Time is also needed to develop, train, and validate the algorithms. In return for these initial investments, the insights gained are much more accurate and relevant within the organization.

Resources

R and Python are common platforms used to build an internal NLP practice. There are various packages available in R for NLP (Kumar & Paul, 2016):

- tm—A widely used package for powerful text-processing, including importing the corpus, metadata management, creating term-document matrices, stop-word removal, stemming, etc.
- RcmdrPlugin.temis—This package is useful for importing and cleaning corpora, terms and document counts, co-occurrences, etc.
- Rweka—Serves as an interface to Weka, an open source software for machine learning. Specifically, for NLP, this can process tokenization and stemming tasks, especially effectively for contiguous alphabetics, string-split to n-grams, etc.

- koRpus—Package with functions for automatic language detection, lexical variability, hyphenation, readability, frequency analyses, and tf-idf.

Python has extensive libraries for conducting NLP. Some of the commonly used ones are:

- Natural Language Toolkit—One of the main tools; it is used for classification, tokenization, tagging, parsing, and semantic reasoning. The library is versatile but can have a steep learning curve.
- Stanford CoreNLP Python—Stanford's CoreNLP program that is written in Java; a ready-to-use toolkit that provides robust techniques for tagging, parsing, entity recognition, pattern learning.
- spaCY—Has standard functionalities and is extremely fast
- TextBlob—provides a simple API for NLP tasks such as part-of-speech tagging, noun phrase extraction, sentiment analysis, classification, translation, etc.
- Polyglot- Primarily for multilingual usage and has features such as language detection and transliteration.

Implications and the Future

Undoubtedly, machine-based NLP has greatly advanced the survey world. However, it is imperative to not blindly over-rely on machine models without understanding specifics. Development of these models require combining linguistic and domain knowledge along with statistical processing to decode complexities of human language. Philosophically, one of the biggest advantages of qualitative research over quantitative research was theory emergence. A question to ponder is whether we are losing that aspect with ML-based techniques. Techniques such as hierarchical LDA need to be further explored to ensure we produce valuable guiding theories that advance I-O psychology.

NLP can also be used for analysis and bias detection in other internally generated open-ended data such as performance reviews, interview feedback, internal blogs or intranet comments, and so on. The future is quite bright and exciting particularly with the emergence of the field of deep learning. Deep learning is a subset of ML that uses supervised and/or unsupervised strategies for automatically learning hierarchical representations to solve more complex real-world problems besides just prediction. Recognizing speech, patterns, pictures, faces, or handwritten numbers are some of those problems, attempting to replicate how human brains process neural signals. Whereas ML generally involves one to two levels of learning, deep learning learns at multiple nodes where each is an output of the previous node and input for the subsequent one. A multi-level architectural learning model is created by fine tuning at every hidden layer and learning automatically from high-volume datasets without requiring manual feature extraction.

Combining deep learning techniques with natural language processing can lead to automated analyses of speech, images, faces, and survey responses instead of typed or written format. Another potential application could be simultaneous automated text analysis as employees type their responses. Language or dialect recognition can benefit global companies, as data can be collected in local dialects without translation errors. With advances in the field of deep learning integrating with NLP, within the bounds of ethics and privacy, we anticipate new avenues of text analytics unimagined before.

References

Abbasi, A., Hassan, A., & Dhar, M. (2014, May). *Benchmarking Twitter sentiment analysis tools*. Presented at the 9th Language Resources Evaluation Conference, Reykjavik, Iceland.

Afflerbach, S., Chatham, C. L., Davis, B. J., Grimme, T. M., Campana, K. L., & Buchanan, J. A. (2014). Reaching across the aisle: The benefits of interdisciplinary work in graduate school. *Industrial–Organizational Psychologist, 52*, 136–142.

Altintzoglou, T., Sone, I., Voldnes, G., Nøstvold, B., & Sogn-Grundvåg, G. (2018). Hybrid surveys: A method for the effective use of open-ended questions in quantitative food choice surveys. *Journal of International Food & Agribusiness Marketing, 30*(1), 49–60.

Banks, G. C., Woznyj, H. M., Wesslen, R. S., & Ross, R. L. (2018). A review of best practice recommendations for text analysis in R (and a user-friendly app). *Journal of Business and Psychology, 33*(4), 445–459. Retrieved from https://doi.org/10.1007/s10869-017-9528-3

Bitter, C., Elizondo, D. A., & Yang, Y. (2010). Natural language processing: A prolog perspective. *Artificial Intelligence Review, 33*, 151–173.

Blei, D. M., & Lafferty, J. D. (2007). A correlated topic model of *Science*. *Annals of Applied Statistics, 1*, 17–35.

Blei, D. M., Ng, A. Y., & Jordan, M. I. (2003). Latent Dirichlet allocation. *Journal of Machine Learning Research, 3*, 993–1022.

Carley, K. (1993). Coding choices for textual analysis: A comparison of content analysis and map analysis. *Sociological Methodology, 23*, 75–126.

Glaser, B. G., & Strauss, A. L. (1967). *The discovery of grounded theory: Strategies for qualitative research*. Chicago, IL: Aldine.

Heimerl, F., Lohmann, S., Lange, S., & Ertl, T. (2014, January). *Word cloud explorer: Text analytics based on word clouds*. Presented at the 47th Hawaii International Conference on System Science, Waikoloa, HI. Retrieved from https://ieeexplore.ieee.org/stamp/stamp.jsp?arnumber=6758829

Ignatow, G., & Mihalcea, R. (2017). *Text mining: A guidebook for the social sciences*. Los Angeles, CA: SAGE Publications.

Jackson, K. M., & Trochim, W. M. K. (2002). Concept mapping as an alternative approach for the analysis of open-ended survey responses. *Organizational Research Methods*, *5*(4), 307–336.

Kumar, A., & Paul, A. (2016). *Mastering text mining with R*. Birmingham, England: Packt Publishing.

Liu, Y., Wang, J., & Jiang, Y. (2016). PT-LDA: A latent variable model to predict personality traits of social network users. *Neurocomputing*, *210*, 155–163.

Lohmann, S., Heimerl, F., Bopp, F., Burch, M., & Ertl, T. (2015, July). *ConcentriCloud: Word cloud visualization for multiple text documents*. Presented at the 19th International Conference on Information Visualisation, IEEE, Barcelona, Spain.

Looker, E. D., Denton, M. A., & Davis, C. K. (1989). Bridging the gap: Incorporating qualitative data into quantitative analyses. *Social Science Research*, *18*(4), 313–330.

Nielsen, F. A. (2011). A new ANEW: Evaluation of a word list for sentiment analysis in microblogs. Proceedings of the ESWC2011 Workshop on "Making Sense of Microposts": Big things come in small packages. *CEUR Workshop Proceedings*, *718*, 93–98.

Pang, B., & Lee, L. (2008). Opinion mining and sentiment analysis. *Foundations and Trends in Information Retrieval*, *2*, 1–135.

Payne, S. L. (1965). Are open-ended questions worth the effort? *Journal of Marketing Research*, *2*(4), 417–419.

Pennebaker, J. W., Boyd, R. I., Jordan, K., & Blackburn, K. (2015). *The development and psychometric properties of LIWC2015*. Austin, TX: University of Texas at Austin.

Pennebaker, J. W., Booth, R. J., Boyd, R. L., & Francis, M. E. (2015). *The development and psychometric properties of LIWC2015* [Computer Software]. Austin, TX: Pennebaker Conglomerates. https://repositories.lib.utexas.edu/bitstream/handle/2152/31333/LIWC2015_LanguageManual.pdf

Pennebaker, J. W., & Francis, M. E. (1996). Cognitive, emotional, and language processes in disclosure. *Cognition and Emotion*, *10*, 601–626.

Roberts, C. W. (Ed.). (1997). *Text analysis for the social sciences: Methods for drawing statistical inferences from texts and transcripts*. Mahwah, NJ: Lawrence Erlbaum Associates.

Stone, P. J., Bales, R. F., Namenwirth, J. Z., & Ogilvie, D. M. (1962). The General Inquirer: A computer system for content analysis and retrieval based on the sentence as a unit of information. *Behavioral Science*, *7*, 484–494.

Wang, Y., & Xu, W. (2018). Leveraging deep learning with LDA-based text analytics to detect automobile insurance fraud. *Decision Support Systems*, *105*, 87–95.

Wattenberg, M., & Viégas, F. B. (2008). The word tree, and interactive visual concordance. *Visualization and Computer Graphics*, *14*(6), 1221–1228.

Wilson, T., Wiebe, J., & Hoffman, P. (2005, October). *Recognizing contextual polarity in phrase-level sentiment analysis*. Proceedings of the Conference on Human Language Technology and Empirical Methods in Natural Language Processing, Vancouver, BC, Canada, pp. 347–354.

14

Is the Engagement Survey the Only Way?

Alternative Sources for Employee Sensing

Madhura Chakrabarti and Elizabeth A. McCune

Since the early 1990s employee sensing has undergone a drastic journey. The 1990s saw a slow and steady adoption of employee satisfaction surveys among large organizations, followed by their digitization in the early 2000s, when paper-and-pencil surveys were replaced with online ones. In 2008, a seminal article on employee engagement (Macey & Schneider, 2008), its measurement, and its relationship with business outcomes played a critical role in changing the conversation. Organizations started focusing more on measuring engagement than satisfaction or morale as they realized that employee engagement is multifaceted and goes much beyond understanding if "I am satisfied with my job." Beginning around 2010, the business and Human Resources (HR) environment began to call for the consumerization or the "appification" of HR characterized by, among other things, the ability to give instant feedback, receive notifications, and iterate constantly (Bersin, 2015). This fundamental shift is resulting in the generation of data from a multitude of sources, in greater magnitude, and in much greater frequency than before. It has led to a world of employee data where in many cases an online survey capturing employee engagement once a year is deemed insufficient.

In this chapter, we will discuss a variety of employee sensing[1] mechanisms beyond the engagement survey; most of which focus on data sources relevant to employee sensing (e.g., data from internal communications and collaboration platforms, health and well-being data) and a few others that touch upon techniques for data analytics (e.g., organizational network analysis). For clarity, we have grouped the data sources into a simple 2×2 framework (see Figure 14.1) leveraging two dimensions: those requiring passive versus active data-collection strategies and those leveraging data sources internal versus external to the organization.

Madhura Chakrabarti and Elizabeth A. McCune, *Is the Engagement Survey the Only Way?* In: *Employee Surveys and Sensing.* Edited by: William H. Macey and Alexis A. Fink, Oxford University Press (2020). © Society for Industrial and Organizational Psychology.
DOI: 10.1093/oso/9780190939717.003.0014

	Passive	Active
Internal	Network data Internal communication portals Biometrics and sociometrics HR and IT service requests Performance management data	Engagement surveys Onboarding surveys Exit surveys Structured qualitative input Health and well-being data
External	Work history, skills, and capabilities Public, large-scale industry and census databases	Employee reviews on external sites

Figure 14.1. A broad classification of various employee sensing mechanisms.

Passive data sources are those that are collected as part of the employee's regular workflow, day-to-day interactions with colleagues, or other compliance-oriented activities. *Active* sources are those for which the data are being collected with the explicit purpose of seeking reactions, input, and/or feedback from employees. *Internal* data sources are those that exist within and are owned by the employee and/or the organization and/or a third party appointed by the organization. *External* data sources are those that exist outside the organization and for which the organization does not have ownership. In the following sections, different data sources and techniques for employee sensing are described in detail, followed by examples, advantages, and considerations, where appropriate.

Internal-Passive Sources

Network Data

The networked organization is becoming the norm for how work gets done today. Eighty-eight percent of global organizations report that they are reorganizing to flatter, more networked team structures (Agarwal, Bersin, Gaurav, Schwartz, & Volini, 2018). Metadata collected from e-mail exchanges[2] and team collaborations platforms like Microsoft Teams and Slack can be powerful data sources to understand if certain employee interaction patterns are predictive of higher retention, better productivity, etc. within an organization. Some form of organizational network analysis (ONA) (Cross, Gray, Gerbasi, & Assimakopoulos, 2012) is often leveraged to analyze these passive data sources to understand individual employee networks, how teams work with one another, and whether some connections across individuals or teams are more important than others (Cross & Prusak, 2002).

Use case: Ramco Systems, an enterprise software provider offering solutions in aviation, human capital management, and more, underwent a significant business transformation. Company leaders believed that in addition to changing its offerings to clients, long-term success depended on creating a culture of transparency and developing and maintaining strong communications networks externally and internally. Ramco implemented an ONA platform to promote a culture of collaboration. In one of the many use cases, the platform collected and analyzed data from Ramco's various communications systems and was able to use this information to onboard its newly hired sales employees faster. Specifically, ONA was used to identify the important relationships of previous and existing high performers, and that information was shared with newly hired employees to emulate. As a result, the onboarding time reduced by two thirds for the new employees (Chakrabarti, 2018).

Internal Communication Portals

Internal social media channels (e.g., Yammer, Chatter, Workplace) are also a potent and regular source of employee sentiment. Employees interact with each other, share knowledge, celebrate wins, and react to organizational announcements on these portals. Using text analytics (e.g., sentiment analysis, topic modeling) on these conversations, organizations can understand the topics being discussed and the sentiment toward those topics at any given point in time.

Use case: Microsoft has a robust employee listening system that includes an annual census, an always-on survey, an onboarding survey, and an exit survey. In addition to the insights gathered via these surveys, Microsoft's leadership wanted visibility to more spontaneous and unstructured dialogues that were happening across the company. The solution was a weekly summary of the topics being discussed by employees in a small number of active, company-wide Yammer groups. The weekly summary provides visibility into the topics with the highest levels of engagement (defined by clicks, likes, comments, and reshares), the overall sentiment associated with the topic (positive, mixed, negative), and a short description of the topics. These summaries are leveraged by leaders, communications teams, and HR teams across Microsoft for quick, timely insights into employee sentiment.

Advantages and Considerations for the Use of Network Data Sources and Internal Communication Portals

Focus on Actual Behaviors

Day-to-day employee behaviors (e.g., how often they connect with others) can be strong indicators of important outcomes (e.g., likelihood to stay with the organization) above and beyond the attitudinal measures often collected through engagement surveys (Carboni, Cross, Page, & Parker, 2019). For example, if an individual contributor emerges as the center of a network for solving technical challenges, it can be a powerful signal of a high-performing employee.

Constant Stream of Data

Unlike annual engagement surveys or quarterly pulses that take place at certain time points, network and communication data generate a steady stream of information throughout the year. It can be, under some circumstances, a more accurate reflection of how employees collaborate, communicate, and engage with each other.

Outcomes Beyond Employee Engagement

By looking at employee interaction patterns via communication and collaboration data, organizations can directly predict outcomes like innovation (Arena, Cross, Sims, & Uhl-Bien, 2017), sales effectiveness (Chakrabarti, 2018), and functional clarity (McDowell, Horn, & Witkowski, 2016)—useful outcomes that go beyond just understanding levels of employee engagement.

Data Privacy

Data privacy concerns apply to all data sources discussed in this chapter, though e-mail data are often considered particularly sensitive. Any organization that seeks to leverage any form of e-mail data for analysis should engage with the appropriate internal privacy, legal, and HR partners and keep the employee perspective and expectations about how their data might be used at the forefront of decision-making. In order to avoid redundancy within this chapter and across this book (see Chapter 24), data privacy will not be listed again; but please do note that data privacy considerations apply to every data source described.

Technology Investments

Passive ONA and sentiment analyses on communications and collaboration data require advanced capabilities and technology investments. Organizations embarking on the employee sensing journey may not be able to afford these investments, though small pilots or project-based engagements with vendors can be a useful starting point.

Potential Bias in Content

Research on online reviews indicates that such reviews may represent the extremely positive and extremely negative experiences rather than the typical experience (Klein, Marinescu, Chamberlain, & Smart, 2018). In the case of internal communication platforms, similar patterns of bias could emerge along with a unique set of challenges. For example, posts may only highlight specific negative experiences that are perceived as being more acceptable to complain about publicly (e.g., inadequate parking, office, or cubicle arrangements). The same phenomena regarding the perceived safety in speaking up could also cause the data to appear overly celebratory or positive.

Biometrics

The use of radio frequency identification (RFID) technology, including biometrics and similar tracking mechanisms, is expanding to employee sensing in the form of wearable sensors such as badges and wristbands that include a scannable chip and even subcutaneous chips. The tracking devices typically have sensors or microphones attached to them that help collect employee data like the employee's location, time spent at a single location, tone of voice, heart rate, bodily movements, etc. These devices have historically served compliance-oriented purposes such as time and attendance tracking for employees but are proving to be valuable sources of data to understand how work gets done ("There Will Be Little Privacy," 2018). Other outcomes for which biometric data may be helpful include more effective organizational design (e.g., regrouping and relocating employees based on frequent interactions among them), increased collaboration (e.g., receiving a nudge to have coffee with a remote colleague who happens to be in the building for a day), identifying unusual workplace behaviors that can be strong indicators of fraudulent activities (e.g., employees frequently visiting areas in the workplace that are uncommonly visited), and a more secured work environment (e.g., secure entry into buildings using retinal scans, preventing nonemployees from entering the work building).

Use case: There are several examples of organizations that have leveraged biometric and similar data to improve experiences and key outcomes for employees. For example, Bank of America studied interactions among employees using microchips and found that most productive workers are part of a close-knit group with whom they maintain strong relationships. In order to facilitate strong collaborative relationships among its employees, the bank introduced group breaks instead of individual breaks (Gotfryd & Tenin, 2014). As yet another example involving a key employee outcome, Gilbane Building Company reduced the time it takes for safety professionals to arrive at an accident site by 91% with the help of wearable sensors capable of detecting a fall that can put a worker's life in danger. Instead of relying on a co-worker to see and report the accident, workers were able to receive immediate help from the safety team thanks to the alert raised by the tracking device (Swedberg, 2018).

Advantages and Considerations in the Use of Biometric Data Sources

Ability to Course-Correct

Most of the tracking mechanisms used today are able to remind or nudge employees in real time. For example, a few hospitals in the United States use the RFID technology to track if nurses have washed their hands after certain patient activities. In cases where they forget, the technology sends a reminder. Unlike survey methodologies where the course correction may take months and sometimes even years, biometrics and related technologies can do so as events are happening.

Applicability to Blue-Collar Work

Many traditional sensing techniques rely on employees to complete online surveys, which, while a relatively simple task for the typical knowledge worker, can be inconvenient or not possible for a blue-collar employee.

Sensor data may be particularly valuable for roles where other approaches to employee sensing are impractical given the day-to-day tasks of the employee. The ambient nature of the data collection prevents disruption in daily routines while simultaneously providing valuable data across a range of employee activities.

Technology Precision

Precision of the activities being recorded by the sensors is a crucial factor underlying biometrics and related techniques. If the activity does not get recorded, the sensor may flag an employee as not having followed the right process. These challenges can be addressed over time as precision improves with more data.

Hawthorne Effect

When employees are aware that their physical movements, whom they talk to, and how they react are being recorded, they may behave differently, at least initially, which can then skew the results. However, over time this effect may fade, especially when coupled with appropriate communication and use of these data by the organization.

Service Request and Performance Management Data

Service Request Data

Analyzing the nature of HR or IT service requests can lead to valuable employee sensing insights. For example, an organization might have phenomenal engagement survey scores on its new rating-less performance management system, but if a high volume of HR service requests indicate a lack of knowledge around how and when managers should give feedback, it can point to the need for additional training and support around the new system.

Performance-Management Data

The performance-management system can also generate useful employee sensing data (e.g., peer-to-peer feedback, annual goals). Some companies are beginning to mine employee goals data using natural language processing to generate a match score among different pairs of employees. A high match score between two employees indicates that they have common goals and aspirations. If the two employees belong to two different parts of the organization, they are nudged to collaborate or, at the very least, meet one another.

Advantages and Considerations in the Use of Service Request and Performance Management Data

Leverage Existing Data
The single biggest advantage of using performance-management system data or HR ticket-management data is convenience as such data require no extra effort, budget, or time to collect.

Complementary (or Alternative) Viewpoints
In organizations where the annual engagement survey is considered the "single source of truth" for all things talent-related, data sources outside of the survey can often provide more nuanced and realistic insights. For example, if "tools and processes" score low every year in the engagement survey, HR or IT ticket data can help shed light on the specific challenges employees experience in that area.

Other Common Considerations

Unique Data Structures
Existing data sources can come in different formats, structured and unstructured, at different levels such as individual or team. As a result, it often requires advanced data-integration and analytics capabilities (e.g., natural language processing, merging separate sources of text data).

Data Access and Expertise
Accessing these data sources can be challenging because their ownership may reside within separate teams. Further, strong partnerships with the data owners to not only access the data but also understand the typical anomalies in the data (e.g., the frequency of e-mail exchanges during the summer months in Europe may not be representative of an average month, limiting the appropriateness of generalizing conclusions drawn from those 2 months of data) are critical before proceeding with any analyses.

Internal-Active Data Sources

The most commonly used employee sensing mechanism in the internal-active quadrant is the engagement survey or related surveys (e.g., exit survey, onboarding survey), yet because the goal of this chapter is to focus on alternative sources of employee sensing, surveys will not be discussed. See Chapter 5 for an overview on life-cycle surveys and Chapter 10 for surveys focused on employee preferences. Additionally, focus group–like methods (e.g., town halls) can be active interventions that provide deep insights from qualitative data. Please refer to Chapter 7 for a detailed discussion on similar types of employee sensing.

This section discusses sensing mechanisms designed to collect pure qualitative feedback from employees, in large volumes, separate from the traditional "comment questions" in an engagement survey.

Structured Qualitative Input

Based on the notion of collective intelligence or the "wisdom of the crowd" (Surowiecki, 2005) that says that the individual is never as smart as the crowd, crowdsourcing has most commonly been used for generating ideas and problem-solving on a specific topic. Organizations using this technique typically post a challenge on an internal crowdsourcing platform. It is kept open for several days, and employees are encouraged to post their solutions or ideas on the platform. Organizations often close the challenge by awarding the top ideas with special events like a lunch with the chief executive officer. In some cases, the ideas get converted to prototypes or pilots, though in other cases, they remain as ideas.

Use case: IBM used crowdsourcing methodology to rebuild its performance-management system in approximately 90 days. The company realized that the way employees work had changed, yet the performance-management system had not. In an effort to align the performance-management system with the way work is done, the company listened to its 380,000 employees through a crowdsourcing activity. The "challenge" posted by the chief HR officer received 75,000 views and 2,000 comments (Zillman, 2016). Using text analytics, the feedback was categorized into themes that were used to redesign a new way of assessing employee performance through an app-based system that allows employees to set shorter-term goals with more frequent feedback per quarter from managers.

Advantages and Considerations in the Use of Structured Qualitative Input

Employees at the Center
Crowdsourcing-type activities are changing the nature of employee sensing from employees as providers of feedback to employees as active participants, that is, those with a stake in the outcome. It helps in designing talent and other processes with the employees, not just for them.

High Level of Transparency and Visibility
Structured, qualitative feedback mechanisms allow for a certain level of transparency that is difficult to achieve elsewhere. Employees can see in real time what their peers and leaders think about a specific topic and do not have to wait for HR to present the results from a survey.

Risk of Delayed or No Concrete Outcomes
Crowdsourcing activities may lose momentum after the initial energy around collecting employee ideas, selecting the best ideas, analyzing themes, and identifying winners. Organizations may fail to sustain the momentum for subsequent activities by converting the best ideas into solutions and executing them.

Lack of Control
In many qualitative conversations, there is very little control over the nature of the conversation, and employees may suggest and build energy around ideas that the organization is not able to implement. In addition, concerns may be raised that warrant further investigation, and following up to address those concerns could be a challenge depending on the size of the organization and the level of engagement in the crowdsourcing activity.

Employee Health and Well-Being Data

Mental, physical, and financial health can have a strong bearing on how and whether employees show up at work (Quick & Tetrick, 2011). Thanks to a significant portion of employees feeling burnt out[3] and associated costs that can range from \$125 to \$190 billion a year (Garton, 2017), employee wellness conversations are becoming mainstream as part of employee engagement programs. Additionally, emerging technology solutions that help capture wellness data from employees are acting as catalysts to bring the topic to the forefront.

Health and wellness data can be powerful sources for employee sensing. Examples include, but are not limited to, self-reported nutrition, exercise, and sleep data; health data from wearable devices that include daily movement and exercise data; basic health measures from on-site health screenings such as blood pressure, weight, height, blood sugar, cholesterol, and basal metabolic rate; and health insurance and prescription cost data.

Advantages and Considerations in the Use of Employee Health and Well-Being Data

Takes into Account Employees' Multiple Needs

Mental and physical well-being are important precursors to employee engagement, and by capturing different indicators of well-being, organizations can help to support all aspects of employees' lives that impact their productivity at work.

High Sensitivity of Health Data

Employees may feel uncomfortable providing health and well-being data even under opt-in arrangements because of the highly sensitive nature of such data. A strong rationale behind why the data are being collected and how an employee may personally benefit from sharing them can help strengthen their value proposition. Also important to note is that health data are highly regulated and have specific privacy protections (e.g., Health Insurance Portability and Accountability Act).

External-Passive and External-Active Data Sources

External Employee Reviews, Skills and Capabilities, Job Portals, and Industry Databases

External Employee Reviews

As consumers, we have become used to giving real-time, always-on feedback to retailers and service providers with whom we engage. Similarly, rating our positive and negative experiences with our employers on public forums (e.g., Glassdoor.com, Indeed.com, Blind) is becoming common and can be a rich external source for employee sensing. In addition, a set of techniques, typically referred to as *webscraping*, can be applied to collect and mine publicly available unstructured data, thus enabling analysis of these data sources (Hernandez, Newman, & Jeon, 2015).

Employee Work History and Skills and Capabilities

A second data source is employee work history and skills and capabilities, available mostly through professional networking sites (e.g., LinkedIn). The data can be analyzed to learn about skills and capabilities available in a specific market and in some cases also predict future employee behaviors (e.g., likelihood to leave the organization). For example, some human capital-management firms have solutions that use employee data from professional networking sites along with internal data to predict important and nontraditional outcomes such as "risk of being approached" (versus a more traditional attrition risk analysis) in order to help prevent unexpected turnover. *Use case*: Doctors Without Borders (or Médecins Sans Frontières) has developed a career platform (http://career.msf.be/) that outlines the various job families in the organization along with typical career paths, required skills, and competencies, all of which are publicly available. Such nontraditional ways of employee sensing, when used in conjunction with employee survey results, can produce valuable insights around key drivers of engagement (e.g., perception of career growth).

Job Portals

Data from aggregated job portals could be another source for employee sensing and the market in which employees operate. By analyzing these data, organizations can get a sense of which types of positions and skills and capabilities are in high demand in the labor market at different locations, what kind of talent is hard to find, what positions are competitors hiring for the most, etc. These data can be used to help provide context on a wide range of employee perceptions, such as compensation equity and fairness perceptions, which may be lower for employees who are in high demand in the market.

Public, Large-Scale Industry, and Census Databases

As organizations think of using publicly available data, it is important to also think about public databases that can be used in tandem with internal and external employee data. For example, www.datausa.io is an open platform that provides public US government data in a visually organized fashion, categorized by critical issues in the United States in areas such as jobs, skills, and education across geographies and industries. Other open-access sources like 10k forms, US Bureau of Labor Statistics (www.bls.gov), patents (e.g., patents.google.com), and the O*Net (www. onetonline.org) can also be valuable sources when layered on top of internal employee data.

Use case: A large marketing services firm in the United States, uses its peers' 10k forms to calculate and compare revenue per employee against its own data. The organization also leverages data from US Bureau of Labor Statistics and combines them with salary and common job title data from sources like Glassdoor.com to calculate industry-specific human capital cost benchmarks that are meaningful to its business leaders.

Advantages and Considerations in the Use of External Employee Reviews, Skills and Capabilities, and Job Portal Data

Multidimensional Data Points
The multitude of data points derived from a single employee review for example helps develop multidimensional insights like average rating of a company combined with sentiment, which could also be parsed into views from present versus past employees.

Volume of Data
Depending on the question one is trying to solve, public data sources can provide massive volumes of data. For example, searching for employee feedback on top retail organizations can yield 20,000 positive and negative reviews alone.

Little Control over the Data
How frequently employees share their reviews, at what point, and the accuracy of the information provided are entirely determined by the employee and the platform that helps collect the data. Organizations have little control over the design of data collection. As a result, this can create limitations in the analyses like making valid comparisons (e.g., some organizations may

only have 30 reviews because of a lack of social media presence, whereas competitors may have 3,000).

Acceptable Use of Data

Acceptable use of publicly available employee data, especially where the true owner of the data (the individual) has intentionally made the information public, is a topic rife with discussion and debate.[4] As the Global Data Protection Regulations and other data regulations evolve, acceptable-use policies will gradually emerge. Partnering with the legal team within the organization is crucial prior to leveraging external sources for employee data.

Creating a Listening Architecture Leveraging Multiple Sensing Mechanisms

As evidenced by the examples in this chapter, using multiple sensing mechanisms to listen to employees is no longer a distant promise. Many organizations are doing so at different levels, whether by linking data from various stages of the employee life cycle (e.g., onboarding survey, engagement survey, exit survey) or across disparate data sources (e.g., badge scanning, e-mail metadata, and engagement surveys).

We recommend that organizations start with a listening architecture as an organizing principle as they try to make sense of exponentially increasing sources of employee information. In designing a listening architecture, organizations can begin by identifying existing employee sensing mechanisms used within the organization and then creating a prioritized list of other listening channels that they would like to include going forward.

Once the existing and desired listening mechanisms have been identified, take steps toward integrating the data generated from the existing listening channels into one single platform or data lake. Many such data (e.g., compensation, performance management, employee demographics) may already reside on a single platform like an HR information system, but others (e.g., talent-acquisition data, engagement data) may need to be pulled from a different platform. This step requires significant investments in terms of time and money, especially when leveraging a third-party solution for data integration. Alternatively, many organizations build their own integrated platform or use off-the-shelf ones. Having a single platform where all employee sensing data exist together may take time to build, but investing in a "single source of truth" is worth the effort. It is also important to note that data from some listening channels may never be integrated into the central platform, either because of privacy laws or because of its unstructured nature (e.g., anonymous employee reviews). Organizations should also work to build intelligence around each of the different sources by documenting how the data are being used, at what cadence they are collected and analyzed, who gets to see the results, etc. This process will help identify, for example, data sources that get tracked but remain underutilized (e.g., employee badge data).

Finally, tools and technology are foundational to all employee listening mechanisms. Once the data available across the listening architecture have been compiled, the tools used for accessing, analyzing, and visualizing the data should support the needs across the organization. In most cases, organizations will likely need multiple tools, or at least multiple versions of a tool, to support users ranging from front-line managers, HR teams, and data scientists to executives. Such tools leveraging employee listening data sources should also guide users to relevant insights and action.

Notes

1. The term *employee sensing* has been used throughout this chapter to refer to both active and passive ways of gathering employee information that can include, but are not limited to, demographics, working styles, work history, and interactions with colleagues. Other terms like *employee listening* have been used interchangeably in this chapter to not sound repetitive.
2. *E-mail metadata* refers to the transactional elements of e-mail exchanges (e.g., recipient and sender fields, time and date stamps for sent and received e-mails, whether attachments are included, nature of the communication—e-mail versus meeting invitation) that can be translated to key metrics (e.g., response time, active working hours, number of connections).
3. A recent Gallup study found that 23% of employees feel burnt out at work very often or always, while another 44% feel burnt out sometime (Wigert & Agrawal, 2018).
4. This refers to the LinkedIn versus HiQ Labs court case around using publicly available employee data on LinkedIn. As of March 2018, the court ruled in favor of HiQ Labs temporarily, stating that as long as the data are publicly available, LinkedIn cannot block HiQ from scraping it (*hiQ Labs, Inc. v. LinkedIn Corporation*, 2018).

References

Agarwal, D., Bersin, J., Gaurav, L., Schwartz, J., & Volini, E. (2018). The hyper-connected workplace: Will productivity reign? Retrieved from https://www2.deloitte.com/insights/us/en/focus/human-capital-trends/2018/network-of-teams-connected-workplace.html

Arena, M., Cross, R., Sims, J., & Uhl-Bien, M. (2017). How to catalyze innovation in your organization. *MIT Sloan Management Review, 58*(4), 38–47.

Bersin, J. (2015). HR technology for 2016: 10 big disruptions on the horizon. Retrieved from https://legacy.bersin.com/uploadedfiles/disruptions-for-2016.pdf?aliId=66864491

Carboni, I., Cross, R., Page, A., & Parker, A. (2019). Network drivers of success: How successful women manage their networks. Retrieved from https://connectedcommons.com/wp-content/uploads/2019/03/invisible-network-drivers-of-womens-success.pdf

Chakrabarti, M. (2018). Ramco uses organizational network analysis to improve sales effectiveness and measure employee engagement. Deloitte. Retrieved from https://www.trustsphere.com/wp-content/uploads/2018/04/Bersin_Ramco_201802-17pp.pdf

Cross, R., Gray, P., Gerbasi, A., & Assimakopoulos, D. (2012). Building engagement from the ground up. *Organizational Dynamics, 41*(3), 202–211.

Cross, R., & Prusak, L. (2002). The people who make organizations go—or stop. *Harvard Business Review.* Retrieved from https://hbr.org/2002/06/the-people-who-make-organizations-go-or-stop

Garton, E. (2017, April 6). Employee burnout is a problem with the company, not the person. *Harvard Business Review.* Retrieved from https://hbr.org/2017/04/employee-burnout-is-a-problem-with-the-company-not-the-person

Gotfryd, A., & Tenin, R. (2014). RFID in the employment context: The struggle between individual privacy and corporate efficiency. Timely Tech. Retrieved from http://illinoisjltp.com/timelytech/tag/employee-tracking

Hernandez, I., Newman, D., & Jeon, G. (2015). Twitter analysis: Methods for data management and a word count dictionary to measure city-level job satisfaction. In S. Tonidandel, E. King, & J. Cortina (Eds.), *Big data at work: The data science revolution and organizational psychology* (pp. 64–114). New York, NY: Routledge.

hiQ Labs, Inc. v. LinkedIn Corporation. (2018). No. 17-16783. Retrieved from https://www.ca9.uscourts.gov/media/view_video.php?pk_vid=0000013344

Klein, N., Marinescu, I., Chamberlain, A., & Smart, M. (2018, March 6). Online reviews are biased. Here's how to fix them. *Harvard Business Review.* Retrieved from https://hbr.org/2018/03/online-reviews-are-biased-heres-how-to-fix-them

Macey, W. H., & Schneider, B. (2008). The meaning of employee engagement. *Industrial and Organizational Psychology, 1*, 3–30.

McDowell, T., Horn, H., & Witkowski, D. (2016). *Organizational network analysis: Gain insight, drive smart.* Deloitte. Retrieved from https://www2.deloitte.com/content/dam/Deloitte/us/Documents/human-capital/us-cons-organizational-network-analysis.pdf

Quick, J. C., & Tetrick, L. E. (2011). *Handbook of occupational health psychology* (2nd ed.). Washington, DC: American Psychological Association.

Surowiecki, J. (2005). *The wisdom of crowds.* New York, NY: Random House.

Swedberg, C. (2018). RFID cuts worker alert response time in half. *RFID Journal.* Retrieved from https://www.rfidjournal.com/purchase-access?type=Article&id=1762 0&r=%2Farticles%20%2Fview%3F17620

There will be little privacy in the workplace of the future. (2018, March 28). *The Economist.* Retrieved from https://www.economist.com/special-report/2018/03/28/ there-will-be-little-privacy-in-the-workplace-of-the-future

Wigert, B., & Agrawal, S. (2018, July 12). Employee burnout, part 1: The 5 main causes. Gallup. Retrieved from https://www.gallup.com/workplace/237059/employee-burnout-part-main-causes.aspx

Zillman, C. (2016, February 1). IBM is blowing up its annual performance review. *Fortune.* Retrieved from http://fortune.com/2016/02/01/ibm-employee-performance-reviews

SECTION 2
ANALYZING DATA TO TELL THE SURVEY STORY

15

Mechanics of Survey Data Analysis

Melinda J. Moye and Alison L. O'Malley

We address some of the important issues involved in collecting, analyzing, and reporting survey data from a practitioner-based perspective. We begin by discussing topics to address while in the survey-planning stage, review key components to include in reports and ways to present data in manager reports, and conclude with basic considerations surrounding statistical modeling including handling of missing data.

Data Structure

The decisions you make at the outset of your survey cycle, long before you begin to collect data, are critical to the success of your overall survey program and can either facilitate or constrain your analyses. In this section, we review differences between confidential or anonymous surveys, how to use your organizational structure to set up reports, and administration methods.

Confidential or Anonymous Surveys

An early decision is whether to administer a confidential or an anonymous survey. In confidential surveys, the survey administration team and/or a third-party survey supplier has access to respondents' identity, but that identity is used only for aggregated analysis purposes. In anonymous surveys, there is no trace of respondents' identity. Administrators of confidential surveys need to determine whether to preload a data file that includes demographics from the human resources information system (HRIS) or to add the demographic items either at the beginning or end of the survey. Whenever possible, we recommend confidential surveys as there are many advantages to this methodology such as shorter surveys, ease of precollected data from

Melinda J. Moye and Alison L. O'Malley, *Mechanics of Survey Data Analysis* In: *Employee Surveys and Sensing*. Edited by: William H. Macey and Alexis A. Fink, Oxford University Press (2020). © Society for Industrial and Organizational Psychology.
DOI: 10.1093/oso/9780190939717.003.0015

the HRIS, ability to track responses longitudinally, and enhanced statistical modeling. Anonymous surveys are sometimes preferred when the administrator does not have the respondent's trust in the process. Demographics that are often useful in reporting and for conducting additional analyses include the following:

- Division within the company
- Country
- Factory/office location
- Type of employee such as administrative or production employee
- Organizational tenure
- Early career versus mid-career
- Function within the organization
- Gender
- Race/ethnic background (United States only)
- Job type (manager versus individual contributor)
- Job grade/level
- Geographic region
- Full-time versus part-time employee

One advantage of adding demographic data from an HRIS data file is that they enable you to shorten your survey. However, they do not provide the opportunity to further customize demographics beyond what is available in the HRIS (e.g., gender as dichotomized or measured with alternative response options) or to gain information that may not be tracked in the HRIS. For example, someone may have a mentor within the organization, although the mentoring relationship may not be captured through the formal mentoring process. Other employees may informally telework 1 or 2 days per week, but they might not have a formal teleworking arrangement documented in the HRIS. This type of information may be missed if you rely solely on loading data from what is available in your HRIS. Administering a confidential survey also enables you to link to other data that might be helpful when analyzing survey results such as performance-management or succession-planning ratings.

Regardless of the decision, organizations must be transparent with employees in terms of who has access to their data and how they will be used. Given that the General Data Protection Regulation was passed in the European Union in May of 2018, it is critical that employees surveyed in the European Union encounter a privacy statement informing them of their right to access their data (see Chapter 24 for more information). Organizations will often work with third-party survey providers to administer surveys so that no one in the organization can see individual survey responses. Without access to individual survey responses, individual-level longitudinal questions cannot be explored. For instance, if we wish to establish how employees differ in their responses over time on the basis of having a particular experience (e.g., undergoing coaching), we cannot answer this with an anonymous survey. To increase self-sufficiency and extract full value from your data, it is helpful if someone within your organization or a third-party supplier has access to consistently applied unique identifiers that enable them to build and test statistical models. For a deeper discussion of the strengths and weaknesses of identified employee surveys, see Saari and Scherbaum (2011).

What demographic variables to include and how to structure the data load file will determine the types of reports that can be run and how data can be reported on the back end. For example, often in addition to displaying direct report lines within department reports, many organizations want to see survey results broken out by division of the organization, geographical region, country, factory/office location, and type of employee (e.g., administrative versus production). All such variables must be in the load file or included in the demographic portion of the survey.

Organizational Hierarchy

If using data from an HRIS, it is important to work with the administrator to ensure that the organizational hierarchy is appropriately represented in the data load file as well as key demographics so that the structure of reports can be built correctly. In addition, if using an organizational hierarchy snapshot to build reports, you will want to use the date the snapshot was taken so that survey respondents complete the survey according to the position they were in at the time the snapshot was taken. This is particularly important if you are including items that have "manager or supervisor" as the referent. To ensure accurate interpretation of results, respondents need to know that their results will roll up to the manager they were reporting to at the time that the organizational hierarchy snapshot was taken, not the date that they completed the survey. It is important to draw a line in the sand and create this distinction; otherwise, there will be confusion as to which manager the respondent's results apply. Survey teams often receive requests to change or update the hierarchy after the snapshot was taken to reflect a recent organizational change. While an organizational hierarchy can be reconfigured to reflect organizational changes, we do not recommend this practice.

Administration Method

An additional consideration is whether to administer the survey online, on paper, or as some combination of the two. The trend for the majority of organizations is to move toward online administration to reduce cost and reduce the time it takes to administer the process from the beginning to the end. Benefits of online administration include live response rate tracking, no printing and shipping of paper surveys, no shipments held up in customs, and no manual scanning of paper surveys or transcription of written comments once they are received. Organizations will have survey data files ready much sooner and with fewer errors than if they had to wait to add the paper survey data. Further, this allows you or your third-party survey provider to start generating reports much sooner as well as faster access to the complete data file in order to conduct additional analyses.

Item Design

When designing surveys, it is important to determine if you want to include open-ended items along with closed-ended items. Closed-ended items take less time to answer than open-ended items and facilitate comparison of responses across respondents, groups, and time. An advantage to including some open-ended items in a survey is that it allows employees to respond from their own viewpoint without having to use the predetermined response options on the survey and to provide insights on issues that were not included in the closed-ended items (Church & Waclawski, 2001). Please see Chapters 12 and 13 for a more in-depth discussion of item types and their use.

Data Cleaning and Missing Data

Regardless of the data-collection method, it is essential to evaluate the adequacy of the data provided. Two sets of decisions are relevant here. The first is to establish rules for identifying careless respondents. The second is to determine procedures for handling missing data.

Identifying Careless Respondents

It is not unusual that some respondents approach the task of survey completion in a less than conscientious manner, rushing through the process seemingly at random. It is appropriate in these circumstances to remove these cases from the data file. The challenge is in establishing the rules by which these decisions are made. Some useful criteria include (1) survey completion times below a threshold, (2) a lack of variance in responses (e.g., all 3s), and (3) demographic variable combinations that are illogical or impossible.

Missing Data

Before reporting item-level results and proceeding to multivariate analysis, it is essential that analysts understand the extent to which data are missing from their data set. Data can be missing at three levels: the item, scale, or survey level (i.e., a person does not submit any survey data). *Response rate*, a ratio of the total number of completed surveys to the number of requested surveys, provides a metric for survey-level nonresponse. *Response rate bias* occurs when the results from the subsample of people who completed the survey differ from results that would be obtained with no missing data. *Loss of data* means a loss of information and an increase in error variance, so it is important to consider why data are missing. Rubin's (1976) typology describes three missing data mechanisms. When data are *missing completely at random*, the pattern of missingness arises from a truly random process. When data are *missing at random*, missingness in part is associated with the observed data. When data are *missing not at random*, missingness is dependent on the missing data values. In practice, missing not at random is of limited value as it is extremely difficult to establish. If data are missing completely at random, then there is little need for concern as parameter estimates will not be impacted. However, if there are systematic gaps in the data such as employees higher in the organizational hierarchy failing to respond to items about trust in leadership or employees who score lower on engagement having higher levels of nonresponse, then problems such as decreased statistical power and biased parameter estimates emerge (Roth, 1994).

We recommend (1) using all available data and (2) reporting and statistically handling missingness at the item level. For starters, maintain a column showing the percentage of missing data for each item in a table of descriptive statistics. It is critical to document and share decisions surrounding missing data so that subsequent analysts can understand why results may not match. In order to make use of all available data for statistical modeling purposes, we encourage the use of maximum likelihood estimation (MLE) or multiple imputation (MI) approaches that model the uncertainty associated with missing data. MLE uses a log likelihood function to identify the population parameters that have the greatest likelihood of producing the sample data. MI entails imputing multiple values for each missing data value, producing several complete data sets whose estimated parameters and standard errors are then pooled. MLE and MI can be accomplished using most statistics packages. For instance, the R package missForest, available from the Comprehensive R Archive Network (https://cran.r-project.org/), is a nonparametric imputation method that can handle a variety of data types. Baraldi and Enders (2010) provide detailed, accessible descriptions of how MLE and MI work.

Although commonly applied, we do not recommend using listwise or pairwise deletion to handle missing data issues. Listwise deletion, also known as "complete case analysis," entails removing all incomplete cases from the data set. Pairwise deletion, or "available case analysis," is best understood through the context of a correlation matrix; cases are excluded when data are missing from one or both variables for an individual. Thus, the pairwise n will be larger than the listwise n. We urge readers to note that default methods in statistical programs such as SPSS are rarely the preferred method for handling missing data.

Further, some discrepancies between output generated in R and SPSS are attributable to how missing data are treated, which in turn impacts how the correlation matrix is constructed. A similar issue arises when conducting factor analysis and the need to be mindful of packages' default rotation method. Ultimately, this comes down to variations in algorithmic approaches—what happens "behind the scenes." Even within analysis software, there is variability in how to perform a computation. For instance, SPSS has five different methods for the calculation of percentiles. We encourage analysts to be aware of the potential for different values to be generated by the same data depending upon the software chosen for statistical analysis and to look to the documentation as more detailed understanding becomes necessary. The use of tools such as R Markdown can facilitate communication as data change hands.

Reporting Elements

Factors or Dimensions

Dimensions in reports are often determined by leadership/stakeholder preferences versus empirically or theoretically driven themes. In order to help managers more easily make sense of survey results, especially when the survey includes a relatively large number of items, it is often helpful to group responses to survey items into meaningful subscales using a blend of factor analysis and an overall a priori strategy. For example, some organizations include employee engagement and manager effectiveness indices on their survey reports. Given that every survey should have a defined purpose with meaningful groups of items, we argue that once you have collected some initial data, you could confirm the constructs or dimensions on your survey by using confirmatory factor analysis versus exploratory factor analysis. If you are using exploratory factor analysis, you do not make any a priori assumptions about relationships among factors. However, we would argue that as survey practitioners/researchers you should have a good idea of what items should cluster together. Exploratory factor analysis enables analysts to remove items that double-load with predictor and criterion measures within the survey. Confirmatory factor analysis uses the statistical methodology of structural equation modeling that tests the hypothesis that the items are associated with specific factors. For a more detailed discussion on factor analysis, see Pedhazur and Schmelkin (1991).

Means or Percent Responding

When reporting survey results, you must determine how the results will be displayed in manager reports (see Chapter 19 on data visualization for more information). Often, survey results will be displayed by recoding responses into categories of favorable, neutral, and unfavorable. For example, the total percentage of respondents who responded with "Strongly Agree" or "Agree" would be collapsed into "percent favorable." Less common is to report all response frequencies (e.g., "Strongly Agree," "Agree," "Neither Agree nor Disagree," "Disagree," "Strongly Disagree"), report results in terms of mean scores, or use net-promoter scores. Often, the reason for collapsing survey responses into categories is to maintain anonymity. Reporting on each response category or on measures of dispersion can increase managers' sensitivity in terms of who in their teams may have provided outlier ratings (Macey, 1996). For example, if a manager has six respondents who indicated strongly agree to an item and one who provided a strongly disagree response, the manager may be tempted to try to determine who provided the negative response. Other reasons why most organizations and survey consulting groups report scores in terms of percent favorable versus means include (1) ease of interpretation, especially for those managers who have a modest statistics background; (2) the tendency for outliers to skew results in small groups; (3) a tendency for means to be misleading when you have a bimodal distribution of scores on an item; and (4) most survey benchmark data are reported in terms of "percent favorable" (Long, 2014).

Understanding Variability

We urge practitioners to pay close attention to full item response distributions as the conclusions reached can vary depending on the shape of the item response distribution (Rivers, Meade, & Fuller, 2009). Considering evidence that team outcomes are likely to be highest when managers' and employees' perceptions of climate are strongly positive and in agreement (Bashshur, Hernández, & González-Romá, 2011), there is value in examining whether there is consensus within a group of respondents. Furthermore, some items are designed to be interpreted at the group level (see Chapter 18 for more on this point). An aggregate rating may not do justice to its constituent parts, as in a team where half of the respondents provide very low ratings and the other half provide very high ratings (Ioannidis et al., 2007). Although it is rare for survey vendors to provide an indication of the extent of agreement among group members, statistical significance tables for the observed variance in ratings compared to the variance of a theoretical distribution with no agreement and the average deviation index are available (Smith-Crowe, Burke, Cohen, & Doveh, 2014).

Comparisons: Item History, Norms, and Benchmarks

When setting up the format for manager survey reports, you may wish to leave space for a history column if applicable. If organizations have used an item previously, they often include the score of the item from the previous administration or a "+" or "−" to indicate how much an item has increased or decreased from the previous administration. Often, organizations find within-group history comparisons helpful in showing trends. As practitioners consider whether results meaningfully differ between survey administrations, it is important to note that seemingly minor changes between survey administrations can impact response distributions or interitem correlations. Ultimately, it is important to establish whether the item(s) of interest actually differs over time or whether the item functions differently (Carter, Kotrba, & Lake, 2014). Item response theory methods can indicate whether there is differential item functioning across measurements and whether there are item or context effects such that results are influenced by changes in question form (e.g., wording, response options) rather than differences in the focal construct itself. Analysts working in global contexts are encouraged to consider how language and cultural differences show up in survey data by assessing measurement equivalence (Ryan, Chan, Ployhart, & Slade, 1999).

Organizations also find it helpful to include across-group comparisons (e.g., comparisons to peer teams, other layers in the hierarchy). Organizations may also want to add an internal company benchmark and/or an external norm benchmark if available (see Chapter 11 on benchmarks). Some organizations also include an internal benchmark such as the average percent favorable score for the organization. Another common practice is for organizations to include an internal benchmark based on the direct report workgroups that rank in the top 25% within the organization on an index or dimension score (e.g., the Employee Engagement Index). This gives workgroups a higher benchmark to compare to. Many survey consulting firms have developed their own set of external norms from their clients over a period of years and are able to break the norms down by type of industry such as manufacturing or finance. When using external norms, you want to make sure you are using the exact item wording. However, small changes such as "company name" in place of "my organization" are permissible. In addition, some organizations include Mayflower Group benchmarks (see Chapter 11).

Minimum n Rules

Organizations typically establish rules to prevent individual employees from being linked to their responses. In particular, it is common to determine the minimum number (n) of respondents needed before a report will be generated. Thus, an important element for reporting is to determine the minimum n rules for manager reports and to clearly communicate the rules up front to survey respondents. For example, you must determine the number of respondents a manager will need in order to generate a report. To clarify, the rule is determined not by the number of employees managers have on their team but by the number of employees who actually respond to the survey. As mentioned, there may be a tendency for managers who have low scores to try to figure out who on their teams provided the low scores, and this is much easier to do when the minimum n size for reports is small. Survey teams will want to provide training to managers to emphasize the importance of acting on the survey results appropriately and not to try to identify respondents. Typically, organizations will provide manager-level reports for teams with 5–10 respondents.

Servicing Additional Report Requests and Privacy Concerns

Another consideration is to ensure that you are protecting anonymity when managers ask for additional ad hoc reports. For example, if a manager received a team report that included seven responses and then wanted to add in two matrixed employees, we would argue that this request should be declined given that when you only add two responses you will be able to tell how these two responses impacted the original overall report results. We maintain that, at a minimum, the difference between an original report and an additional ad hoc report where you are adding responses must be three or greater. Analysts who wish to take advantage of the data-visualization capabilities in tools such as Tableau are encouraged to remain mindful of the need to set filters for group size, taking care not to produce views that violate the minimum n stipulations. When producing dashboards and configuring user access, take care when establishing how dashboard users can interact with the data (e.g., who can download detailed data views).

Reporting Statistical Significance

Survey practitioners often get questions from leadership on whether there is a statistically significant difference between team scores or between current team and previous team scores. In order to determine if there is a statistical difference between two sets of scores, you would need to calculate the confidence interval around the observed difference. The confidence interval helps you determine if there is a large enough difference relative to the amount of error in the data to be considered legitimate rather than due to chance (Levenson, 2014). For survey results that have a small number of respondents, the confidence interval would need to be fairly large. Given that we do not typically calculate confidence intervals for all of the survey items, we often use guidelines to determine if differences between scores are meaningful. Often, survey consulting firms will share rules of thumb with their clients to use with managers who receive reports. For example, if the number of survey respondents in the smallest team is 100 or more, you may want to look for differences in percent favorable of 5% or more. If the team sizes you are comparing are 50–99 respondents, you may want to look for differences in percent favorable of 10% or more. Finally, when you are comparing survey responses in small groups of fewer than 50, you may need to look for differences in percent favorable of 15% or greater to indicate meaningful distinctions.

Model-Building

This section introduces the need to go beyond item-level results to examine relationships between predictors and criterion measures. Only through multivariate statistical analysis can we establish which factors have statistically and practically significant impacts on outcomes such as engagement or turnover intentions. These ideas are expanded upon in Chapter 16.

Multicollinearity

As we employ statistical approaches, it is important to consider multicollinearity as survey items tend to be highly intercorrelated. Variance inflation factors (VIFs) provide a measure of the severity of multicollinearity. In general, multicollinearity decreases the stability of regression coefficient estimates. Practitioners may encounter the rule of thumb that a VIF greater than 10 indicates severe multicollinearity that ought to be handled by dropping one or more of the predictors that is highly correlated with other predictors; but dropping predictors shifts the model that is being tested, and it is ill-advised to arbitrarily toss items out of the prediction equation. This consideration of how comprehensive of a model to test introduces us to the *model bias–variance trade-off*, where we are confronted with the risk of underutilizing available predictor data and in turn underpredicting the outcome of interest (e.g., engagement) in the current sample and future samples.

Predictive Analytics

If practitioners intend for survey data to inform predictive modeling efforts, it is important to keep in mind that traditional regression-based statistical models may not generalize to new data sets (Yarkoni & Westfall, 2017). In such instances, the arrived-upon model does not perform as well when users attempt to forecast what has not yet been observed. This is problematic in the event that decision makers want to go beyond the current data set and gain some sense of what is likely to be the case in the future. Stated more plainly, it is possible that pursuing good model fit can compromise an analytics team's ability to make good predictions (Yarkoni & Westfall, 2017). If practitioners face a need to predict outcomes for a new sample, they may wish to consider more modern prediction methods that apply model tuning parameters to balance the model bias–variance trade-off and arrive upon an appropriately complex model. For an overview of modern prediction methods, such as ridge regression that introduces a ridge tuning parameter to handle multicollinearity among predictors and lasso (least absolute shrinkage and selection operator) and least angle regression that optimize variable selection through less "greedy" fitting techniques than stepwise regression, see Putka, Beatty, and Reeder (2017). This said, Macey and Daum (2017) note that within organizations predictor weights tend to be quite stable.

Analysts who wish to combine model interpretability with statistical rigor may be particularly interested in classification and regression trees (CARTs), a type of decision tree methodology which is better at detecting nonlinearity and interactions. Classification trees apply to dichotomous outcomes (e.g., employees who stayed versus left the company), and regression trees involve continuous outcomes. Whereas in traditional regression approaches a single model represents the entire data set, CARTs use a recursive partitioning method to create trees where each node or leaf of the tree has a model attached to it. A parent node splits into two groups that are most different with respect to the outcome measure. For example, in a turnover analysis the parent node may split based upon whether or not employees are enrolled in the company's medical insurance plan. The tree-growing methodology progresses from there by assessing which of the remaining independent variables results in the best split according to the selected splitting criterion (Lemon, Roy, Clark, Friedmann, & Rakowski, 2003). *Bagging* (i.e., bootstrapping a sample and aggregating predictions from a multitude of trees) and boosting are extensions of CART that can improve model stability and predictive power. The R package caret can implement all of these models. Kuhn and Johnson's (2013) text on applied predictive modeling is a good resource for readers who wish to learn more about the predictive modeling process.

Person-Centered Statistical Approaches

The preceding paragraphs focused on variable-centered statistical approaches. Although it is tempting to focus on the predictive power of certain data elements, questions can arise about distinctions between "types" of employees. Analyses that speak to this are known as *person-centered approaches*. Breaking with the assumption made by variable-centered approaches that variables are similarly related across the population, person-centered approaches model population heterogeneity. The population is broken down into mutually exclusive subpopulations (profiles) with similar response patterns, and the goal is often to determine predictors of subpopulation membership. For instance, people analytics teams may be motivated to use survey data to create distinct profiles of stayers and leavers (Woo & Allen, 2014), of commitment (Meyer, Stanley, & Parfyonova, 2012), or of engaged, disengaged, and actively disengaged employees. Person-centered approaches may hold particular intuitive appeal to practitioners as the notion of constellations of variables invites consideration of "recipes" for desired outcomes (e.g., retaining high potentials). Person-centered approaches include methods such as cluster analysis and latent class or latent profile analysis, depending on whether observed variables are categorical or continuous.

Conclusion

Our intent was to help practitioners think through scenarios that will inform their survey administration including which survey vendors with whom to partner, and the following chapters will expand on many of the ideas we presented. We hope these points ultimately enable decision makers to reach accurate conclusions and allocate resources appropriately to obtain desired results.

References

Baraldi, A. N., & Enders, C. K. (2010). An introduction to modern missing data analyses. *Journal of School Psychology, 48*(1), 5–37. doi:10.1016/j.jsp.2009.10.001

Bashshur, M. R., Hernández, A., & González-Romá, V. (2011). When managers and their teams disagree: A longitudinal look at the consequences of differences in perceptions of organizational support. *Journal of Applied Psychology, 96*, 558–573. doi:10.1037/a0022675

Carter, N. T., Kotrba, L. M., & Lake, C. J. (2014). Null results in assessing survey score comparability: Illustrating measurement invariance using item response theory. *Journal of Business and Psychology, 29*, 205–220. doi:10.1007/s10869-012-9283-4

Church, A. H., & Waclawski, J. (Eds.). (2001). *Designing and using organizational surveys: A seven-step process.* San Francisco, CA: Jossey-Bass.

Ioannidis, J., Patsopoulos, N., Kavvoura, F., Tatsioni, A., Evangelou, E., Kouri, J., Contopoulos-Ioannidis, D., & Liberopoulos, G. (2007). International ranking systems for universities and institutions: A critical appraisal. *BMC Medicine, 5*, 30. doi:10.1186/1741-7015-5-30

Kuhn, M., & Johnson, K. (2013). *Applied predictive modeling.* New York, NY: Springer.

Lemon, S. C., Roy, J., Clark, M. A., Friedmann, P. D., & Rakowski, W. (2003). Classification and regression tree analysis in public health: Methodological review and comparison with logistic regression. *Annals of Behavioral Medicine, 26*(3), 172–181.

Levenson, A. (2014). *Employee surveys that work: Improving design, use, and organizational impact.* San Francisco, CA: Barrett-Koehler Publishers.

Long, D. (2014, July 21). 5 reasons not to use mean scores when interpreting employee engagement survey results. Decisionwise. Retrieved from https://www.decision-wise.com/5-reasons-not-to-use-mean-scores-interpreting-employee-engagement-survey-results/

Macey, W. H. (1996). Dealing with the data: Collection, processing, and analysis. In A. I. Kraut (Ed.), *Organizational surveys: Tools for assessment and change* (pp. 204–232). San Francisco, CA: Jossey-Bass.

Macey, W. H., & Daum, D. L. (2017). SKDA in context. *Industrial and Organizational Psychology, 10*(2), 268–277. http://dx.doi.org/10.1017/iop.2017.18

Meyer, J. P., Stanley, L. J., & Parfyonova, N. M. (2012). Employee commitment in context: The nature and implication of commitment profiles. *Journal of Vocational Behavior, 80*(1), 1–16. https://doi.org/10.1016/j.jvb.2011.07.002

Pedhazur, E., & Schmelkin, L. (1991). *Measurement, design and analysis: An integrated approach*. Hillsdale, NJ: Erlbaum.

Putka, D. J., Beatty, A. S., & Reeder, M. C. (2017). Modern prediction methods: New perspectives on a common problem. *Organizational Research Methods, 21*(3), 689–732. https://doi.org/10.1177/1094428117697041

Rivers, D. C., Meade, A. W., & Fuller, W. L. (2009). Examining question and context effects in organization survey data using item response theory. *Organizational Research Methods, 12*(3), 529–553. http://dx.doi.org/10.1177/1094428108315864

Roth, P. L. (1994). Missing data: A conceptual review for applied psychologists. *Personnel Psychology, 47*(3), 537–560. https://doi.org/10.1111/j.1744-6570.1994.tb01736.x

Rubin, D. B. (1976). Inference and missing data. *Biometrika, 63*(3), 581–592.

Ryan, A. M., Chan, D., Ployhart, R. E., & Slade, L. A. (1999). Employee attitude surveys in a multinational organization: Considering language and culture in assessing measurement equivalence. *Personnel Psychology, 52*(1), 37–58. https://doi.org/10.1111/j.1744-6570.1999.tb01812.x

Saari, L. M., & Scherbaum, C. A. (2011). Identified employee surveys: Potential promise, perils, and professional practice guidelines. *Industrial and Organizational Psychology, 4*, 435–448. https://doi.org/10.1111/j.1754-9434.2011.01369.x

Smith-Crowe, K., Burke, M. J., Cohen, A., & Doveh, E. (2014). Statistical significance criteria for the r_{wg} and average deviation interrater agreement indices. *Journal of Applied Psychology, 99*, 239–261. http://dx.doi.org/10.1037/a0034556

Woo, S. E., & Allen, D. G. (2014). Toward an inductive theory of stayers and seekers in the organization. *Journal of Business and Psychology, 29*, 683–703. https://doi.org/10.1007/s10869-013-9303-z

Yarkoni, T., & Westfall, J. (2017). Choosing prediction over explanation in psychology: Lessons from machine learning. *Perspectives on Psychological Science, 12*(6), 1100–1122. https://doi.org/10.1177/1745691617693393

16

Taking Action to Drive Change Through Survey Key Driver Analysis

Jeff W. Johnson

The more actionable the results of an organizational survey, the more valuable they are to the end user. The mean score or the percentage of favorable responses is not enough to identify the areas in which interventions will have the most impact on changing attitudes. One way to make survey data more actionable is through the application of survey key driver analysis (SKDA). *SKDA* is a general term describing statistical procedures for identifying priorities from among a larger set of topics measured by a survey. A frequent challenge when interpreting survey results is determining which topics warrant the greatest attention. Assuming a well-designed survey that taps into the issues that are important to the organization, a properly applied SKDA can be a powerful tool in this regard.

The *key drivers* of a particular outcome (e.g., employee engagement) are the survey topics that are most highly associated with the outcome. Although causality cannot be definitively determined from survey responses, it is assumed that how respondents feel about these topics has the most impact on driving their responses to outcome items. By determining the relative importance of each survey topic to a particular outcome, SKDA suggests where attention should be focused to have the greatest impact on that outcome, helping decision makers prioritize action to drive meaningful change.

SKDA reduces the burden on decision makers who must digest voluminous survey results, focusing their attention on areas that are within their control and important for influencing outcomes. By simplifying and organizing results, decision makers are more engaged in the process and more likely to take action on specific, actionable goals. Absent SKDA, decision makers are likely to speculate about which areas should be addressed, possibly based on (a) their own biases or anecdotal experiences, (b) the lowest-scoring items,

Jeff W. Johnson, *Taking Action to Drive Change Through Survey Key Driver Analysis* In: *Employee Surveys and Sensing.* Edited by: William H. Macey and Alexis A. Fink, Oxford University Press (2020). © Society for Industrial and Organizational Psychology.
DOI: 10.1093/oso/9780190939717.003.0016

(c) scores that have decreased over time, or (d) what seems easiest to address (Rotolo, Price, Fleck, Smoak, & Jean, 2017).

The focus of this chapter is how to analyze survey data to help set priorities. A detailed explication of how to identify relevant themes and design a survey to best measure them is beyond the scope of this chapter (see Chapter 12). With regard to the data analysis itself, a well-designed survey containing relevant themes is assumed. The SKDA process presupposes that an appropriate model has already been identified (Klein et al., 2017).

SKDA Methods

Over the years, researchers have used a wide variety of statistical procedures for determining the relative importance of predictor variables (e.g., survey topics). Some examples include the increase in R^2 associated with adding a predictor to the model (Darlington, 1968), the semi-partial correlation (Bring, 1994), and the product of the standardized regression coefficient and zero-order correlation (Hoffman, 1960; Thomas, Hughes, & Zumbo, 1998). The most popular methods have been zero-order correlations and standardized regression coefficients (Johnson & LeBreton, 2004), which have the advantages of being easy to compute using standard statistical software packages and familiarity to those with a basic knowledge of statistics, but they are inadequate for determining predictor importance (e.g., Darlington, 1968; Hoffman, 1960).

The problem centers around the correlations between predictor variables. When predictors are uncorrelated, zero-order correlations and standardized regression coefficients are equivalent. The squares of these indices sum to R^2, or the proportion of variance in the outcome variable that is explained by the predictor variables, so the relative importance of each variable can be expressed as the proportion of predictable variance for which it accounts. When predictor variables are correlated (i.e., *multicollinearity*), these indices are no longer equivalent, do not sum to R^2, and take on very different meanings. Squared correlations represent the unique contribution of each predictor by itself, whereas squared regression coefficients represent the incremental contribution of each predictor when combined with all remaining predictors.

To illustrate, consider a researcher who wants to determine how each specific survey topic contributes to employee engagement. Regression coefficients are inadequate because employees do not consider the incremental amount of satisfaction they derive from each aspect of the company while holding the others constant when evaluating how engaged they are. Zero-order correlations are also inadequate because employees do not look at each aspect of the company independent of all the others. Rather, employees consider all the aspects simultaneously and implicitly weight each aspect relative to the others in determining their overall engagement level.

Johnson and LeBreton (2004) defined *relative importance* as "the proportionate contribution each predictor makes to R^2, considering both its direct effect (i.e., its correlation with the criterion) and its effect when combined with the other variables in the regression equation" (p. 240). They reviewed many alternative statistical importance measures and found that almost all of them have significant shortcomings. The primary problem with most of these indices is that they often provide nonsensical results such as negative or zero importance for variables that should be important under conditions that are common in survey research (e.g., high intercorrelations).

Today, the dominant procedures for measuring relative importance are the general dominance statistic used in Budescu's (1993) dominance analysis (DA) (first suggested by Lindeman, Merenda, & Gold, 1980) and relative weight analysis (RWA) (Johnson, 2000). These indices (a) yield importance weights that represent the proportionate contribution each predictor makes to R^2, (b) consider a predictor's direct effect and its effect when combined with other predictors, and (c) provide importance estimates that make sense from a conceptual and logical standpoint.

General DA weights are computed as the average of each predictor's (p) squared semipartial correlation across all $p!$ possible orderings and subsets of the predictors. This defines predictor importance as the average contribution to R^2 across all possible orderings of all subset regression models (Budescu, 1993).

Relative weights are computed by transforming the predictors to a set of new variables that is as highly related as possible to the original set of predictors but in which individual predictors are uncorrelated with each other (i.e., orthogonal). The outcome variable is regressed on the orthogonal variables, and the squared standardized regression coefficients unambiguously represent the relative importance of these variables. The original predictors are then regressed on the orthogonal variables. The relative importance of the uncorrelated variables to the original predictors is also unambiguous because regression coefficients are assigned to the uncorrelated variables. Relative weights are computed by combining the indices representing the relative importance of the uncorrelated variables to the outcome variable and the indices representing the relative importance of the uncorrelated variables to the original predictors (Johnson, 2000).

Practically speaking, it makes no difference whether DA or RWA is used to conduct SKDA because the two methods produce almost identical results despite being very different approaches to evaluating predictor importance (Johnson, 2000; LeBreton, Ployhart, & Ladd, 2004; LeBreton & Tonidandel, 2008; Tonidandel & LeBreton, 2010). The average difference between dominance weights and relative weights is often in the third decimal place when examined across thousands of simulated data sets (Tonidandel & LeBreton, 2011).

In this chapter, I focus on RWA as the SKDA method because it is the most commonly used relative importance procedure by practitioners (Macey & Daum, 2017) and relative weights are easier to compute than dominance weights (Tonidandel & LeBreton, 2011). The recommendations presented in this chapter apply equally to either method.

SKDA Example

Dalal, Baysinger, Brummel, and LeBreton (2012) surveyed 191 employees to determine the key drivers of three types of employee performance. The criteria were self-ratings of employee behavior relevant to (a) task performance, (b) organizational citizenship behavior, and (c) counterproductive/deviant workplace behavior. The predictors were measures of (a) positive affect, (b) negative affect, (c) perceived organizational support, (d) work centrality, (e) job involvement, (f) employee engagement, (g) job satisfaction, and (h) organizational commitment. Each topic was measured with multiple items that were rolled up into a scale score. RWA was used to evaluate the relative importance of the predictors to each criterion separately. Results are displayed in Table 16.1.

Table 16.1 suggests a number of conclusions. For example, employee engagement made a relatively strong contribution to the prediction of all three outcomes, while organizational commitment had little impact on any. Negative affect had the strongest relationship with both task performance and counterproductive behavior but had very little impact on organizational citizenship behavior. Work centrality and positive affect were strong

Table 16.1 Relative Importance of Employee Attitudes to Three Types of Employee Behavior

	Outcome		
Survey Topic	Task Performance $(R^2 = .23)$	Organizational Citizenship Behavior $(R^2 = .22)$	Counterproductive Work Behavior $(R^2 = .18)$
Positive affect	.03	.12	.04[a]
Negative affect	.38[a]	.08[a]	.56
Perceived organizational support	.09	.10	.14[a]
Work centrality	.04[a]	.19[a]	.02
Job involvement	.11[a]	.06	.01[a]
Employee engagement	.15	.25	.13[a]
Job satisfaction	.16	.14	.06[a]
Organizational commitment	.04	.06	.03[a]

Note. Relative weights are presented as a proportion of R^2. Results are adapted from Dalal et al. (2012).
[a]Relationship between predictor and outcome is negative.

predictors of organizational citizenship behavior but contributed little to the other two outcomes.

Table 16.1 clearly demonstrates that key drivers depend on the outcome of most interest. If the goal is to decrease counterproductive behaviors, hiring employees who are low on negative affect is recommended. If increasing organizational citizenship behaviors is of most interest, working to increase employee engagement should have the most impact. Increasing engagement could be done by developing a survey measuring specific topics that are expected to impact engagement and conducting SKDA to identify the key drivers of engagement.

It may be the case that a survey measures multiple important outcome variables that are of equal interest and leaders want to identify the key drivers that will have the most impact on all of them. In this case, an option is to conduct a multivariate RWA (LeBreton & Tonidandel, 2008) or DA (Azen & Budescu, 2003), which considers all outcome variables simultaneously while accounting for their intercorrelations. Dalal et al. (2012) conducted a multivariate RWA and found that negative affect (31%), employee engagement

(15%), and job satisfaction (12%) had the most impact across all three outcome variables.

Criticism of SKDA

Cucina, Walmsley, Gast, Martin, and Curtin (2017) delineated a number of criticisms of SKDA that warrant mention here, and they went so far as to call for a moratorium on the use of SKDA by survey providers. This article engendered several responses to address these points. I briefly summarize each of the criticisms and the responses in this section, then provide additional detail in the following section by offering recommendations for conducting SKDA. It should be noted that most of Cucina et al.'s criticisms were based on the use of correlations or stepwise regression as the SKDA technique, so these criticisms do not apply to the use of RWA or DA.

Criticism 1. Standard Deviations Impact SKDA Results

Cucina et al. (2017) argued that survey items with smaller standard deviations (SDs) are less likely to be related to the outcome variable because low variance limits the size of the correlation coefficient. In an example data set based on a survey of federal employees, they found a correlation of .62 between item SD and the correlation between that item and the outcome variable. The implication is that survey topics that most respondents agree are problems would be unlikely to come out of SKDA as key drivers and that key drivers are primarily determined by respondent agreement.

Several responses addressed this criticism by presenting analyses of other survey data that did not replicate this finding. Hyland, Woo, Reeves, and Garrad (2017) examined survey data from 20 diverse organizations and found a mean correlation between item SD and item–outcome correlation of .05. Klein et al. (2017) found a correlation of .12 between item SD and item–outcome correlation in their own normative employee survey database. Because Cucina et al. (2017) included items in their analysis that were not appropriate to include in SKDA, Macey and Daum (2017) reanalyzed their data using a subset of just the appropriate items and found a correlation of .45. They also completed this analysis for other outcome variables and found the correlation to be negative in both cases across three different survey administrations. These more extensive analyses indicate that item variance does not have a meaningful impact on SKDA results.

Criticism 2. SKDA Capitalizes on Chance

Cucina et al. (2017) suggested that SKDA capitalizes on chance because a priori hypotheses are typically not made. I argue that hypotheses typically are made because the survey developer selects items to include on a survey that measure things that are thought to have some relationship with the outcome of interest. For example, a job satisfaction survey includes items that measure different facets of job satisfaction, based on literature review, previous research, or employee focus groups. The hypothesis is essentially that all constructs measured by the survey are related to the criterion, and the SKDA is conducted to determine the relative strength of these relationships (Johnson, 2017; Macey & Daum, 2017).

Criticism 3. Random Item Selection Performs as Well as SKDA

Cucina et al. (2017) showed that randomly choosing a subset of items yielded nearly as high an R^2 as choosing items based on stepwise regression after cross-validating, concluding that random selection approximated the results of stepwise regression. Macey and Daum (2017) analyzed the same data in a different way, however, and found that the R^2 for the three most important items identified in the SKDA was substantially higher than the average R^2 for three randomly selected items across 1,045 replications. Because survey items tend to be highly intercorrelated, any set of items will probably have a similar R^2 (Johnson, 2017). Regardless, the purpose of SKDA is explanation, not prediction. SKDA is intended to explain how variables contribute to the prediction of a criterion, not to select the subset of variables that maximizes prediction (Johnson, 2000). Two highly correlated items with similar correlations with the outcome variable are likely to have similar relative weights, but one will not add much to prediction beyond the other. Similarly, an item with a small correlation with the outcome variable may meaningfully increase the R^2 if it is uncorrelated with the other items already included, but that does not make it a key driver of the outcome.

Criticism 4. Latent Factor Structure Could Explain SKDA Results

Cucina et al. (2017) proposed that an alternative explanation for the correlations between specific items and the outcome is that they are indicators of the same latent variable rather than being true key drivers. This is not an issue, however, because the latent structure underlying survey responses can be described as a hierarchical factor model with the overall evaluation at the highest level and the more specific facets beneath it. For example, an employee's overall job satisfaction is clearly determined by the employee's attitudes toward specific aspects of the job. The outcome variable measures the same factors as those measured by the more specific items to the extent that constructs lower in the hierarchy contribute to the construct at the higher level.

Criticisms 5 and 6. Lack of Situational and Temporal Specificity

Cucina et al. (2017) contended that survey items represent universal constructs and that relationships between specific facets and overall evaluations should generalize across situations and time, with SKDA differences across situations or time due to sampling or measurement error. This line of thinking ignores the literature on person–environment fit (Su, Murdock, & Rounds, 2015), vocational interests (Holland, 1997), work adjustment (Dawis & Lofquist, 1984), and attraction–selection–attrition theory (Schneider, 1987), all of which are based on individual differences in work preferences and the importance placed on elements of the job and organization. Although there certainly are consistencies in drivers of many outcome variables, there are differences in the strength of these relationships. For example, Meyer, Stanley, Herscovitch, and Topolnytsky's (2002) meta-analysis found that variables such as role ambiguity, role conflict, distributive justice, and procedural justice had strong correlations with organizational commitment; but the corrected mean correlations had wide credibility intervals, indicating that there are substantive moderators influencing the size of the correlations. In other words, the strength of the relationships involving these variables varied by setting.

The purpose of SKDA is to identify generalities across individuals within an organization or business unit to target the issues that will have the greatest impact on the most people. What those issues are depends on the configuration of individuals within the organization, which depends on who the organization attracts and hires. For example, pay satisfaction is probably a more important driver of job satisfaction in a Wall Street brokerage firm than in a nonprofit charitable foundation.

It is also possible that attitudes and relationships with overall evaluations change over time, especially if there has been a significant organizational change or an influx of new people. Rotolo et al. (2017) described SKDA as a snapshot in time and said we should not expect key drivers to maintain the same impact over time as organizations and their operating environments evolve. The purpose of SKDA is to identify the set of variables on which to take action in a given organization at a given point in time to improve a given outcome (Scherbaum, Black, & Weiner, 2017). This can only be done by conducting a local survey and analyzing the data to identify key drivers of the outcome of interest, not by conducting a literature review or consulting a meta-analysis.

Recommendations

Cucina et al. (2017) also discussed issues regarding sample sizes and causation, but these and other methodological issues are easily addressed if the recommendations presented in this chapter are followed. In this section, I address the most frequent methodological questions that arise concerning SKDA.

Types of Variables

When determining if an item is appropriate for including as a predictor or an outcome in SKDA, the primary considerations are distributional properties and item content.

Distributional Properties
All SKDA procedures are based to some extent on the correlations between variables, so the types of variables that are appropriate for SKDA

are the same types that would be appropriate for any kind of correlational analysis. Correlational analyses assume that variables are measured on an interval or continuous scale, but response scales for survey items are really at the ordinal level, meaning that scores can be rank-ordered meaningfully. Nevertheless, analyses of ordinal variables are common and not problematic when the assumption of approximately equal intervals between scale points is reasonable. A "Strongly Disagree" to "Strongly Agree" rating scale is approximately interval, but an item with a response scale like 1 = none, 2 = 1 or 2, 3 = 3 to 10, 4 = more than 10 clearly violates the interval-level assumption and would not be appropriate for inclusion in SKDA. Also, a survey item with a scale that has its most favorable point in the middle (e.g., "Too Much," "About Right," "Too Little") is not appropriate for SKDA. I recommend that survey items have a minimum of four scale points, but dichotomous items (e.g., yes/no) can be used as predictor variables. The logistic regression variants of RWA (Tonidandel & LeBreton, 2010) or DA (Azen & Traxel, 2009) should be used with dichotomous outcome variables.

If scale scores are created from multiple items measuring different aspects of the same topic, a mean score across items would approximate a continuous scale. The items composing the scale score should be measured on the same response scale, and standardizing the items before computing the scale score will ensure that items with more variance will not implicitly be given more weight (Oswald, Putka, & Ock, 2015). Factor analysis is recommended to ensure that items are indicators of the same construct, and reliability analyses should demonstrate that the items are internally consistent.

To ensure that items are meeting distributional assumptions, Rotolo et al. (2017) recommended checking that (a) predictor and outcome variables have similar skewness and kurtosis, (b) there are no outliers having inordinate impact on the relationships between variables, and (c) there are no nonlinear relationships.

Item Content

Not every item on a survey is appropriate for inclusion in SKDA. Some items have purposes other than to measure topics that may be drivers of an overall evaluation (e.g., to communicate company values or track product quality; Rotolo et al., 2017). SKDA assumes a causal relationship between the predictors and the outcome, so predictors should measure aspects that can reasonably be assumed to influence the outcome variable. Potential key drivers should be specific, actionable survey topics over which the organization has some control. The organization cannot directly control the outcome variable, so predictor items should measure issues that could be changed by the organization in order to influence employee opinions about those issues, which in turn influence the overall evaluation.

Similarly, the outcome variable must measure something that could reasonably be expected to be influenced by the predictors. For example, a measure of overall satisfaction with the company is an appropriate outcome variable if the predictors are measures of satisfaction with specific aspects of the company.

Scales versus Items

There are pros and cons associated with using either individual survey items or composites of items that form scale scores as the predictors in SKDA. Items have the advantage of being more specific and therefore more actionable than scale scores. Scale scores have the advantages of (a) being more reliable than items, (b) keeping the number of predictors to a more manageable and interpretable level, and (c) being more continuous than ordinal-level items.

The most important limitation of item scores is that the relative weights for single items can be misleading if there are differing numbers of items measuring similar topics. The importance of highly correlated items measuring a single topic is spread out more or less symmetrically among them, so a large number of items measuring one topic would tend to get smaller relative weights than a small number of items measuring an equally important topic.

Lundby and Johnson (2006) suggested a two-step procedure for creating actionable recommendations when a survey consists of multiple items measuring different topics. First, compute scale scores for groups of items measuring a similar topic and use these scale scores as the predictors in RWA. This produces a meaningful estimate of importance for each survey topic. To report on the importance of single items, the scale-level RWA is followed up with separate RWAs of the items within each topic. If some aspects of a topic are more important than others, this analysis would identify the specific areas to target for improvement.

Sample Size

The sample size for SKDA should not be smaller than that appropriate for conducting multiple regression, but there is no minimum sample size appropriate in all situations. Lindeman et al. (1980) suggested that a useful rule of thumb for multiple regression is a sample size of at least 100, or 20 times the number of variables, whichever is larger. Hyland et al. (2017) demand a minimum of 250 respondents for conducting SKDA. Although rules of thumb are generally inadequate (Maxwell, 2000), they are probably helpful as a starting point. I recommend computing standard errors around relative weights and differences between relative weights to evaluate the level of confidence we should have in our conclusions.

Standard Errors and Significance Tests

SKDA is usually conducted on a sample from a population, so the level of confidence we can have in the results depends on the stability of the importance weights. We are often interested in how confident we can be that one survey topic is more important than another or if the relative importance of a survey topic is significantly different across groups. There is no sampling error theory for relative weights or DA weights, but confidence intervals can be estimated using a bootstrap approach (Azen & Budescu, 2003; Johnson, 2004). "Bootstrapping" is a nonparametric procedure for estimating standard errors on the basis of repeated random samples (with replacement) from a sample (Efron, 1979). Relative weights are calculated within each subsample, and the SDs across subsamples represent the standard error of each relative weight. Confidence intervals can be constructed around relative weights to make confidence statements about the value of individual relative weights in the population. When comparing relative weights within a sample to determine if one predictor is significantly more important than another, confidence intervals must be computed around the differences between relative weights (Johnson, 2004).

When comparing relative weights across populations (e.g., discrete business units), Johnson (2004) showed that confidence intervals should be constructed around the difference between two independent proportions (e.g., Moore & McCabe, 1989). This requires that relative weights be expressed as proportions of the predictable variance, which is recommended to control for differences in R^2 across samples. Significant differences (i.e., the confidence interval does not include zero) should be interpreted as differences across populations in the importance of a predictor relative to the other predictors in the model.

It is also possible to determine whether a relative weight is significantly different from zero, even though the confidence interval around a relative weight will never include zero because relative weights cannot be negative. Tonidandel, LeBreton, and Johnson (2009) showed that adding a random variable to the model (which by definition has no importance) allows one to compute a confidence interval around the difference between each study variable and the random variable. If the confidence interval does not include zero, the relative weight for the study variable is significantly different from zero.

Measurement Error

Johnson (2000) cautioned RWA users to consider the relative reliabilities of the predictors when interpreting relative weights. Differences in the reliability of measurement can affect any SKDA method because the magnitude of the correlation between two variables is influenced by the quality of the measures. Unreliability suppresses correlations, so correlations between less reliable variables will be suppressed more than correlations between more reliable variables. With SKDA, we are really interested in the relative importance of one construct (e.g., satisfaction with leadership) to another (e.g., organizational commitment), rather than the relative importance of a measure of one construct to a measure of another.

Johnson (2004) showed how wide disparities in the reliabilities of measures can lead to meaningful differences when comparing relative weights computed on measured variables and relative weights computed on latent variables. The researcher should compute coefficient alphas for all survey topics and consider whether the disparity between reliabilities may meaningfully influence the results of the SKDA.

Magnitude of R^2

R^2 measures the proportion of variance in outcome variable scores that can be accounted for by an optimally weighted linear combination of predictor scores in multiple regression. The magnitude of R^2 must be considered when interpreting SKDA results. A small R^2 means that the most important predictors are still relatively unimportant, in an absolute sense. For example, if scores on survey topics only account for 20% of the variance in the outcome scores, that means that 80% of the variance is still left unaccounted for. A low R^2 may be an indication that there are important variables that are not being measured by the survey.

Relative weights and DA weights will always sum to the R^2 obtained from an ordinary multiple regression analysis. Any observed discrepancy is likely due to different data being used in each analysis, such as using pairwise deletion of missing cases for one analysis and listwise deletion for the other.

Assuming Causality

SKDA is based on correlational analyses, and correlation does not mean causation. Therefore, using the term *key driver* requires an inferential leap because saying that opinions on specific survey topics drive overall opinions assumes a causal relationship. In some cases, it is possible that a person's overall level of satisfaction could drive his or her responses to specific items. To some extent, a third variable such as positive affectivity could influence responses to both specific and outcome items. Nevertheless, it is reasonable to expect that an overall evaluation would be influenced by a person's opinions on specific attributes related to that evaluation, so the assumption of causality is not a great leap. It is the responsibility of the researcher to ensure that business leaders understand that causation cannot be proven and to choose language carefully in presenting SKDA results (Klein et al., 2017). The whole point of SKDA is to identify areas in which organizational resources should be invested, so we must balance a common-sense understanding of the limits of correlational analyses with an honest appraisal of the likely direction of causality.

Understanding Importance Weights

Relative weights or DA weights should never be computed and interpreted without also examining the correlations and regression weights associated with each predictor. These importance weights are always positive, so the correlations are necessary to determine if the relationship between the predictor and the outcome is positive or negative. Comparing correlations and regression weights can help the researcher understand if the importance effect is primarily because of a large direct effect or a large indirect effect in conjunction with the other variables in the model (Johnson & LeBreton, 2004).

On rare occasions, examining correlations and regression coefficients can identify a suppressor variable in the model. A *suppressor variable* is a predictor that is uncorrelated with the outcome variable but adds significantly to its prediction by removing irrelevant variance from one or more other predictors, thus increasing the predictive power of the other predictors. Including or excluding the suppressor variable causes difficulties in interpretation of SKDA results. When a suppressor variable is operating, the proper approach is to compute the partial correlation matrix controlling for the suppressor variable and submit the partial correlation matrix to SKDA (Johnson, 2016; Thomas et al., 1998).

Conclusion

In this chapter, I advocated for the use of RWA (Johnson, 2000) or DA (Budescu, 1993), as opposed to problematic indices such as correlations or multiple regression, to obtain quantitative importance weights to identify key drivers when analyzing survey data. SKDA can be a powerful tool for driving organizational change, but like any tool, it can do more harm than good if it is not used properly. Cucina et al. (2017) had many criticisms of SKDA, but their criticisms were actually about the improper application of SKDA, not about the tool itself. The point of this chapter was to make recommendations for the proper use of SKDA, which, if followed, should ameliorate these types of concerns.

Although SKDA is a powerful tool, it is not the only tool in the toolbox. To get the most out of survey data, we should also examine things like trends over time, external benchmarks, comments, and linkages with other outcomes (Rotolo et al., 2017). Evidence from multiple methods (e.g., focus groups, stakeholder interviews) can be used to support SKDA results to provide stronger arguments for setting priorities (Klein et al., 2017). SKDA results are a starting point for helping the client make sense of the data rather than an automatic action plan developer (Hyland et al., 2017).

The most difficult part of the survey process usually comes after the data have been collected and the organization must decide what to do with the results. This typically involves some sort of prioritization process in which a larger set of potential issues is narrowed down to a smaller set of priorities for action. Without information on the relative importance of each issue with respect to a specified outcome, the default strategy is to focus on survey items or topics with the lowest scores, which may not have much of an impact on the outcomes that are really of interest. SKDA is an important step forward in helping to set priorities for action that will lead to meaningful organizational change.

References

Azen, R., & Budescu, D. V. (2003). The dominance analysis approach for comparing predictors in multiple regression. *Psychological Methods, 8*, 129–148.

Azen, R., & Traxel, N. (2009). Using dominance analysis to determine predictor importance in logistic regression. *Journal of Educational and Behavioral Statistics, 34*, 319–347.

Bring, J. (1994). How to standardize regression coefficients. *American Statistician, 48*, 209–213.

Budescu, D. V. (1993). Dominance analysis: A new approach to the problem of relative importance of predictors in multiple regression. *Psychological Bulletin, 114*, 542–551.

Cucina, J. M., Walmsley, P. T., Gast, I. F., Martin, N. R., & Curtin, P. (2017). Survey key driver analysis: Are we driving down the right road? *Industrial and Organizational Psychology, 10*, 234–257.

Dalal, R. S., Baysinger, M., Brummel, B. J., & LeBreton, J. M. (2012). The relative importance of employee engagement, other job attitudes, and trait affect as predictors of job performance. *Journal of Applied Social Psychology, 42* (Suppl. 1), E295–E325.

Darlington, R. B. (1968). Multiple regression in psychological research and practice. *Psychological Bulletin, 69*, 161–182.

Dawis, R. V., & Lofquist, L. H. (1984). *A psychological theory of work adjustment.* Minneapolis, MN: University of Minnesota Press.

Efron, B. (1979). Bootstrap methods: Another look at the jackknife. *Annals of Statistics, 7*, 1–26.

Hoffman, P. J. (1960). The paramorphic representation of clinical judgment. *Psychological Bulletin, 57*, 116–131.

Holland, J. L. (1997). *Making vocational choices: A theory of vocational personalities and work environments* (3rd ed.). Odessa, FL: Psychological Assessment Resources.

Hyland, P. K., Woo, V. A., Reeves, D. W., & Garrad, L. (2017). In defense of responsible survey key driver analysis. *Industrial and Organizational Psychology, 10*, 277–283.

Johnson, J. W. (2000). A heuristic method for estimating the relative weight of predictor variables in multiple regression. *Multivariate Behavioral Research, 35*, 1–19.

Johnson, J. W. (2004). Factors affecting relative weights: The influence of sampling and measurement error. *Organizational Research Methods, 7*, 283–299.

Johnson, J. W. (2016, April). *Using relative weight analysis when suppressor variables are operating.* Symposium conducted at the 31st Annual Conference of the Society for Industrial and Organizational Psychology, Anaheim, CA.

Johnson, J. W. (2017). Best practice recommendations for conducting key driver analyses. *Industrial and Organizational Psychology, 10*, 298–305.

Johnson, J. W., & LeBreton, J. M. (2004). History and use of relative importance indices in organizational research. *Organizational Research Methods, 7*, 238–257.

Klein, C., Synovec, R., Zhang, H., Lovato, C., Howes, J., & Feinzig, S. (2017). Survey key driver analysis: Perhaps the right question is, "are we there yet?" *Industrial and Organizational Psychology, 10*, 283–290.

LeBreton, J. M., Ployhart, R. E., & Ladd, R. T. (2004). A Monte Carlo comparison of relative importance methodologies. *Organizational Research Methods, 7*, 258–282.

LeBreton, J. M., & Tonidandel, S. (2008). Multivariate relative importance: Extending relative weight analysis to multivariate criterion spaces. *Journal of Applied Psychology, 93*, 329–345.

Lindeman, R. H., Merenda, P. F., & Gold, R. Z. (1980). *Introduction to bivariate and multivariate analysis.* Glenview, IL: Scott, Foresman and Company.

Lundby, K. M., & Johnson, J. W. (2006). Relative weights of predictors: What is important when many forces are operating. In A. I. Kraut (Ed.), *Getting action from organizational surveys: New concepts, methods, and applications* (pp. 326–351). San Francisco, CA: Jossey-Bass.

Macey, W. H., & Daum, D. L. (2017). SKDA in context. *Industrial and Organizational Psychology, 10*, 268–277.

Maxwell, S. E. (2000). Sample size and multiple regression analysis. *Psychological Methods, 5*, 434–458.

Meyer, J. P., Stanley, D. J., Herscovitch, L., & Topolnytsky, L. (2002). Affective, continuance, and normative commitment to the organization: A meta-analysis of antecedents, correlates, and consequences. *Journal of Vocational Behavior, 61*, 20–52.

Moore, D. S., & McCabe, G. P. (1989). *Introduction to the practice of statistics.* New York, NY: W. H. Freeman and Company.

Oswald, F. L., Putka, D. J., & Ock, J. (2015). Weight a minute . . . what you see in a weighted composite is probably not what you get! In C. E. Lance & R. J. Vandenberg (Eds.), *More statistical and methodological myths and urban legends* (pp. 187–205). New York, NY, and London, England: Routledge.

Rotolo, C. T., Price, B. A., Fleck, C. R., Smoak, V. J., & Jean, V. (2017). Survey key driver analysis: Our GPS to navigating employee attitudes. *Industrial and Organizational Psychology, 10*, 306–313.

Scherbaum, C. A., Black, J., & Weiner, S. P. (2017). With the right map, survey key driver analysis can help get organizations to the right destination. *Industrial and Organizational Psychology, 10*, 290–298.

Schneider, B. (1987). The people make the place. *Personnel Psychology, 40*, 437–453.

Su, R., Murdock, C., & Rounds, J. (2015). Person–environment fit. In P. J. Hartung, M. L. Savickas, & W. B. Walsh (Eds.), *APA handbook of career intervention* (Vol 1, pp. 81–98). Washington, DC: American Psychological Association.

Thomas, D. R., Hughes, E., & Zumbo, B. D. (1998). On variable importance in linear regression. *Social Indicators Research, 45*, 253–275.

Tonidandel, S., & LeBreton, J. M. (2010). Determining the relative importance of predictors in logistic regression: An extension of relative weight analysis. *Organizational Research Methods, 13*, 767–781.

Tonidandel, S., & LeBreton, J. M. (2011). Relative importance analysis: A useful supplement to regression analysis. *Journal of Business and Psychology, 26*, 1–9.

Tonidandel, S., LeBreton, J. M., & Johnson, J. W. (2009). Determining the statistical significance of relative weights. *Psychological Methods, 14*, 387–399.

17

Linkage Analysis

Tying Employee Attitudes to Business Outcomes

Shawn M. Del Duco, Patrick K. Hyland, David W. Reeves,
and Anthony W. Caputo

If assessment is the basis for organizational change, as many practitioners argue, then it comes as no surprise that employee surveys find organizational researchers among their most vocal advocates. But what about the uninitiated? How do practitioners convince business executives, for example, not only of the importance of surveying their employee population at a given time but also of continuing to invest in what are typically costly survey programs year over year? Linking employee attitudes, as measured by organizational surveys, to important outcomes, such as employee turnover and performance, provides a compelling business case for executives to invest both emotionally and fiscally in employee surveys.

A Brief History of Linkage Analysis

Linkage analysis is a modern framework for evaluating the impact organizational attitude surveys have on business outcomes. Over the past century, research on job attitudes has mushroomed and become increasingly sophisticated (Judge, Weiss, Kammeyer-Mueller, & Hulin, 2017). As technology continues to advance our ability to administer and leverage organizational surveys, business leaders and practitioners collect more varied data on employees than ever before. Since 2006, about three out of four large organizations survey their employees in some capacity (Kraut, 2006).

Despite their rising popularity, the influx of data created from frequent organizational surveying poses a challenge for organizational researchers to demonstrate the impact surveys have on actual organizational performance. When researchers from The Engagement Institute (2014) asked nearly 100

Shawn M. Del Duco, Patrick K. Hyland, David W. Reeves, and Anthony W. Caputo, *Linkage Analysis* In: *Employee Surveys and Sensing*. Edited by: William H. Macey and Alexis A. Fink, Oxford University Press (2020). © Society for Industrial and Organizational Psychology.
DOI: 10.1093/oso/9780190939717.003.0017

organizations to list the common analytical challenges they were facing, over 40% indicated that their organization was not effective at connecting attitudinal survey data to business outcomes. The challenge is that doing so takes substantial time and effort. Determining whether employee attitudes, as measured by surveys, lead to business performance requires the integration and analysis of multiple data sources. However, understanding the link between employee attitudes and other organizational data, such as those from a human resources information system (HRIS) and performance measures, often provides organizations and business leaders the breakthrough insights they are searching for.

Over the past four decades, linking employee perceptions of the work environment to individual and organizational performance has become increasingly important to business leaders. Since Schneider and colleagues first found a positive, statistically significant relationship between employee perceptions of customer service and actual customer service ratings (Schneider & Bowen, 1985; Schneider, Parkington, & Buxton, 1980), linking employee attitudes with various other data sources has garnered more appeal. Despite much of the research being conducted at the time indicating no strong evidence for such relationships (Brayfield & Crockett, 1955; Lawler & Porter, 1967; Organ, 1977; Schwab & Cummings, 1970; Vroom, 1964), Iaffaldano and Muchinsky (1985) conducted a meta-analysis to empirically test whether job satisfaction and job performance were related and found that they were. Since then, empirical research demonstrating the link between job attitudes and business performance has flourished. Tornow and Wiley's (1991) study both replicated and extended the findings of Schneider and Bowen (1985), finding positive relationships between employee and customer perceptions of service quality and measures of organizational performance. This research ultimately showed that an organization's bottom line is largely based on its ability to create compelling employee experiences (Wiley, 1996).

Heskett, Jones, Loveman, Sasser, and Schlesinger (1994) further explored these linkages by building a model of organizational effectiveness referred to as the *service–profit chain*. The service–profit chain was one of the first models to detail the importance of internal and external service and how they are linked to an organization's financial performance (Heskett et al. 1994; Heskett, Sasser, and Schlesinger, 1997). More research emerged linking job attitudes and service quality to organizational adaptability (Angle & Perry, 1981), turnover (Wiley, 1996), customer retention (Ashworth,

Higgs, Schneider, Shepherd, & Carr, 1995), and managerial effectiveness (Johnson, 1995).

This process of connecting employee survey data (e.g., job attitudes, job satisfaction, employee engagement, employee affect) with objective measures of business performance (e.g., sales, profit, productivity) and other key organizational performance indicators such as customer satisfaction, turnover, and absenteeism was formalized in Jack W. Wiley's 1996 publication "Linking Survey Results to Customer Satisfaction and Business Performance." There, Wiley defined linkage analysis as a process of "integrating and correlating data collected from employees with data in other key organizational databases" (Wiley, 1996, p. 330).

Since then, the linkage research model has been renamed the *high-performance model* (Wiley, 1996; Wiley & Campbell, 2006) and has been used to link leadership practices and the employee experience with customer satisfaction and business performance. Employee attitudes and perceptions of the work environment at the individual, group, and organizational levels has now been empirically linked to outcomes such as employee performance (Judge, Thoresen, Bono, & Patton, 2001; Judge et al., 2017; Salanova, Agut, & Peiro, 2005), organizational citizenship behaviors (Organ & Ryan, 1995), unit-level profit and productivity (Harter, Schmidt, & Hayes, 2002), service quality (Brown & Lam, 2008; Hogreve, Iseke, Derfuss, & Eller, 2017; Piening, Baluch, & Salge, 2013), customer loyalty (Salanova et al., 2005), sales and financial performance (Benkhoff, 1997; Gong, Law, Chang, & Xin, 2009; Piening et al., 2013; Sung & Choi, 2014), safety (Harter et al., 2002), and absenteeism and turnover (Grotto, Hyland, Caputo, & Semedo, 2017; Saari & Judge, 2004). Thanks to this large body of research, we can now leverage linkage analysis and the linkage research model as an effective foundational framework to demonstrate the value of organizational attitude surveys (Macey, 2007; Wiley, 1996; Wiley & Campbell, 2006).

The Linkage Analysis Process

Linkage analysis generally proceeds through several main steps. In this section, we briefly review these steps and present common challenges that routinely arise throughout the process.

Determining one or more research questions is the first and most important step in conducting linkage analysis. Regardless of the analytical technique employed, a well-articulated research question (or set of questions) will guide decisions at each of the remaining stages in the process; for example, the time lag needed between the collection of predictor and outcome variables. An example of a clear research question would be "Do employees who volunteer in community outreach programs report higher levels of employee engagement than employees who do not volunteer in such programs?"

Upon determining one or more research questions to explore, the next step is to identify available data. An overlooked benefit of linkage research is that it often highlights current gaps in a company's data ecosystem. Predictor and outcome variables used in most linkage studies typically come from different data sources within a company. However, when faced with a paucity of objective outcome measures, researchers will often risk common source bias and conduct linkage analyses with predictor and outcome variables drawn from a single data source. A common example of this type of analysis is attempting to predict an employee's intention to stay with a company based on that employee's work perceptions gathered at the same time (through the same methodology). In such a scenario, it is difficult to posit that one variable predicts another variable. The units of analysis included in a linkage study are largely predicated on the availability of data and the business owners of those data within organizations.

The units of analysis included in a linkage study impact both the analytical technique to be employed as well as the intervention that follows from the analysis. It is common for predictor and outcome variables to be collected at different levels of measurement. For example, a study correlating employee perceptions with organizational performance might include data collected at both the individual level and the team level. In such cases, a decision must be made as to whether to aggregate individual-level data to align with team-level data (and risk losing valuable between-subject variability) or employ more sophisticated, multilevel analytical approaches. It is imperative for both predictor and outcome variables that meaningful variability exists at the chosen unit of analysis. It is equally important that there is clear accountability associated with the selected units of analysis. For example, if retail stores are chosen as the units of analysis and store managers are managers in name only (i.e., managers have little decision-making authority), then it would be prudent to aggregate store-level data to the district or regional level or wherever a sufficient degree of decision-making authority resides. The ultimate aim of linkage analysis is to determine actionable leverage points for making organizational improvements, and if units of analysis are not targeted at an actionable level, then the analysis runs the risk of becoming an empty exercise of simply satisfying curiosity.

After identifying one or more research questions, identifying available data sources, and determining the units of analysis, the next step is to conduct the analysis. The choice of analytical technique is determined by the framing of the research question, as well as the nature of the data being analyzed. While analytical approaches serve unique purposes, all of the approaches described here and elsewhere in this book measure the degree to which two or more variables are related.

At the most basic level, simple descriptive statistics such as means can be compared between groups to determine if meaningful and statistically significant differences exist. These types of approaches are particularly useful when dealing with very limited data sets (i.e., small data sets with relatively few variables). For examining group differences using larger data sets consisting of many variables, analysis of variance (ANOVA) is a powerful approach. The ANOVA family of techniques ranges from basic comparisons of two groups on a single outcome of interest to comparisons of three or more groups across multiple outcomes, while accounting for the effect of extraneous variables. It is often the case that both the predictor and outcome variables in a linkage analysis are continuous (as opposed to discrete groupings). In these instances, correlation and regression techniques are often employed. A simple, two-variable (i.e., bivariate) correlation analysis examines the strength and direction of the linear relationship between two continuous variables. An example of such an analysis would be examining the relationship between employee age and salary. Similar to ANOVA, correlation and regression techniques can account for the effect of extraneous variables. While the number and nature of available regression techniques are too numerous for a detailed treatment in this chapter, logistic regression is a technique worth highlighting due to its popularity in the context of employee turnover prediction. Logistic regression is often used when the outcome variable in a linkage analysis is categorical (e.g., employees who left the company versus those who stayed with the company). Relative weights analysis (RWA) is a popular regression approach. An advantage of RWA is that it allows for the evaluation of the unique contributions made by each predictor simultaneously for an outcome of interest (see Chapter 16). Structural equation modeling (SEM) represents a sophisticated, multistage analytical approach that includes latent variables, or factors, that are indicated by measured variables. While the use of this technique alone does not allow for causal inferences, SEM provides robust tests of the directionality of relationships among a multitude of variables. Finally, machine learning techniques such as support vector machines represent powerful modeling approaches for examining very large data sets with many variables. Machine learning techniques are particularly useful in the early stages of an analysis, when the nature of the relationships within a data set are unknown. The results from exploratory analyses are often used to build rich theoretical models, which can later be tested using confirmatory techniques.

Upon completion of the initial analyses, linkage findings should be cross-validated (i.e., replicated). This is particularly important in the absence of a research-based, theoretical framework to guide the analysis. In the enviable scenario in which a researcher has data to spare, a best practice is to reserve a portion of the original data set (extracted in a randomized fashion) for replicating the analysis results found with the larger data set.

Common Challenges and Solutions

Even when following a rigorous set of steps, it is possible that issues may arise while trying to conduct linkage analyses. In this section, we cover some of the more common issues that may arise and offer possible solutions to addressing these issues. While problematic, these issues do not in themselves doom a linkage analysis to failure and may be overcome with methodological and theoretical adjustments to your analysis.

Time-Lag Issues

Time-lag issues are relatively easy to overcome when performing linkage analysis, but many individuals may overlook them. An issue with establishing a time lag during linkage analysis is ensuring an appropriate level of lag between assessment of the intervention and assessment of the outcomes. These lags should be based on the best available research and theory. For example, when assessing turnover, a lag of 6 months to 1 year is appropriate from the previous survey assessment, to ensure that you are capturing the current reasons for an employee's departure. However, for other linkage analyses a longer lag may be appropriate, such as when assessing the impact of certain training programs, which could take up to 2 or 3 years to show a true impact on performance.

Statistical Power

A more difficult challenge that can occur while performing linkage analysis is a lack of power, typically due to a low sample size. Many business metrics are only gathered at a group level such as a business unit, function, or location. Due to this, the sample size is only as large as the number of clear units that can be identified. In some situations, such as large retailers, this does not cause an issue; but in other situations, where the sample size is substantially lower, a possible solution must be found. In some situations, it is possible to utilize traditional significant testing statistics (e.g., correlation, regression) to investigate these possible linkages; however, this is most likely to be successful in areas where the effect sizes are quite large, which is not always the case while conducting linkage analysis. When effect sizes are smaller and accompanied by a small sample size, traditional significance testing might be unrealistic. In these instances, it is important to consider the value that descriptive statistics can have in understanding patterns in data. Analyzing and displaying relationships can help uncover relationships that might be hidden by traditional analysis techniques or simply not be discovered due to the lower power of the analysis to discover these relationships.

Restriction of Range

Restriction of range is an issue that occurs often in linkage research, especially when dealing with issues such as safety records and turnover. Due to the relative low occurrence of these incidences, it is not uncommon to have a linkage data set with only 10% to 5% occurrence in the population. There are several methodological solutions to these issues. First, it is important to use the most appropriate analysis method, such as Poisson regression for outcomes such as near-miss incidences (i.e., count data) or logistic regression for dichotomous outcomes such as turnover. The econometric literature provides a more in-depth introduction to the application of Poisson regression to count data (e.g., Winkelmann, 2008). Beyond choosing the correct analysis method when dealing with a restricted outcome, it is important to ensure that the outcome is as clearly-defined as it possibly can be. For example, when working with turnover data, it is important to target a refined measure of turnover, preferably focusing on what is most important for the business (e.g., voluntary, regrettable, high potential turnover). In addition to ensuring that the measure is clearly-defined, utilizing control variables is important to remove other noise that can be captured in the outcome variable.

Null and Nontheoretical Findings

Finally, while conducting linkage analysis one may find null relationships or, worse, relationships that run counterintuitively to predictions and theory. In these situations, there are several strategies that one can follow. Similar to the way that descriptive statistics and figures can be helpful in understanding relationships where the analysis power is low, they can also be helpful in understanding if there are outliers that are causing null or counterintuitive relationships. For example, when examining the relationship between employee engagement and sales performance, it is possible that certain shared demographics are causing certain poor-performing locations to also have higher than average employee engagement scores. Through examination of scatterplots, etc., it is possible to identify these and examine them as separate entities to refine the analysis sample as much as possible. In addition to attempting to identify any outliers that may exist, it is important that the measures being used in analysis are as uncontaminated by systematic noise as possible. Control variables in the modeling process can be of great use in removing the impact of many possible unit demographics that could be impacting outcomes (e.g., location square footage, employee group tenure, bonus structuring, socioeconomic status of the surrounding area, etc.). After removing many of these effects through inclusion as control variables, it is possible to get a more precise look at how certain independent variables are impacting business outcomes.

Linkage Analysis Case Studies: Three Examples from the Field

For organizations seeking to improve performance, linkage analysis is a powerful technique that can help leaders, managers, and employees understand complex workplace dynamics, identify performance drivers and barriers, and determine where to invest time, energy, and resources. Linkage analysis can be used to evaluate a wide range of management decisions, human capital strategies, and organizational initiatives—from hiring and onboarding practices to leader development programs and customer service campaigns. The following is a brief overview of three case studies that showcase how linkage analysis can be used to generate data-based insights.

Identifying Attitudinal Antecedents of Employee Turnover

In many organizations, talent retention is a top priority. Considering the high cost of employee turnover, this makes sense: One recent study found that turnover costs (e.g., separation costs, replacement costs) range from 90% to 200% of the exiting employee's salary (Allen, Bryant, & Vardaman, 2010). Faced with increasing levels of attrition in the wake of an extensive organizational restructuring, one company sought to determine if it could identify attitudinal predictors of turnover. As a first step, researchers determined what data were available for analysis. Fortunately, the company conducted a nonanonymous engagement survey on an annual basis, and it maintained an HRIS database that tracked employee attrition (both regrettable and nonregrettable) daily. Using these data, it linked individual employee survey results from a 2015 organization-wide engagement survey with HRIS attrition data from 2016. In total, it assembled a linkage database with survey results and attrition/retention status for over 10,000 employees. It then conducted logistic regression analyses to determine if attitudes measured on the 2015 engagement survey predicted retention/attrition a year later. The company found that responses to three survey items predicted turnover behavior 1 year later. Employees were significantly more likely to stay with the company when they (a) believed their career goals could be met, (b) were confident in the future of the organization, and (c) believed that senior leaders acted with integrity. Based on this information, the company took steps to clarify career paths, train managers on how to conduct stay interviews (Finnegan, 2015), and initiate a leadership listening tour to increase communication and connection between executives and employees in the wake of the restructuring.

Exploring the Relationship Between Leader Personality and Leader Effectiveness

For decades, scholars and practitioners have sought to understand the factors that hinder leader and manager effectiveness. In a review of the literature, Hogan, Hogan, and Kaiser (2010) noted that personality-based factors emerge as a common source of managerial derailment. Motivated by these findings, one company sought to explore the relationship between its leaders' personality traits and their effectiveness. As a first step, researchers linked various metrics, including leaders' personality assessment data, their multirater feedback results, and their direct reports' engagement and turnover data. Next, the research team conducted a series of concurrent and time-lagged correlational and regression analyses. Several significant relationships across the data sources emerged. For example, leaders who were more conscientious (based on a personality assessment) demonstrated significantly more customer-focused behaviors (based on 360-feedback from colleagues). Also, leaders who demonstrated higher levels of self-regulation (based on 360-feedback) had significantly lower levels of team turnover. Based on these findings, the company started providing leaders with more comprehensive reports and coaching that integrated feedback on their personality, values, and behavior and the impact they were having on their team.

Using Linkage Analysis to Reduce Accidents

In the United States, 5,190 workers died from work-related injuries in 2016 (Bureau of Labor Statistics). It has been estimated that workplace deaths and injuries result in costs of over $48 billion annually (Goetsch, 1996). Moreover, 35 million workdays are lost each year because of accidents and injuries (Cascio, 1998). For many companies, particularly those in the energy and manufacturing industries, finding ways to create a safer work environment is a critical management priority. One company was interested in exploring the relationship between employee attitudes, as measured on an annual employee survey, and workplace accidents. Researchers found that workplace accidents were less likely to occur in teams with highly motivated employees. In fact, they found that over the course of 4 years, accident rates progressively increased in teams with low morale and decreased in teams with high morale. These findings make sense considering our knowledge of engagement and safety. Both require strong leadership, effective management, and a work environment that balances organizational performance goals with employees' physiological and psychological needs. Based on these findings, the company started identifying teams with persistently low engagement levels and providing additional manager training, safety training, and support from human resource business partners.

Practical Considerations: Turning Linkage Results into Organizational Action

Empirical insights do not always lead to organizational action. Even the most compelling linkage findings will not lead to learning or improvement if results are difficult for organizational members to comprehend or translate into new behaviors, norms, or practices. We have found that linkage analysis is more likely to lead to positive change when researchers take three important steps: (a) ensure that statistics are understandable, (b) learn from positive deviants, and (c) involve organizational members in the data interpretation and action-planning process. Here is a brief overview of what we've learned regarding turning linkage results into action.

Ensure Key Decision Makers Understand the Statistics

Linkage researchers should make a concerted effort to communicate results in a way that is clear, compelling, and transparent. We have found that linkage studies come to life when they are framed within a story. Stories are "important cognitive events, for they encapsulate, into one compact package, information, knowledge, context, and emotion" (Norman, 1994, p. 146). By presenting linkage studies in a simple narrative arc, with a clear beginning (i.e., what did we study and why?), a middle (i.e., what did we find, and what didn't we find?), and an end (i.e., based on these results, what are the organizational implications?), researchers can help organizational stakeholders understand key messages without getting lost in the data. Graphs, charts, path models, and outlier profiles are visually compelling ways to depict results (see Chapter 19). Translating statistical equations into clear contingency statements with bottom-line results (e.g., this means that if we improve team effectiveness scores by 5%, we can expect to see a 10% boost in customer satisfaction levels) is also a powerful way to make findings meaningful. Ensuring that audience members understand foundational research methods and statistical concepts is also critical. For example, if correlational analyses were conducted, it is important to explain that correlation does not imply causality. In cases where the research sample was large, it may be important to distinguish between statistical significance and practical significance and utilize effect sizes to clarify the magnitude of findings.

Learn from Positive Deviants, Outliers, and Exceptions to the Rule

Linkage analysis is a powerful way to identify and explore relationships between variables. But results do not always explain why relationships exist. Results do not always shed light on how high-performing leaders, employees, or units achieve exceptional results. We have found that positive deviance analysis (Pascale, Sternin, & Sternin, 2010) can help researchers develop a deeper understanding of empirical results, providing insights into contextual factors, environmental conditions, critical behaviors, and workplace practices, which, in turn, drive performance. This strengths-based, problem-solving approach is based on the observation that, in every social system, there are certain individuals, groups, or teams that succeed while others fail. By finding these outliers and determining the unique behaviors and strategies that they use to succeed, organizational members can learn from each other. Linkage results can be leveraged to find both positive and negative deviants. Through interviews and observations, linkage researchers can gain insights about performance drivers, best practices, and critical differentiators.

Involve Organizational Members in Data Interpretation and Data Actioning Processes

Imposed change efforts rarely work. We have found that linkage studies are more likely to lead to positive organizational change when leaders, managers, and employees are fully involved in reviewing results, interpreting findings, identifying issues and root causes, and developing solutions and action plans. Based on the core tenets of action research and organization development (see Burke, 1982), we have found that linkage research projects are most successful when researchers and organizational members work together in a collaborative, collegial, and inquisitive way. Rather than presenting results to stakeholders, researchers should seek to engage in a discussion with organizational members. In other words, the linkage results should be a conversation starter, that is, a way to help leaders, managers, and employees start to make sense of relationships and dynamics within their organization. By providing stakeholders with data-based insights and allowing organizational members to interpret those results in the context of their strategic goals, cultural tendencies, competitive challenges, and people initiatives, they are more likely to engage with their data, explore organizational dynamics, and commit to meaningful action.

The Increasing Importance of Linkage Analysis in a Big Data World

Technological advances are making it easier to gather, integrate, and analyze massive amounts of information on an ongoing basis, which is creating new opportunities for organizations to learn more about their employees, their customers, and their work environments. But as noted in the section "A Brief History of Linkage Analysis," many organizations are struggling to connect employee data with business outcomes. This might be because many organizations have not thought carefully or critically about their employee research program.

As we look to the future, we think that employee research programs must move from stand-alone surveys, assessments, and databases to an integrated, evidence-based understanding of employee performance and behavior. We believe that leaders, managers, and decision makers should question popular management myths and generalized findings from the field and demand the kind of organization-specific insights that can only be produced by integrating and analyzing data on a regular basis. And we think that linkage analysis should become a standard research practice in more organizations.

References

Allen, D. G., Bryant, P. C., & Vardaman, J. M. (2010). Retaining talent: Replacing misconceptions with evidence-based strategies. *Academy of Management Perspectives*, *24*, 48–64. doi:10.5465/AMP.2010.51827775

Angle, H., & Perry, J. (1981). An empirical assessment of organizational commitment and organizational effectiveness. *Administrative Science Quarterly, 26*(1), 1–14. doi:10.2307/2392596

Ashworth, S. D., Higgs, C., Schneider, B., Shepherd, W., & Carr, L. S. (1995, May). *The linkage between customer satisfaction data and employee based measures of a company's strategic business intent.* Paper presented at the Tenth Annual Conference of the Society for Industrial and Organizational Psychology, Orlando, FL.

Benkhoff, B. (1997). Ignoring commitment is costly: New approaches establish the missing link between commitment and performance. *Human Relations, 50,* 701–726.

Brayfield, A. H., & Crockett, W. H. (1955). Employee attitudes and employee performance. *Psychological Bulletin, 52*(5), 396–424. doi:10.1037/h0045899

Brown, S. P., & Lam, S. K. (2008). A meta-analysis of relationships linking employee satisfaction to customer responses. *Journal of Retailing, 84*(3), 243–255. doi:10.1016/j.jretai.2008.06.001

Bureau of Labor Statistics, U.S. Department of Labor, The Economics Daily, 5,190 fatal work injuries in the United States during 2016 on the Internet at https://www.bls.gov/opub/ted/2017/5190-fatal-work-injuries-in-the-united-states-during-2016.htm (visited January 17, 2020).

Burke, W. W. (1982). *Organization development: Principles and practices.* New York, NY: Little, Brown & Company.

Cascio, W. F. (1998). *Managing human resources.* Boston, MA: Irwin-McGraw-Hill.

Engagement Institute. (unpublished manuscript). 2014 quarter four pulse survey results: Engagement related measurement challenges.

Finnegan, R. P. (2015). *The stay interview: A manager's guide to keeping the best and the brightest.* New York, NY: AMACOM.

Goetsch, D. L. (1996). *Occupational safety and health* (2nd ed.). Englewood Cliffs, NJ: Prentice Hall.

Gong, Y., Law, K. S., Chang, S., & Xin, K. R. (2009). Human resources management and firm performance: The differential role of managerial affective and continuance commitment. *Journal of Applied Psychology, 94,* 263–275. doi:10.1037/a0013116

Grotto, A. R., Hyland, P. K., Caputo, A. W., & Semedo, C. (2017). Employee turnover and strategies for retention. In H. W. Goldstein, E. D. Pulakos, J. Passmore, & C. Semedo (Eds.), *The Wiley Blackwell handbook of the psychology of recruitment, selection and employee retention* (pp. 445–472). Chichester, England: Wiley-Blackwell. doi:10.1002/9781118972472.ch21

Harter, J. K., Schmidt, F. L., & Hayes, T. L. (2002). Business-unit-level relationship between employee satisfaction, employee engagement, and business outcomes: A meta-analysis. *Journal of Applied Psychology, 87,* 268–279. doi:10.1037//0021-9010.87.2.268

Heskett, J. L., Jones, T. O., Loveman, G. W., Sasser, W. E., Jr., & Schlesinger, L. A. (1994). Putting the service-profit chain to work. *Harvard Business Review, 72*(2), 164–170.

Heskett, J., Sasser, W. E., & Schlesinger, L. (1997). *The service profit chain: How leading companies link profit and growth to loyalty, satisfaction, and value.* New York, NY: Free Press.

Hogan, J., Hogan, R., & Kaiser, R. B. (2010). Management derailment. In S. Zedeck (Ed.), *American Psychological Association handbook of industrial and organizational psychology* (Vol. 3, pp. 555–575). Washington, DC: American Psychological Association.

Hogreve, J., Iseke, A., Derfuss, K., & Eller, T. (2017). The service profit chain: A meta-analytic test of a comprehensive theoretical framework. *Journal of Marketing, 81*, 41–46. doi:10.1509/jm.15.0395

Iaffaldano, M. T., & Muchinsky, P. M. (1985). Job satisfaction and job performance: A meta-analysis. *Psychological Bulletin, 97*(2), 251–273. doi:10.1037/0033-2909.97.2.251

Johnson, J. W. (1995, May). *Linking management practices and service orientation to customer satisfaction.* Paper presented at the Tenth Annual Conference of the Society for Industrial and Organizational Psychology, Orlando, FL.

Judge, T. A., Thoresen, C. J., Bono, J. E., & Patton, G. K. (2001). The job satisfaction–job performance relationship: A qualitative and quantitative review. *Psychological Bulletin, 127*, 376–407. doi:10.1037/0033-2909.127.3.376

Judge, T. A., Weiss, H. M., Kammeyer-Mueller, J. D., & Hulin, C. L. (2017). Job attitudes, job satisfaction, and job affect: A century of continuity and of change. *Journal of Applied Psychology, 102*(3), 356–374. doi:10.1037/apl0000181

Kraut, A. I. (Ed.). (2006). *Getting action from organizational surveys: New concepts, methods and applications.* San Francisco, CA: Jossey-Bass.

Lawler, E. E., & Porter, L. W. (1967). The effect of performance on job satisfaction. *Industrial Relations, 7*, 20–28. doi:10.1111/j.1468-232X.1967.tb01060.x

Macey, W. H. (2007). Linkage research and analyses. In S. G. Rogelberg (Ed.), *Encyclopedia of industrial and organizational psychology* (pp. 459–460). Thousand Oaks, CA: Sage Publications.

Norman, D. A. (1994). *Things that make us smart: Defending human attributes in the age of the machine.* New York, NY: Perseus Books.

Organ, D. W. (1977). A reappraisal and reinterpretation of the satisfaction–causes–performance hypothesis. *Academy of Management Review, 2*(1), 46–53. doi:10.5465/AMR.1977.4409162

Organ, D. W., & Ryan, K. (1995). A meta-analytic review of attitudinal and dispositional predictors of organizational citizenship behavior. *Personnel Psychology, 48*(4), 775–802. doi:10.1111/j.1744-6570.1995.tb01781.x

Pascale, R., Sternin, J., & Sternin, M. (2010). *The power of positive deviance: How unlikely innovators solve the world's toughest problems.* Boston, MA: Harvard Business Press.

Piening, E. P., Baluch, A. M., & Salge, T. O. (2013). The relationship between employees' perceptions of human resource systems and organizational performance: Examining mediating mechanisms and temporal dynamics. *Journal of Applied Psychology, 98*, 926–947. doi:10.1037/a0033925

Saari, L. M., & Judge, T. A. (2004). Employee attitudes and job satisfaction. *Human Resource Management, 43*, 395–407. doi:10.1002/hrm.20032

Salanova, M., Agut, S., & Peiro, J. M. (2005). Linking organizational resources and work engagement to employee performance and customer loyalty: The mediation of service climate. *Journal of Applied Psychology, 90*(6), 1217–1227. doi:10.1037/0021-9010.90.6.1217

Schneider, B., & Bowen, D. E. (1985). Employee and customer perceptions of service in banks: Replication and extension. *Journal of Applied Psychology, 70*, 423–433. doi:10.1037/0021-9010.70.3.423

Schneider, B., Parkington, J. J., & Buxton, V. A. (1980). Employee and customer perceptions of service in banks. *Administrative Science Quarterly, 25*(2), 252–267. doi:10.2307/2392454

Schwab, D. P., & Cummings, L. L. (1970). Theories of performance and satisfaction: A review. *Industrial Relations, 9*(4), 408–430. doi:10.1111/j.1468-232X.1970.tb00524.x

Sung, S. Y., & Choi, J. N. (2014). Multiple dimensions of human resource development and organizational performance. *Journal of Organizational Behavior, 35*, 851–870. doi:10.1002/job.1933

Tornow, W. W., & Wiley, J. W. (1991). Service quality and management practices: A look at employee attitudes, customer satisfaction, and bottom-line consequences. *Human Resource Planning, 14*(2), 105–115.

Vroom, V. R. (1964). *Work and motivation.* New York, NY: Wiley.

Wiley, J. W. (1996). Linking survey results to customer satisfaction and business performance. In A. I. Kraut (Ed.), *Organizational surveys: Tools for assessment and change* (pp. 330–359). San Francisco, CA: Jossey-Bass.

Wiley, J. W., & Campbell, B. H. (2006). Using linkage research to drive high performance: A case study in organizational development. In A. I. Kraut (Ed.), (2006). *Getting action from organizational surveys: New concepts, methods and applications* (pp. 150–182). San Francisco, CA: Jossey-Bass.

Winkelmann, R. (2008). *Econometric analysis of count data.* Berlin, Germany: Springer-Verlag.

18

Optimizing Differences Between Groups Is Important

Examples from Applied Settings

Paul D. Bliese, Eliza W. Wicher, and Dhuha Abdulsalam

An employee's response to a single survey item often undergoes two transformations before being converted into information used by practitioners and researchers. First, the response may be combined with responses from similar items to create a scale score. Constructs such as engagement, burnout, work–family conflict, and work overload are often assessed using multi-item scales as a way to enhance the measurement properties (e.g., reliability, validity) of the construct being assessed. Literature on measurement validation underlying this first transformation process is well developed and represents a mainstay of applied psychology research and practice (e.g., Hinkin, 1998; Pedhauzer & Schmelkin, 1991).

Second, survey item responses or scale scores are often aggregated to higher-level units. Many firms, for instance, aggregate employee engagement data to the level of the team (or higher) by calculating group averages for teams of direct reports under specific managers, sections, divisions, business units, and so on. Human resources (HR) departments may spend considerable time interpreting and acting upon responses averaged across managers and other higher-level entities. One important side note of the aggregation process is that employee confidentiality on engagement surveys is often maintained by ensuring that individual responses are aggregated across a minimum number of respondents (e.g., typically between three and five) prior to being reported. Employees are assured that summary information will be generated and that individual responses will not be examined.

In this chapter, we are specifically interested in examining the properties of items that undergo the second transformation. We show that items that appear, on the surface, to be similar can display quite different properties

Paul D. Bliese, Eliza W. Wicher, and Dhuha Abdulsalam, *Optimizing Differences Between Groups Is Important* In: *Employee Surveys and Sensing*. Edited by: William H. Macey and Alexis A. Fink, Oxford University Press (2020).
© Society for Industrial and Organizational Psychology.
DOI: 10.1093/oso/9780190939717.003.0018

when aggregated to higher-level units. Specifically, we show that some items do a particularly good job of differentiating higher-level units, while other items do a relatively poor job. At a practical level, understanding whether an item does or does not differentiate among higher-level units matters because this property of an item ultimately impacts the item's utility. For an item to be useful as a feedback tool or to help guide strategic policy, the item (or scale) must differentiate across relevant groups. For instance, a firm that decides to focus on developing managers as a way to enhance their human capital would likely use some form of engagement data from direct reports as an information source. For aggregated information from direct reports to be valuable, however, the average responses from direct reports on the engagement item(s) would need to differentiate among managers. HR departments and managers often seek to prioritize items or scales for action-planning given limitations of time and resources. They often do so based on the favorability of results. More specifically, results that appear unfavorable are prioritized for action-planning over other items or scales. Prioritization decisions are often made in the absence of information about how well the item or scale differentiates units at any given level in the organization and therefore may not be focused on the correct level of the organization to achieve the desired impact.

From a practical perspective, our interest in the ability of items to differentiate among higher-level entities is also motivated by what we see as pressure to shorten engagement surveys (see Chapters 1 and 4). Finally, we are also interested in exploring how items behave when aggregated to a higher-level entity because this type of data transformation is used among academic and applied researchers who assess group-level constructs such as cohesion, leadership, and safety climate (Chan, 2019). Research in these areas routinely asks group members to rate the construct prior to averaging responses at the group level. The resulting group means are used to represent the group-level construct. This form of group-level measurement is commonly referred to as a *composition process* (Kozlowski & Klein, 2000) or a fuzzy composition process (Bliese, 2000). Because researchers often measure group-level constructs using scale scores, it is important to ensure that the items going into the scale score are optimized in terms of differentiating higher-level entities.

Researchers and practitioners are well aware that specific items underlying a scale score differ in the degree to which they reflect the construct of interest. For instance, items used to assess a construct such as emotional burnout vary with respect to item–total correlations and factor loadings.

One of the most important aspects of the measurement validation process surrounds identifying items that are both viewed as valid indicators of the measured construct and strong in terms of high factor loadings and item–total correlations. Interestingly, it is common for items to appear similar in terms of face validity and/or with respect to being seen by experts as capturing the underlying construct but to nonetheless differ in terms of factor loadings. It can be hard to predict which items will do well in terms of measurement validation, which is why researchers working in this area typically initially generate a large number of possible candidate items.

What is less understood is that items can also display considerable variability with respect to the higher-level transformation. That is, items can vary in meaningful ways in their ability to differentiate groups, with some items doing much better than other items in terms of detecting group differences (Bliese, Maltarich, Hendricks, Hofmann, & Adler, 2019). Researchers and practitioners may experience difficulty in predicting which items will be particularly good at differentiating between groups (although we provide some guidelines with respect to writing items that can facilitate between-group differentiation). For instance, Bliese et al. (2019) reported that three very similar-looking items used to assess group cohesion showed substantially different ability to differentiate among groups. The wording of the items, though, gave no strong signals about which specific items might or might not be good at differentiating groups with respect to cohesion.

While several different approaches can be used to identify items that differentiate across groups, Bliese et al. (2019) focused on the intraclass correlation coefficient type 1, or ICC(1) (Bartko, 1976; Bliese, 2000). The ICC(1) can be estimated from a simple one-way analysis of variance (ANOVA) model or from a mixed-effects model (e.g., Pinheiro & Bates, 2000; Raudenbush & Bryk, 2002). ICC(1) values can also be estimated with relatively few groups (<30), unlike other methods such as multilevel confirmatory factor analysis that can also be used to identify item-level differentiation but require 50 or more groups (Bliese et al., 2019). When used on an item-by-item basis, the ICC(1) provides an estimate of the degree to which the item differentiates groups. For instance, an ICC(1) value of .10 indicates that 10% of the variance in employees' responses to a survey item can be explained by the groups to which they belong.

In our experience, ICC(1) values associated with group membership tend to range between .05 and .25 (5%–25%). Importantly, however, items that comprise the same scale can have different ICC(1) values even though the items may appear similar in terms of face validity. One key implication associated with the variability in the ICC(1) is that researchers and practitioners can (and in our minds should) leverage information about item-level ICC(1) values when constructing scale scores and when selecting items that will be eventually aggregated to a higher level (e.g., the workgroup).

In this chapter, we show that practitioners can think about item-level ICC(1) values as being functionally equivalent to factor loadings when selecting items or developing scales that are intended for use when items or scales are going to be aggregated to represent a higher-level group. We further illustrate findings similar to those reported in Bliese et al. (2019) and show that information obtained in level-1 measurement validation (e.g., item–total correlations or factor loadings) is largely independent of the item-level ICC(1) information. The implications of our illustrations are that optimizing the measurement properties of a scale using typical established validation procedures may do little to enhance between-group differentiation, and thus, a singular reliance on typical, established validation procedures may be limiting the degree to which data from engagement surveys provide useful, actionable information for firms. Ultimately, our goal is to provide concrete and practical information optimizing the value of items used in engagement surveys.

Differentiating Groups

Firms routinely collect employee engagement survey data with the up-front expectation that results will be aggregated to higher-level units prior to making inferences. In many cases, results are calculated and reported at the level of the manager, and a manager is provided with aggregate information (e.g., means) summarizing responses from his or her direct reports. While it may not be immediately obvious, between-group differentiation is a fundamental assumption underpinning the use and value of aggregate measures. That is, aggregate data are provided to managers with the expectation that managers have some influence over the construct.

For instance, consider surveys collected from platoons in support of US Army soldiers deployed to Iraq in 2009 as part of the Mental Health Advisory Team VI (US Army, 2009). During the Iraq War, the US Army was concerned about whether soldiers experienced barriers to receiving mental health services. If barriers existed, the US Army was interested in finding ways to reduce them to facilitate care-seeking. When ratings were averaged by platoon, the item stating "My leadership discourages the use of mental health services" had an ICC(1) of .01 (US Army, 2009, p. 38), suggesting that only 1% of the variance in a soldier's response could be explained by group membership. In contrast, the item stating "It is too difficult to get to the location where the mental health specialist is" had an ICC(1) of .09, or 9% of the variance.

ICC(1) values for the first item suggest that a strategy focused on emphasizing small unit leaders' role in terms of encouraging mental health services would be unlikely to produce meaningful change. In contrast, the ICC(1) of .09 for the second item suggests that a larger strategy targeted toward identifying platoons reporting challenges reaching care would potentially be effective. The point is that the ICC(1) values could help the larger organization prioritize resources and focus intervention strategies at (a) the correct level and (b) the correct intervention leverage point. In this example involving resource constraints, having information on what not to focus effort on is just as important as having information about where to focus efforts.

Examining ICC(1) values can also help firms avoid treating random error as something meaningful that requires attention at a specific group level. For instance, assume that a response to a survey item about work–family conflict is dichotomized so that a group mean represents the percent of "agree" and "strongly agree" responses. If the overall level of work–family conflict is 40%, we might observe the group means in Figure 18.1 from 50 teams, each of which has 10 members. It would be tempting to make negative inferences about the managers of the three teams with 70%–80% work–family conflict and make positive inferences about the managers of the seven teams with 10%–20% work–family conflict.

The values in Figure 18.1, however, represent nothing more than random error. The observed distribution was generated by randomly assigning group IDs to a vector of 1s and 0s with a 40% probability of a 1 and calculating group means for the 50 randomly assigned group IDs.[1] While the percentages appear to represent meaningful differences, an ICC(1) value would correctly identify that the distribution in Figure 18.1 does not reflect any type of meaningful group difference (ICC[1] = -.002[2]). Note that while it may seem odd to estimate an ICC(1) on a dichotomous variable, simulations suggest that ICC(1) values based on one-way ANOVA models perform reasonably well even if the outcome is dichotomous (Ridout, Demétrio, & Firth, 1999).

In addition to examining ICC(1) values, practitioners may want to examine consistency in patterns across time. For instance, if the patterns we see in Figure 18.1 are entirely random, then a subsequent data collection will generally find that groups in the extreme move toward the center ("regression to the mean"). In nonstatistical terms, the extreme groups have virtually nowhere to go except toward the mean (they cannot really become more extreme). In concrete terms, referring back to Figure 18.1, group number 18 (the group with the lowest value of work–family conflict) and group number 22 (the group with the highest level of work–family conflict) are likely to move toward the middle.

Unfortunately, in our experience, ICC(1) estimates and ANOVAs are rarely conducted in practice. Furthermore, researchers and practitioners tend to give too much weight to current results without considering patterns over time. In our example data in Figure 18.1, we might have reason to be

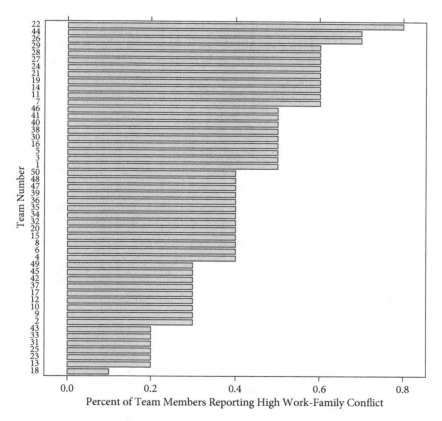

Figure 18.1. Aggregated and sorted levels of work–family conflict for 50 groups.

concerned about group 22 if it continued to remain in the top few positions over two or three data collections. In the absence of ANOVA results, ICC(1) results, and/or data from groups over time, however, it would be prudent to avoid putting too much emphasis on group 22's rating from just this one time period. We suspect that many firms may be routinely wasting effort in an attempt to "manage" random variability, in part because data from relatively small groups (10 direct reports on average) can be quite variable and appear to be showing meaningful differences, as is the case with Figure 18.1.

These two examples (barriers to care in the US Army and random work–family conflict) illustrate the importance of testing for between-group differentiation in applied settings. Both examples also involve single-item measures. In research settings, multi-item scales may be more common than single-item indices; nonetheless, the selection of items that comprise the scale can dramatically influence the ICC(1) value of the scale score (Bliese et al., 2019). More specifically, if one creates a scale score comprised of four items with small ICC(1) values, the ICC(1) value for the scale score will generally be small. In contrast, if four items with large ICC(1) values are selected, the ICC(1) value for the scale score will typically be large. Thus, issues surrounding the ability of an item to differentiate groups is important regardless of whether using single-item indices or scales.

In applied settings, the ability to differentiate groups can help focus resources and avoid trying to manage random variability. In both research settings and applied practice, differentiating groups is equally important for understanding how group membership influences hypothesized relationships between variables. As demonstrated by Bliese, Maltarich, & Hendricks (2018), group means based on underlying data with ICC(1) values of 0 will "inherit" any correlation observed in the raw unaggregated data. For instance, if 1,000 x and y variables (e.g., employee ratings of work overload and of work–family conflict) have a correlation of .60 and group IDs are arbitrarily assigned to create 100 groups of size 10, the group means from the 100 groups will also have a correlation of .6.[3]

A researcher looking only at the correlation of .60 based on the 100 group means of work overload and work–family conflict could incorrectly infer that managers play some important emergent or incremental (Hofmann & Gavin, 1998) role in this relationship. In other words, based on these results, a researcher could incorrectly infer that something about how different managers deal with work overload in their groups is related to the groups' work–family conflict. In the presence of ICC(1) values of 0, a more reasonable conclusion would be that employees within work groups differ from each other with respect to their views of both work overload and work–family conflict. Perhaps some attribute of the employee, such as marriage status or whether the employee has children, explains the individual differences across employees. If, however, these employee-level perceptions are independent of the manager (ICC[1] is 0), any observed correlation involving group means reveals nothing positive or negative about any specific manager. In the end, a significant correlation involving group means may reflect nothing more than an underlying individual-level relationship (Lincoln & Zeitz, 1980). Again, our point is that ICC(1) values are helpful not only in terms of informing researchers and practitioners on how to identify whether managers (and other groups) really differ but also in terms of thinking about managers' potential impact on some of the drivers of outcomes of interest.

Interpreting Low ICC(1) Values

In the simulated context of Figure 18.1 or the example arbitrarily assigning group means to pairs of x and y variables mentioned above ("Differentiating Groups"), an ICC(1) value of 0 is easy to interpret because we understand how the data were generated. In applied settings, however, a low ICC(1) is more challenging to interpret. On the one hand, a low ICC(1) value could indicate that groups simply are not differentiated on the construct of interest in their teams. That is, a low ICC(1) value could indicate that the distribution of responses across teams is roughly equivalent to the distribution of mean values that would have been observed if responses from team members were randomly assigned to different managers. Low ICC(1) values on important variables may also occur if a firm actively manages the variable of interest. For instance, if a firm has an outstanding manager training program and is proactive about removing supervisors who are ineffective, the overall variance associated with direct reports' perceptions of leadership would likely be diminished, thereby decreasing the ICC(1). Because many firms monitor and actively manage important outcomes, a low ICC(1) may accurately reflect a lack of meaningful differences among groups.

On the other hand (and a more problematic situation), a low ICC(1) value could be the product of measurement validation processes that failed to select items that differentiate groups. Items and scales might have been selected in ways that met conventional norms of internal consistency and validity but nonetheless failed to detect between-group differences. To elaborate on this point, when we observe that an item such as "My leadership discourages the use of mental health services" has an ICC(1) value of .01, we assume that the low value reflects a lack of differentiation on the construct. That is, we assume that leaders are not viewed as differing in terms of inhibiting the use of mental health. It is also possible, though, that something about the wording of the item does a poor job of differentiating leaders at the platoon level. Perhaps, for instance, the stem of "my leadership" is too vague, and ICC(1) values would have been much higher if the item had asked "Leaders in my platoon discourage. . . ." Or perhaps the target of "mental health services" is adding error to the responses, and the item would differentiate better if it had stated "the brigade's behavioral health officer." Or, finally, perhaps the item would have exhibited stronger ICC(1) values if it had included a clear referent to the platoon such as "My leadership discourages our platoon members from. . . ." Our point is not to be critical of the item but simply to note that a lot of choices go into items and that these choices may very well influence ICC(1) values. As a consequence, to make a claim that lower-level leadership is not a key factor in inhibiting mental health, it would be important to have several different items and show that ICC(1) values were low in all cases.

In basic and applied research, similar concerns exist. A key goal of multilevel research is to test theory by building statistical models that include contextual group-level variables. As hinted at in our example involving x and y variables mentioned above ("Differentiating Groups"), the ICC(1) value of the scale score plays a key role in whether contextual group-level variables such as shared perceptions of team leadership add unique variance to mixed-effects models (see also Bliese, 1998). Consequently, when a variable fails to add incremental variability, two potential interpretations are possible. First, the group-level variable may add nothing to a mixed-effects model because the variable plays no important theoretical role in the processes of interest. Alternatively, however, a group-level variable may add nothing because the measurement validation of the construct was done in a way that selected items failed to capture differences between groups.

These examples illustrate the importance of developing measures that differentiate groups and highlight the risks associated with developing items that are deficient in terms of group differentiation. We should be asking not just whether it is possible to create deficient group-level measures but whether our standard procedures are likely to be producing deficient group-level measures. To answer this question, we present a detailed analysis of item-level ICC(1) values from an engagement survey conducted in a large company. In the analysis, we show that items assessing similar constructs vary with respect to ICC(1) values and that typical measurement validation procedures would fail to identify items with good differentiation.

Description of the Sample

Data were collected in 2014, 2015, and 2016 from a single firm with respondents who spanned different job functions and levels. Employees were grouped based on their direct manager. The 2014 data represented 7,008 individual respondents in 604 groups with a mean group size of 7.6 and a range of 5–26 employees per group. The 2015 data represented 8,805 individual respondents in 704 groups with a mean group size of 7.9 and a range of 5–28 employees per group. The 2016 data represented 15,015 individual respondents in 1,436 groups with a mean group size of 8.5 and a range of 5–29 employees per group.

Example 1: Referents Matter (Broad vs. Focused Referents)

Many firms are interested in promoting the diversity of their workforces. Strategically, however, firms may vary with respect to how they choose to promote diversity. One option would be to encourage hiring managers to promote diversity within their teams. If a firm elected to choose this option, then it would be important to develop items that aligned to this strategy and to examine how managers were assessed by their employees on this diversity. Consider two items used by our example firm:

> Item 1: My manager encourages an environment where individual differences are valued.
> Item 2: [FIRM NAME] encourages and promotes diversity of backgrounds, talents, and perspectives.

The two items differ in several ways, but one of the most salient is that the first item clearly focuses on "My manager." While both items assess aspects of diversity, in the 2014 data, the ICC(1) value at the manager level for item 1 (.17) is substantially stronger than the ICC(1) at the manager level for item 2 (.11). Another way to think about this is that item 2 is only 64.7% as "efficient" as item 1 in terms of differentiating managers.

We emphasize that both items are reasonable in the global sense of assessing diversity, so the selection of items depends on the eventual intended use. If the firm plans to provide feedback and develop strategies at the level of the manager, then item 1 is preferable. If the goal is to obtain an overall assessment of the firm, then item 2 may be fine with the caveat that it is hard to know exactly what employees consider when asked to rate "the firm"—employees could be assessing any level of senior executive, for instance.

As a second example, consider the following two items focused on promoting high performance:

Item 3: My manager inspires high performance through his or her leadership.
Item 4: People here challenge each other to meet higher standards of performance.

Again, the items differ in a number of ways, but a salient difference is that the first item focuses on the manager. The ICC(1) in the 2014 data for item 3 is .21, and that for item 4 is .13. Item 4 is only 61.9% as efficient in differentiating teams as item 3. As with the previous example, if the firm is going to provide feedback to managers with the expectation that managers are responsible for promoting high performance among subordinates, item 3 is clearly superior. Providing feedback to managers based on item 4 would introduce unnecessary error by using an item that was significantly worse at differentiating managers. Item 4 might be more appropriate for assessing a team-level construct such as intrateam collaboration, although the referent "people here" is likely still ambiguous. If an organization was interesting in tracking and promoting intrateam collaboration, the ICC(1) could probably be increased by specifically asking employees to consider other team members instead of "people here." Overall, however, these examples speak to the choice of referent in survey design and how that might be evaluated in practice.

Example 2: The Stability of ICC(1) Values

A logical question to ask about the ICC(1) values in both the example involving promoting diversity and the example involving promoting high performance is whether the differences between ICC(1) values are stable. We can answer this question two different ways. First, we can estimate confidence intervals around the ICC(1) values to get a sense of whether we would likely see large differences in another sample (wide confidence intervals). Second, we can examine the temporal stability of the ICC(1) values by estimating values on additional data from the years 2015 and 2016. If ICC(1) values show narrow confidence intervals and return values that are similar across years, we can infer that the ICC(1) results we reported from 2014 reflect properties of the items.

To estimate confidence intervals for the ICC(1), we use a different R package (ICCest function in ICC package). Consequently, the ICC(1) estimates may vary slightly as there are several different analytic ways to estimate ICC(1) values (see Bliese, 2000). Table 18.1 provides estimates of the ICC(1) values and the confidence intervals for the four items discussed in example 1 in all three time periods. Notice that ICC(1) estimates have fairly narrow confidence intervals and that the ICC(1) values are stable across time.

Table 18.1 The Stability of ICC(1) Values

Item	ICC(1) 2014	ICC(1) 2015	ICC(1) 2016
1. My manager encourages an environment where individual differences are valued.	.17 (.148–.191)	.16 (.140–.178)	.17 (.155–.185)
2. [FIRM NAME] encourages and promotes diversity of backgrounds, talents, and perspectives.	.11 (.093–.132)	.11 (.089–.122)	.09 (.075–.100)
3. My manager inspires high performance through his or her leadership.	.21 (.189–.235)	.19 (.170–.210)	.20 (.185–.216)
4. People here challenge each other to meet higher standards of performance.	.13 (.106–.146)	.13 (.112–.147)	.14 (.131–.160)

Note. Numbers in parentheses represent the 95% confidence interval for the ICC(1) values.

At a practical level, these results imply that ICC(1) values from a reasonably large sample will likely replicate in future samples.

One caveat to the point about temporal stability is that if a firm actively manages the construct, the ICC(1) value might change. In our example, if an initiative is put into place that focuses on helping managers whose teams report low values on item 1, which asks whether "individual differences are valued," the firm would likely experience an overall increase (firm-wide) on the average value and an associated decrease in the ICC(1).

Example 3: Different Constructs Likely Have Different ICC(1) Values

The previous examples highlight the importance of wording items in ways that focus the respondent on the level at which feedback will be provided. That is, if items are going to be aggregated to the level of the manager, then focusing the items on the manager or workgroup appears to increase the ICC(1) values. Presumably, however, constructs likely vary in the degree to which they display between-group variation. For instance, consider the following four items:

Item 1: Our work processes are well organized and efficient.
Item 2: Processes and procedures allow me to effectively meet my customers' needs.
Item 3: At [FIRM NAME], we are always searching for the next great idea.
Item 4: Good ideas are adopted here regardless of who suggests them or where they come from.

None of these items explicitly reference the manager or workgroup; however, the first two items, which focus on work processes and procedures, have ICC(1) values of .20 and .22, respectively, in the 2014 data. The second two items, which focus on innovation and idea generation, have ICC(1) values of .11 and .12, respectively, in the 2014 data.

While this is a simple example, it suggests that managers are viewed (by their teams) as having more differentiation (e.g., a larger impact) in terms of setting and maintaining work processes than in terms of fostering new ideas. Obviously, there are many caveats to this statement, not the least of which is that before drawing this conclusion it would be prudent to develop items that explicitly focused on the manager and workgroup. That is, perhaps an item that stated "My manager makes sure that our workgroup is always searching for the next great idea" would show substantial increases in ICC(1) values. Ultimately, however, it seems likely that constructs will vary with respect to ICC(1) values and that some of this variation will depend on whether the construct is likely observable and concrete (work processes and procedure) or more abstract (idea generation).

We note that ICC(1) values on constructs that explicitly refer to states that the respondent experiences (e.g., "In the last two weeks, I have felt. . . .") tend to have low ICC(1) ratings. For instance, researchers have found that well-being-type measures tend to have ICC(1) values of around .05 (Bliese 2006; Murray & Short, 1995). We suspect that many constructs of interest to applied psychologists and practitioners (e.g., commitment, job satisfaction, turnover intention) may have low ICC(1) values because such items focus the employee on his or her internal state.

Example 4: ICC(1) Values and Individual Psychometrics

Our final example further illustrates a point detailed by Bliese et al. (2019), who demonstrated that individual psychometrics do not provide the same information as ICC(1) values. As noted, firms often use single items and report aggregate results from single items. Even so, even in applied settings, there are advantages to developing measurement systems that rely on multi-item scales to help ensure that items are reliably assessing constructs of interest. For instance, an engagement survey might ask three items about how a manager promotes diversity in his or her workgroup with the idea that the three items comprise a reliable measure of diversity. Showing that respondents are internally consistent on these three items helps support the idea that diversity promotion is being reliably assessed.

Importantly, however, the common indices used to evaluate items for internal consistency provide virtually no information about whether the item is particularly good at differentiating groups. To illustrate this point, consider Table 18.2. The table lists four items from the 2014 survey that are internally consistent as a measure of "engagement" (Cronbach's alpha of .87) along with factor loadings from a confirmatory factor analysis. The measure of internal consistency, the factor loadings, and the fit indices (confirmatory factor index = .986; Tucker Lewis index = .959; normed fit index = .986; root

Table 18.2 ICC(1) Values and Individual Psychometrics of the 2014 Engagement Scale

Item	Factor Loading	ICC(1)
1. I feel energized by my job.	.745	.15
2. I would recommend [FIRM NAME] as a great place to work.	.824	.16
3. Working at [FIRM NAME] inspires me to do my best.	.816	.10
4. If I were offered a comparable position with similar pay and benefits at another company, I would stay with [FIRM NAME].	.783	.11

Note. Cronbach's alpha = .87.

mean square error of approximation = .115; standardized root mean squared error = .020) suggest that a scale of engagement based on these four items would be reliable.

Notice, however, that the four items vary with respect to how well they differentiate groups. The first two items have ICC(1) values of .15 and .16, and the second two items have ICC(1) values of .10 and .11. These ICC(1) differences are not captured by the factor loadings. Indeed, if one used the factor loadings to down-select items to a three-item scale, a likely candidate for omission would be item 1 ("I feel energized by my job") because it has the lowest factor loading. Unfortunately, eliminating this item would work against detecting differences across groups because item 1 has one of the higher ICC(1) values.

Scale development is complex, and developing valid and reliable scales is challenging (see also Chen, Mathieu, & Bliese, 2004). We do not advocate that items for scales assessing group-level constructs be based solely on ICC(1) values; however, we do encourage both practitioners and researchers to use ICC(1) information when selecting items.

Conclusion

The ability to differentiate groups has important implications in both applied and research settings. Unfortunately, relatively little attention has been devoted to optimizing between-group differentiation. In this chapter we have shown that items on engagement surveys differ substantially with respect to their ability to differentiate groups and have argued that both researchers and practitioners should examine item-level ICC(1) values when developing surveys where results will be aggregated to the group level.

Notes

1. Appendix A provides code to replicate Figure 18.1 and estimate ICC(1) values in R statistical software. Appendix B provides code for estimating an ICC(1) in SPSS.
2. Negative ICC(1) values are possible if estimated using ANOVA models. ICC(1) values estimated in mixed-effects models, however, have a minimum value of 0.
3. Code is provided in Appendix A.

References

Bartko, J. J. (1976). On various intraclass correlation reliability coefficients. *Psychological Bulletin, 83*, 762–765.

Bliese, P. D. (1998). Group size, ICC values, and group-level correlations: A simulation. *Organizational Research Methods, 1*, 355–373.

Bliese, P. D. (2006). Social climates: Drivers of soldier well-being and resilience. In A. B. Adler, C. A. Castro, & T. W. Britt (Eds.), *Military life: The psychology of serving in peace and combat. Operational Stress* (Vol. 2, pp. 213–234). Westport, CT: Praeger Security International.

Bliese, P. D. (2000). Within-group agreement, non-independence, and reliability: Implications for data aggregation and analysis. In K. J. Klein & S. W. Kozlowski (Eds.), *Multilevel theory, research, and methods in organizations* (pp. 349–381). San Francisco, CA: Jossey-Bass.

Bliese, P. D., Maltarich, M. A., & Hendricks, J. L. (2018). Back to basics with mixed-effects models: Nine take-away points. *Journal of Business and Psychology, 33*, 1–23.

Bliese, P. D., Maltarich, M. A., Hendricks, J. L., Hofmann, D. A., & Adler, A. B. (2019). Improving the measurement of group-level constructs by optimizing between-group differentiation. *Journal of Applied Psychology, 104*, 293–302.

Chan, D. (2019). Team-level constructs. *Annual Review of Organizational Psychology and Organizational Behavior, 6*, 325–348.

Chen, G., Mathieu, M. J., & Bliese, P. D. (2004). A framework for conducting multilevel construct validation. In F. Dansereau & F. J. Yammarino (Eds.), *Research in multi-level issues. Multi-level issues in organizational behavior and processes* (Vol. 3, pp. 273–303). Oxford, England: Elsevier Science.

Hinkin, T. R. (1998). A brief tutorial on the development of measures for use in survey questionnaires. *Organizational Research Methods, 1*, 104–121.

Hofmann, D. A., & Gavin, M. B. (1998). Centering decisions in hierarchical linear models: Implications for research in organizations. *Journal of Management, 24,* 623–641.

Kozlowski, S. W. J., & Klein, K. J. (2000). A multilevel approach to theory and research in organizations: Contextual, temporal and emergent processes. In K. J. Klein & S. W. Kozlowski (Eds.), *Multilevel theory, research, and methods in organizations* (pp. 512–553). San Francisco, CA: Jossey-Bass.

Lincoln, J. R., & Zeitz, G. (1980). Organizational properties from aggregate data: Separating individual and structural effects. *American Sociological Review, 45,* 391–408.

Murray, D. M., & Short, B. (1995). Intra-class correlation among measures related to alcohol use by young adults: Estimates, correlates and applications in intervention studies. *Journal of Studies on Alcohol, 56,* 681–694.

Pedhauzer, E. J., & Schmelkin, L. P. (1991). *Measurement, design and analysis: An integrated approach.* Hillsdale, NJ: Lawrence Erlbaum.

Pinheiro, J. C., & Bates, D. M. (2000). *Mixed-effects models in S and S-PLUS.* New York, NY: Springer.

Raudenbush, S., & Bryk, A. (2002). *Hierarchical linear models: Applications and data analysis methods* (2nd ed.). Thousand Oaks, CA: Sage.

Ridout, M. S., Demétrio, C. G. B., & Firth, D. (1999). Estimating intraclass correlation for binary data. *Biometrics, 55,* 137–148.

US Army. (2009). Mental Health Advisory Team (MHAT) VI: Operation Iraqi Freedom 07-09 Report. Retrieved from https://armymedicine.health.mil/Reports

Appendix A

R Statistical Code

```
#####################################
#Code to generate Figure 1 and estimate the ICC(1)
#####################################
set.seed(426431)
DATA<-data.frame(WFC=rbinom(500,size=1,prob=.4),GRPID=rep(1:50,10))
TDAT<-sort(tapply(DATA$WFC,DATA$GRPID,mean))
library(lattice)
win.graph() # opens a graphic window in the Windows operating system
barchart(TDAT,ylab="Team Number,"
xlab="Percent of Team Members Reporting High Work-Family Conflict,"col="grey")
library(multilevel)
tmod<-aov(WFC~factor(GRPID),DATA)
ICC1(tmod)
#############################################
# Create two correlated variables; assign arbitrary group IDs
# and estimate a group-level correlation
#############################################
library(MASS)
set.seed(101313)
```

```
#create two random variables with correlation of .60
TDAT<-mvrnorm(n=1000, mu=c(0, 0),
Sigma=matrix(c(1, .60, .3, 1), nrow=2))
IND.DAT<-data.frame(X=TDAT[,1],Y=TDAT[,2],GID=rep(1:100,each=10))
#Estimate the individual correlation
nrow(IND.DAT)
cor(IND.DAT[,1:2])
#Create 100 group means from groups with 10 members
GRP.DAT<-aggregate(IND.DAT,list(IND.DAT$GID),mean)
#Estimate the correlation among the 100 group means
nrow(GRP.DAT)
cor(GRP.DAT[,2:3])
########################
#Example code to read in data and estimate
# the ICC(1). Assumes raw data in csv format with
# column for group ID and columns for items
########################
data <- read.csv(file.choose())
names(data)
########################
#Estimate ICC(1) values
########################
library(multilevel)
mult.icc(data[,c("item1","'item2,"'item3")],data$groupid)
########################
#Estimate confidence intervals for the ICC(1)
########################
library(ICC)
ICCest(data$groupid, data$item1)
```

Appendix B

SPSS Syntax for ICC(1)

```
VARCOMP item1 BY groupid
/RANDOM=groupid
/OUTFILE=VAREST ('C:\Program Files\VAREST.sav')
/METHOD=REML
/CRITERIA=ITERATE(50)
/CRITERIA=CONVERGE(1.0E-8)
/DESIGN
/INTERCEPT=INCLUDE.
GET FILE = "C:\Program Files\VAREST.sav" /DROP = ROWTYPE_ VARNAME_.
RENAME VAR (VC1 VC2 = BETWEEN WITHIN).
COMPUTE ICC=BETWEEN/(BETWEEN+WITHIN).
LIST.
```

19

Data Visualization

Evan F. Sinar

Data visualization comprises a set of techniques and principles to graphically represent quantitative information. Well-designed data visualizations use visual properties such as position, length, angle, and color to efficiently explore and compellingly convey data sets of any size. Compared to traditional text- or table-based methods for summarizing and communicating data, visualizations produce stronger understanding, memorability, and engagement for audiences and stakeholders. Despite these advantages, data visualization is an underused and suboptimized approach for many survey researchers and practitioners who have ample access to the prerequisite data sources and influence opportunities to deploy these techniques effectively.

Workplace surveys remain key and explainable drivers of insight about employee attitudes, voice, and predicted behaviors for many organizations (Judd, O'Rourke, & Grant, 2018). Adoption of visualization techniques will allow the survey practitioner to better leverage survey findings by attracting and focusing attention of—and, often, investment from—organizational stakeholders. This chapter overviews key guidelines for effectively visualizing survey data to highlight the visualization types and techniques most aligned to survey data-gathering and business applications and recommends tools and resources for incorporating visualization into one's own survey practices.

Visualization's Potential for Survey Research

Awareness and application of data visualization have surged alongside the use of new and prolific "big data" information sources such as wearable sensors, Internet of things devices, social media, and point-of-sale transaction data. The big data context has also been an impetus for early discussions of visualization applied to management science (e.g., Sinar, 2015; Tay et al., 2017).

Evan F. Sinar, *Data Visualization* In: *Employee Surveys and Sensing.* Edited by: William H. Macey and Alexis A. Fink, Oxford University Press (2020). © Society for Industrial and Organizational Psychology.
DOI: 10.1093/oso/9780190939717.003.0019

However, most visualization techniques are also very well suited to several defining characteristics of survey-driven data collection regardless of the magnitude of these data sets. Survey data are readily visualized because they are often highly structured, numerical (though they can still include free-text responses to specific questions), comparative (e.g., across participant groups), and repeated (e.g., spanning time and repeated administrations).

Visualization's relevance for survey research applications is further accentuated by how adeptly survey methods and outputs complement big data approaches. Big data research is often exploratory; surveys typically center on a predetermined set of questions and hypotheses. Big data research requires heavy extract, transform, and load activities when preprocessing data; survey researchers are better able to shape data gathering and quality assurance at the time of collection (Baker, 2017). This allows survey data to be advanced more quickly and more confidently to the visualization stage of analysis. Well-constructed surveys can be the antithesis of and a natural counterpart to big data (Callegaro & Yang, 2018).

Visualization Proficiency and Objectives for Survey Analysis

For survey analysis purposes, data visualization can be used for two major purposes: to explore and explain survey data sets. Data visualization aids survey data exploration by allowing the researcher or audience to detect relationships, patterns, and variation within the data sets as they progress through the earliest stages of analysis. Visualization techniques are well suited to diagnosing issues with data quality such as outliers and unexpected distributions (Borovina Josko & Ferreira, 2017). Deployed as "graphical descriptives," visualization approaches can surface awareness and elicit action about key survey data parameters such as skewness, residual linearity, homogeneity of variance, and the presence of overly influential data points (Tay, Parrigon, Huang, & LeBreton, 2016).

Data visualization can serve an explanatory function by helping survey researchers convey complexity in a format that is more approachable to and engaging for a broad audience. Pandey, Manivannan, Nov, Satterthwaite, and Bertini (2014) found visually presented information to be more persuasive to and produce more attitude change with an audience compared to the same information presented in tables. Al-Kassab, Ouertani, Schiuma, and Neely

(2014) found that when visualization techniques were used, managers' information synthesis and processing abilities while making decisions were improved. Kernbach, Eppler, and Bresciani (2015) found that business strategies presented visually garnered greater attention, stronger agreement, heightened recall, and more positive presenter ratings compared to when the same information was presented in bulleted lists.

Audience Considerations

Survey researchers must proactively identify and align their visualization approaches to both the audience and the modality of their data presentation. Facing an audience with low familiarity with or preference for visualized data, a researcher should consider a more extensive orientation preamble to raise awareness and openness of the visualization methods being used. Ultimately, a researcher's goal should be to gain a deep understanding of the insights, decisions, and actions being sought for a particular business audience. If audiences, even for the same underlying survey data set and study, vary dramatically on these factors, a researcher may be better served by creating a different presentation for each distinct audience than attempting— often fruitlessly—to produce a single visualization-based presentation for all groups.

Senior executives are a key stakeholder group for many visualization presentations as they often operate at the intersection of complex, strategic decision-making and oversight of large swaths of survey data-generating segments of the organization (see Chapter 20). Moore (2017) identified six instructive data visualization properties matching the expectations of executive decision makers:

1. *Data relevance, integrity, and accuracy*: Established through deliberate qualification of data before they are visualized, information about data cleaning can be shared as an overlay to the visualization itself or an explicit component of the presentation.
2. *Integration of multiple data sources*: Complex, strategic decisions will often require analyses and visualizations that synthesize and align several distinct data sources. Survey researchers can draw on multivariate methods or "small multiples" approaches to show different data sources in a progressive, easily comparable panel view.

3. *Clarity, intuitiveness, and pattern-spotting*: Visualizations that reduce complexity toward a clear, concise message of trends and insights are better received by executives. Survey researchers can maximize clarity by adopting effective graphical principles such as minimalistic use of color and avoidance of excessive visual adornments that do not convey data (e.g., three-dimensional effects, redundant or overly verbose labeling).

4. *Decision enabling but not decision formulating*: Senior audience decisions are typically informed but not conclusively made on the basis of a single or even a set of visualizations. Accordingly, survey researchers should draw conclusions from the data they visualize including recommendations for action and progression. However, they should remain open to further questions (and, often, follow-up visualizations) to explore additional facets of the decision to be made by the executive team.

5. *Confidence, professionalism, and knowledge of subject matter*: Analyst confidence, professionalism, and know-how are evident in visualization design choices and accompanying explanations for the rationale and insights derived from the data.

6. *Creation of a "wow" factor*: Senior executives—most of whom have seen hundreds of data tables, dashboards, and traditional visualizations such as bar and pie charts—respond positively to beyond-the-norm visualization techniques. Accordingly, more distinctive and unique visualizations can improve memorability and impact (Borkin et al., 2013).

Modality Considerations

Design choices can vary based on the format in which the visualization is displayed. For large-group formats such as slide-based presentations, screen sizes, lighting, projector resolutions, color saturation, and room depths can vary widely. Presenters should confirm visualization legibility beforehand in the room and with the projector which will be used, making any adjustments needed to improve the audience's view of the material. This may involve increasing font and graphics size, enhancing graphical contrast, and adding annotations, highlights, or callout boxes to denote key points.

Printed report formats can draw on the advantages of higher-resolution graphics in print format and close-up inspection of the material. Annotations and explanations can be positioned alongside visualizations, whereas in slide-based presentations these must be listed on-screen or vocalized by the speaker. Researchers must evaluate the robustness of their visualizations to black-and-white or grayscale, recognizing that distinctions using color as a graphical property may not extend to print formats that don't retain the full color scale. Sites such as Colorbrewer (http://colorbrewer2.org) generate color schemes that are safe for printing, photocopying, and color-blindness.

Interactivity is a third major form of visualization modality—formats that allow the audience to visually explore the survey data sets themselves, typically through specialized software for this purpose. Interactive visualizations move beyond static views to offer dynamic perspectives on survey data sets, thereby expanding the engagement and utility of visualization approaches in scenarios where interactivity is appropriate. Interactivity is particularly useful with audiences whose diverse perspectives will benefit the research effort as these individuals will often detect patterns and propose explanations the original researcher may not have considered. The UK's Ofcom organization has produced an excellent example of an interactive view of survey results (Ofcom, 2018).

As an overview of interactive visualization techniques in the hypothetical context of an employee engagement survey, I draw on and explicate a seven-category framework for visualization interactivity proposed by Soo Yi, Kang, Stasko, and Jacko (2007):

1. *Select*: To mark a particular case of data for additional investigation or later reference. For example, selecting an outlier department in which average engagement scores are much lower than other groups.
2. *Explore*: To shift the visualization to a different segment of the data set. For example, shifting from a visualization of the highest-engagement work teams in Europe to the same rank-ordered view for teams in Asia.
3. *Reconfigure*: To sort, change axis or date ranges, reset the baseline, or otherwise alter the visualization perspective. For example, to change the visualization from a 1-year to a 3-year view of engagement trends.
4. *Encode*: To visually express a data property by changing an element's size, color, shape, or another graphical parameter. For example, highlighting a particular region's engagement scores within a cross-region visualization when presenting to senior leaders.

5. *Abstract/elaborate*: To shift the visualization to a different level of the data structure, either higher or lower in the hierarchy. For example, elevating from a country-level view of engagement scores by function to a region-level view of engagement scores by country.
6. *Filter*: To limit the number of data elements displayed in the visualization. For example, to filter out employees with tenures greater than 10 years in a visualization of engagement score change over time.
7. *Connect*: To detect associations between similar data elements across visualizations. For example, to identify the subset of departments which are each above the median on three specific facets of engagement and below the median on the remaining facets.

Design Principles

A survey researcher's design choices have critical consequences for the most important goal of any visualization—accurate understanding of the visualized data patterns by the audience. Researchers can maximize clarity by drawing on extensive research comparing interpretative accuracy of foundational visual properties that are the basis for every visualization. Summarizing decades of prior research, Lunbald (2015) rank-ordered 10 core visual features from most to least accurate for nominal, ordinal, and interval/ratio data (Table 19.1): position, length, angle, area, volume, shape, color hue, saturation, contrast, and texture. Differences expressed using visual features

Table 19.1 Core Visual Features Ordered by Accuracy

	Nominal Data	Ordinal Data	Interval/Ratio Data
More accurate	Position	Position	Position
	Color hue	Contrast	Length
	Texture	Saturation	Angle
	Contrast	Color hue	Area
	Saturation	Texture	Volume
	Shape	Length	Contrast
	Length	Angle	Saturation
	Angle	Area	Color hue
	Area	Volume	Texture
Less accurate	Volume	Shape	Shape

higher on these lists are more accurately interpreted; those lower on the lists produce under- or overestimates of true numerical differences. By understanding how features shape accuracy, survey researchers can plan their visualization design to maximize clarity. They can also avoid poor visualization practices such as using volume instead of length to depict differences in interval/ratio data since the latter often produce skewed interpretations or using shape to denote differences among ordinal data groupings.

As a general practice, researchers should exclusively use the top four visual features whenever possible. That is, use only position, length, angle, and area to show differences among data on continuous scales. Or if data have been grouped into categories ordinally, use only position, contrast, saturation, and color hue (when selecting color hues, it is important to also consider color-blindness and often, for corporate presentations, brand standards) to distinguish data elements while maintaining high accuracy. The visual features in this section are referenced alongside overviews of visualization categories and specific types: each type uses one or more of these properties to show data distinctions.

Data Source Considerations

Survey researchers should consider several characteristics when evaluating and preparing their data sets for visualization. Certain properties of survey data can, when in place, substantially boost the applicability of the visualization techniques discussed in this chapter. Though large volumes of data are not essential for visualizations, the advantages of visualized forms of data presentation over tables or text will increase commensurately with the magnitude and complexity of the survey data set. As with other forms of talent-focused analytics, baseline thresholds for data cleanliness and quality should be exceeded before proceeding with visualizations.

Beyond data that fulfill basic quality standards, data gathered across multiple time periods—for example, when the same survey is administered repeatedly—can be readily visualized to display longitudinal trends. With regular "pulse surveys," a growing trend for employee engagement data-gathering (see Chapter 4; Bersin, 2017), the class of visualizations designed specifically for longitudinal research questions will become increasingly relevant. Multivariate survey data, such that each case is defined on many distinct dimensions (e.g., attitudes, demographics, recommendation intentions), also draw on visualization's strengths. Visualization is also well matched to survey data segmented into nested groups such as department, job title, or tenure range. Map-based survey data—for example, resulting from a global survey administration—are aligned with geographical visualization methods. If the survey includes open-ended components (e.g., free-response text fields), text-centered visualization methods can be useful for conveying key themes, though typically after preprocessing of the raw text responses. Specific visualization types associated with data set profiles are discussed in more depth in the following section.

Visualization Types Matched to Survey Purposes

A researcher's choice of data visualization type should be matched to the intended goal of a specific survey analysis. Drawing on a visualization framework defined by Kirk (2012), I propose five distinct categories aligned to common survey purposes. For the five categories, I list sample survey research questions they answer in business settings, several representative types within the category, which graphical principles each uses to encode data (based on the list in Table 19.1), and genericized examples of each type.

First are visualization types designed to compare values across groups (Table 19.2 and Figure 19.1). In this type, data are categorized into groups, and these groups are compared to each other based on an aggregate property, often an average or count. Group comparison visualizations include slopegraphs, alluvial diagrams, and more commonly used forms such as bar charts. Survey data categorizing individual cases into job levels, functions, departments, and demographic groups such as race, gender, and generation are well suited to group comparison visualizations. Slopegraphs, well suited to group comparisons, show how group scores vary across variables

Table 19.2 Group Comparison Visualizations

To answer business questions such as	Which regions have shown the strongest year-to-year increase in engagement scores? How do proportions of at-risk employees differ between organizational functions?		
Visualization type	Slopegraph	Alluvial diagram	Bar/column chart
Display data using	Angle, position	Area, position	Length

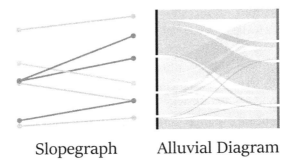

Slopegraph　　Alluvial Diagram

Figure 19.1. Slopegraph and alluvial diagram examples.

or between two time periods. Alluvial diagrams show patterns for how cases flow between categories. Bar and column charts represent data as length of bars and columns, respectively.

Second are visualizations to display connections or relationships among variables (Table 19.3 and Figure 19.2). Visualizations of this type show how two or more variables covary. Survey data spanning multiple continuous or categorical variables (e.g., pairing survey data with outcome data) are well

Table 19.3 Connection/Relationship Visualizations

To answer business questions such as	Which engagement facets have the strongest relationship with employee turnover? Which departments share common profiles in their engagement responses by factor?		
Visualization type	Bubble plot	Scatterplots	Parallel coordinates
Display data using	Position and area	Position	Position

Bubble Plot　　　Scatterplot　　Parallel Coordinates

Figure 19.2. Bubble plot, scatterplot, and parallel coordinates examples.

Table 19.4 Hierarchical/Part-to-Whole Visualizations

To answer business questions such as	Which departments have the largest number of low-engagement employees? Looking across all departments nested within regions, which are the problematic "hot spots"? Which engagement patterns are consistent across all functions within a region, and which are more variable across functions?		
Visualization type	Circle packing	Tree map	Sunburst
Display data using	Area	Area	Area

suited to connection/relationship visualizations. Connection/relationship visualizations include visual correlation matrices, scatterplots, and parallel coordinates. Visual correlation matrices depict relationship magnitude as larger-area circles within a grid. Scatterplots show how strongly increases in one variable relate to increases in a second variable; by adding bubble size as a third visual property as a bubble plot, they can also show which cases in the scatterplot have the largest number of members (e.g., larger departments are shown by larger circles). Parallel coordinates show multivariate data by arraying variables along an x-axis and connecting the relative positions of each data element by lines spanning all variables.

Third are visualizations to represent hierarchical or part-to-whole associations (Table 19.4 and Figure 19.3). Survey data with data structured into hierarchies (e.g., departments nested within regions) are well suited to hierarchical/part-to-whole visualizations. Common hierarchical/part-to-whole visualizations include circle packing, tree maps, and sunburst charts. Circle packing diagrams encode each group's size by area of its corresponding

Circle Packing   Tree Map   Sunburst

Figure 19.3. Circle packing, tree map, and sunburst examples.

Table 19.5 Over-Time Visualizations

To answer business questions such as	Which survey response groups become proportionally larger or smaller over time? When did year-to-year engagement score increases and decreases peak?			
Visualization type	Horizon chart	Stream graph	Bump chart	Line chart
Display data using	Area, saturation	Area, position	Area, position	Angle, position

circle and can depict other values such as average engagement score by hue of the circle. Tree maps display data within a rectangular layout and size data elements based on group size or another relative value. Rectangles can also be subdivided based on a lower level of the hierarchy to be represented. Sunbursts also show weighted hierarchical structures, but instead of subdividing the shape, they extend it outward to additional layers of depth. Because of this, they are often better at showing multilevel structures. For both tree maps and sunbursts, color can also be introduced as a visual property similar to a heat map—for example, using darker green to indicate stronger engagement levels for a group or subgroup.

Fourth are visualization types that illustrate change over time (Table 19.5 and Figure 19.4). Survey data occurring over time—for example, multiple administrations of a company-wide pulse survey—are well suited to over-time visualizations. Over-time visualizations include horizon charts, stream graphs, bump charts, and line charts. Horizon charts display changes in time-series data (e.g., year-over-year increases or decreases) by placing both negative and positive values on the vertical scale, showing negative values with an alternate color or saturation and above the "horizon" baseline alongside

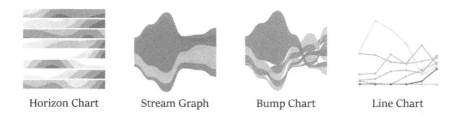

Horizon Chart   Stream Graph   Bump Chart   Line Chart

Figure 19.4. Horizon chart, stream graph, bump chart, and line chart examples.

Table 19.6 Geospatial Visualizations

To answer business questions such as	Where within our global operations are engagement scores highest and lowest? Which region has the largest number of at-risk leaders?	
Visualization type	Choropleth	Dot map
Display data using	Color, hue, saturation	Area, position

positive values. Stream graphs use area to show the relative magnitude of a group across time period, and bump charts additionally show the rank order of groups (groups positioned higher on the y-axis for a particular time period are larger than groups positioned lower). Line charts show the change in a data value across time periods.

Fifth are visualizations that overlay data representations onto maps or other geographic structures (Table 19.6 and Figure 19.5). Survey data spanning countries or regions are well suited to geospatial visualizations. Geospatial visualization types include choropleth maps and dot maps. Choropleth maps encode existing geographic structures (typically countries or states) with color hues, saturations, or contrasts that vary based on data properties such as score levels or number of cases. Dot maps place circles scaled by a data property onto geographic structures.

Although this summary of visualization types attempts to curate a subset of visualizations within each category based on applicability to survey

Choropleth Map   Dot Map

Figure 19.5. Choropleth and dot map examples.

research, a multitude of additional types exists. A comprehensive resource for perusing an expanded range of visualization types is The Data Visualisation Catalogue (Ribecca, 2017). For each of 60 (at the time of this writing) visualization types, the site provides a description, characteristics, functions, similar charts, generation tools, and real-world examples. For additional discussion of and "in the wild examples" for seven of the visualization types which are relatively uncommon in practice but that have high potential for further use in survey research—slopegraphs, parallel coordinates, alluvial diagrams, sunbursts, circle packing, streamgraphs, and horizon charts—see Sinar (2016).

Visualizing Text Data

As organizations accumulate open-response and other forms of unstructured data at increasing rates within and alongside workplace surveys, text analysis is emerging as a distinct and powerful application for visualization methods (see Chapter 13). Although similar to other forms of data visualization in that text frequencies and sentiments must first be coded as quantitative variables, text-centric visualizations are distinct in that they represent words and phrases directly within the graphical views. Text visualization methods appear to be advancing even more rapidly than quantitative visualization techniques: the Text Visualization Browser (Kucher & Kerren, 2015). presents over 400 visualization techniques, searchable and sortable as they apply to various analytic tasks.

Three common text visualization types (Table 19.7) include word clouds, word trees, and bubble lines. Word clouds, which size words based on their frequency in a corpus, despite their near-ubiquity and susceptibility to data

Table 19.7 Text Visualizations

To answer business questions such as	Which terms are most used by leaders to describe the development programs we offer? Has our shift to open-office floor plans caused related terms to be cited more often in the "what can we improve" field of our engagement survey?		
Visualization type	Word cloud	Word tree	Bubble lines
Display data using	Text size	Position, text size	Area, position

misrepresentation (e.g., certain words will appear visually larger simply because of their number of letters), are nonetheless highly intuitive and versatile. Word clouds also gain sophistication when they are split by group membership to show how certain terms are used more by one group than another (e.g., do higher-tenure employees use words or phrases more than those with lower tenure?) or when sentiment is applied as an additional visual property (e.g., determining the color or saturation of a term). Word trees also size words based on their frequency but extend this concept by showing the most commonly paired words to the target, either before or after. For a survey project, researchers can visualize the most commonly appearing words after "my manager," for example, or before "needs improvement." Bubble lines encode word or term frequency as circle size and place these circles along an x-axis continuum representing either a timescale or within a single document (e.g., to show if certain terms are used more often in the survey administrations following a major company restructuring, compared to those before).

Evidence-Based Visualization Best Practices and Risks

An extensive research program by Borkin and colleagues (2013, 2016) has validated many of the recommended graphical principles on the audience impact of visualizations. These researchers found that memorability was maximized with visualizations that were colorful, included human figures, and used unique rather than common graphical types. More recently, Garwood, Jones, Clements, and Miori's (2018) study of clarity in data visualization showed that more concise visualizations—those without extraneous elements—produced higher postpresentation comprehension rates for the audience of business managers.

Turning to unintentionally deceptive forms of visualization that should be avoided, Pandey, Rall, Satterthwaite, Nov, and Bertini (2015) investigated the impact of four common types of visualization deception: truncating bar chart y-axes to start at a value other than 0, encoding a quantity as the radius rather than the area of a circle, adjusting the aspect ratio of a graph to change the apparent slope of a line, inverting the y-axis so that the shift from low to high on the graph is displayed as a downward-sloping line. These researchers found that all four deceptions indeed created misunderstandings about the true data patterns and should be avoided as a result.

Foundational Techniques

Agnostic to specific graphical types, four foundational techniques can be useful for survey researchers deploying visualizations in their own work.

1. *Orienting*: This can include presenting a "mock-up" visualization to familiarize the audience with the layout of the graphic before proceeding to the actual data. This keeps the discussion focused on the intended story rather than on clarifications about the visualization type itself.

2. *Contrasting*: Researchers can accentuate a visualization's contrast—and resulting memorability—by using focal colors and highlights to draw attention to the most notable cases or patterns in the data. This can also include using visual properties to denote when a displayed difference exceeds a threshold for statistical or practical significance.

3. *Sequencing*: Well-sequenced visualizations—those that progress through multiple distinct data views in a planned and logical order—will immerse the audience in the larger story the researcher is seeking to convey. In a survey project, this could involve shifting from a global to a regional to a department-level view of data to sharpen emphasis on the most noteworthy portions of the data but only after the broader organizational landscape is established. One useful sequencing model is to emulate the panel-based structure of comics—Bach, Riche, Carpendale, and Pfister (2017) describe and detail this concept in an extremely creative article about "data comics."

4. *Annotating*: By annotating data visualizations with supplementary information, survey researchers can more clearly communicate key data-driven insights, observations, and recommendations. Annotations also reduce working memory demands for the audience (Shah & Hoeffner, 2002), which in turn shifts the balance of an audience discussion away from basic clarification questions and toward more sophisticated co-exploration and planning next-step actions. With visualizations for survey projects, annotations can include information about time frames and provenance of data, trigger events for score shifts, and include a title that clearly outlines recommendations and rationales.

Visualization Tools

One of the most important recent trends in data visualization has been the shift from programming-focused visualization tools (e.g., R, D3.js) to tools that prioritize design and ease of use over programming aptitude. While toolsets like R remain highly robust platforms for generating visualizations, I focus here on three tools that are either open source or readily available and that often require just a few minutes to move from a well-organized data set to a preliminary visualization, contingent on further postgeneration annotation and refinement.

1. *RawGraphs* (*http://rawgraphs.io/*): RawGraphs is an open-source site into which researchers can import or paste their data. Once imported, the platform offers 21 types of configurable visualizations and exports to vector graphics files which can be further edited and saved at any resolution needed.
2. *Voyant* (*http://voyant-tools.org/*): Voyant is a versatile online platform for processing text-based data from quantitative and qualitative survey projects. It produces numerous text visualization types: word clouds, word trees, and bubble lines, as well as more than a dozen other visualizations for analyzing and displaying a text corpus.
3. *Microsoft Excel*: The newest versions of Excel can generate many of the recommended visualizations: bar charts, line charts, scatterplots, choropleth maps, tree maps, and sunbursts—additional visualizations with high utility for survey research can be created with add-ins or templates.

Concluding Comments

Survey researchers will face continued pressures to represent their data in accessible, approachable ways, for both technical and nontechnical audiences. Fortunately, survey information is natively well suited to data visualization techniques due to its structure, blend of quantitative and qualitative elements, and nature to include comparative, over-time, and geospatial features. By aggressively pursuing data visualization techniques for their memorability and decision impact, survey researchers can accelerate their ability to catalyze commitment, adoption, and action for business audiences. This chapter sought to overview key tips, techniques, and tools for visualizing survey data effectively, in alignment with common questions for this form of research.

References

Al-Kassab, J., Ouertani, Z. M., Schiuma, G., & Neely, A. (2014). Information visualization to support management decisions. *International Journal of Information Technology & Decision Making, 13*, 407–428.

Bach, B., Riche, N. H., Carpendale, S., & Pfister, H. (2017). The emerging genre of data comics. *IEEE Computer Graphics and Applications, 38*(3), 6–13.

Baker, R. (2017). Big data: A survey research perspective. In P. P. Biemer, E. De Leeuw, S. Eckman, B. Edwards, F. Kreuter, L. Lyberg, C. Tucker, & B. West (Eds.), *Total survey error: Improving quality in the era of big data* (pp. 47–70). Hoboken, NJ: Wiley.

Bersin, J. (2017). HR technology disruptions for 2018: Productivity, design, and intelligence reign. Retrieved from https://www.isaconnection.org/assets/documents/2018BersinHRTechDisruptionsReport.pdf

Borkin, M. A., Bylinskii, Z., Kim, N. W., Bainbridge, C. M., Yeh, C. S., Borkin, D., . . . Oliva, A. (2016). Beyond memorability: Visualization recognition and recall. *IEEE Transactions on Visualization and Computer Graphics, 22*(1), 519–528.

Borkin, M. A., Vo, A. A., Bylinskii, Z., Isola, P., Sunkavalli, S., Oliva, A., & Pfister, H. (2013). What makes a visualization memorable?. *IEEE Transactions on Visualization and Computer Graphics, 19*(12), 2306–2315.

Borovina Josko, J. M., & Ferreira, J. E. (2017). Visualization properties for data quality visual assessment: An exploratory case study. *Information Visualization, 16*(2), 93–112.

Callegaro, M., & Yang, Y. (2018). The role of surveys in the era of "big data." In D. L. Vannette & J. A. Krosnick (Eds.), *The Palgrave handbook of survey research* (pp. 175–192). Cham, Switzerland: Palgrave Macmillan.

Garwood, K. C., Jones, C., Clements, N., & Miori, V. (2018). Innovations to identifying the effects of clear information visualization: Reducing managers time in data interpretation. *Journal of Visual Literacy, 37*, 40–50.

Judd, S., O'Rourke, E., & Grant, A. (2018, March 14). Employee surveys are still one of the best ways to measure engagement. *Harvard Business Review.* Retrieved from https://hbr.org/2018/03/employee-surveys-are-still-one-of-the-best-ways-to-measure-engagement

Kernbach, S., Eppler, M. J., & Bresciani, S. (2015). The use of visualization in the communication of business strategies: An experimental evaluation. *International Journal of Business Communication, 52*(2), 164–187.

Kirk, A. (2012). *Data visualization: A successful design process.* Birmingham, England: Packt.

Kucher, K., & Kerren, A. (2015, April). Text visualization techniques: Taxonomy, visual survey, and community insights. In *2015 IEEE Pacific Visualization Symposium (PacificVis)* (pp. 117–121). IEEE. Retrieved from https://textvis.lnu.se/.

Lunbald, P. (2015, June 23). Second pillar of mapping data to visualizations: Visual encoding. Retrieved from https://blog.qlik.com/visual-encoding.

Moore, J. (2017). Data visualization in support of executive decision making. *Interdisciplinary Journal of Information, Knowledge, and Management, 12,* 125–138.

Ofcom (2018). *Communications Market Report.* Retrieved from https://www.ofcom.org. uk/research-and-data/multi-sector-research/cmr/cmr-2018/interactive.

Pandey, A. V., Manivannan, A., Nov, O., Satterthwaite, M. L., & Bertini, E. (2014). *The persuasive power of data visualization.* Public Law and Legal Theory Working Paper 474. New York, NY: New York University.

Pandey, A. V., Rall, K., Satterthwaite, M. L., Nov, O., & Bertini, E. (2015, April). How deceptive are deceptive visualizations? An empirical analysis of common distortion techniques. In B. Begole (Ed.), *Proceedings of the 33rd Annual ACM Conference on Human Factors in Computing Systems* (pp. 1469–1478). New York, NY: ACM.

Ribecca, S. (2017, April 17). Which chart reference pages are the most popular? Retrieved from https://datavizcatalogue.com/blog/most-popular-chart-reference-pages/.

Shah, P., & Hoeffner, J. (2002). Review of graph comprehension research: Implications for instruction. *Educational Psychology Review, 14*(1), 47–69.

Sinar, E. F. (2015). Data visualization. In S. Tonidandel, E. King, & J. Cortina (Eds.), *Big data at work: The data science revolution and organizational psychology* (pp. 115–157). New York, NY: Taylor & Francis.

Sinar, E. F. (2016, February 14). 7 data visualization types you should be using more (and how to start). Retrieved from https://medium.com/@EvanSinar/7-data-visualization-types-you-should-be-using-more-and-how-to-start-4015b5d4adf2

Soo Yi, J., Kang, Y., Stasko, J. Y., & Jacko, J. A. (2007). Toward a deeper understanding of the role of interaction in information visualization. *IEEE Transactions on Visualization and Computer Graphics, 13*(6), 1224–1231.

Tay, L., Ng, V., Malik, A., Zhang, J., Chae, J., Ebert, D. S., . . . Kern, M. (2017). Big data visualizations in organizational science. *Organizational Research Methods, 21*(3), 660–688.

Tay, L., Parrigon, S., Huang, Q., & LeBreton, J. M. (2016). Graphical descriptives: A way to improve data transparency and methodological rigor in psychology. *Perspectives on Psychological Science, 11*(5), 692–701.

20

Creating and Delivering
the Executive Presentation

Telling the Story of the Survey

Sarah R. Johnson

Organization surveys today are vastly different from those in the early days of the process. Theories, metrics, technology, and approaches have all changed over the decades since the first surveys were administered in organizations; and many of the chapters in this book have alluded to the evolution of the survey process. One component of the survey process that has remained absolutely essential to success is the presentation of survey results to senior leaders in the organization. Even in this age of big data and easy access to all manner of analytics, a presentation of survey findings to executives remains a valuable component of the survey process. When carefully crafted and skillfully delivered, this presentation has the ability to inform, educate, challenge, and inspire senior leaders to take action. The purpose of this chapter is to provide guidance, based on research and practice, which enables survey professionals to get maximum impact from the executive presentation of organizational survey results.

Executive presentations have evolved alongside survey and research practices generally. Advances in technology have resulted in new tools for creating, displaying, and disseminating graphics and the presentation deck. The growing field of data science has enabled analysis of quantitative and qualitative survey responses along with extensive demographic data and business performance metrics. Presentations can be made virtually, eliminating the need to bring geographically dispersed leaders into the same room at the same time to review the findings of the survey. And ever-increasing daily meeting requirements for leaders have compressed many presentations from extensive data reviews to short, carefully curated decks that summarize only a handful of the most important findings.

Sarah R. Johnson, *Creating and Delivering the Executive Presentation* In: *Employee Surveys and Sensing.* Edited by: William H. Macey and Alexis A. Fink, Oxford University Press (2020). © Society for Industrial and Organizational Psychology.
DOI: 10.1093/oso/9780190939717.003.0020

There are four fundamental steps to creating an informative executive presentation that inspires productive and honest conversation and results in meaningful actions:

- Clarify the objective
- Create the story
- Find the right format
- Deliver the presentation

These elements work together to create an opportunity for the survey staff to influence leaders and truly become a strategic partner for managing human capital in the organization.

Clarifying the Objective

What is the purpose of the presentation, and what is the result the survey team hopes to achieve? One common answer to this question is "to brief senior leaders and drive change." Fair enough. But brief them on what and to what end? Given the vast amount of data that the typical survey can produce, significant effort must be made to edit the many topics that could be covered to the small number that must be covered. Human working memory is limited, and the members of your audience will only be able to recall three or four chunks of information or key points (Clark & Mayer, 2007). If the survey presentation includes, for example, 10 themes, the reality is that not only won't your audience remember all 10 but each audience member is likely to walk away remembering a unique set of three to four chunks of information; and the presentation will fail to convey a consistent, complete, and lasting message to the audience.

Without a clear objective, the presentation is nothing more than a collection of slides displaying a variety of data cuts. Without a clear objective, the audience may think the presentation was interesting but at the same time be entirely unclear as to why they are being given the information, how it is relevant to them, and what, if anything, they need to do as a result. A presentation without a clear objective is a missed opportunity.

Human Resources (HR) functions and industrial–organizational (I-O) psychologists have long aspired to be strategic partners to the business in general and to organization executives in particular. Being a strategic partner entails understanding the organization's strategic objectives, what needs to happen for those objectives to be achieved, and what is standing in the way of achieving the objectives. Each of these should inform not only the content of the organization's survey but how the data are analyzed, summarized, reported, and acted upon. For maximum impact, the presentation of results should reflect not what is most interesting in the results but what is most relevant to helping the organization accomplish its strategy and achieve its objectives.

Generally, there is not one single leader, or one defined group, who is solely able to act on survey results. Typically, many different leaders and leadership teams need to be briefed on survey results and in entirely different ways. It is critical for the survey team to identify the end game(s). What action is required as a result of the presentation? Specific answers to this question may only become clear once the data from the survey have been analyzed. Specific survey findings may necessitate unique presentations to different leaders and/or staff groups who need to have this information and are in the best position to act. For example, an analysis of results for high-potential employees is of great value to the team that manages the leadership succession process. Data on employees' understanding of the organization's ethical conduct guidelines and whether they feel safe reporting violations should be shared with internal counsel. The point is that the right data and insights need to be delivered to the right audience.

Creating the Story

A good presentation should contain all of the same elements as a story, including a compelling plot with just the right amount of detail, featuring vibrant personas the audience can relate to and an ending that inspires and compels action. Stories engage the whole brain and are more memorable than simply facts and figures. To that end, recall the writing guidance you may have received in middle school, the 5 Ws: who, what, when, where and why. Considering each of these when creating a presentation will yield a compelling story.

Who?
Who is the audience for the presentation? The audience could include the top leaders of the organization, the board of directors, staff groups, managers, or

employees themselves. Each of these potential audiences has different needs for information, topical interests, and comfort with data. Each potential audience consumes information differently, which means that a presentation created for one audience can easily miss the mark with another if not modified to suit. Identifying and understanding the audience is a crucial first step in the process.

"Who" can also represent the various subgroups in the survey data, from regions and business units to programmers and production employees. It is unnecessary (and potentially impossible) to address all employee subgroups in the presentation, so the presenter must determine which subgroups are of greatest interest to the audience, whether from a strategic perspective or an action-ownership perspective. Some subgroups may have a differential impact on the success of the organization, necessitating significant attention in the presentation. Others are of interest because they are under the purview of the audience as their subordinates or because they may be impacted by programs and practices within the control of members of the audience. It is critical to match the most meaningful slice of the organization with the right audience.

What?

"What" can be approached in two ways. First of all, the "what" can be thought of as fulfilling an information need on the part of the audience. What do they want to know, what topics are of greatest value to them, and what information do they need to successfully execute their jobs? But the "what" may also represent what the audience needs to hear. In this respect, the presentation may focus on new insights, new information, or new topics that the audience is not aware of but needs to know more about. The first approach to "what" is providing the information the audience wants; the second is providing the information the audience does not yet know they want or need, such as emerging trends or data patterns, unexpected findings, or experimental topics. It is important to identify the "what" in the context of recent events in the marketplace or the organization, current strategic initiatives, or the results of other studies or initiatives. Pulling the thread from these other sources of information through to the survey results can help the audience grasp the full meaning and implications of the information that is being presented.

In any case, it is essential to provide the audience with the data and insights that are most relevant to their role in the organization and their ability to effect change. If the "what" is not correctly paired with the right "who," the presentation may be interesting but will solicit a "so what?" or "who cares?" reaction.

There will be times when the "what" is good news. Survey scores may have improved, and actions put in place to address previously identified issues are showing promising returns. There are other times when some or all of the "what" could be perceived as bad news or at the very least a difficult message to deliver. Good news and bad news can be equally difficult to share.

Good news will be a relief to the audience, and they may justifiably take credit for actions that led to this success. But too much good news can lead to complacency, meaning there is no apparent need to take action. Leaders can walk away from a presentation of positive news with a sense that the organization is doing well and that there is nothing urgent or pressing that requires action. Good news can be interpreted to mean that leadership can turn their attention to other things and not worry about these issues until the next survey rolls around. Bad news can also elicit complacency, if the "what" is constructed in a way that does not lend itself to action or if the "what" is interpreted to mean that things in the organization are so bad that very little or nothing can be done. Many presenters are uncomfortable presenting the bad news, and there is an understandable tendency to down-play the findings, justify them in some way, or skirt blame for what might be a disastrous situation. This approach doesn't serve the organization well, nor does it give leaders all the information they need to successfully guide the organization.

In both cases, good news and bad news, the best approach is to include the "but," such as "the survey indicates that employees are highly engaged and our previous actions are yielding promising results, but we need to continue to monitor the situation to insure continued effective implementation of actions, as well as scan the environment to get ahead of potential threats to engagement." When it comes to bad news, the "but" should reference bright spots in the organization (e.g., "scores are low across most units, but there are several units that have done well and provide useful lessons for improvement" or "results indicate serious issues in the new division, but we are confident that these actions, if implemented quickly, can yield improvements"). In general, it is helpful to discuss good news first and then layer in the bad. Starting the presentation with bad news can create defensiveness and an unwillingness to truly listen to the discussion of results.

When?

Given the pace of change in the business world, data and insights, like French fries, are always best when fresh. Presenting survey data long after they have been collected could beg the question as to whether the findings are still valid or if time has shifted the work environment or rendered the identified issues moot. Recently collected data have greater face validity with audiences than data that could be perceived as obsolete.

"When" can also refer to how quickly action needs to take place. Urgent issues may require quick action in order to limit potential negative impacts. Emerging issues may lend themselves to more study with no need for immediate action. In any event, the presenter should provide the audience with guidance as to how quickly actions need to be taken to address the issues raised.

Where?

Organizations are complex organisms, generally comprised of a wide variety of skill groups, locations, regions, business units, levels of authority, and product lines, to name just a few of the potential areas of differentiation. Is the issue systemic across all groups (less likely) or localized in a few groups (more likely)? Where is action likely to result in the greatest positive impact on the organization? Where will the pain be greatest if action is not taken?

It is fair to say that actions that are overly homogenized to suit every organizational subunit will not yield much impact. Designing actions to suit every employee generally results in not suiting any specific employee very well. It is far better to use the presentation to identify the subgroup(s) of the organization where actions are most needed or will yield the most benefit to the organization. For example, focusing attention on critical skill groups, those employees whose skills are difficult to acquire and have significant impact on achieving the organization's goals, will identify specific issues and the actions necessary to insure that this critical asset is protected and nurtured. Turning the audience's attention toward a manufacturing site that is responsible for producing the next generation of products or the call-center employees who have a direct influence on customer satisfaction may be far more productive than looking at all data for all employees in all locations and job groups. The best advice is to avoid boiling the ocean but rather seek out those islands that offer the greatest promise to the organization.

Why?

Like several of the other Ws, "why" has two meanings. The first is analytically focused and is a response to questions such as the following: Why is this insight occurring? Why is engagement declining (or improving)? Why are we losing key talent? Why are some managers successful leaders of people and others struggle to build relationships? Why are researchers afraid to take risks and create innovative solutions? Analysis of the quantitative data via driver analyses, correlations, or a deep demographic analysis can yield clues. Qualitative data in the form of written comments can provide detailed insight into issues raised in the survey results. Comments are best utilized to illustrate the qualitative findings, adding valuable specificity to a finding that may feel amorphous to the audience. It is important to report findings, of course; but without answering the "why" question, audience members are left to come to their own conclusions, which may be heavily influenced by their own biases or experiences or just plain wrong. Delivering insights that explain and educate the audience will lead them to implement actions that are well informed and have the potential to succeed.

Organizational leaders have access to an overwhelming amount of data and information, and the organization's survey is no different. Between the combination of responses to survey questions, dozens of demographic variables, plus the ability to link to business performance metrics, there is the potential for an endless number of analytics and insights. This brings us to the second meaning of "why." The "what" of survey findings and insights is nearly limitless, so it is important to ask "why." Why do leaders need to know this? Why will this information make a difference to the organization's success? It comes down to editing; there are many potential nuggets of information that could be included in the presentation, but some more important than others to share.

Leaders are busy people, and the time survey researchers have to influence them is limited, so it is essential to edit the topics in the presentation ruthlessly. Too much information is confusing, and when a lot is presented in a short amount of time, there is limited opportunity to go into the detail necessary to provide good insight. Presentations cluttered with too many topics and insights quickly lose their focus, which inevitably limits their impact on the audience and on potential actions. Asking "Why is this insight/analysis/finding critical to this audience, and why is it essential to take action now?" will assist in the editing process and yield a presentation that provides the most essential information to the audience. It makes sense to provide different insights and analyses to different audiences.

Putting the 5 Ws Together

Consider the following real-world examples of leader presentations that considered who, what, when, where, and why.

A large, global, and heavily diversified and decentralized organization conducts an annual survey of all employees.

- *Who*: The presentation to the chief executive officer (CEO) focuses exclusively on the executive population.
- *Why*: In this decentralized model the CEO owns responsibility for the engagement, development, and succession of executive talent across the various entities to insure the future success of the organization. Driver analysis, thematic analysis of comments, and contextualizing the results provide reasons for absolute scores and trends.
- *What*: The CEO needs to know not only whether employees have trust and confidence in these leaders but also how these leaders feel about the organization and if there are any potential performance or turnover concerns. Reviews of the data provide insights into the population and suggest necessary actions to be taken.
- *Where*: Analyses identify the business units, regions, or levels of leader (e.g., director, vice president, senior vice president) that may be at risk or struggling to perform.
- *When*: The outcomes of the analysis and the story reveal just how urgently actions need to be taken.

A global customer experience outsourcing organization provides call-center services to many clients, from retailers to cable television providers.

- *Who*: Senior leaders who manage the call centers want to understand the perspective of the thousands of call-center employees who interact with millions of customers each week.
- *What*: Like many companies in this industry, turnover in the call center is high, so it is essential to monitor current levels of engagement in the call center and which employee experiences in the organization influence engagement and can reduce turnover. Reporting the data by location can be used to take local action to address local issues.

- *Why*: Understanding the antecedents to turnover can vastly improve customer satisfaction and lower costs.
- *Where*: Results for each data center and client pinpoint specific pain points that can be addressed via local leadership.
- *When*: Data are collected continuously via onboarding and exit surveys and the annual census survey so that corrective actions can be taken quickly.

Either of these examples would be incomplete if one of the 5 Ws was missing. What made these presentations successful was that the right information was presented to the right audience. Clarifying and editing the story along with matching the story to the audience enhance the odds that meaningful action will be taken and change will occur.

Finding the Right Format

Most discussions of the 5 Ws also include an H: "how." In the context of creating presentations of survey data to share with leaders, "how" refers to the construction of the actual presentation. A thoughtful analysis of the audience, their preferred method of receiving this type of information, and their level of comfort with data and analytics will inform the outline and flow of the presentation, the degree of detail used in explaining the data, and the design of the meeting itself. It is also important to consider the relationship between the presenter and the audience. A good relationship may allow the presenter to be more provocative in the analysis of the results and the message of the presentation.

The "how" of the survey presentation is entirely contextual, and determining the best format to tell the story that has been carefully crafted from survey data depends on the audience and the circumstances. The following is a list of considerations that will influence the "how":

- *Is the audience adept with data*? There are many approaches to analyzing survey data and displaying the findings of these analyses. Approaches to data analysis and data visualization are addressed in Chapter 19, so there is no need to discuss the many options here. Suffice it to say that the data analysis and visualization choices must fit the capabilities of the audience. If the analyses and visuals are complicated and unknown to the audience, much of the presentation will be spent in explanation and justification of this approach. Long explanations of methodologies and graphics leave less time for insights and discussion and run the risk of either alienating the audience or losing their interest and focus. Use the simplest approach to data analysis that will yield critical insights, and edit visuals so that they are clear, concise, and easily understood without a lengthy explanation.

- *How much time is allotted, and how long are attention spans?* There is a distinct trend toward shorter presentations, some with as few as 10 slides of data and insight. Agendas often get squeezed, and the time allotted for the presentation may shrink from 90 minutes to 15. It is essential that the survey team has crafted a short elevator speech, or even a tweet, that summarizes the most critical insight and guidance the leader must take from the presentation. It is wise to craft this speech after data analysis but before creating the presentation deck. Once developed, it will inspire how the presentation unfolds via slides and visuals.

- *In person or virtually?* Virtual meeting technology has enabled employees to collaborate in real time, despite working miles and even continents apart. While efficient, virtual meetings can result in less interaction and discussion among attendees; and without visual cues from attendees' faces and body language, it can be difficult for the presenter to determine if the message is clearly understood or accepted by the audience. As a rule, in-person presentations and discussions are preferred but not always realistic given geographic constraints.

- *Pictures or prose?* While presentation tools such as PowerPoint or Keynote are commonly used in organizations, some companies in general and some executives in particular distrust presentation decks. They may believe that decks leave out key information or gloss over critical details. Realistically, many presentations of survey results (or any other topic, for that matter) communicate little if the presenter is not alongside to share the message that the slides represent. There are instances where prose, or a written summary of the results, is the appropriate vehicle for communicating findings or simply documenting the details of the presentation for future reference. Executives who are unable to meet either in person or virtually may benefit from a well-written and concise summary that includes words and pictures. There are many tools that can be used, from white papers to infographics to interactive tools. Regardless of format, visuals are better remembered than lines of text (Vogel, Dixon, & Lehman, 1986). The combination of visuals and words, either spoken or written, enables dual-channel processing and will be remembered far better by the audience (Mayer, 2010).

- *Static or dynamic?* Real-time survey technology provides a virtually unlimited ability to run queries and burrow into the survey database. Some presenters have supplemented their static deck of slides by switching over to the live survey reporting site to respond to a question or a hypothesis posed by one of the attendees. There is research to suggest that such interactions with tools and images can yield better recall and comprehension (Lutz & Lutz, 1977), but accessing a live site can derail the meeting if the presenter struggles to create the right query or find the relevant data or if a curious and persistent meeting participant insists on focusing on the live site rather than the materials that have been prepared. This is an advanced option and requires excellent meeting participant and time management, not to mention good technology, to be effective.
- *Presentation or workshop?* Presentations of survey results can be used effectively as a data resource included in the context of a larger set of activities. For example, a daylong meeting of leaders may start with a deep dive into survey results, followed by a discussion facilitated by an HR leader or organization development specialist. The leaders might then work together to develop strategies for managing policies and practices, guided by the survey results. The intent of this format is to encourage the involvement of leaders to drive change but also to allow them to see the value of employee and survey data to inform strategy and policy in the organization. Inviting conversation and debate during the session will create active involvement and ownership of the results and subsequent actions.

Deliver the Presentation

Presentations require presenting, and an important and sometimes overlooked detail is exactly who will make the presentation to senior leaders. The presenter should be viewed as credible, knowledgeable about the information being presented, and in the best position to drive home the message of the presentation and to inspire action. The best choice of presenter is also dependent upon the content of the message and the expected audience.

Difficult messages, such as poor or declining survey results, mistrust of senior leaders, or low scores from the senior leaders who participated in the survey, may need to be presented by a messenger who is the least likely to be shot or the most likely to survive being shot. Potential presenters may include members of the survey team, internal HR consultants, internal HR executives, or external survey consultants who have been working with the internal survey team on the project.

- *Members of the internal survey team*: These individuals are the most familiar with the strategy, design, and workflow of the survey project. Often, members of the survey team are professionals with graduate degrees in I-O psychology, making them comfortable with explaining data and analyses. However, these professionals may not be well established with the leadership team or seen as experts. If internal staff have not developed this relationship with leaders and are not yet able to speak with authority, it is best to use them in a supporting role during the presentation, providing details and commentary while another individual leads the presentation.

- *Internal HR leader*: This is generally the executive to whom the survey team ultimately reports or the organization's head of HR. This individual usually is known to the leadership and has a good relationship with them as the head of HR often serves on the organization leadership council. While this individual has credibility with leaders, he or she isn't always an authority on the survey and interpretation of results so will require technical support from others when making the presentation.

- *External consultant*: Most senior leaders view external consultants as industry experts, which consequently affords them credibility and authority to speak about data trends and industry best practices. External consultants are typically the best presenters when the message to leaders is complex or uncomfortable or if the internal survey team is not comprised of subject matter experts. External consultants are seen as neutral bystanders; they are not enmeshed in internal organization politics, have no particular ax to grind, and are consequently viewed as unbiased. An external consultant has the luxury of not being an employee of the organization, which makes him or her more willing to candidly say what needs to be said and the most likely to survive being shot when delivering an unpleasant message. The external consultant will also benefit from having an internal staff person in the room to provide support for the presentation in the way of data and/or administrative details about the process.

It is always a good idea to provide a brief preview of the survey results and messaging to a senior leader who can serve as an advocate in the meeting. This might be the head of HR, assuming this person is not delivering the presentation, or the CEO, in the event the presentation is being made to a group of leaders. In this instance, the CEO can reinforce the messages and role-model active listening, involvement, and action-planning. Previews can provide helpful insight for modifying the presentation or tweaking the messages to provide maximum impact to the audience.

When designing the flow of the meeting itself, it is important to leave a significant amount of time for discussion as questions and comments from the audience are always valuable and reinforce understanding. Even better is designing the flow of the data to encourage self-discovery of the overall findings. Create a plot for the story, a logical flow of data that will lead the audience to an inevitable conclusion about the findings and what needs to happen next. This involves more exposition of findings and less telling, but ultimately leaders will achieve greater ownership of the results when they feel they have discovered them on their own. Discovery is frequently achieved by challenging the thinking and beliefs of the audience. Consider presenting survey results in a way that provokes their thinking, such as directing the attention of the audience to a critical population, or pushes on their assumptions about the organization, its employees, or the future of the workforce.

Final Thoughts

Organizational surveys are one of the most strategic activities that an HR function can undertake. The survey is one of the few organization initiatives that involves every employee subgroup and all segments of the organization. When well designed, survey results provide valuable insight for organizational effectiveness and organizational success. The presentation of survey results is key to influencing the organization at the very top, shaping the thinking of senior leaders and how they lead the organization. It is essential to the success of the organization's survey program as a strategic tool and enabling HR to be a true strategic partner to leaders.

References

Clark, R., & Mayer, R. (2007). *e-Learning and the science of instruction: Proven guidelines for consumers and designers of multimedia learning*. Hoboken, NJ: Pfeiffer.

Lutz, K. A., & Lutz, R. J. (1977). Effects of interactive imagery on learning: Application to advertising. *Journal of Applied Psychology*, *62*(4), 493–498.

Mayer, R. (Ed.). (2010). *Cambridge handbook of multimedia learning*. New York, NY: Cambridge University Press.

Vogel, D. R., Dixon, G. W., & Lehman, J. A. (1986). *Persuasion and the role of visual presentation support: The UM/3M study* (Report No. MISRC-WP-86-11). Minneapolis, MN: University of Minnesota.

21
Action Taking Augmented
by Artificial Intelligence

Sara P. Weiner and Melissa McMahan

Taking action is unequivocally the most important aspect of any employee survey program. The age-old principle that surveys conducted without action taking "may hurt you rather than help you" (Viteles, 1953, p. 394) is as true as ever. To achieve the return on investment senior leaders have come to expect from survey practices, there must be well-understood and universally adopted action taking and follow-up processes in place. Visible, meaningful action demonstrated by managers and senior leaders on an ongoing basis is critical to building employees' trust that their feedback is valued and can make a difference, and to successfully leveraging a survey program to achieve organizational goals. With the shift toward more frequent pulsing (for more on pulse surveys, see Chapter 4), expectations around meaningful action taking are even higher.

More than 20 years ago, Hinrichs (1996) described a three-legged stool required for a successful survey: measurement, reporting, and employee-involved action taking. Yet, despite decades of research and practice aimed at improving the effectiveness of action taking, including the introduction of online reporting that has been commonplace for well over a decade (Barbera & Young, 2006), many organizations continue to struggle to achieve adoption and accountability and, in turn, to realize meaningful change. We believe we are now at a pivotal point in survey history, where the advances in survey technology such as those offered under the umbrella of artificial intelligence (AI) have the power to be a game changer if coupled with evidence-based and forward-thinking industrial and organizational (I-O) psychology practices. AI has greatly facilitated our ability to quickly determine the actions that will matter most, and when combined with updated organizational practices, the benefits of employee surveys can be fully realized. In this chapter, we propose an approach to action taking summarized simply as *take action that matters,*

Sara P. Weiner and Melissa McMahan, *Action Taking Augmented by Artificial Intelligence* In: *Employee Surveys and Sensing.* Edited by: William H. Macey and Alexis A. Fink, Oxford University Press (2020). © Society for Industrial and Organizational Psychology.
DOI: 10.1093/oso/9780190939717.003.0021

communicate, and repeat frequently, which combines sound I-O practices executed with AI-augmented solutions to enable an agile, accurate, and effective action response to every organizational survey. As we will describe, action taking will only be successful if companies have sound practices and technology that can align to and enable those practices. This combination makes it as easy as possible for managers to complete the most critical steps of a survey: engaging teams in understanding results; selecting critical areas for focus; identifying actions that matter most to employees and the business; and ultimately integrating action-taking practices into ongoing business practices.

Clarifying Terminology

Action Taking versus Action Planning

We feel *action planning* is a misleading term that undermines the criticality of, and accountability around, taking meaningful action on employee feedback. The best-laid plans are meaningless if they are not effectively executed. To underscore this point, we advocate for replacing the term *action planning* with *action taking*.

AI

With or without AI, action taking is a discipline unto itself. In the context of action taking, AI augments and amplifies human abilities that inform and accelerate decision making. AI can be defined as a set of algorithms and techniques that mimic human intelligence (Chen, 2017) after data are used to train the system. For the purposes of this chapter, we include smart algorithms, machine learning, natural language processing (NLP), and deep learning all under the umbrella of AI.

Platform

A survey platform is a combination of hardware architecture and software applications.

Challenges to Action Taking

Historically, action-taking processes have been cumbersome and siloed from everyday business practices. They required heavy lifting by both Human Resources (HR) and managers who received lengthy static reports and action-taking manuals that demanded a heavy cognitive load to effectively interpret and often necessitated participation in time-consuming, one-size-fits-all training (Hinrichs, 1996). Results typically took weeks, even months, to process and disseminate, largely due to inefficient manual processes and technology and oftentimes due to a heavily orchestrated level-by-level cascade for releasing results down the organization. While this type of cascade may be a purposeful choice, the trade-off is that results have reduced relevancy by the time managers receive them, a challenge that is more pronounced in today's business world of agility and speed. Alternatively, some organizations choose to keep results at the top, thereby disabling action taking at the local level where it is critically important to realizing improvements in key outcomes. As has long been understood in organizational development, all members of an organizational system need to be involved to affect the most positive organizational change (French, 1969).

While technological enhancements over the years have helped to reduce manual steps and improve reporting speed, access, and accuracy, until recently, they have not delivered the dynamic results and personalized guidance that managers are accustomed to receiving when using other business intelligence tools. Even with the recent trend of shorter surveys or pulses, managers may still struggle with interpreting people data and/or integrating those people data with their business data to determine the best course of action for their teams.

Another obstacle to successful action taking is due to a specific mindset. Many leaders and managers still view people data as owned by HR and expect their HR partners to drive the action-taking process, rather than viewing it as ongoing leadership responsibility and strategic imperative. As a result, managers with many competing demands on their time may deprioritize or delegate action taking, particularly when a compelling business case has not been made to demonstrate that taking the time to understand and improve the employee experience can also improve their ability to achieve their business goals. In our experience, linkage research (see Chapter 17; also, Schneider, Macey, Lee, & Young, 2009; Wiley, 1996) is the most effective mechanism for demonstrating this business case and capturing the attention of leaders and managers yet is oftentimes not available due to insufficient data, technology, or capability.

The Opportunity: Keeping Pace with Change

To improve adoption and accountability around action taking, it is our belief that survey practices and technology must align with how the world, and the way in which we interact and lead, is changing. We are in an environment characterized by volatility, uncertainty, complexity, and ambiguity (Giles, 2018). Church and Burke (2017) describe the rate and complexity of change as accelerating at an exponential pace. In this rapid-cycle economy, organizations need solutions that allow them to nimbly respond to the ever-changing expectations and needs of customers, employees, and managers. Regardless of where you sit in an organization, the need to adopt more real-time, agile practices is evident; and it's no different in the survey space. Let's take a brief look at the importance of these changes vis-à-vis survey practices and technology.

We Live and Work in a Real-Time, Highly-Connected World

The rapid advancement and adoption of connected technologies and AI-based solutions (e.g., customer service chatbots, Alexa and Siri, rideshare and other apps) have dramatically changed our lives. At work, the changing landscape of data accessibility, volume, speed, variety, and veracity—often referred to as "big data" and operationalized through AI methods—has produced "unimaginable new insights" (Church & Dutta, 2013, p. 24) and greatly impacted the expectations of managers and employees. In our experience, managers now expect dynamic business intelligence tools that allow them to immediately gain insights, determine the best course of action, and monitor the impact of those actions on their goals. Similarly, employees expect an easily accessed, interactive vehicle to share their thoughts and feedback in real time and to receive a meaningful and timely response from leadership in return.

Work Has Become Even More Team-Centric

While teams and informal networks have always been important, today's companies depend on effective collaboration across the organization—what we refer to as *network performance*—more than ever to achieve results at speed and scale. Teams now come in many forms, such as virtual teams with employees spread around the globe, cross-functional project teams, and the rapidly growing "gig workforce" (Thibodeaux, 2018) that provides on-demand, transient staffing. To optimize performance and engagement, organizations must provide technology that facilitates inclusion and connection, along with practices that support managers in helping every type of team member feel a sense of purpose and connection to the company. (Note: There are legal considerations to address regarding co-employment perceptions that could arise when surveying contingent workers.)

Managers Serve as Facilitators of Connection and Continuous Improvement

Employees today need their managers to coach, inspire, and empower them. To do so successfully, managers must value and facilitate two-way communication and meaningful connection with their employees. Google found that managers who lead in this way have more engaged, high-performing teams (Bariso, 2018). To that end, we believe managers can greatly benefit from receiving people insights on a more frequent basis such as quarterly pulses (versus annual or less frequent surveys) to fuel more ongoing, authentic conversations with their teams around improving the employee experience and to stay on top of team engagement. To avoid a perception of oversurveying and the concomitant risk of survey fatigue, we recommend that the number and quality of surveys and pulses be thoughtfully managed across the company (Weiner & Dalessio, 2006).

AI-Augmented Solutions and Forward-Thinking Practices

Taking into consideration the aforementioned historical challenges and how the world of work is changing, our recommended approach—*take action that matters, communicate, and repeat frequently*—ensures leaders, managers, and employees are supported and empowered at every step of the action-taking process. It starts with easy, real-time access to survey results and insights and a greater level of personalized guidance than was possible in the past to help managers and teams focus on the **areas that matter most**, have effective discussions with shared accountability for taking action at all levels, and maintain an ongoing feedback loop to discuss and fine-tune actions taken based on survey feedback for maximal impact (Black, 2017). It's important to note that accountability for action taking goes hand in hand with empowerment. Each level of leadership, along with each individual employee, can directly influence aspects of the employee experience; and together all must work to create a positive environment.

We can now leverage AI-powered technology in revolutionary ways to remove unnecessary complexities, deliver real-time prescriptive and predictive analytics, provide insights and guidance that previously have been unavailable, and most importantly drive more agile behaviors and practices to achieve meaningful, sustainable change. AI-powered technology is faster and as (or more) accurate than humans if trained well and based on unbiased data. Simply put, the amount of data that machines can handle and the insights they can yield far exceed human capacity. For example, when looking for key drivers of engagement, the machine can instantaneously and simultaneously review top correlates, trends over time, comparisons to internal and external benchmarks, patterns across all available demographics and other attributes, and responses to open-ended questions. As a result, AI can quickly guide leaders, managers, and employees to the most important areas for focus in their organization.

There are many examples of how AI can be used to transform the action-taking component of any survey program. Here, we describe a number of AI capabilities and provide some tips for best leveraging these capabilities in any organization.

Accelerated Insights to Action

Managers need easy-to-implement guidance specifically designed to help them quickly answer questions such as "Which results should I use to understand how my team is doing?" "What are our priorities for improvement?" "How do I share results with my team?" and "What actions can we take to have the greatest impact?" In organizations that shift to more frequent pulsing, this guidance becomes all the more important to address the common concern that there is insufficient time between pulses to understand results and have an impact on scores.

AI can simplify and accelerate the first steps of action taking for managers—results analyses and interpretation—thereby minimizing time spent analyzing and maximizing time spent on more important activities such as having conversations with their teams about actions for improvement. At a minimum, AI provides each manager with an instantaneous summary of key metrics (e.g., engagement score), top drivers of those metrics, bright spots (areas of strength) and hot spots (areas of concern), and prepopulates an action plan with recommended focus areas and actions (behavioral tips and development resources) for addressing those areas. The manager can then decide if those are the best areas for focus given the context of the business and input from the team, but nonetheless the up-front heavy lifting is done.

To further understanding of quantitative results, NLP of comment data can provide context and deeper meaning, thus leading to a more appropriate action response. NLP has evolved far beyond the content analysis available years ago (Kulesa & Bishop, 2006) and can now instantaneously analyze an infinite number of comments to reveal key topics and themes, solution-focused comments, representative comments, and relationships among comments as well as with scalar items. For example, a manager's quantitative results may show career opportunity as the top driver of engagement for the team, yet NLP could reveal that 75% of the employees who rated this scalar item poorly described issues concerning on-the-job learning opportunities such as mentoring, rotational assignments, or job shadowing. Looking at the quantitative results alone may have led the manager to rely on HR to institute an organization-wide career path communication strategy or revisit the promotions process, but with these comment themes, the manager is empowered to take action on what matters most to the team—that is, finding ways to provide team members with new on-the-job learning opportunities, many of which are within the manager's ability to impact immediately.

It's important to take a moment to underscore the impact of NLP technology. NLP is one of the most transformative aspects of AI for all survey users as it opens the door to including more open-ended questions plus commenting ability (e.g., after scalar questions) in survey design. NLP also greatly accelerates data processing and the accuracy of results. Historically, survey program owners and HR may have limited the number of commenting opportunities on surveys due to the burdensome process of reviewing and coding thousands (or hundreds of thousands) of comments, oftentimes frustrating survey responders who wanted more opportunity to express how they were feeling in their own words. Now with NLP, survey responders feel more supported in communicating their experiences, managers gain a deeper understanding of those experiences, and HR and the survey team can focus on organization-wide issues and other value-add activities.

At every step of the action-taking process, today's survey platforms can also include action-taking guidance—both the action content itself (e.g., behavioral tips on how to improve career conversations) and the action-taking process steps (e.g., hold a transparent feedback discussion with your team within 1 week) to ensure managers understand their responsibilities and best practices for success. This is done in a more personalized, faster, and less stressful way than in the past. The survey team should work with the platform provider to ensure the guidance is appropriate and accurate for their company (e.g., fits the culture and survey philosophy, links to available resources such as a learning system). Outside of the platform, the survey team can develop communications such as FAQs about the survey approach and how the platform works (e.g., how recommended focus areas are determined) to ensure managers and employees trust the insights and recommendations they receive.

Ongoing Personalized Manager Coaching

Successful action taking extends beyond the immediate period after survey close. To realize meaningful, sustainable change, AI can help managers keep the action-taking dialogue with their teams alive between surveys to ensure actions are having the desired impact, as well as to help them integrate action-taking conversations into their ongoing business conversations. AI-driven chat bots and smart nudges (Bersin, 2019) can provide managers with recommended behaviors and steps that are personalized for them and delivered in the moments they need them most. Even with the best of intentions, managers have many competing demands on their time, so this virtual "coach in a box" can help improve adoption and build capability and habits.

Nudge theory has two foundational components, the first is *choice architecture*, whereby people can be influenced by the order and context in which things are presented to them; the second is *libertarian paternalism*, which directs people to what will be a good outcome for them without mandating they make that decision (Thaler & Sunstein, 2008). In the action-taking context, nudges can be simple reminders, but they are most effective when they provide guidance to show managers the best, most rational choices based on what the system knows about them for achieving the results they would like to see. For example, let's say a manager's focus area from the last survey was collaboration skills. Because an AI-powered platform can be configured to use multiple types of data (e.g., people, operational; see "Connecting the Dots Across Different Types of Data" below), it can suggest behavioral action items on effective collaboration to populate the manager's development goals for performance management as well as nudge them with behavioral tips on the day of an important cross-functional meeting. It's up to the manager to decide what to do next: whether to accept that guidance or choose another approach. This technical support is a significant step forward in creating greater manager capability, empowerment, and accountability around action taking and, as a result, lessening dependence on HR.

It is important to note that the aforementioned AI-driven insights and guidance, along with role-based permissions and confidentiality protections, can help put HR and senior leaders at ease about simultaneously releasing results to all levels of management, a practice we recommend to enable an agile and effective action response across the organization. As discussed, many organizations still depend on a cascade approach or keep results at the top, usually due to concerns about appropriate use of data and controlling the messaging about results. Senior leadership and HR will be more comfortable about releasing results at the same time to all managers when they understand that the appropriate guardrails and guidance have been put in place. To do so successfully, the survey team should ensure they are able to explain what underlies the technology and the in-product guidance; collaborate on defining who has permission to see which data; and create communications to build understanding and trust for leaders, managers, and employees.

Organization-Wide Action

Mid-level and senior leaders also need guidance on addressing multiple layers of action taking—that is, choosing the one to two things they will focus on as managers of their direct report teams, as well as the areas to address across their larger organizations. AI can guide individual leaders through this process, as well as help align efforts across the company for greater impact and efficiency by identifying when multiple teams are working on the same focus areas and providing customized suggestions for collective efforts. The survey team plays a role here in ensuring that in-product guidance and communications help managers navigate these layers of individual and collective action taking without getting lost in analysis paralysis or trying to boil the ocean (as the sayings go!).

AI can also guide senior leaders toward larger organizational issues they uniquely have the power to impact individually or as a senior leadership team across the enterprise. Based on our observations across hundreds of organizations of all different sizes and industries, the data clearly show that individual managers do not own all drivers of engagement; some drivers are under the direct, and sometimes sole, influence of senior leaders (see also Chapter 8). While managers may be the voice to communicate decisions from senior leadership to their teams, the actions and behaviors of senior leaders are highly visible and can make a huge difference in organizational engagement. HR plays an important role in coaching senior leaders to model effective leadership behaviors as well as action-taking behaviors in response to the survey feedback. In fact, we have seen organizations change their culture around the use of surveys from one of being "held" accountable to one where all levels of management "feel" accountable for driving change after they observe senior leaders demonstrating ownership of issues under their influence and effective action-taking behaviors (i.e., transparently sharing results, taking action that matters, communicating, and repeating frequently).

Connecting the Dots Across Different Types of Data

Managers often wonder how their survey results relate to other data they receive. Historically, data have been presented in a siloed manner, analyzed independently, and even sometimes offered conflicting perspectives. Now, some platforms can support seamless integration of all types of survey program results (onboarding, engagement, exit, etc.) together with other people and operational data (e.g., performance goals, turnover, promotion metrics, customer satisfaction), providing a holistic view and data story for managers and HR. This capability helps managers understand how all of their data combine to provide a complete picture of their organization and provides clarity on the best course of action. For example, managers in larger organizations could see which leadership behaviors measured in multi-rater surveys are associated with higher engagement to help prioritize areas for focus. Integrated platforms can also do the administrative work for managers by, for example, auto-populating suggested activities from their action plans in their performance development goals (e.g., how to improve collaboration skills) and tracking progress in both places.

At a more macro level, HR centers of excellence and program owners can instantaneously gain tremendous within- and across-program insights to help them continuously improve programs and ensure investment in the right initiatives. For example, talent acquisition and development teams can see which aspects of an onboarding program have had the greatest impact on new-hire engagement. Similarly, HR business partners can use this information to prioritize their coaching efforts where they are needed most, as well as connect managers for peer-to-peer support.

Predictive Models

As discussed, managers at all levels are more likely to take ownership of their data when there is a compelling business case that doing so will improve their business results. To that end, linkage analysis has been conducted for decades, but the advent of AI makes it much more accessible. A great first step is leveraging an attrition model provided through a survey platform. This predictive model identifies patterns of responses across companies that have been shown to predict attrition, and that collective model of attrition risk can then be applied to any company's results. Machine learning can later be used to improve the model over time. This approach enables "needle in a haystack" capabilities not possible by humans, allowing every possible permutation of demographic variables (e.g., top sellers in Japan with 3–5 years of tenure; engineers by gender and location) to be explored so that attrition risks can be flagged (within confidentiality requirements) and appropriate and timely targeted action can be taken.

Once there is sufficient volume and quality of survey and attrition data, a bespoke company-specific predictive model could be incorporated into the platform using that company's own attrition data. Similarly, models with business outcomes such as customer satisfaction scores can be used to demonstrate how results on survey items (e.g., trust in leadership) are related to key business outcomes and ensure managers are focused on the top drivers of those outcomes in action taking. While business outcome data can be fed into a survey platform to give managers access to these types of analyses, the survey team should first take great care to ensure data quality is at an acceptable level, that it is the right unit of analysis (e.g., teams, divisions), and that the analysis technique itself is well understood. Ideally, given the complexity around predicting business outcomes due to the many variables that play a role in such outcomes, the linkage model should initially be run outside of the system by data scientists, I-O psychologists, or other experts in data modeling and reviewed with business leaders until the model is sufficiently refined to ensure both statistical and face validity (for more on linkage analysis, see Chapter 17). Once developed, however, the model can be applied within the platform instantaneously on any new data, without having to repeat this time-consuming process outside of the platform.

Organizational Learning

Machine learning can detect which actions chosen by managers to address certain organizational issues have had the greatest impact on outcome measures and, as a result, more often suggest those actions to leaders facing similar issues in the future. HR can then ensure investments are made in people practices that support these high-impact efforts (e.g., leadership training, organizational effectiveness initiatives). An integrated system across all stages of the employee life cycle (from candidate to alumnus) that is linked to operational and business data wherever possible, and a commitment to continuously update action-taking guidance, will result in a true understanding of that organization (e.g., contributors to retention, performance, customer satisfaction) with the most efficacious responses to challenges.

Keeping Pace with Organizational Change

With the rapid pace of change, organizations are restructuring more than ever. Historically, accurately capturing organizational hierarchies in survey technology took weeks to program and, therefore, could not keep up with organizational changes, oftentimes rendering outdated results. As a result, managers would often deprioritize or dismiss the results as not reflective of their current organizations and abandon their action-taking activities. Technology enables organizational hierarchies to be reorganized (while ensuring confidentiality standards are maintained) so results for the new combinations of employees (or groups) can be seen in real time, thereby ensuring relevant data (for more on survey data analysis, see Chapter 15). That being said, the team an individual is part of affects that person's perceptions and survey responses so it is important to keep in mind that results created using new combinations of employees to reflect an updated organizational structure will only approximate what those results would have been had those employees been working together as part of an intact team at the time of the survey. This issue is an important consideration for HR and survey program owners in determining whether or not to reconfigure results. In either case, the selected approach should be communicated up front to managers and employees.

AI Limitations and Considerations

Using AI also presents some challenges. Virtually unlimited analysis and insights provided by AI can be overwhelming or risk confidentiality if delivered without effective guidance and protections. There is also a risk that spurious correlations can surface given all the data available (e.g., when running hundreds of correlations, some will be statistically significant just by chance); therefore, limitations should be put in place to avoid these statistical issues. In addition, humans need to interpret the results to determine if relationships make sense. Leaders, managers, and HR still need to interpret AI-powered insights vis-à-vis the context of their organization. Managers must take the time to consider the insights within their business context and discuss those insights with their teams to ensure they have the most complete picture prior to moving to action taking. Interpreting results is still art plus science even with AI, as it should be.

As stated, the survey team needs to fully understand the survey platform to ensure any in-product guidance, permissions/restrictions, confidentiality protections (such as ensuring combinations of data meet minimum n requirements, or that filtered results are not permitted to be run and compared in order to avoid exposing individuals), and the like are appropriate for their culture, leadership capability, and survey practices. In addition, the survey team should provide aligned supplementary communications and training resources. Finally, the survey team needs to assess and understand AI bias-detection and correction approaches, and ensure their practices adhere to the European Union's General Data Protection Regulation guidelines (see Chapter 24) or other legal restrictions.

Another challenge may be limited transparency on how an AI-powered system works. It only takes one bad experience or example, especially if highly publicized, for people to distrust AI. The survey team should ask questions of the provider (whether a vendor or internal) about the foundational I-O research that was used to create the action-taking features and content in any platform they plan to implement. In addition, they should ask about the data and processes used to train the system, for example, "How do we know that the suggested actions will have desired effects?" "How was the model developed to assess attrition risk?" "What data were used to develop the taxonomy of themes in the NLP?" "What processes and tools are being used to ensure bias is minimized?" AI tools need feedback mechanisms and a way to train algorithms to get more accurate and smarter. One concern is whether some demographic groups are underrepresented in a data set, in which case they won't be selected by the algorithm, thus leading to bias (Zielinski, 2017). Humans must continue to ensure the machine is learning from relevant, accurate, and unbiased data. For example, training data should include representation from all groups who may be surveyed. Equally critical, NLP should be trained based on comments made by employees in organizational surveys, rather than non-employee experience data such as customer survey comments or random discussions in public social-media forums. There are also tools available, and being developed, to assist specifically with detecting and then correcting bias (Spadafora, 2018). The only way to achieve the benefits we have outlined is to ensure there is rigorous research and unbiased training underlying the technology.

As discussed, it is important that the survey team thoughtfully communicates decisions around the aforementioned areas to build trust in the platform. While higher-level communications and FAQs are appropriate for managers and employees, more in-depth communications and training should be provided to HR business partners to ensure they fully understand the survey platform and can vouch for its trustworthiness.

Conclusion

We recognize that organizations are under more pressure than ever to achieve lofty results; thus, it is critical to help leaders and managers realize that continuously improving the employee experience and the success of their people will strengthen and enable their organization's business success.

When all levels of leadership can see how focusing on the employee experience, including engagement, has positive effects on the business metrics they track and the attainment of organizational goals, it is a hugely compelling argument to pay attention to the employee survey and make the time to *take action that matters, communicate, and repeat frequently*. Furthermore, when they see how AI can greatly simplify the survey process, making it more agile, thoughtfully guiding and nudging them, and enabling the integration of survey results into ongoing business cycles, they will be more compelled to prioritize action-taking efforts. Due to the speed, simplification, and personalization afforded through AI, more frequent surveys become very useful in running the business by enabling leaders, managers, and HR to maintain an ongoing focus on improving the employee experience. In addition, it's important to recognize that leaders and managers have influence on people's lives outside work—with their families, friends, and communities. Leveraging AI technology to take action that matters and to influence the employee experience in authentic and meaningful ways thus has far-reaching effects.

The present and the future are exciting in terms of AI-augmented action taking. Yet, AI is not a self-sustaining or stand-alone tool in the action-taking process. When coupled with science-based practices and a focus on transformation, a concomitant shift in mindsets, behaviors, and habits of leaders, managers, employees, and HR is possible. HR has a critical role in facilitating this transformation. Having access to complete, digestible, and prescriptive information immediately, coupled with personalized on-demand guidance, empowers managers to shift to a place of independence. This approach can influence an organizational culture that supports managers being treated as the owners of their own data versus having to rely on HR to understand results, see a new data cut of interest, or know what to do next. Simultaneously, HR then has time to work on things that are systemic, provide resources or targeted coaching to leaders and managers, encourage those who are not engaged in the process, and identify best practices that can be shared to help others. In addition, HR can help managers shift to more agile people practices by securing their buy-in through demonstrated business impact (the "so what" element); giving them real-time data and easy-to-use business intelligence tools that seamlessly integrate with other data sources and readily become a natural part of their everyday business practices; providing coaching in the very moments managers need it; and identifying cross-organizational opportunities to improve impact. That is,

HR plays a critical role, not by micromanaging change management but by enabling agile behavior change and inculcating new capabilities and habits.

Action taking today is a substantially different process from what it was even 10 years ago thanks to AI and modern organizational practices. Technology-fueled guidance today covers far more analyses to arrive at personalized suggestions for action in the moments when it is needed most and does it all instantaneously, versus the cumbersome, rule-based applications of the past. Taking advantage of AI-powered survey technology coupled with evidence-based and forward-thinking organizational practices supports the entire organization and is essential to leverage as a competitive advantage.

Acknowledgments

We thank the editors for their herculean effort in compiling this book and their thoughtful and helpful feedback on earlier versions of this chapter. We also thank Vivian Chou for her outstanding assistance on the initial literature review.

References

Barbera, K. M., & Young, S. A. (2006). Online Reporting: Real time, real impact, real opportunities. In A. I. Kraut (Ed.), *Getting action from organizational surveys: New concepts, technologies, and applications* (pp. 213–237). San Francisco, CA: Jossey-Bass.

Bariso, J. (2018). Google spent a decade researching what makes a great boss. It came up with these 10 things. Inc. Retrieved from https://www.inc.com/justin-bariso/google-spent-a-decade-researching-what-makes-a-great-boss-they-came-up-with-these-10-things.html

Bersin, J. (2019, October 28). HR technology market 2019: Disruption ahead. *Enterprise Alumni*. Retrieved from https://enterprisealumni.com/news/alumni-research/hr-technology-market-2019-alumni/

Black, J. (2017). Getting managers to actively improve employee engagement: Is your approach data-informed? Retrieved from https://medium.com/glint-od-science/getting-managers-to-actively-improve-employee-engagement-is-your-approach-data-informed-787311b31057

Chen, F. (2017, July 15). AI and deep learning [Video file]. Retrieved from https://www.youtube.com/watch?v=ht6fLrar91U

Church, A. H., & Burke, W. W. (2017). Four trends shaping the future of organizations and organization development. *OD Practitioner, 49*, 14–22.

Church, A. H., & Dutta, S. (2013). The promise of big data for OD: Old wine in new bottles or the next generation of data-driven methods for change? *OD Practitioner, 45*, 23–31.

French, W. (1969). Organization development objectives, assumptions and strategies. *California Management Review, 12,* 23–34.

Giles, S. (2018, May 9). How VUCA is reshaping the business environment and what it means for innovation. *Forbes.* Retrieved from https://www.forbes.com/sites/sunniegiles/2018/05/09/how-vuca-is-reshaping-the-business-environment-and-what-it-means-for-innovation/#6ff721c5eb8d

Hinrichs, J. R. (1996). Feedback, action planning, and follow-through. In A. I. Kraut (Ed.), *Organizational surveys: Tools for assessment and change* (pp. 255–279). San Francisco, CA: Jossey-Bass.

Kulesa, P., & Bishop, R. J. (2006). What did they really mean? New and emerging methods for analyzing themes in open-ended comments. In A. I. Kraut (Ed.), *Getting action from organizational surveys: New concepts, technologies, and applications* (pp. 238–263). San Francisco, CA: Jossey-Bass.

Schneider, B., Macey, W. H., Lee, W. C., & Young, S. A. (2009). Organizational service climate drivers of the American Customer Satisfaction Index (ACSI) and financial and market performance. *Journal of Service Research, 12,* 3–14.

Spadafora, A. (2018, September 19). IBM launches AI bias tool. *ITProPortal.* Retrieved from www.itproportal.com/news/ibm-launches-ai-bias-tool/

Thaler, R. H., & Sunstein, C. R. (2008). *Nudge: Improving decisions about health, wealth, and happiness.* New York, NY: Penguin Books.

Thibodeaux, W. (2018). How the rise of the gig economy is boosting the social status of temp and flex workers. *Inc.* Retrieved from https://www.inc.com/wanda-thibodeaux/how-rise-of-gig-economy-is-boosting-social-status-of-temp-flex-workers.html?cid=search

Viteles, M. S. (1953). *Motivation and morale in industry.* New York, NY: W. W. Norton & Company.

Weiner, S. P., & Dalessio, A. T. (2006). Oversurveying: Causes, consequences, and cures. In A. I. Kraut (Ed.), *Getting action from organizational surveys: New concepts, technologies, and applications* (pp. 294–311). San Francisco, CA: Jossey-Bass.

Wiley, J. W. (1996). Linking survey results to customer satisfaction and business performance. In A. I. Kraut (Ed.), *Organizational surveys: Tools for assessment and change* (pp. 330–359). San Francisco, CA: Jossey-Bass.

Zielinski, D. (2017, August 16). Artificial intelligence can boost HR analytics, but buyer beware. *SHRM.* Retrieved from https://www.shrm.org/resourcesandtools/hr-topics/technology/pages/artificial-intelligence-can-boost-hr-analytics-but-buyer-beware.aspx

SECTION 3
CHALLENGES AND OPPORTUNITIES

22

Rediscovering the Art of Surveys for Organization Change

Allan H. Church and Janine Waclawski

Imagine receiving a link to a survey and that when you open it up it explains what your senior leadership is trying to achieve over the next 12–18 months. Imagine there are messages to employees that explicitly describe the new values, behaviors, or expectations for the workplace. Further, the message says the chief executive officer (CEO) will share the findings with all employees. Would that inspire you? In fact, when was the last time you took a survey where you learned something new about what your organization was doing at a strategic level?

What you are reflecting on are *surveys for change*. These are surveys designed to create a desired need for changing the current state. They do this by articulating what is important to the organization and by making a commitment to sharing results and taking action at multiple levels. While surveys for change share many of the same elements as other types of organizational survey programs, there are some key differences as well. Those are the focus of this chapter. Paradoxically enough, while the use of surveys for providing the most senior leaders with insights continues to increase, the impact of surveys for driving organizational transformation appears to be on the decline (Fermin, 2014).

Why is this distinction important? One of the factors working against the survey process over the past decade has been the call by consultants in trade publications to abandon more traditional annual or biannual census-driven survey methodologies in favor of alternative approaches (often which they are selling). Other factors include ongoing pressures around cost and timeliness of traditional large-scale survey approaches. Recent trends in the marketplace have pushed these goals to the very limits of measurement quality. Therefore, it is no wonder that organization development (OD) and change-focused survey efforts have diminished. The rise and arguable overuse of

Allan H. Church and Janine Waclawski, *Rediscovering the Art of Surveys for Organization Change* In: *Employee Surveys and Sensing*. Edited by: William H. Macey and Alexis A. Fink, Oxford University Press (2020). © Society for Industrial and Organizational Psychology.
DOI: 10.1093/oso/9780190939717.003.0022

pulse surveys (Colihan & Waclawski, 2006) along with the ubiquitous nature of self-service online survey applications and the popularity of firm-based benchmarking efforts have all contributed to this. Even the concept of engagement, as popular as it is, has come under fire, largely because of the misuse of the concept (Church, 2016).

Unfortunately, the recommended cure for the field's issues with contemporary organizational surveys does not appear to be any better. While the data collected from short pulse surveys or some of the new "non-survey survey" technologies might be intriguing, none of the results are likely to aid in driving a desired culture. Ironically, these same types of trade-press authors often point to the need for follow-up efforts such as employee focus groups to dig deeper into underlying issues raised by bland or limited data from poorly designed surveys. In short, in an effort to reduce cost and increase speed, they have added more time, money, and resources required to conduct focus groups to identify the challenges in the first place.—that is, assuming that the organization wants to use the data for something meaningful like driving a change agenda.

While many practitioners continue to promote the use of good strategic survey practice and measurement constructs, fewer highlight the use of surveys specifically for transformational interventions. It is our intent to remind readers of what we consider to be the lost art of surveys for change and discuss why this methodology is so important for industrial–organizational (I-O), OD, and Human Resources (HR) practitioners to better understand and re-establish as a key approach.

Evolution of Surveys for Change

The survey began as a tool for measuring employee attitudes and behaviors in the post–Second World War era. The modern survey as we known it originated in the 1950s and grew in popularity through the 1970s and 1980s with the rise of such industry consortia as The Mayflower Group (Johnson, 1996). Employee attitude surveys became common in organizations with an emphasis on measuring key sets of attitudes and attributes of the culture. Many of the measured content and practices regarding effective surveys today were created or had their roots based in that time period. While the emphasis tended to be on measuring and tracking opinions over time, action-planning became increasingly important as external pressures began to change the nature of the employment contract.

The Rise of Surveys for OD and Change

It was in this context in the 1980s and 1990s that surveys for large-scale organizational change became a phenomenon. Following on the heels of significant business growth, external consulting efforts specializing in organizational change became the new trend. OD practitioners in particular began leveraging surveys both for diagnostic purposes and to intentionally drive key messages, content, and interventions into the organization via the survey itself (Burke, Coruzzi, & Church, 1996; Church, Margiloff, & Coruzzi, 1995; Church & Waclawski 2001; Kraut & Saari, 1999). For example, surveys were used at NASA for years following the *Challenger* accident to determine the impact, develop action plans, and measure progress toward driving positive change in both management practices and the culture over time (Burke, 2018). Similarly, surveys were used after the SmithKline Beecham merger (Burke & Jackson, 1991) to set expectations and measure the shift toward the new "simply better" culture outlined by the new CEO of the merged company.

The commonality in these examples is that the surveys in question were explicitly designed and used to drive a transformation effort in an organization. Based on the early work of Lewin (1958), expanded on by Beckhard and Harris (1987), the concept is simple. Data create dissatisfaction with the current state, which in turn creates a felt need for change. When we consider that OD is defined as the "the process of increasing organizational effectiveness and facilitating personal and organizational change through the use of interventions driven by social and behavioral science knowledge" (Burke, 2011), it is easy to see how survey results could play a key role in the entire change process. In fact, the survey is a particularly powerful method for OD because it highlights the present state, communicating what is important for the future, facilitating action-planning, and measuring progress (Waclawski & Church, 2002). This is evident in the increasing emphasis on action-planning and accountability in the survey practitioner literature over time (Church, Kuyumcu, & Rotolo, 2016; Kraut, 1996, 2006).

A Shifting Focus to Bright, Shiny "Survey" Objects

Although the increasing adoption of surveys in organizations over the past two decades has given rise to many positive trends in technology, action-planning, and analytics, it has also contributed to what we believe is a significant decline in the practice of surveys for change. The reasons for this are many, including (1) the democratization of survey technology, (2) the rise of important but often misunderstood constructs by management such as engagement (Church, 2016; Macey & Schneider, 2008), and (3) methodological misunderstandings and misalignments between the purpose of surveys and what different types of survey techniques (e.g., pulse vs. census) and new "non-survey survey" methods (e.g., crowdsourcing and active listening tools) can offer. This has given rise to the need for bright, shiny objects even in the survey arena (Rotolo et al., 2018), which has only served to muddy the concept of surveys for change.

Many survey programs serve multiple purposes. A recent benchmark study of The Mayflower Group highlights this trend (see Table 22.1). Overall, 86% of member companies noted two distinct purposes to their primary survey program and 39% noted three. While it is a positive that 18% are taking a surveys for change approach and almost a third include change as a secondary goal, the primary drivers today are monitoring trends for senior executives (82%) and local action-planning (71%).

So what exactly are surveys for change? For example, does having a few questions in an existing survey about a new program or initiative (e.g., launching a health and wellness agenda or flex-work policy) or conducting organization-wide pulse surveys on a special topic (e.g., sustainability)

Table 22.1 Benchmark Summary of Survey Purpose

Purpose of Company Survey	First Selection	First or Second Selection
Provide data for senior executives to monitor employee attitudes/engagement	50%	82%
Provide data for local action-planning efforts	32%	71%
Drive a large-scale organizational change agenda	18%	32%

Note. N = 28 responses. Table reflects cumulative responses, and therefore, column 2 adds to more than 100%.

A total of 24 companies picked 2 options, and 11 companies picked all 3 options.

count? We would suggest that the answer is no. While the topics themselves may be about change initiatives, unless they meet specific criteria, they would not be considered a survey for large-scale change.

Clarity of Purpose Matters

Over the past 50 years, organizational surveys have been employed for a number of different purposes at the system (total company), group (reflecting business units, functions, or teams), and individual (managerial) levels. As many authors of strategic survey applications have noted (see Chapter 2), the key to an effective survey process is identifying and aligning the purpose of the survey content, process, and outcomes to the critical needs of the business. While almost anyone today, regardless of their background, can create and launch a survey in under 5 minutes, without having an aligned process the results are likely to have limited impact. This may be acceptable for certain types of needs (e.g., informing a presentation or business case), but it falls short of a survey for change. Moreover, even using a comprehensive off-the-shelf survey from a well-established consulting firm is unlikely to meet the criteria. Except in rare cases, the content will not be aligned with your cultural language and strategy.

As noted, surveys for change help create "dissatisfaction with the current state," assist people in understanding what the future state looks like, and provide data on how to get there. Thus, the communications, questions asked, and action-planning processes need to be very specific and customized to each change initiative to have maximum impact. Otherwise, the survey tool is simply informing the effort, not helping to drive it.

Differentiating Characteristics of Surveys for Change

In general, surveys for change share common elements with other quality survey designs (e.g., quality item construction, use of benchmarks where appropriate, senior leadership alignment, transparency of communications, protecting confidentiality of responses, linkage analytics and diagnostics, reporting and follow-up mechanisms). The key differences fall into three areas. Together they represent the criteria for assessing whether a survey is change-focused or not.

The Survey Reflects a Social Systems Perspective

In the context of OD and transformation, systems refer not to information technology but to a social systems theory (Katz & Kahn, 1978) approach to diagnosing and working through change in organizations. In this context, organizations are seen as being comprised of a number of different interdependent subsystems with a variety of inputs and outputs that impact one another. This means considering the interplay between factors across multiple levels such as leadership, culture, values, mission and strategy, work unit climate, reward systems, and structure.

In the content of surveys for change, the focus shifts from employee attitudes about targeted areas or constructs to a wider range of factors. Some of these include senior leadership behaviors or actions, perceptions of operations across business units, clarity and relevance of a new mission or vision at multiple levels, or accountability for managers behaving in ways that reinforce the new culture. The survey focus (both the item content and the way results are analyzed and actioned against) is directed toward the transformation effort itself.

This is why leadership alignment and sponsorship (ideally the CEO) are so critical to surveys for change. While it is important for any survey program to have senior support, for a change effort to be successful it requires full integration across all interventions planned or enacted. Although there are many examples of this process from a consulting approach (e.g., surveys being designed to drive a new culture following a merger or new CEO transition), one of the more compelling and close to home for us was PepsiCo's cultural focus on diversity and inclusion in the early 2000s. Although the case has been described in depth elsewhere from different angles (e.g., Church, Rotolo, Shull & Tuller, 2014; Thomas & Creary, 2009), following are some key elements:

CEO-led initiative (focused on both workforce composition and culture change)

supported via a social systems approach linked to new behaviors (via 360 feedback)

linked to new cultural indicators introduced through the launch of a custom 60-item inclusion survey and reinforced through one of the early examples of a targeted pulse survey effort (and later integrated into the ongoing organizational health survey program) aligned to hiring, promotion, and turnover processes

reinforced by mandatory inclusion training for all professionals in the company

tracked by HR dashboards and analytics (including linkage research)

linked to internal employee resource group action-planning efforts and highly visible external advisory boards

aligned to the new business and people dual performance-management process

recognized through consistent messaging from and highly visible CEO decisions

In sum, the survey was not the intervention itself, but rather it was integral to and linked with a fully integrated change-management agenda over a multi-year approach. While not every survey for change needs to follow this level of effort, this example provides one of the more comprehensive models.

The Survey Content Is Actionable, Relevant, and Strategic (and Usually Customized)

Whatever the purpose of an organizational survey, good I-O practice would suggest it needs to have items that are well written and provide meaningful information to key stakeholders. In some cases, and for some survey purposes, those stakeholders may be a somewhat limited set of individuals (e.g., the senior leadership team or a group of front-line supervisors), and not all content is equally relevant for everyone. As noted, it is critical to understand the purpose of the survey effort to ensure that the approach is fully aligned. What differentiates surveys for change in this context is that the items on the survey should be highly specific to the change or transformation itself.

The questionnaire content (and response scales) should target strategic topics related to the change (e.g., regarding the desired shift in the culture, new leadership behaviors, or ways of working), and the data collected must be both relevant and actionable in the context of the change agenda. Asking questions about topics that are tangential to the effort is fine if they are based on ongoing initiatives or common standard benchmarks (e.g., for tracking trends in engagement or comparison of pre-/post-intervention success on core attitudes of interest such as manager capability), but you should avoid the "kitchen sink" approach if possible. It is important to remember that surveys convey what is important to the organization and the survey sponsor. If the content reflects a jumble of ideas, initiatives, and pet items (all probably well intended), the focus of the effort will be lost on employees.

Although there are different approaches to building a change-focused survey, one of the more comprehensive and effective methods is to base the content on an organizational systems framework. There are a number of these available in the academic and practitioner literatures (e.g., Burke & Litwin, 1992) which have proven useful in shaping survey design content as well as the broader intervention set and change agenda overall. While some consulting firms have their own approaches, they pose more challenges for customization because (a) their model constructs are proprietary and (b) their item content is generally fixed or limited to a range of choices. Although using standardized items can be helpful, if the purpose is driving a targeted organizational change effort, it is highly unlikely that anyone else's standard items will either convey what is important or measure what is critical to your agenda. This same argument holds when considering 360 feedback for OD interventions (Church & Burke, 2019).

Having a model for change from which to drive your survey content is only part of the issue of relevance though. Often, there are challenges due to a lack of a formal survey strategy, a limited understanding of how surveys for change work, and the inability to identify and place limits on appropriate content areas. From a survey strategy perspective and to ensure that surveys for change work as intended, it is critical that the purpose is clearly articulated and that item content is aligned. Figure 22.1 provides two options for approaching surveys for change (integrated and tiered or mass-customized).

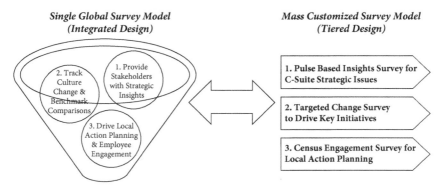

Figure 22.1. Design choices for organizational surveys for change.

A survey for change can be a stand-alone process or a component of a larger process (as 33% of The Mayflower Companies indicated). If driving a transformation process is the primary intent, you should consider launching a separate survey for change, at least initially to provide a laser focus on the effort. Moving to independent and clearly articulated survey models could help meet the needs of different survey stakeholders while preserving the clear purpose and intent of each survey. Later, the content can be reintegrated (as in the PepsiCo diversity and inclusion example), once the groundwork for change has taken hold. What is critical is that the strategy for your organizational survey program is clear and well articulated. Employees need to understand why this survey differs from other types of tools used in the company. Importantly, HR and line leaders often need the same level of education.

The Survey Results Are Communicated and Used by Employees

So far we have focused primarily on the front-end strategy, purpose, and content of surveys for change. The third key differentiator concerns the outcome of the process, that is, how the results from the survey are shared and the accountability mechanisms for driving change in the workplace. Once again, the distinction can be subtle in that survey action-planning has become a major focus for most large-scale programs. However, the emphasis on transparency, reporting to the lowest level of accountability possible (while protecting confidentiality of respondents), institutionalizing formal mechanisms for taking action, and tracking improvement is what differentiates surveys for change.

If we follow the OD mindset, surveys for change should be operating at the level of an individual manager who can affect positive improvements in employee engagement, working conditions, recognition, development, communications, team dynamics, and growth in his or her immediate work environment. For the data-based feedback model to work, the results must be given to managers and their teams to review, discuss, and create energy to move forward together (Nadler, 1977). This means that surveys for change must have transparency as a core value embedded in the process. Any survey that does not have the results shared with employees at a significantly meaningful level of detail cannot be a change-based survey regardless of what it measured. How could it be expected to impact anything if employees don't understand what happened? For managers and employees to enact change, they must have the data in hand both initially (the driver for the change) and ongoing as a mechanism for tracking progress (accountability for change).

This isn't just about providing managers with deep insight tools at their fingertips as some consulting firms like to promote (though technology is certainly enabling a different way of thinking about what managers can take from their data) but instead about the dialogue of change between people at work. From an OD perspective the energy for change comes from the process as much as the insights themselves. Further, it is this "energy for change" that is the key mechanism needed to overcome organizational inertia or resistance. Thus, the communications from and actions taken by the most senior leaders play a key role. If the proper expectations are not set or there is misalignment between intent and outcomes, the survey for change will not work and could cause more harm than good.

OD efforts are defined by three elements: (1) data to initiate change, (2) social science theory and systems-level thinking, and (3) a normative perspective regarding how organizations and people grow and develop (Waclawski & Church, 2002). From a transparency and accountability perspective, the normative value of connecting back to employees is critical. In fact, feedback itself is one of the core values of OD. Moreover, the data feedback stage in the classic OD consulting paradigm focuses on shared interpretation of the results even before the intervention stage. In other words, in an OD and change approach to surveys, the process of change for employees begins with the "what" when the survey questions are asked and the "how" when those expectations are refined during the sharing of results and the commitment from senior leaders to take action. Unfortunately, some senior leaders would prefer to focus on advanced statistics and insights (and not their transparency), which are critically important but not the solution at the employee level in a survey for change paradigm. Different but related challenges occur when one attempts to use pulse surveys for change efforts as there is often perceived lack of ownership and accountability for action at the managerial level, and a large percentage of employees have generally not been communicated to about the effort.

Another challenge we see in the use of surveys for change is that senior leaders have a difficult time observing the impact of localized change efforts at the top of the organization. This is due to the "diminishing effect of observational change" that occurs in most standard survey programs. Simply put, between administrations there are likely to be fluctuations due to many factors (e.g., interventions or lack thereof) that result in improvements or declines in results. If these are not directed at a unified cultural and behavioral shift, they are likely to cancel each other out and not be seen at the most senior level of the survey outcome as the change having an impact (see Figure 22.2). This is why change efforts (and surveys for change) require a consistent and holistic agenda, not just a survey by itself.

In many organizations of sufficient size or scale when a large-scale change effort is launched or components of an existing survey are used to measure action-planning efforts, the change occurs at multiple levels. The more specific the feedback, the more likely the change will result. But in many instances, there will be large pockets of the organization where either the focus is lost or managers do nothing with the results. This can result in no apparent change at the aggregate level or even negative employee perceptions of things getting worse (Church et al., 2012; Church & Oliver, 2006). In addition, the scale of perceived meaningful impact for senior leadership begins to diminish simply by the law of averages and large numbers.

An understanding of where the real improvements happened and didn't happen at the local level and why is crucial for driving change. Was it because there was a sudden vacuum of support from the top, managers, or even HR when the results didn't come back as positively as they would have liked? Everyone is quick to create their own survey questions but not always willing to act on (or even share) the results they produce. Was it because the

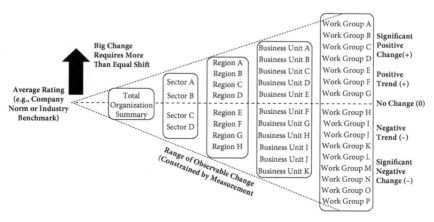

Figure 22.2. The diminishing effect of organizational layers on observable change.

results weren't shared or there was a lack of interest? If the change effort is not fully engaged, perhaps those lower in the organization simply didn't find the survey content relevant, compelling, or even actionable for them. This takes us back to content and strategy.

From OD and change lens, all of this means finding and reinforcing those great examples and taking additional action where the wrong outcomes occurred. Clearly, this type of approach to surveys for change requires a level of commitment to accountability and follow-up beyond just "Did the action-planning process happen?" and "Did we see a change in the engagement score?" mentality. It requires a true commitment to what it takes to transform an organization and understand the dynamics and systems implications of why and where change happens.

Next, we describe a brief case example of how internal HR practitioners can use surveys for change within an existing larger system.

Building an Agile Marketing Organization

Several years ago one of the authors was assigned to be the HR business partner (HRBP) to the chief marketing officer (CMO) of a signature operating unit of a global consumer products organization. The CMO was new to the department and the business sector. The HRBP had been with the team for many years and knew the context well. As a result, the CMO relied heavily on his HRBP to help him understand the culture and how the team was perceived by its cross-functional partners. Based on these observations, along with a deep diagnosis of the results from the annual survey, it was clear that the department needed to undergo significant transformation to make it more effective.

Fortunately, the annual survey process was ingrained in the culture as a core change-management tool, and the insights served as a compelling rallying cry for change. The CMO and HRBP used the survey results diagnostically to help identify several levers for intervention: culture, leadership, structure, and capability. From a culture standpoint, it was clear that the department was heavy siloed, resistant to change, and not agile as a result. Teams within the department didn't work together effectively, and the connectivity to other departments (e.g., Finance, Sales, and supply chain in particular) was poor. This made the development and execution of effective marketing programs difficult and slow. Often, initiatives would be far into the development phase, and the team would learn at the 11th hour that the plans weren't feasible or supported by other functions. In addition, the behaviors of the team leaders as well as the structure reinforced this mentality. Teams were not designed or rewarded for collaborating with one another, and leaders were focused on their team goals, not those of the department or the larger business sector. Lastly, there were capability gaps in digital marketing (which was emerging at the time) and in collaboration skills. In short, the CMO and HRBP had their work cut out for them and decided the function needed to be changed from the ground up. They knew that this was going to be a multiyear, multipronged approach to change and required a broader systems perspective.

In this case not only was the core survey process used to identify the areas that needed to change but the team also developed a custom pulse survey to both communicate the CMO's new expectations (i.e., ways of working) and measure progress toward the goals they had laid out collectively. One of these areas was agility. As part of the transformation initiative, they worked with an outside consulting firm to bring agile working techniques to the department. For marketing, this was primarily focused on breaking down silos by creating lean, cross-functional teams for key initiatives like new product launches and big marketing promotions like the Super Bowl (both of which required multifunction alignment and approval). The agile process also included leveraging technology platforms such as Slack and Trello to drive co-creation and working collaboratively in real time. The introduction of new ways to conduct meetings was also a key component. Techniques were adapted from those used in smaller entrepreneurial environments that focus on the accelerated launch of minimum viable products versus overbaking and perfecting ideas.

This was a very different way of working and was extremely uncomfortable for many of the seasoned leaders. The CMO experienced a fair amount of resistance and used several measures to counteract this. They included the formation of a CMO council (i.e., a group of high-potential leaders who were thirsty for change and influential in the department) and a targeted monthly pulse survey to reinforce the key messages and track impact over time. Results were immediately shared with the CMO and discussed with his direct reports and the CMO council. The purpose was to make course corrections and continue the dialogue of change. Figure 22.3 provides sample items and interventions identified as a result of the initial diagnosis and ongoing survey process.

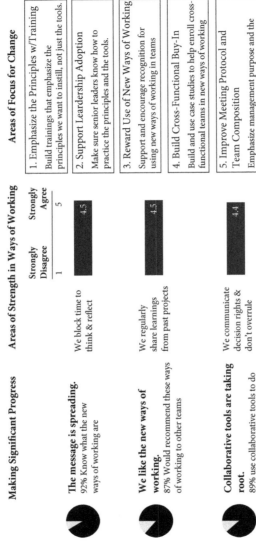

Figure 22.3. Agile ways of working survey results for marketing function. SLAM = Self-Organizing, Lean, Autonomous and Multidisciplinary.

Years later, the agile methodology remains active within the function. In addition, the agile tools and ways of working have spread to other parts the company (both functions and business sectors around the world). This was a data-driven transformation. The initial diagnostic power of the core internal survey results was the key enabler, and the follow-up targeted pulse surveys provided the cultural reinforcement and accountability to ensure that the change was "sticky" enough to outlast even its original executive sponsor.

Developing Capability for Surveys for Change

There is a final point to be made about survey capability in general. We believe that the changing nature of technology and our cultural obsession with real-time data and insights have led to the "commoditization and democratization of surveys" at a broader level. This shift in turn has led to the devaluation of their perceived impact among senior leaders for any purpose including driving change. Perhaps this is simply a reflection of the adage "familiarity breeds contempt"; however, we think there is more to it than that. We see a widening capability gap as well.

While clearly some organizations have internal efforts focused on surveys for change, in others we have witnessed the survey function being dismantled as leaders shift their attention toward the latest bright, shiny objects. We have also seen fewer and fewer new entrants to the field being deeply skilled in this technique. We believe it is paramount that academic programs in OD, I-O, and HR include an emphasis on data-driven methods for change and that surveys remain one of the core tools taught beyond a single lecture. We also believe that industry groups and professional societies (e.g., Society for Industrial and Organizational Psychology, Society for Human Resource Management, Association for Talent Development) should redouble their efforts to ensure that this capability is not lost at the practice level.

Conclusion

Surveys for change represent a unique and arguably somewhat lost art when it comes to current practice today. In this chapter we have outlined the case for surveys for change, described the factors which differentiate these types of surveys, and provided some examples of ways in which organizations can bring back this focus and capability. Also, equally importantly, we have discussed why surveys for change are such an important capability and how they can make a significant difference in the successful transformation of organizations today.

References

Beckhard, R., & Harris, R. T. (1987). *Organizational transitions: Managing complex change* (2nd ed.). Reading, MA: Addison-Wesley.

Burke, W. W. (2011). *Organization change: Theory and practice* (3rd ed.). Thousand Oaks, CA: Sage.

Burke, W. W. (2018). *Organization change: Theory and practice* (5th ed.). Thousand Oaks, CA: Sage.

Burke, W. W., Coruzzi, C. A., & Church, A. H. (1996). The organizational survey as an intervention for change. In A. I. Kraut (Ed.), *Organizational surveys: Tools for assessment and change* (pp. 41–66). San Francisco, CA: Jossey-Bass.

Burke, W. W., & Jackson, P. (1991). Making the SmithKline Beecham merger work. *Human Resource Management, 30,* 69–87.

Burke, W. W., & Litwin, G. H. (1992). A causal model of organizational performance and change. *Journal of Management, 18,* 523–545.

Church, A. H. (2016). Is engagement overrated? Five questions to consider before doing your next engagement survey. *Talent Quarterly, 9,* 1–7.

Church, A. H., & Burke, W. W. (2019). Strategic 360 for organization development. In A. H. Church, D. W. Bracken, J. W. Fleenor, & D. S. Rose (Eds.). *The handbook of strategic 360 feedback.* New York, NY: Oxford University Press.

Church, A. H., Golay, L. M., Rotolo, C. T., Tuller, M. D., Shull, A. C., & Desrosiers, E. I. (2012). Without effort there can be no change: Reexamining the impact of survey feedback and action planning on employee attitudes. In A. B. Shani, W. A. Pasmore, & R. W. Woodman (Eds.), *Research in organizational change and development* (Vol. 20, pp. 223–264). Bingley, England: Emerald Group.

Church, A. H., Kuyumcu, D., & Rotolo, C. T. (2016, April 28). Driving change through organizational surveys. In R. W. Griffen (Ed.), *Oxford bibliographies in management.* New York, NY: Oxford University Press. Retrieved from http://www.oxfordbibliographies.com/view/document/obo-9780199846740/obo-9780199846740-0089.xml

Church, A. H., Margiloff, A., & Coruzzi, C. A. (1995). Using surveys for change: An applied example in a pharmaceuticals organization. *Leadership and Organization Development Journal, 16*(4), 3–11.

Church, A. H., & Oliver, D. H. (2006). The importance of taking action, not just sharing survey feedback. In A. Kraut (Ed.), *Getting action from organizational surveys: New concepts, technologies and applications* (pp. 102–130). San Francisco, CA: Jossey-Bass.

Church, A. H., Rotolo, C. T., Shull, A. C., & Tuller, M. D. (2014). Inclusive organization development: An integration of two disciplines. In B. M. Ferdman & B. Deane (Eds.), *Diversity at work: The practice of inclusion* (pp. 260–295). San Francisco, CA: Jossey-Bass.

Church, A. H., & Waclawski, J. (2001). *Designing and using organizational surveys: A seven-step process.* San Francisco, CA: Jossey-Bass.

Colihan, J., & Waclawski, J. (2006). Pulse surveys: A limited approach with some unique advantages. In A. Kraut (Ed.), *Getting action from organizational surveys: New concepts, technologies and applications* (pp. 264–293). San Francisco, CA: Jossey-Bass.

Fermin, J. (2014, September 9). 12 mind-blowing employee survey statistics. Officevibe. Retrieved from https://www.officevibe.com/blog/employee-surveys-infographic

Johnson, R. H. (1996). Life in the consortium: The Mayflower Group. In A. I. Kraut (Ed.), *Organizational surveys: Tools for assessment and change* (pp. 285–309). San Francisco, CA: Jossey-Bass.

Katz, D., & Kahn, R. L. (1978). *The social psychology of organizations* (2nd ed.). New York, NY: John Wiley & Sons.

Kraut, A. I. (2006). *Getting action from organizational surveys: New concepts, technologies, and applications.* San Francisco, CA: Wiley-Bass.

Kraut, A. I. (1996). *Organizational surveys: Tools for assessment and change.* San Francisco, CA: Jossey-Bass.

Kraut, A. I., & Saari, L. M. (1999). Organization surveys coming of age for a new era. In A. I. Kraut & A. K. Korman (Eds.), *Evolving practices in human resource management: Responses to a changing world of work* (pp. 302–327). San Francisco, CA: Jossey-Bass.

Lewin, K. (1958). Group decision and social change. In E. E. Maccoby, T. M. Newcomb, & E. L. Hartley (Eds.), *Readings in social psychology* (pp. 197–211). New York, NY: Holt, Rinehart, and Winston.

Macey, W. H., & Schneider, B. (2008). The meaning of employee engagement. *Industrial and Organizational Psychology, 1*(1), 3–30. Retrieved from https://doi.org/10.1111/j.1754-9434.2007.0002.x

Nadler, D. A. (1977). *Feedback and organization development: Using data-based methods.* Reading, MA: Addison-Wesley.

Rotolo, C. T., Church, A. H., Adler, S., Smither, J. W., Colquitt, A. L., Shull, A. C., Paul, K. B., & Foster, G. (2018). Putting an end to bad talent management: A call to action for the field of industrial and organizational psychology. *Industrial and Organizational Psychology, 11*(2), 176–219. Retrieved from https://doi.org/10.1017/iop.2018.6

Thomas, D. A., & Creary, S. J. (2009). *Meeting the diversity challenge at PepsiCo: The Steve Reinemund era (Case: 9-410-024).* Boston, MA: Harvard Business School Publishing.

Waclawski, J., & Church, A. H. (2002). Introduction and overview of organization development as a data-driven approach for organizational change. In J. Waclawski & A. H. Church (Eds.), *Organization development: A data-driven approach to organizational change* (pp. 3–26). San Francisco, CA: Jossey-Bass.

23

Employee Survey Research

A Critical Review of Theory and Practice

Lewis K. Garrad and Patrick K. Hyland

Employee survey research has become common practice in modern organizations. In the mid-1990s researchers found that over 70% of US organizations surveyed their employees on an annual or biannual basis (Paul & Bracken, 1995). More recently, researchers at The Engagement Institute (Ray, Hyland, Dye, Kaplan, & Pressman, 2013) found that over 80% of global organizations survey their employees on a regular basis, with an increasing number administering regular pulse surveys throughout the year.

While employee surveys are popular, this methodology has its limitations. Many of the fundamentals of employee survey research were established in the early part of the 20th century (Jacoby, 1988). But a lot has changed in the world of work, the field of psychology, and the practice of management over the past 100 years. By evaluating the extent to which the discipline has kept pace with new developments and discoveries, we can identify methodological weak spots and opportunities for improvement and progress.

In this chapter, we conduct a critical review of employee survey research theory and practice. We start by exploring the theoretical foundations of employee survey research in context of new perspectives about work, organizational change, and workplace dynamics. Then we highlight common methodological and analytical mistakes that researchers in the field often make. Finally, we provide recommendations for improving the way employee research is conducted in today's business environment.

Lewis K. Garrad and Patrick K. Hyland, *Employee Survey Research* In: *Employee Surveys and Sensing*. Edited by: William H. Macey and Alexis A. Fink, Oxford University Press (2020). © Society for Industrial and Organizational Psychology.
DOI: 10.1093/oso/9780190939717.003.0023

The Theoretical Foundations of Employee Survey Research

The origins of employee survey research can be traced back to the 1920s, when organizations started using questionnaires to assess worker morale and improve employee relations (Jacoby, 1988). Following the development of the Thurstone procedure for attitude assessment (Thurstone & Chave, 1929), an increasing number of companies started conducting employee surveys (Schneider, Ashworth, Higgs, & Carr, 1996). In the 1940s, Rensis Likert and Kurt Lewin each founded research centers that advanced and refined organizational survey research methods (Burke, 2002). In the decades that followed, field work by researchers like Floyd Mann (1957), David Nadler (1977), and Ben Schneider (e.g., Schneider, Parkington, & Buxton, 1980) helped establish employee survey research as a core practice in the field of organization development and industrial–organizational psychology.

Today, surveys are typically used to gather employee feedback about a range of topics (e.g., employee engagement, job satisfaction, leader effectiveness, team collaboration, and workplace efficiency). While the content and structure of employee surveys often vary across organizations, there are three main activities that characterize all well-designed organizational survey projects.

- *Careful measurement.* Employee surveys are designed with a specific goal in mind: to measure personal perceptions in an objective way. In their primer on survey research, Church and Waclawski (2017) highlight the importance of measurement, defining employee surveys as "a systematic process of data collection designed to quantitatively measure specific aspects of organizational members' experience as they relate to work" (p. 3). Because accurate measurement is the sine qua non for any employee survey, survey researchers and practitioners place heavy emphasis on developing and utilizing well-designed items and scales, valid and reliable indices, and representative and generalizable research samples.
- *Robust data analysis.* After survey data have been collected, they are subjected to robust statistical analysis. Using various techniques, researchers seek to generate insight from survey responses. For

example, descriptive statistics are often computed to gain a basic understanding of the data. Comparative measures—based on either internal norms, between-group difference tests, longitudinal results, or external benchmarks—are used to identify high and low scores and positive and negative trends. If open-ended questions are included in the survey, content-coding techniques are often used to convert written comments into quantifiable themes. Correlational, regression, and relative weights analysis, along with structural equation modeling, is often conducted to identify relationships between variables and determine key drivers of important outcomes. On occasion, linkage analysis is conducted to explore the relationship between employee attitudes and other organizational metrics like customer satisfaction, store sales, or product defects.

- *Collective feedback and action planning.* After data analysis is conducted, survey results are often shared broadly with organizational members. Influenced by Lewin's seminal thinking about change (i.e., data can unfreeze groups and create change) and action research (i.e., stakeholders should be involved in any research effort focused on creating collective change), Likert and Mann emphasized the importance of involving employees, managers, and leaders in the process of interpreting results, identifying areas for change, and developing plans for improvement. Based on his field experience, Mann (1957) noticed that employees tended to become frustrated and cynical when managers did not review results and involve them in the action-planning process. Decades later, Nadler noted that surveys create expectation for action, noting that "the mere act of data collection generates energy around those activities that are being measured" and "creates expectations that the data collection will have consequences" (1996, p. 180).

All research paradigms are based on a set of philosophical assumptions about the nature of reality (i.e., ontology), the process of knowledge-building (i.e., epistemology), and the essence of what is right and wrong (i.e., axiology) (Patton, 2002). These philosophical assumptions influence the kinds of questions that researchers raise, the methods they use to study those questions, and the conclusions they reach (Chilisa & Kawulich, 2012).

Inherent in the three main survey activities are a set of basic assumptions about the nature of organizations, the correct way to do research, and the appropriate way to treat people in work settings. From an ontological perspective, the logic of employee survey research is influenced by both general systems theory (von Bertalanffy, 1950) and the field of cybernetics (Wiener, 1948). As a result, survey researchers tend to view organizations as open systems and place great importance on feedback as a source of organizational self-regulation and survival (Katz & Kahn, 1978). Organizational change is assumed to be a teleological, episodic, and time-bound process, progressing in a linear, rational, goal-oriented way (Van de Ven & Poole, 1995). From an epistemological standpoint, the practice of employee survey research was greatly shaped by the scientific thinking of the first half of the 20th century, which emphasized reductionism, determinism, and equilibrium as core principles (Hayles, 1991). Influenced by the philosophical perspectives of positivism, functionalism, and social determinism, survey researchers seek to make sense of workplace phenomena by using nomothetic methods—often focused on contextual factors—to discover underlying patterns of behavior, test hypotheses, identify causal relationships, determine universal truths, and produce pragmatic solutions (Burrell & Morgan, 1979). In terms of axiology, Lewin, Likert, Mann, and other early organization development practitioners emphasized that employee survey research should be conducted in a way that promotes humanistic values, participative processes, and democratic ideals (Burke, 1997).

Employee survey research is clearly founded on reasoned philosophical principles. But new theory and research highlight potential limitations, liabilities, and blind spots associated with this methodology. In the decades following the establishment of the employee survey field, new scientific perspectives—based on different philosophical assumptions—have been advanced. For example, interpretivism—which emerged as a critique of the positivism paradigm in the mid-20th century—contends that idiographic techniques and qualitative methods are the best ways to understand and interpret human behavior (Hudson & Ozanne, 1988; Neuman, 2000). Complexity theory is causing scientific communities to shift their focus from reductionism, predictability, and linearity to holism, uncertainty, and nonlinearity (Grobman, 2005). Complex adaptive systems theory, an outgrowth of complexity theory, is leading some organizational researchers and practitioners to question if open systems theory is sophisticated enough to understand chaotic, disruptive, and emergent organizational dynamics. Finally, a growing body of cross-cultural research (for example, see Dickson, Den Hartog, & Mitchelson, 2003) calls into question whether Western norms and ideals—like participative leadership and democratic decision-making—are valued by non-Western employees.

More than 50 years ago, Abraham Kaplan (1964) cautioned researchers to beware of the law of the instrument—the tendency to design research studies based on one's methodological expertise. "It comes as no particular surprise," he said, "to discover that a scientist formulates problems in a way which requires for their solution just those techniques in which he himself is especially skilled" (p. 28). For organizational researchers, this means it is critical to carefully consider the limitations of employee surveys, particularly in light of new paradigms, emerging frameworks, and global findings.

Assuming that surveys are the only effective way to investigate workplace research questions and initiate organizational change is a mistake. To guard against overutilizing employee surveys, researchers should think carefully about the best way to explore various organizational phenomena and consider a variety of options. Edmondson and McManus (2007) introduced a contingency framework for conducting field research that provides a helpful set of recommendations. They argue that the best way to produce high-quality field research is to create a fit between research methodology and level of knowledge. When a body of knowledge or a theory is new and research support is limited, they recommend using qualitative research techniques (e.g., interviews, observations, ethnographies) and pattern analysis to generate new insights in an inductive way. When a body of knowledge is growing and developing, having received mixed support, they recommend deploying both qualitative and quantitative research methods and exploratory analyses to expand knowledge. And when a body of knowledge or theory is well established, they recommend using quantitative research techniques, like surveys, and conducting formal hypothesis-testing in a confirmatory way. By utilizing a framework like this, organizational researchers can ensure that they are deploying employee surveys in a judicious way.

From Theory to Practice: Common Methodological and Analytical Mistakes

Even when employee surveys are the best available method for investigating workplace questions, methodological and analytical errors can undermine the accuracy, validity, and utility of results. In this section, we highlight three common methodological concerns that employee survey researchers often overlook, along with three common analytical mistakes they often make.

While survey strategies vary across organizations, there are some normative practices. Surveys are often administered to a population of employees (e.g., either a sample or a census) at a given point in time (e.g., annually, quarterly, monthly, daily, ad hoc), with a series of questions asking about work-related attitudes, feelings, behaviors, perceptions, and preferences. Employee surveys usually include items that measure proposed predictor and criterion variables. Once data collection is complete, researchers typically conduct various analyses (e.g., correlational analysis, key driver analysis, structural equation modeling) to determine if empirical relationships exist.

From a methodological perspective, survey researchers often ignore three potentially confounding factors when they follow these practices.

- *Overlooking the limitations of cross-sectional design.* Many researchers use a cross-sectional design when conducting organizational surveys. Cross-sectional surveys are often used because they are easy to administer, allowing a researcher to get a snapshot of workforce attitudes at a particular point in time by administering a survey (often anonymously) to current employees. Assuming that a representative sample completes the survey, cross-sectional design allows researchers to understand prevalence rates and explore associations between variables. To understand the extent to which attitudes change over time, researchers who use this design usually compare survey results across a number of administrations and calculate trend scores, either at the overall organization, business unit, or team level.

   While this approach can provide a directional indication of change-over-time trends, it can also lead to inaccurate conclusions, particularly if the employee population changes between survey administrations. For example, various researchers and practitioners have found that a honeymoon exists at work: New hires often have very favorable attitudes when they first join an organization (e.g., Johnson, 2018). If a number of new employees join an organization during the course of a year, their positive attitudes could impact overall organizational survey results, leading researchers to conclude that workforce attitudes are improving (when in fact the honeymoon effect is elevating results). The only way to arrive at accurate change-over-time assessments and causal conclusions is to use a longitudinal survey design. This requires a researcher to track attitudes at the individual level and make comparisons based only on employees who complete all surveys over a given time period. Fortunately, new technology is making this easier to do. Using human resources information system data and Web-based surveys, an increasing number of organizations are now conducting identified, confidential surveys. But even when organizations do conduct identified surveys, many researchers continue to compare total organization, unit, or team results across time, failing to consider or explore how hiring, turnover, or other changes in the composition of the workforce may impact trend results. This can lead to inaccurate findings and faulty conclusions. When exploring survey trends, researchers should either limit their analysis to a within-person longitudinal design or at least ensure that cross-sectional comparisons are based on comparable organizational samples (e.g., similar size, response rate, percentage of new hires, demographic composition) and highlight possible interpretive risks.

- *Ignoring common method bias and the necessary conditions for claiming causality.* Many organizational surveys seek to determine both how employees feel about their work experience and why they feel the way they do. Researchers often take data collected from a single survey and conduct correlational and key driver analysis to evaluate the extent to which survey items and dimensions are related with each other. When empirical relationships are discovered, they are often presented as being part of a potential causal chain (e.g., key driver results suggest that if we clarify career paths, employees are more likely to be motivated). There are two methodological problems with this approach. First, it does not take into account the potential systematic measurement error that could be caused by method variance, which is the "variance that is attributable to the measurement method rather than to the construct of interest" (Bagozzi & Yi, 1991, p. 426). This means that statistical relationships discovered between items or dimensions measured by a single survey may not be valid or accurate. As Podsakoff and colleagues note in their seminal article on common method bias (Podsakoff, MacKenzie, Lee, & Podsakoff, 2003), method variance can inflate or deflate the amount of observed variance between attitudinal constructs, causing researchers to erroneously under- or overstate the size of the relationship between variables. Second, concluding that causal relationships exist between survey items or dimensions measured at a single point in time is bad practice. While any good survey researcher or practitioner knows that correlation does not imply causation, some leaders, managers, and employees may not.

Fortunately, there is a straightforward way to correct for both problems. Creating a temporal separation between measuring predictor variables and criterion variables is one way researchers can reduce method variance (Podsakoff et al., 2003). It also allows researchers to establish time precedence, one of the necessary conditions for demonstrating causality. Many organizations are currently administering regular pulse surveys (e.g., weekly, monthly, or quarterly). By conducting statistical analyses across surveys, rather than within surveys, researchers can control for common method bias and test for causal relationships.

- *Surveying only the evaluating and remembering self.* Typically, organizational surveys ask employees to make global evaluations about work based on retrospective reflections. Employees are often presented with a statement (e.g., "My job makes good use of my skills and abilities") and then are instructed to use a Likert scale to indicate the extent to which they agree with the statement. Sometimes survey items explicitly direct employees to reflect on events or experiences that have happened in the past (e.g., "Over the past month, how often has your manager provided you with helpful feedback?").

  Well-being research by Daniel Kahneman and his colleagues suggests that these types of survey items only assess part of the phenomenon of work. Through a series of studies, they discovered that people's moment-by-moment assessment of events can be quite different from their after-the-fact, reflected evaluation of those same events. For example, Wirtz, Kruger, Scollon, and Diener (2003) found that respondents' experience of their vacation assessed using day-by-day event-sampling surveys was notably different from their evaluation of vacation assessed by a series of postvacation survey items. Based on findings like these, Kahneman and Riis (2005) emphasize the importance of measuring both moment-by-moment experiences and retrospective evaluations. "Evaluation and memory are important on their own," they say, "because they play a significant role in decisions, and because people care deeply about the narrative of their life. On the other hand, an exclusive focus on retrospective evaluations is untenable if these evaluations do not accurately reflect the quality of actual experience" (p. 289).

For organizational researchers seeking to develop a comprehensive understanding of their work environment, this line of research has important implications. Retrospective and evaluative assessments of critical workplace events (e.g., starting a new job, receiving a promotion, working on a team, going through an organizational change) may not provide a fully accurate understanding of the employee experience. By using experience sampling techniques like the Day Reconstruction Method (Kahneman, Krueger, Schkade, Schwarz, & Stone, 2004) or daily diaries, researchers may be able to generate new insights about a range of important topics. According to Fisher and To (2012), these methodologies are particularly well suited for "studying dynamic within-person processes involving affect, behavior, interpersonal interactions, work events, and other transient workplace phenomena" (p. 865).

From an analytical perspective, survey researchers often make three mistakes when they analyze and interpret survey data.

- *Mistake 1: Assuming more is better.* Many survey practitioners and researchers assume that positive attitudes are good and that the more positive attitudes are, the better. The positive psychology movement has been influential in advancing the idea that positive emotions and attitudes result in better outcomes (Peterson, Park, & Sweeney, 2008) citing examples which show that people with positive mindsets often experience more creativity and better well-being (e.g., Fredrickson & Branigan, 2005; Tugade, Fredrickson, & Feldman Barrett, 2004). But there are three potential drawbacks that come with consistently positive survey results.

  1. Strongly favorable attitudes may prevent organizational leaders from engaging in the critical process of reflection and change. Organizational change experts like Lewin and Kotter have long emphasized the importance of using disruptive data to unfreeze organizations and create an impetus for change (Cummings, Bridgman, & Brown, 2016). If employees are satisfied with the way things are, organizations may struggle to break out of the status quo.

  2. Research suggests that employees in some roles may actually benefit from a sense of dissatisfaction at work. For example, studies have found that creative people are more likely to experience negative affect (Akinola & Mendes, 2008) and antisocial behavior (Gino & Ariely, 2012), which makes engaging them more of a challenge. For these people, often it is their frustration that drives their action (Norem & Cantor, 1986).

3. It is also possible that some attitudes and states are better measured via an ideal-point approach rather than a dominance approach, which intrinsically assumes that stronger endorsement of an item is predictive of increased outcomes. For example, research shows that people who are overly optimistic about their current performance tend to raise less energy and therefore prepare less effectively for the future (Kappes, Oettingen, Mayer, & Maglio, 2011). Research (e.g. Halbesleben, Harvey, & Bolino, 2009) also shows that highly engaged employees suffer more work–family interference. The implication is that some attitudes and employee states may actually be more beneficial if they fluctuate (as noted by George, 2010) rather than being maintained at a consistently high level.

All together these concerns mirror the patterns often seen with other psychological traits where curvilinear relationships between variables are common. The "too much of a good thing" effect has been found for everything from intelligence (Antonakis, House, & Simonton, 2017) to personality (Le et al., 2011). More is not always better—this is an important point that survey researchers and practitioners should keep in mind as they interpret survey data and share results with organizational members.

- *Mistake 2: Overemphasizing contextual factors.* Most employee surveys focus on measuring climate factors and shared employee experiences. This is because researchers primarily seek to understand how contextual and situational factors—like teamwork and leader effectiveness—impact organizational outcomes like engagement or retention. While this is not an illogical strategy per se, this focus has led to a lack of practical integration between the psychology of individual differences and perceptions of workplace experience.

This is important because recent research suggests that individual factors like personality play a significant role in how people think and feel about their work. For example, a meta-analysis published in 2018 established that around 50% of the variance in an employee's work engagement (as measured by the Utrecht Work Engagement Scale) is predicted by personality and character variables (Young, Glerum, Wang, & Joseph, 2018). Given the relative stability of personality in most people during their work life (DelVecchio & Roberts, 2000), this finding implies that variables like engagement are heavily influenced by the nature of the people selected into the organization. It also helps to underscore the importance of understanding the interactions between individual and situational factors. For example, the way people construct their views about work can be rather personal, and research into how employees experience meaningfulness in their job shows significant individual variance (Bailey & Madden, 2015), even for people doing the same work. Actions that focus only on situational factors are therefore likely to have limited impact.

- *Mistake 3: Assuming survey results will lead to change.* Publicly available data on employee attitudes rarely show much change. For example, Harter (2018) reported that the percentage of engaged employees "has ranged from a low of 26% in 2000 and 2005 to the recent six-month high of 34% in 2018. On average, 30% of employees have been engaged at work during the past 18 years." With a tiny variation of only 4% from the average, it's difficult to argue that survey programs focused on engagement actually change anything. Why do people seem so stubborn in their opinion about work?

A principal assumption of the employee survey process is that leaders have the capacity and willingness to use employee feedback to create change. Yet this assumption has not always held true for several reasons. First, if leadership style is a function of leader personality (Judge, Bono, Ilies, & Gerhardt, 2002) and employee experiences are related to leadership style (Martin, Guillaume, Thomas, Lee, & Epitropaki, 2016), then the stability of leader personality limits behavioral change unless the leader applies sustained effort and learning. Second, individual employee personality also plays a significant role in determining how people respond to surveys, reducing the impact a leader can have on the situational factors that drive the feedback.

Next, as leaders have become more aware of the role that broader systemic and cultural issues play in determining organization performance (e.g., Judge & Cable, 1997), survey researchers have expanded their questions to wider and more complex issues of organization effectiveness. These elements of organization functioning are hard to change and usually require significant coordinated activity across various teams and leaders simultaneously. The role of senior leadership has been found to be also critical, with studies demonstrating that factors like chief executive officer personality playing a role in culture development (O'Reilly, Caldwell, Chatman, & Doerr, 2014). The effort involved to achieve the type of coordinated shift that is needed is usually beyond the resources many organizations are willing to apply unless they are in dire need.

Combined, these issues mean that it can be difficult for any individual manager to effect change. The risk is that many then become disillusioned and frustrated with the employee survey process and/or become passive participants.

Looking Beyond Employee Surveys: Building Better Employee Research Programs

When employee surveys are carefully planned and rigorously designed, the data they generate can produce powerful insights, foster meaningful change, enhance the employee experience, and improve organizational performance. But, as we've argued in this chapter, surveys have limitations. When researchers and practitioners misuse this methodology or assume it is the only way to learn from their employees, they run the risk of creating faulty feedback loops, misguided conclusions, and organizational blind spots.

In recent years, various experts have argued that evidence-based human resources (e.g., Rousseau & Barends, 2011), advanced people analytics (e.g., Waber, 2013), organizational sense-making (Weick & Sutcliffe, 2015), and organizational learning (Hess, 2014) are critical in today's volatile and uncertain business environment. In light of these arguments, we think organizations should develop a broad set of research capabilities that extend beyond traditional employee surveys. For organizational researchers and practitioners seeking to build a best-in-class employee research program, we recommend focusing on four practices.

- *Learn to use multiple methodologies.* Surveys can be effective for measuring well-tested theories. But so much of what organizations need to learn about in today's fast-paced world is nascent, emergent, nuanced, and complex. For some research questions, qualitative methods may yield the best insights. Technological advances in artificial intelligence, computer-assisted text analysis, and natural language processing are making it easier to analyze extensive amounts of unstructured data in efficient and effective ways.
- *Assess phenomena at multiple levels.* Richard Hackman (2003) wrote a compelling article about learning more by crossing levels. His main point was that because most organizational dynamics happen at multiple levels, with individual-, group-, and organization-level causes and consequences,

researchers can develop a better understanding of workplace phenomena by conducting research at multiple levels. Using a multilevel approach, researchers could explore team effectiveness, for example, by assessing team member personalities, group-level behavior, and organization-level culture. Unfortunately, many researchers do not take this approach, instead focusing on just one level of analysis. As a result, they often develop a limited understanding of organizational dynamics.

- *Integrate multiple data sets.* Many organizations have fallen into the habit of relying on single-survey correlational and/or key driver analysis to make significant organizational decisions. As noted, this type of analysis is prone to common method bias. These days, most organizations have robust effectiveness, performance, and productivity metrics. By linking these data with attitudinal data, researchers and practitioners can conduct analyses that are more sophisticated, more valid, and potentially more insightful for their organizations.

- *Engage multiple stakeholders.* In our opinion, the best employee research programs create insight, energy, and direction for organizational members. With that in mind, we think that organizational researchers and practitioners should think carefully about how to design research assessments, analyses, and feedback mechanisms that empower and energize everyone from front-line employees to C-suite leaders. Is our research actually motivating employees? Is it helping managers and leaders be more effective? Is it truly improving the work environment and organizational effectiveness? These are the kinds of questions we think researchers should ask themselves on a regular basis.

As we look to the future, we think that employee surveys should continue to play a critical role in employee research programs. But we also think that the smartest organizations will develop and deploy a comprehensive set of research tools and methodologies to understand their workforce.

References

Akinola, M., & Mendes, W. B. (2008). The dark side of creativity: Biological vulnerability and negative emotions lead to greater artistic creativity. *Personality and Social Psychology Bulletin, 34*(12), 1677–1686. doi:10.1177/0146167208323933

Antonakis, J., House, R. J., & Simonton, D. K. (2017). Can super smart leaders suffer from too much of a good thing? The curvilinear effect of intelligence on perceived leadership behavior. *Journal of Applied Psychology, 102*(7), 1003–1021. doi:10.1037/apl0000221

Bagozzi, R. P., & Yi, Y. (1991). Multitrait–multimethod matrices in consumer research. *Journal of Consumer Research, 17*, 426–439.

Bailey, C., & Madden, A. (2015, October). Time reclaimed: Temporality and the experience of meaningful work. *Work, Employment, & Society, 31*(1), 3–18. doi:10.1177/0950017015604100

Burke, W. W. (1997). The new agenda for organization development. *Organization Dynamics, 25*(1), 7–21.

Burke, W. W. (2002). *Organizational change: Theory and practice.* Thousand Oaks, CA: Sage.

Burrell, G., & Morgan, G. (1979). *Sociological paradigms and organizational analysis.* Aldershot, England: Gower.

Chilisa, B., & Kawulich, B. B. (2012). Selecting a research approach: Paradigm, methodology and methods. In C. Wagner, B. B. Kawulich, & M. Garner (Eds.), *Doing social research: A global context* (pp. 51–61). London, England: McGraw-Hill.

Church, A. H., & Waclawski, J. (2017). *Designing and using organizational surveys: A seven step approach.* San Francisco, CA: Jossey-Bass.

Cummings, S., Bridgman, T., & Brown, K. G. (2016). Unfreezing change as three steps: Rethinking Kurt Lewin's legacy for change management. *Human Relations, 69*(1), 33–60. Retrieved from https://doi.org/10.1177/0018726715577707

DelVecchio, W. F., & Roberts, B. W. (2000). The rank-order consistency of personality traits from childhood to old age: A quantitative review of longitudinal studies. *Psychological Bulletin, 126*(1), 3–25.

Dickson, M. W., Den Hartog, D. N., & Mitchelson, J. K. (2003). Research on leadership in a cross-cultural context: Making progress, and raising new questions. *Leadership Quarterly, 14*(6), 729–768.

Edmondson, A., & McManus, S. (2007). Methodological fit in management field research. *Academy of Management Review, 32*, 1155–1179. Retrieved from http://dx.doi.org/10.5465/AMR.2007.26586086

Fisher, C. D., & To, M. L. (2012). Using experience sampling methodology in organizational behavior. *Journal of Organizational Behavior, 33*(7), 865–877. Retrieved from https://doi.org/10.1002/job.1803

Fredrickson, B. L., & Branigan, C. (2005). Positive emotions broaden the scope of attention and thought-action repertoires. *Cognition & Emotion, 19*(3), 313–332. doi:10.1080/02699930441000238

George, J. M. (2010). More engagement is not necessarily better: The benefits of fluctuating levels of engagement. In S. L. Albrecht (Ed.), *New horizons in management. Handbook of employee engagement: Perspectives, issues, research and practice* (pp. 253–263). Cheltenham, England, and Northampton, MA: Edward Elgar.

Gino, F., & Ariely, D. (2012). The dark side of creativity: Original thinkers can be more dishonest. *Journal of Personality and Social Psychology, 102*(3), 445–459.

Grobman, G. (2005). Complexity theory: A new way to look at organizational change. *Public Administration Quarterly, 29*(3), 351–384.

Hackman, J. R. (2003). Learning more from crossing levels: Evidence from airplanes, orchestras, and hospitals. *Journal of Organizational Behavior, 24*, 1–18.

Halbesleben, J. R., Harvey, J., & Bolino, M. C. (2009). Too engaged? A conservation of re-sources view of the relationship between work engagement and work interference with family. *Journal of Applied Psychology, 94*(6), 1452–1465. doi:10.1037/a0017595

Harter, J. (2018). Employee engagement on the rise in the U.S. Gallup. Retrieved from https://news.gallup.com/poll/241649/employee-engagement-rise.aspx

Hayles, K. (1991). *Chaos and order: Complex dynamics in literature and science.* Chicago, IL: University of Chicago Press.

Hess, E. D. (2014). *Learn or die: Using science to build a leading-edge learning organization.* New York, NY: Columbia University.

Hudson, L. A., & Ozanne, J. L. (1988). Alternative ways of seeking knowledge in con-sumer research. *Journal of Consumer Research, 14,* 508–521. Retrieved from http://dx.doi.org/10.1086/209132

Jacoby, S. M. (1988). Employee attitude surveys in historical perspective. *Industrial Relations, 27*(1), 74–93. Retrieved from https://doi.org/10.1111/j.1468-232X.1988.tb01047.x

Johnson, S. R. (2018). *Engaging the workplace: Using surveys to spark change.* New York, NY: ASTD.

Judge, T. A., Bono, J. E., Ilies, R., & Gerhardt, M. W. (2002). Personality and leadership: A qualitative and quantitative review. *Journal of Applied Psychology, 87*(4), 765–780. Retrieved from http://dx.doi.org/10.1037/0021-9010.87.4.765

Judge, T. A., & Cable, D. M. (1997). Applicant personality, organizational culture, and organization attraction. *Personnel Psychology, 50,* 359–394. doi:10.1111/j.1744-6570.1997.tb00912.x

Kahneman, D., Krueger, A. B., Schkade, D. A., Schwarz, N., & Stone, A. A. (2004). A survey method for characterizing daily life experience: The day reconstruction method (DRM). *Science, 306*(5702), 1776–1780.

Kahneman, D., & Riis, J. (2005). Living, and thinking about it: two perspectives. In F. A. Huppert, N. Baylis, & B. Keverne (Eds.), *The science of well-being* (pp. 285–306). New York, NY: Oxford University Press.

Kaplan, A. (1964). *The conduct of inquiry: Methodology for behavioral science.* San Francisco, CA: Chandler.

Kappes, H. B., Oettingen, G., Mayer, D., & Maglio, S. (2011). Sad mood promotes self-initiated mental contrasting of future and reality. *Emotion, 11*(5), 1206–1222.

Katz, D., & Kahn, R. L. (1978). *The social psychology of organizations.* New York, NY: Wiley.

Le, H., Oh, I. S., Robbins, S. B., Ilies, R., Holland, E., & Westrick, P. (2011). Too much of a good thing: Curvilinear relationships between personality traits and job performance. *Journal of Applied Psychology, 96*(1), 113–133. doi:10.1037/a0021016

Mann, F. C. (1957). *Research in Industrial Human Relations. Studying and cre-ating change: A means to understanding social organization.* (Publication No. 17). Champaign, IL: Industrial Relations Research Association.

Martin, R., Guillaume, Y., Thomas, G., Lee, A., & Epitropaki, O. (2016). Leader–member exchange (LMX) and performance: A meta-analytic review. *Personnel Psychology, 69*(1), 67–121. Retrieved from https://doi.org/10.1111/peps.12100

Nadler, D. A. (1977). *Feedback and organization development: Using data-based methods.* London, England: Addison-Wesley.

Nadler, D. A. (1996). Setting expectations and reporting results: Conversations with top management. In A. I. Kraut (Ed.), *Organizational surveys: Tools for assessment and change* (pp. 177–203). San Francisco, CA: Jossey-Bass.

Neuman, W. L. (2000). *Social research methods qualitative and quantitative approaches* (4th ed.). Needham Heights, MA: Allyn & Bacon.

Norem, J. K., & Cantor, N. (1986). Defensive pessimism: Harnessing anxiety as motivation. *Journal of Personality and Social Psychology, 51*(6), 1208–1217.

O'Reilly, C. A., Caldwell, D. F., Chatman, J. A., & Doerr, B. (2014). The promise and problems of organizational culture: CEO personality, culture, and firm performance. *Group & Organization Management, 39*(6), 595–625. Retrieved from https://doi.org/10.1177/1059601114550713

Patton, M. Q. (2002). *Qualitative research and evaluation methods* (3rd ed.). Thousand Oaks, CA: Sage Publications.

Paul, K. B., & Bracken, D. W. (1995). Everything you always wanted to know about employee surveys. *Training & Development, 49*(1), 45–49.

Peterson, C., Park, N., & Sweeney, P. J. (2008). Group well-being: Morale from a positive psychology perspective. *Applied Psychology, 57,* 19–36. doi:10.1111/j.1464-0597.2008.00352

Podsakoff, P. M., MacKenzie, S. B., Lee, J. Y., & Podsakoff, N. P. (2003). Common method biases in behavioral research: A critical review of the literature and recommended remedies. *Journal of Applied Psychology, 88,* 879–903. Retrieved from http://dx.doi.org/10.1037/0021-9010.88.5.879

Ray, R., Hyland, P. K., Dye, D., Kaplan, J., & Pressman, A. (2013). The DNA of engagement. Retrieved from https://www.conference-board.org/councils/councildetail.cfm?councilid=1058

Rousseau, D. M., & Barends, E. G. (2011). Becoming an evidence-based HR practitioner. *Human Resource Management Journal, 21,* 221–235. doi:10.1111/j.1748-8583.2011.00173.x

Schneider, B., Ashworth, S. D., Higgs, A. C., & Carr, L. (1996). Design, validity, and use of strategically focused employee attitude surveys. *Personnel Psychology, 49*(3), 695–705. Retrieved from http://dx.doi.org/10.1111/j.1744-6570.1996.tb01591.x

Schneider, B., Parkington, J. J., & Buxton, V. M. (1980). Employee and customer perceptions of service in banks. *Administrative Science Quarterly, 25,* 252–267.

Thurstone, L. L., & Chave, E. J. (1929). *The measurement of attitude.* Oxford, England: University of Chicago Press.

Tugade, M. M., Fredrickson, B. L., & Feldman Barrett, L. (2004). Psychological resilience and positive emotional granularity: Examining the benefits of positive emotions on coping and health. *Journal of Personality, 72*(6), 1161–1190.

Van De Ven, A. H., & Poole, M. S. (1995). Explaining development and change in organizations. *Academy of Management Review, 20,* 510–540. http://dx.doi.org/10.2307/258786

Von Bertalanffy, L. (1950). An outline of general systems theory. *British Journal of the Philosophy of Science, 1,* 134–165.

Waber, B. (2013). *People analytics: How social sensing technology will transform business and what it tells us about the future of work.* Upper Saddle River, NJ: FT Press.

Weick, K. E., & Sutcliffe, K. M. (2015). *Managing the unexpected: Sustained performance in a complex world.* Hoboken, NJ: John Wiley & Sons.

Wiener, N. (1948). *Cybernetics; or control and communication in the animal and the machine.* Oxford, England: John Wiley & Sons.

Wirtz, D., Kruger, J., Scollon, C. N., & Diener, E. (2003). What to do on spring break? The role of predicted, on-line, and remembered experience in future choice. *Psychological Science, 14*(5), 520–524.

Young, H. R., Glerum, D. R., Wang, W., & Joseph, D. L. (2018). Who are the most engaged at work? A meta-analysis of personality and employee engagement. *Journal of Organizational Behavior, 39,* 1330–1346. Retrieved from https://doi.org/10.1002/job.2303

24

From Identified Surveys
to New Technologies

Employee Privacy and Ethical Considerations

Lise M. Saari and Charles A. Scherbaum

Employee surveys and privacy issues have become more complicated with
the movement toward identified surveys, integrated databases, expanded
analytics, and the advancement of technology. Survey practitioners are increasingly involved with integrated data initiatives that include identified employee survey data (Ducey et al., 2015; Saari & Scherbaum, 2011).
Technological advances in machine learning, artificial intelligence, and ambient data collection are also occurring at the time of writing this chapter.
These new technologies are developing at a fast pace and present new
challenges, including privacy and ethical considerations (King, Tonidandel,
Cortina, & Fink, 2016; Waber, 2018). Survey professionals and industrial–
organizational (I-O) psychologists are increasingly working between the
colliding forces of legal/ethical frameworks, on the one hand, and rapidly
moving technology advances, on the other hand.

Employee surveys have successfully transitioned in earlier times to new
technologies (Kraut & Saari, 1999; Thompson, Surface, Martin, & Sanders,
2003). Online surveys were introduced in the 1980s, and it is now commonplace for surveys to be administered via computers and smartphones.
With the transition from paper to computer-based surveys, a major focus
of survey practitioners was ensuring employee privacy and building trust
(Church & Rotolo, 2011; Fenlason & Suckow-Zimberg, 2006). As employee
surveys evolve further into new technologies, it is important to retain the
original tenet of I-O psychology: "promoting human welfare through the
various applications of psychology to all types of organizations" (Sashkin &
Prien, 1996).

Lise M. Saari and Charles A. Scherbaum, *From Identified Surveys to New Technologies* In: *Employee Surveys and
Sensing.* Edited by: William H. Macey and Alexis A. Fink, Oxford University Press (2020). © Society for Industrial and
Organizational Psychology.
DOI: 10.1093/oso/9780190939717.003.0024

The purpose of this chapter is to review and provide recommendations on data privacy and ethical considerations related to employee attitude measurement, including new technologies. The chapter starts with a discussion of data privacy and related data protection issues. This is followed by a review of the ethical considerations related to employee surveys, including the ever-changing legal landscape. We then summarize select new technologies that collect employee attitude data and discuss the challenges they pose. Finally, we close with recommendations for the use of employee surveys and evolving technologies.

Resources used as the basis for this chapter include the I-O psychology literature, the ethics literature, legal regulations related to privacy, and technology publications. The authors also carried out 10 structured interviews and numerous other discussions with respected, highly experienced I-O psychology survey professionals as well as technology experts.

Data Privacy

Current Trends

Employee surveys have continued to move from anonymous to identified surveys since earlier articles discussed this trend (Saari & Scherbaum, 2011). Identified employee surveys have a unique identifier for each employee taking the survey. The identifying information tied to each employee is supposed to be kept separate, with controls over who has access to the key; but ultimately a person can be identified. Based on the interviews we conducted, it is estimated that over 80% of employee surveys are now identified rather than anonymous surveys.

Another trend is the movement from linkage research (Rucci, Kirn, & Quinn, 1998; Wiley, 1996) toward more extensive integrated analyses. These include human capital analytics and data science initiatives comprised of big data, machine learning, and/or artificial intelligence (King et al., 2016). These developments are based on statistically relating diverse sets of data, including employee data. The inclusion of identified employee survey data as part of these initiatives heightens privacy concerns.

Many new technologies are being proposed that could be used to measure employee attitudes. These include analyzing employees' social media posts, scraping company chats/e-mails for attitude shifts, and measuring emotions through cameras on employees' computers. Some of these technologies, by their very design, raise significant concerns about privacy and possibly violate regulations such as the European Union's General Data Protection Regulation (GDPR).

Data Privacy Risks

One privacy concern with employee attitude data is if they become part of data science initiatives, they will be managed by, and the responsibility of, other professionals such as internal business intelligence or data science professionals (Guzzo, 2016; Putka & Oswald, 2016). The potential for privacy violations depends in large part on the research ethics background of who manages these technologies (Black, Hyland, & Rutigliano, 2011; Weiner, Jolton, Dorio, Klein, & Herman, 2011), and it is likely that they will not have the same ethical training and background as I-O psychology survey professionals.

Another data privacy concern is the possibility of data breaches (Waber, 2018). Data breaches have increased every year since reporting began. In 2018 there were approximately 500 million personal records exposed from over 1,200 security breaches in the United States alone (Identity Theft Resource Center, 2018). This trend is not likely to reverse in the foreseeable future.

Finally, even the highest-integrity survey professionals may be faced with pressures that put privacy protection at risk. For example, if they have demonstrated the ability to predict attrition based on longitudinal employee attitude data, executives may want to know who specifically is likely to leave; or if leading indicators of employee misconduct have been determined, there could be requests to reveal who is predicted to engage in misconduct. Situations such as these can test the ethics of even the highest-integrity survey professional. Moreover, privacy issues arise not just from the potential release of identified personal data but also from the inferences and decisions drawn from the data about an individual (Tene & Polonetsky, 2013).

Employee Perceptions and Data Quality

Against the backdrop of employee survey trends and potential privacy issues, the general public's concern around privacy is on the rise (e.g., Antón,

Earp & Young, 2010). A national survey (National Cyber Security Alliance, 2016) found that 68% of US respondents cited online privacy as a major concern. Couple this with increased data breaches and it is understandable that people have concerns about data privacy.

Trust is an essential feature for obtaining quality data from employee surveys (Froelich, 2011; Morris & Ashworth, 2011). In fact, survey experts (e.g., Church & Rotolo, 2011) advise against using identified surveys in organizations with low-trust environments. Related to the issue of trust, research over many decades has shown that assurances of privacy are important for obtaining high-quality employee survey data. Even in high-trust organizations where identified surveys are implemented with the utmost professionalism, there can be impacts on data quality such as rating inflation and nonresponse (Bowling, 2005; Heerwegh, Vanhove, Matthijs, & Loosveldt, 2005; Sashkin & Prien, 1996; Thompson & Surface, 2007; Tourangeau & Yan, 2007). New technologies that raise privacy concerns could potentially have even greater effects on data quality (Fogel & Nehmad, 2009; Graeff & Harmon, 2002). However, there are some conflicting findings on this topic (e.g., Black et al., 2011). This is an area where more research by both practitioners and academics is needed.

Although privacy is deemed an important right in general, individual differences and societal norms may influence the level of concern around privacy. It has been suggested that certain regions or cultures may have differing views on privacy (Luong, 2011). Employee surveys, which are often global, need to consider varying levels of concern about privacy by employees across the globe. For example, Hessler and Freerks (1995) state that Europeans consider privacy an essential and fundamental human right and therefore may have even stronger views around privacy. In fact, European data privacy regulations reflect this sentiment, as will be discussed in the next section.

Principles that Can Guide Decisions Involving Data Privacy

The effective acquisition, development, and maintenance of human capital in an organization require the collection of data from current or potential employees. These data can take many forms (e.g., selection assessments) and occur at various points in the employee life cycle. Regardless of the form, the collection of employee data raises legal and ethical issues about how the data should be handled and used (Lefkowitz, 2017; Waber, 2018). These data often are of significant consequence to an applicant or employee, and the misuse, misinterpretation, or disclosure of the data could harm the individual or the organization.

Unlike other forms of employee data (e.g., performance evaluations), employee survey data are provided on a voluntary basis and ask the employee to share their attitudes and personal views, often on sensitive topics. There are many purposes for and uses of employee survey data. The purpose and use can frame many of the ethical and privacy considerations. For example, employee survey data can be used to make decisions that have implications for the organization (e.g., organizational change efforts) or consequences for individuals (e.g., manager performance evaluation). In these cases, the ethical considerations take on a different dimension from when there is no consequence for the individual providing the survey data. Thus, there are unique considerations for how these data should be used, maintained, and protected to ensure that employees continue to trust the survey process and provide insights (Saari & Scherbaum, 2011). Among these considerations, data privacy is the primary issue from both an organizational and an employee perspective (Froelich, 2011).

Historically, these data privacy considerations were handled by administering anonymous surveys (Fenlason & Suckow-Zimberg, 2006). Given that anonymous surveys were effective at maintaining the privacy of employee survey data, little attention was devoted to developing best professional practices for the use and protection of employee survey data. However, the proliferation of identified surveys and new technologies to measure attitudes, by their design, identify employees. This requires a complete reconceptualization of data privacy and guidelines for their use (Saari & Scherbaum, 2011).

Although best practice guidelines have been successfully developed in other fields (e.g., Council of American Survey Research Organizations, American Association for Public Opinion), there is no formal set of best practices for employee surveys. However, there are several ethical and legal principles that can be drawn on to identify a set of reasonable guidelines for collecting and using employee survey data. These guidelines can direct current survey practice as well as address the many difficult privacy questions that arise with new technologies. In the remainder of this section, we review these ethical and legal principles.

Belmont Report

Other than the intended use, the collection of employee survey data closely mirrors other forms of human subject research. Thus, the major principles that guide human subject research contained in the Belmont Report (National Commission for the Protection of Human Subjects of Biomedical and Behavioral Research, 1979) can inform employee survey research. The Belmont Report contains three major principles:

- *Respect for people* who enter research voluntarily, with adequate information, and without deception
- *Informed consent*, which includes providing complete information, ensuring comprehension, and voluntariness
- *Privacy/confidentiality*, which includes maintaining privacy and data security and clarifying how long data are retained

These principles have some obvious application to employee survey data. Employees should have choice in completing a survey, should know how it will be used, and should have their data protected (Biga, McCance, & Massman, 2011).

American Psychological Association Ethical Guidelines

The American Psychological Association (APA) has a set of guidelines for the ethical conduct of psychologists in a variety of practice and research settings, including organizational consultation settings (American Psychological Association, 2017). These guidelines build and expand upon the principles in the foundational Belmont Report as well as operationalize what these principles mean for the practice of psychology.

Several sections of the APA ethical guidelines touch on issues that survey practitioners often face. For instance, Section 1.03 addresses conflicts between organizational demands and ethical practice. Section 3.04 states that psychologists have an obligation to avoid doing harm and minimize the potential for harm when it is foreseeable. Section 3.11 states that psychologists have an obligation to disclose, in advance, the possible uses of information gathered, any limits to confidentiality, and who will have access to the information. The psychologist is responsible for making this disclosure to the client and to those who will be affected (e.g., employees).

Section 4 of the APA ethical guidelines specifically focuses on practices and obligations related to privacy and confidentiality. The guidelines in this section outline the responsibility of psychologists to maintain the confidentiality of the information they gather and to disclose any limits to maintaining confidentiality such as laws or organizational policies. Psychologists also have the responsibility to limit intrusions into individuals' privacy by only collecting information needed to provide services at hand.

Data Protection Regulations

Given the frequency of data breaches and general concerns about privacy in the digital age, governments around the globe have enacted or are beginning to enact data privacy regulations. The United States has had inconsistent regulations regarding data privacy. As of the writing of this chapter, specific states have begun enacting data privacy laws. Most notably, California passed comprehensive data privacy laws that substantially increase the protection of individually identifiable information on par with the European Union's. As a result of actions by individual states, there is renewed interest in enacting federal data privacy laws to create a unified framework. Data privacy regulations in the United States will continue to evolve in response to a need for consistency and to keep up with changing technologies and related privacy issues.

In contrast to the United States, the European Union has had consistent data privacy regulations that ensure a high level of protection of individually identifiable information. The European Union has instituted several data privacy frameworks that set the ground rules for use of individually identifiable data, including employee survey data. Beginning with the 1995 Directive on Data Protection, minimum standards were set for the protection of individually identifiable information. In 2018, the European Union replaced this with the GDPR (European Union, 2016), which raises the minimum standards and introduces new requirements.

The GDPR has seven principles that must be followed by organizations handling employee or consumer data from EU countries. The first principle of *notice* requires that information about how the data will be used is provided to survey respondents before the data are collected. This notice must include the current and future uses of the data by the organization and any third parties that the organization contracts with.

The second principle of *choice* requires that the data can be used for purposes other than those originally described only if survey respondents are asked permission. Given the difficulty of obtaining permission at a later point, this principle should encourage careful thought about current and potential future uses of survey data so that employees can be informed and given choice and permission can be acquired at initial data collection.

The third principle, *accountability for onward transfer*, states that if employee survey data are transferred to a third party, the organization transferring the data retains liability for the proper handling of the data. The fourth principle of *security* holds that the organization will take reasonable precautions to protect personal data from loss, misuse, unauthorized disclosure, alteration, or destruction.

The fifth principle of *data integrity and purpose limitation* states that an organization will only collect and use employee data in a manner consistent with the purposes for which it has been authorized by the respondent. The sixth principle of *access* allows a respondent to correct any inaccuracies within reasonable limits or remove his or her data. The seventh principle focuses on *enforcement, recourse, and liability*. If found in violation, an organization can be fined 20 million euros or 4% of annual revenue, whichever is greater.

The GDPR strengthened previous EU requirements including individuals' access to their data, oversight for data privacy protections, and penalties for failure to protect data privacy. Several of the changes have the potential to directly impact the collection and use of employee survey data. Under the GDPR, informed consent must be simple and clear and must accurately describe the intended uses of the data. Consent must be given through active opt-in, and it must be easy to withdraw consent at any point. Additionally, individuals have the right to have their data erased and no longer used.

The GDPR also includes a requirement called *privacy by design*. This principle states that data privacy protections need to be included in the design and development of a system from the beginning and not as an afterthought, which is often the case with new technologies (Dreibelbis, Martin, Coovert, & Dorsey, 2018).

As of the writing of this chapter, the GDPR has been in effect for close to 1 year. All indications are that it is being fully enforced, with violations and fines already occurring. Issues that seem to be at the forefront are inappropriate release or sharing of data, the right to be forgotten (the ability for an individual to request that his or her data be erased), and informed consent violations. To assist organizations in complying with GDPR requirements, the European Union provides a number of guideline documents. These documents cover topics such as transparency, consent, breach notification, and problems with using automated decision-making. The US Department of Commerce (2018) has established a program called Privacy Shield to help US-based organizations comply with these regulations.

Although the specific regulations in Europe, the United States, and elsewhere are likely to continue to evolve, the principles underlying all of them mirror the ethical guidelines in the Belmont Report and the APA's ethical guidelines. Survey practitioners are well advised to follow regulatory developments. We also encourage those in the field to proactively adopt sound ethical practices such as those in the Belmont Report and the APA ethical guidelines (see Biga et al., 2011, and Black et al., 2011, for examples).

New Technologies: Privacy and Ethical Considerations

There are many new technologies related to measuring employees' attitudes that have the potential to impact what data are collected and how the data are used. These technologies may be commonplace when this chapter is read in the future, or other technologies may supplant them.

New technologies provide the potential for positive benefits but also pose challenges for data privacy. In this section, we focus on three key areas where technologies are having impact and likely will in the future: new data-collection methods, data integration and storage, and advanced analytics.

New Data-Collection Methods

Although surveys have been the mainstay of capturing employee attitudes for most of the past century, there is a groundswell of interest in methods that can be used to capture attitudes passively and in as close to real time as possible. For example, there is rapid growth in the use of short-cycle pulse surveys, such as apps that survey employees daily or even multiple times a day. However, these methods are ultimately just a faster and more flexible version of current survey tools.

The truly revolutionary technologies are in *passive* methods of data collection. These methods do not explicitly require awareness by employees that data about them are being collected and analyzed. One example of these passive methods is the use of the "digital self" to gather ambient, text-based data available from social media or company communications. Data can be obtained from social media as well as internal company e-mails and chats to purportedly measure attitudes (McFarland & Ployhart, 2015). For example, Hernandez, Newman, and Jean (2016) describe how Twitter can be used to assess group-level job satisfaction and attitudes. The words from these data sources are text-mined, or sentiment analysis software is applied to identify attitudes.

Another example of passive data-collection methods is physiologically based measures. This range of technologies has been termed *emotive analytics* and purportedly measures attitudes or emotions via image, speech, or even touch. For example, facial emotion recognition (Lozano-Monasor, López Bonal, Fernández-Caballero, & Vigo-Bustos, 2014) has been developed that captures emotions from a computer camera or other cameras. One interviewee shared that a leader somewhat jokingly said there was no need for an employee survey because they could just read the emotions of employees via security cameras located throughout the company. Eye-tracking methodologies have been developed to capture engagement from gaze patterns and pupillometry (Hopstaken, van der Linden, Bakker, Kompier, & Leung, 2016). Technologies have also been developed that analyze recorded speech for tone or emotion (Fayeka, Lecha, & Cavedon, 2017; Scherer, 2003). Other physiologically based measures on the horizon include the use of artificial intelligence methods to identify emotions based on how someone touches a device, such as a phone (Koetsier, 2018).

Related to physiologically based measures are sensor technologies. Employee identification badges and office furniture are joining the Internet of things, allowing sensor technology to collect data on how often and with whom employees interact and where time is spent. These could potentially be used as indicators of employee attitudes, such as if an employee is interacting less with others.

A desirable aspect of these passive technologies for data collection is that they do not require any time of the employee through active involvement in the measurement. However, passive methods do raise significant privacy concerns about the possibility of a lack of informed consent or that employees are even aware the measures are taking place. Another concern with these emerging technologies is the quality of the data and whether they measure what they purport to measure—or if they could be making erroneous attributions about a person (Waber, 2018).

Data Integration and Storage

Existing and emerging technology is allowing for the possibility of an endless number of options to integrate and store data. These can involve data flows that are handled through complex arrangements of contractors, subcontractors, and service providers globally. They are made up of intricate networks of platforms, applications, and the cloud. It may well be the case that it is difficult to know where exactly data actually reside. Although a detailed review of these technologies is beyond the scope of this chapter, it is sufficient to say that the complexity of data storage and transfer adds to the challenges in managing and protecting data privacy. The integration of wide arrays of different types of data into data warehouses and other platforms for retrieval and use poses added privacy challenges. All of these issues frame the "looming crisis" of increased cybersecurity threats due to the exponential nature of technology development with unexpected consequences (Dreibelbis et al., 2018).

Advanced Analytics

Although not a new survey-related technology per se, the rise of data science and the incorporation of employee survey data into these efforts represent an emerging trend. Advanced analytics modeling, including machine learning and artificial intelligence methods, expand the uses of employee survey data and who is managing them. Given that the majority of these analyses are at the individual level, the protection of individual privacy is a substantial concern. If the goal of these analyses is to provide organizational leaders insights to better manage their human capital, how to use these insights to make valid decisions and simultaneously protect individual privacy is important. In addition, the use of artificial intelligence to make automated decisions that may be biased or unfair is a growing concern, and the GDPR has specific guidance on this concern. Therefore, careful thought should be given to how to ethically and legally conduct these advanced analytic initiatives.

Recommendations and Best Practices

Technology and legal regulations related to employee privacy are constantly changing. Regardless of these changes, there are best practice recommendations that can be offered based on the ethical principles discussed in this chapter and the humanistic values that guide the work of I-O psychologists.

> *Have a policy.* Have a clearly stated policy for the collection, use, and protection of individually identifiable data. Whoever is responsible for the data, whether an external vendor or an internal company group, should have an ethics and privacy policy in place.
>
> *Have a privacy clearinghouse.* It is recommended that companies and consulting organizations have a specialized group to review privacy issues for employee surveys, new technologies, and other employee privacy-related needs.
>
> *Clearly inform, use opt-in.* Clearly tell employees before data collection what is being obtained, how it will be used including any decision criteria, how their information will be protected, and whether it may be transferred to a third party. Use opt-in based on a clear, affirmative act and let employees know they can later decide to opt out.
>
> *Do not coerce.* Avoid actual or perceived coercion, such as survey reminders that explicitly state it is known that the employee has not responded.
>
> *Protect identity.* Always separate the identifying information from survey or other data, using nonidentifiable codes and keeping the codes with identifying information in a protected encrypted file that is separated from the data and those who use the data. This practice allows data to be linked from various sources without using the most sensitive identifiers such as employee number.
>
> *Use data responsibly.* Help organizations balance what can be predicted against what should be predicted (Boudreau, 2014). This principle is especially challenging with big data, which incentivize the collection of

any/all data for unanticipated uses and for decisions that may not necessarily be valid.

Keep the original tenets of I-O psychology in mind at all times. When engaged in practice or carrying out research, keep in mind the original humanistic tenets of I-O psychology related to protecting employee welfare (Gloss, Carr, Reichman, Abdul-Nasiru, & Oestereich, 2017; Lefkowitz 2017; Lowman, 2006). Along with the organization perspective, it is important to always keep the employee perspective front and center.

Acknowledgments

The authors thank the experts who provided valuable insights on employee surveys, privacy, and technology issues: Andrew Biga, Justin Black, Kathryn Dekas, Jay Hamlin, Lilia Hayrapetyan, Mathian Osicki, Peter Rutigliano, Jeffrey Saltzman, Mary Kate Stimmler, and Sara Weiner.

References

American Psychological Association. (2017). *Ethical principles of psychologists and code of conduct.* Washington, DC: Author. Retrieved from https://apa.org/ethics/code/ethics-code-2017.pdf

Antón, A., Earp, J., & Young, J. (2010). How Internet users' privacy concerns have evolved since 2002. *IEEE Security and Privacy, 8*(1), 21–27.

Biga, A., McCance, A., & Massman, A. (2011). Identified employee surveys: Lessons learned. *Industrial and Organizational Psychology, 4,* 449–451.

Black, J., Hyland, P., & Rutigliano, P. (2011). Realizing the promise and minimizing the perils of identified surveys: Reports from the field. *Industrial and Organizational Psychology, 4,* 462–467.

Boudreau, J. (2014, September 4). Predict what employees will do without freaking them out. *Harvard Business Review.* Retrieved from https://hbr.org/2014/09/predict-what-employees-will-do-without-freaking-them-out

Bowling, A. (2005). Mode of questionnaire administration can have serious effects on data quality. *Journal of Public Health, 27,* 281–291.

Church, A., & Rotolo, C. (2011). Revisiting the great survey debate: Aren't we past that yet? *Industrial and Organizational Psychology, 4,* 455–459.

Dreibelbis, R., Martin, J., Coovert, M., & Dorsey, D. (2018). The looming cybersecurity crisis and what it means for the practice of industrial and organizational psychology. *Industrial and Organizational Psychology, 11*(2), 346–365.

Ducey, A., Guenole, N., Weiner, S., Herleman, H., Gibby, R., & Delany, T. (2015). I-Os in the vanguard of big data analytics and privacy. *Industrial and Organizational Psychology, 8*(4), 555–563.

European Union. (2016). Regulation (EU) 2016/679 of the European Parliament and the Council. General Data Protection Regulation. Retrieved from https://eur-lex.europa.eu/eli/reg/2016/679/oj

Fayeka, H., Lecha, M., & Cavedon, L. (2017). Evaluating deep learning architectures for speech emotion recognition, *Neural Networks, 92*, 60–68.

Fenlason, K., & Suckow-Zimberg, K. (2006). Online surveys: Critical issues in using the Web to conduct surveys. In A. Kraut (Ed.), *Getting action from organizational surveys* (pp. 183–212). San Francisco, CA: Jossey-Bass.

Fogel, J., & Nehmad, E. (2009). Internet social network communities: Risk taking, trust, and privacy concerns. *Computers in Human Behavior, 25*(1), 153–160.

Froelich, J. (2011). Identifying the ethical (unethical) undercurrent of identified surveys. *Industrial and Organizational Psychology, 4*, 476–478.

Gloss, A., Carr, S., Reichman, W., Abdul-Nasiru, I., & Oestereich, T. (2017). From handmaidens to POSH humanitarians: The case for making human capabilities the business of I-O psychology. *Industrial and Organizational Psychology, 10*, 1–41.

Graeff, T., & Harmon, S. (2002). Collecting and using personal data: Consumers' awareness and concerns. *Journal of Consumer Marketing, 19*, 302–318.

Guzzo, R. (2016). How big data matter. In S. Tonidandel, E. King, & J. Cortina (Eds.), *Big data at work: The data science revolution and organizational psychology* (pp. 336–350). New York, NY: Routledge.

Heerwegh, D., Vanhove, T., Matthijs, K., & Loosveldt, G. (2005). The effect of personalization on response rates and data quality in Web surveys. *International Journal of Social Research Methodology, 8*, 85–99.

Hernandez, I., Newman, D., & Jeon, G. (2016). Twitter analysis: Methods for data management and a word count dictionary to measure city-level job satisfaction. In S. Tonidandel, E. King, & J. Cortina (Eds.), *Big data at work: The data science revolution and organizational psychology* (pp. 64–114). New York, NY: Routledge.

Hessler, R., & Freerks, K. (1995). Privacy ethics in the age of disclosure: Sweden and America compared. *American Sociologist, 26*, 35–53.

Hopstaken, J., van der Linden, D., Bakker, A., Kompier, M., & Leung, Y. (2016). Shifts in attention during mental fatigue: Evidence from subjective, behavioral, physiological, and eye-tracking data. *Journal of Experimental Psychology, 42*(6), 878–889.

Identity Theft Resource Center. (2018). *2018 end-of-yea data breach report.* Retrieved from https://www.idtheftcenter.org/wp-content/uploads/2019/02/ITRC_2018-End-of-Year-Aftermath_FINAL_V2_combinedWEB.pdf

King, E., Tonidandel, S., Cortina, J., & Fink, A. (2016). Building understanding of the data science revolution and IO psychology. In S. Tonidandel, E. King, & J. Cortina (Eds.), *Big data at work: The data science revolution and organizational psychology* (pp. 1–15). New York: Routledge.

Koetsier, J. (2018, August 31). This AI can recognize anger, awe, desire, fear, hate, grief, love . . . by how you touch your phone. *Forbes.* Retrieved from www.forbes.com/sites/johnkoetsier/2018/08/31/new-tech-could-help-siri-google-assistant-read-our-emotions-through-touch-screens/#3f98a8242132

Kraut, A., & Saari, L. (1999). Organization surveys: Coming of age for a new era. In A. Kraut & K. Korman (Eds.), *Evolving practices in human resource management: Responses to a changing world of work* (pp. 302–307). San Francisco, CA: Jossey-Bass.

Lefkowitz, J. (2017). *Ethics and values in industrial-organizational psychology* (2nd ed.). New York, NY: Routledge.

Lowman, R. (Ed.). (2006). *The ethical practice of psychology in organizations* (2nd ed.). Washington, DC: American Psychological Association.

Lozano-Monasor, E., López Bonal, M., Fernández-Caballero, A. & Vigo-Bustos, F. (2014). Facial expression recognition from webcam based on active shape models and support vector machines, *Lecture Notes in Computer Science Book Series, 8868*, 147–154.

Luong, A. (2011). Implications of identified surveys: Culture matters. *Industrial and Organizational Psychology, 4*, 484–486.

McFarland, L., & Ployhart, R. (2015). Social media: A contextual framework to guide research and practice. *Journal of Applied Psychology, 100*(6), 1653–1677.

Morris, D., & Ashworth, S. (2011). We don't need to protect what is already protected. *Industrial and Organizational Psychology, 4*, 473–475.

National Commission for the Protection of Human Subjects of Biomedical and Behavioral Research. (1979). *Belmont Report: Ethical principles and guidelines for the protection of human subjects of research*. Washington, DC: Government Printing Office.

National Cyber Security Alliance. (2016). *2016 TRUSTe/NCSA Consumer Privacy Infographic—US Edition*. Retrieved from http://www.trustarc.com/resources/privacy-research/ncsa-consumer-privacy-index-us

Putka, D., & Oswald, F. (2016). Implications of the big data movement for the advancement of IO science and practice. In S. Tonidandel, E. King, & J. Cortina (Eds.), *Big data at work: The data science revolution and organizational psychology* (pp. 181–212). New York, NY: Routledge.

Rucci, A., Kirn, S., & Quinn, R. (1998). The employee–customer–profit chain at Sears. *Harvard Business Review, 76*, 82–97.

Saari, L., & Scherbaum, C. (2011). Identified employee surveys: Potential promise, perils, and professional practice guidelines. *Industrial and Organizational Psychology, 4*, 435–448.

Sashkin, M., & Prien, E. (1996). Ethical concerns and organizational surveys. In A. Kraut (Ed.), *Organizational surveys: Tools for assessment and change* (pp. 381–403). San Francisco, CA: Jossey-Bass.

Scherer, K. (2003). Vocal communication of emotion: A review of research paradigms. *Speech Communication, 40*, 227–256.

Tene, O., & Polonetsky, J. (2013). Big data for all: Privacy and user control in the age of analytics. *Northwestern Journal of Technology and Intellectual Property, 11*(5), 239–273.

Thompson, L., & Surface, E. (2007). Employee surveys administered online: Attitudes toward the medium, nonresponse, and data representativeness. *Organizational Research Methods, 10*, 241–261.

Thompson, L., Surface, E., Martin, D., & Sanders, M. (2003). From paper to pixels: Moving personnel surveys to the web. *Personnel Psychology, 56*, 197–227.

Tourangeau, R., & Yan, T. (2007). Sensitive questions in surveys. *Psychological Bulletin, 133*, 859–883.

US Department of Commerce. (2018). *Privacy shield framework*. Retrieved from http://www.privacyshield.gov

Waber, B. (2018). The happy tracked employee. *Harvard Business Review*. Retrieved from https://hbr.org/2018/09/the-happy-tracked-employee

Weiner, S., Jolton, J., Dorio, J., Klein, C., & Herman, A. (2011). Attributed surveys from the perspective of practitioners: Providing more value than risk. *Industrial and Organizational Psychology, 4*, 468–472.

Wiley, J. (1996). Linking survey results to customer satisfaction and business performance. In A. Kraut (Ed.), *Organizational surveys: Tools for assessment and change* (pp. 330–359). San Francisco, CA: Jossey-Bass.

25

Managing Workplace Job Attitudes and Performance in Organizations with Labor Unions

James K. Harter and Denise R. McLain

In this chapter, our primary objective is to share research and practical advice resulting from several decades of study with organizations whose employee base includes union members. We shed light on historical context, public sentiment, organizational research evidence, and best practices for management that correspond with positive job attitudes and high performance in organizations.

Employees join labor unions for various reasons. Most labor experts agree that unions have historically existed to increase the utility of employment and to remedy dissatisfying work situations—generally through higher wages, better benefits, and protection against unfair treatment (Getman, Goldberg, & Herman, 1976; Hammer & Avgar, 2005; Zalesny, 1985). Unions exist under an assumption that there is, or should be, some separation between employees and management to protect the worker in situations where management may produce a less than equitable work-reward balance. Research also suggests that organizations have higher value when workers have positive attitudes toward their work and workplace (Edmans, 2012). An important management question emerges in this tug and pull of worker and organizational interests: Can a workplace environment that maximizes what is best for both the worker and the organization be built in a unionized situation?

We will present information in the last two sections of this chapter that indicates the answer can be "yes" if the right management practices are put into place.

James K. Harter and Denise R. McLain, *Managing Workplace Job Attitudes and Performance in Organizations with Labor Unions* In: *Employee Surveys and Sensing*. Edited by: William H. Macey and Alexis A. Fink, Oxford University Press (2020). © Society for Industrial and Organizational Psychology.
DOI: 10.1093/oso/9780190939717.003.0025

Involvement in Unionization and Public Sentiment

Union membership has been on the decline in recent decades. The US Bureau of Labor Statistics (2018) reports that nearly 15 million workers, 11% of the 2018 US workforce, belong to unions. This is a decline from the high of 28% in the 1950s. Union membership is most notable among public sector employees (34%), of whom the highest percentage of union members work in local governments (41%). Private sector union membership is highest in the utilities (23%), transportation and warehousing (17%), telecom (16%), and construction (14%) industries.

The downward trend in unionization has many possible causal explanations. One theory is that automation has both given rise to and caused the reduction in unionization—creating an inverted U–shaped distribution (Dinlersoz & Greenwood, 2012; Thompson, 2012). For example, increases in union membership coincided with increases in manufacturing automation, producing an economy of specialized but less skilled labor jobs that were amenable to unionization.

Over time the information age took center stage. Employers placed a higher income premium on education—workers became less reliant on organized labor because they could improve their income through their own efforts. If projections from automation experts (Frey & Osborne, 2017) are accurate, less skilled jobs will be the first to be replaced in the future—potentially furthering the downward trend in unionization. But this is up for debate as automation has historically created new jobs as well. A surge in automation may have similar outcomes to what was seen in the manufacturing era—for example, a possible increase in skilled-trade jobs that are designed to manage robots and other automation. Union membership may also increase due to unmet workplace or well-being needs in some skilled professions (i.e., nurses or teachers). Gallup polls dating back to 1936 find that general public approval of unions remains high. In fact, the 62% approval rating for unions recorded in 2018 is higher than ratings recorded in the 1970s.

As approval of unions is increasing, the proportion of Americans who say they would like to see labor unions have more influence has also increased—from 25% in 2009 to 39% in 2018—suggesting an increasingly positive sentiment toward unions (Saad, 2018). This shift in sentiment coincides with wage stagnation and increased costs of health care, education, and housing, resulting in less disposable income (Rothwell, 2016).

Overall, public sentiment runs somewhat counter to the downward trend in unionization—most Americans approve of unions and have a relatively positive sentiment toward them. However, the majority believe the influence of unions will continue to diminish despite unions continuing to have an important presence in several industries. Interestingly, labor strikes by teachers, hotel staff, and nurses saw a major uptick between 2018 and 2019. In 2018, more than 400,000 teachers and school staff walked out of their classrooms. And in January of 2019, 30,000 Los Angeles teachers went on strike and demanded greater support for their school systems. As a result, the school district agreed to hire 84 more librarians and 300 more nurses so that every elementary school would have a nurse 5 days a week.

Similarly, Marriott hotel workers went on strike in Boston, San Francisco, San Diego, and five other cities in 2018, angry that their wages were not keeping up with inflation and soaring rent costs at the same time that their company reported a record year for profitability (Wong, 2019).

Considering these changes in public approval and participation in strikes, organizations must effectively lead unionized employees in collaborating both with one another and with non-union employees to produce desired organizational outcomes.

The Job Attitudes of Unionized Employees

Job attitudes have been a significant focus of workplace researchers over the past several decades. Many meta-analyses have documented a substantial and generalizable relationship between job attitudes and performance at the individual level (Harrison, Newman, & Roth, 2006; Judge, Thoresen, Bono, & Patton, 2001; Mackay, Allen, & Landis, 2017) and at the organizational unit level (Harter, Schmidt, Asplund, Killham, & Agrawal, 2010; Harter, Schmidt, & Hayes, 2002; Whitman, Van Rooy, & Viswesvaran, 2010). A recent study reports that the business unit–level relationship between job attitudes and performance is generalizable in industries with both high (manufacturing) and low (retail, finance) union composition (Krekel, Ward, & de Neve, 2019). Organizational leaders are apparently aware of the importance of positive job attitudes as two thirds of American workers report that their organization conducts at least one employee survey per year (Gallup, 2017a).

Researchers have conducted substantial analysis of differences in job attitudes between unionized and non-unionized employees (Hammer &

Avgar, 2005), suggesting that union employees are as satisfied with benefits, wages, and job security as non-union workers but less satisfied with the types of work they are asked to do, their freedom to make decisions, the resources they have to do their jobs, their influence on major workplace decisions, their opportunities for advancement, and their supervision (Bryson, Cappellari, & Lucifora, 2004; Freeman, 1978; Freeman & Rogers, 2006; Kochan & Helfman, 1981; Meng, 1990; Miller, 1990; Pfeffer & Davis-Blake, 1990; Renaud, 2002).

Several theories have been proposed that attempt to explain the logical inconsistency of union workers having lower net job attitudes but also having lower turnover rates. We will not review them all in this chapter but recommend the thorough review provided by Hammer and Avgar (2005). An in-depth analysis by Bryson et al. (2004) found that, after using a propensity score–matching approach to control for job situations and occupational and job characteristics, union workers were less satisfied than a perfectly matched subsample of non-union employees on all facets of work (the wages of union employees offset this difference somewhat but were unable to fully compensate for other job facets).

A variety of studies dispute the idea that unions cause employees to be dissatisfied; the dissatisfaction of union members is real, but some studies suggest that it's due to the working conditions and the attitudes of workers prior to being unionized (Freeman & Rogers, 2006; Laroche, 2016). Overall, these studies confirmed that unionization is negatively related to job satisfaction. The results suggest that the difference in job satisfaction between union members and non-union members can be explained by a selection effect—people often join unions because they are dissatisfied or disengaged. That puts the onus for workplace satisfaction squarely on companies.

The results suggest that managers and the Human Resources department should address workers' expectations, in particular their need to express their discontent with certain elements of their jobs. Gallup has found that it is crucial to have systems to collect employee opinions, ideas, and reactions in the workplace. The local-level manager should be the starting point, while organizational efforts are put in place, such as skip-level meetings, Kaizen events, WorkOut meetings, suggestion boxes, or working groups. The goal of this type of organizational effort is to encourage employee participation and involvement in the attainment of workplace objectives. By providing information to management about employees' collective preferences, these workplace practices can enable organizations to choose a better mix of working conditions, product development, workplace rules, and employee remuneration. This can produce a more satisfied, cooperative, and productive workforce.

According to Freeman and Rogers (2006), employees want their voices to be heard. They desire a role in the decisions that are made for their work environment and have strong ideas about how their involvement could improve their work and the company's output. These findings are similar to those Gallup has seen. All employees want to feel that they are making significant contributions to their workplaces. The way organizations hear and process employees' ideas will shape, to a large degree, whether or not they feel valued for their contributions.

Taylorism is a late 1800s management philosophy attributed to Fredrick Winslow Taylor that treats workers as machines and supports the belief that workers do not have the skill or knowledge to contribute to key process decisions. Belief in Taylorism lingers today, with many companies exhibiting this philosophy in their managing of call centers, manufacturing, and other types of work that follow standard procedures. The use of this management style typically creates the feeling that employees need someone to advocate their voice to management because they are not being asked directly for their opinions.

The need for employees to feel valued—to know that they really make a difference in their organizations—is one of 12 key discoveries made in a multiyear research effort by Gallup (Harter, Schmidt, Agrawal, Plowman, & Blue, 2016). If the ideas, instincts, and intelligence of a company's employees are its competitive advantage, then employees' belief that they are heard regarding key issues is crucial. Nothing is more demoralizing to employees than being excluded from decisions that affect their jobs. Great managers consult with employees regularly to make sure they have input into critical decisions. This does not mean that employees have the final say on the decisions that affect their jobs, but it does mean that when employees' desires and managers' decisions differ, the best managers explain the rationale behind their decisions. These managers help employees to see all sides of a decision and to understand the reasoning behind it. A straightforward explanation can build credibility and communication. Ideas are the building blocks of increased efficiency and new product development. Work environments that encourage employees to share their opinions allow the exchange of new and better ideas, which may lead to greater outcomes. Not all ideas will be successfully implemented, but the process of refining ideas is still productive: It builds employees' confidence in the company and shows them that their efforts can make the company better.

The job attitude facets outlined in Gallup's employee engagement (referred to as Q^{12}) metric can be thought of as basic workplace needs that generalize across work situations, including role clarity (clear expectations, materials, and equipment), individual contribution (opportunities to do what you do best, recognition, feeling cared about, encouraging development), belonging (opinions counting, connection to the organization's purpose, co-worker relationships), and growth (progress discussions and learning opportunities). These elements, while historically descriptive of productive workplaces, are also aligned with workplace expectations for the newer workforce of millennial job seekers (Gallup, 2016).

To understand how unionized environments differ from non-unionized environments, Gallup reviewed first administration Q^{12} data (data collected prior to workplace interventions) from companies within four industries with the highest proportions of unionized employees, each of which has generally lower engagement scores: public administration, health care, manufacturing, and public utilities. To further control for industry and job-type differences, Gallup extracted data only for non-managerial employees within each of the organizations with union representation. The overall data set included 239,459 union-member employees and 42,053 non-union-member employees from 2014 to 2016.

Consistent with prior published research, non-union employees had more positive job attitudes (the average of the 12 formative job attitude–engagement facets): Compared with the overall database of first administration work units, non-union employees scored 8 percentile points higher than union employees.

Table 25.1 shows the differences between union and non-union, non-managerial employees for overall company satisfaction and each job attitude–engagement facet. Non-union employees scored higher on each of the measured facets but to varying degrees. For example, non-union employees scored more than 20 percentile points higher on "supervisor or someone at work cares," "someone encourages development," "opinions count," "co-workers committed to quality," "progress discussions," and "opportunities to learn/grow." The gap was narrowest, less than 10 percentile points, on "know what's expected," "recognition/praise," and "have a best friend at work." The overall direction of the differences, in favor of non-union employees, was consistent across industries.

Table 25.1 Difference in Job Attitude–Engagement Facets Between Union and Non-Union Work Units in Public Administration, Manufacturing, Health Care, and Public Utilities

	Gallup's Q^{12} Elements
Job Attitude–Engagement Facet	Percentile Point Difference Between Union and Non-Union
Overall satisfaction with company	18
1. Know what's expected	4
2. Materials and equipment	15
3. Opportunities to do what I do best	10
4. Recognition/praise	9
5. Supervisor or someone at work cares	22
6. Someone encourages development	21
7. Opinions count	21
8. Connect with mission/purpose	16
9. Co-workers committed to quality	24
10. Have a best friend at work	8
11. Progress discussions	23
12. Opportunities to learn/grow	24

Note. All facets exhibited higher scores for non-union groups. Overall satisfaction asked on a 1–5 scale with 1 = extremely dissatisfied and 5 = extremely dissatisfied. Elements 1–12 asked on a 1–5 scale with 1 = strongly disagree and 5 = strongly agree. For exact item wording, see Harter et al. (2002). The Gallup Q^{12} items are Gallup proprietary information and are protected by law. You may not administer a survey with the Q^{12} items or reproduce them without written consent from Gallup.

These findings suggest that union employees are generally comparable to non-union employees on role clarity, recognition, and close social bonds at work. But they are less comparable on elements indicating involvement, development, and respect for fellow workers.

Challenges to Surveying in a Union Environment

Implementing a survey in a union environment can be difficult. A variety of employee concerns can affect participation, interventions, and follow-up survey implementation.

For example, employees may be concerned that their answers will be shared with location leadership and result in some type of retribution. When employees believe that their opinions are not confidential, it can affect survey responses and data accuracy. Taking a few proactive steps can easily ensure high participation rates:

1. Gain commitment from members of corporate and location leadership that they will listen to the results with an open mind, share the findings with every location, and act on the results to improve the work environment.
2. Provide transparency regarding the reason for the survey and why management is interested in surveying employees.
3. Guarantee confidentiality to achieve a high participation rate. For example, host a webinar for key influencers in every location that allows participants to hear directly from the researcher on how confidentiality will be maintained and how the data will be analyzed and reported back to the parent organization and location leadership. Clearly explain if open-ended items will be utilized and how they will be reported. Create brochures or handouts that explain the process and how data will be utilized. This information should be shared during key communication meetings and posted in prominent areas throughout locations.
4. Meet with local-level union representation to explain the survey process and how results will be utilized. Invite union representation to be a part of results presentations and training meetings.
5. After the survey, send sincere communications thanking individuals for participating, sharing their opinions, and being open to changes that the organization or location needs to make.
6. Provide forums for leadership to share key findings from the survey and how the identified issues will be addressed. Ensure that these forums also highlight what the organization is doing well.

Challenges in Managing a Union/Non-Union Workforce

Both global and US working population data suggest that engaging employees to perform at high levels is not easy (Gallup, 2017b). The findings discussed in the previous two sections in this chapter also suggest that organizations face additional challenges in involving and developing employees who are union members. After reviewing our past work with organizations, we have identified two common systemic performance-management barriers to union-member engagement that need to be overcome in most organizations. These observations provide context for the engagement facets, with the largest gaps between union and non-union employees.

1. *Lack of continuous feedback.* In a union environment, there are often substantially more rules for organizations to follow when providing feedback and development opportunities to teams and individuals. When more processes are required, this can slow down ongoing conversations that influence the effectiveness of teams and individuals. The presence of additional rules may also decrease the engagement of the supervisors who have to follow them.

2. *Stipulations on the work tasks union members can perform.* In many union environments, only employees with certain roles can perform specific work responsibilities. Most organizations face challenges in meeting customer needs that require workers to adjust their priorities. Narrow parameters on work roles and workload can jeopardize performance during "all-hands-on-deck" situations when the organization needs employees to adjust and provide additional discretionary effort. This, then, can transfer to perceptions of pay equity, which can decrease collaboration and support between co-workers and might develop animosity between non-union and union employees when team members perceive that others are not "pulling their weight" or being held accountable for their performance.

Solving these issues is often at the discretion of the union representative and dependent on the quality of the representative's relationship with the organization's location leadership. Some representatives will allow strong performance management and collaboration across roles, while others may leverage the issue to receive some type of benefit from the organization. In both of these scenarios, achieving change takes time and finesse.

Of note, while the industries studied here generally have lower engagement scores than industries such as finance, retail, and services, there is wide variation across organizations in levels of engagement and even wider variation across teams within organizations—for both those comprised of union members and those containing non-union employees. Figure 25.1 depicts the distribution of engagement for union and non-union teams, illustrating that many union and non-union teams' engagement levels are spread across the spectrum of engagement.

This graph also highlights the difference in median engagement between union and non-union teams (the average of the 12 job attitude–engagement facets). Teams within organizations, whether unionized or non-unionized, vary substantially in ways that often reflect how they are managed.

Further, after many survey administrations and management interventions, many of the companies in lower-scoring industries have reached the top decile of the overall engagement database for both union and non-union employees. While the average engagement of union employees starts at a lower level than that of non-union employees, the union employee average exceeds the starting point of the non-union employees after only a few survey administrations and interventions. Gallup has seen significant change in union environments using intentional interventions to better their work environments. For example, a global manufacturing company with approximately 44,000 union employees and 27,000 non-union employees doing the same type of work showed this same pattern. Within 3 years, both groups increased their level of engagement as measured by the Gallup Q^{12}, but the union group had a greater increase than the non-union group. However, it is important to note that the union group started at a lower level of engagement.

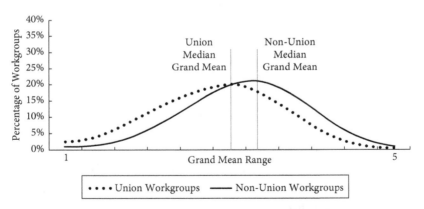

Figure 25.1. The distribution of engagement across unionized and nonunionized teams. Workgroups in highly unionized industries— manufacturing, utilities, and health care.

Note. Gallup Client Workgroup Level Database, 2014–2016. Non-managers only from manufacturing, utilities, and health care organization surveys in their first to third administrations with some unionized workforce. Average of 2.1 survey administrations for both union and non-union groups.

In the following section, we will outline key interventions that increase individual feedback and progress conversations, team-level action-planning, and continual listening approaches from management.

How Unionized Organizations Increased Engagement

The unionized organizations spent conscious time in upgrading the quality of management. Specifically, most of the organizations cited in the earlier research began by enhancing their partnerships with union representatives to create more supportive work environments. Rather than fixate on productivity, these organizations focused on creating a workplace where employees felt like they mattered. Union representatives were generally supportive of the engagement facets outlined in Gallup's Q^{12} metric as long as they were involved in the process and the organizations presented a sincere attempt to work together. In many cases, employee issues were handled before they became grievances; and as employees became more engaged, their productivity increased and they were less likely to have grievances with management.

The following are examples of some of the approaches successful organizations used:

- *Setting an organizational tone* and philosophy, beginning with upper management, that indicated an engaging work environment was as important as creating a safe and productive work environment. This was not limited to issuing statements and was supported by the actions of upper management.
- *Revising the selection of supervisors and managers* to include criteria based on team management capabilities. For a few of the organizations, this meant that selection criteria needed to be upgraded. In the past, selection of supervisors or managers had been based on process and production excellence in prior roles that required no managerial skills or abilities. However, effective managing requires inspiring teams, setting goals, arranging resources, initiating during times of adversity, building committed and collaborative teams, and good decision-making. These organizations set clear criteria for selection into the role of manager rather than making it a "rite of passage" to tenure and advancement.
- *Providing in-house supervisor training.* Most of the organizations promoted supervisors from within the company. Although this was an

efficient model for succession planning, it created a void in management expertise. Many of these employees had worked their way up through the front line without having any type of training or experience in management. The added training covered management development topics such as

- How to listen
- How to deal with conflict
- Performance-management approaches
- How to lead meetings
- How to provide meaningful recognition in daily interaction

- *Providing engagement data to front-line managers* so that they could understand the views of their team members or shifts. It was also expected that every supervisor would have a discussion with the team or shift to identify ways to increase levels of engagement. This communicated to team members that their opinions were important.
    - Additionally, feedback discussions of the data were hosted through creative forums such as safety, huddle, or stand-up meetings.
- *Hiring or promoting managers who had strong management capabilities to positions above front-line supervisors.* These managers were then able to help coach and develop the current supervisors' management talent. The organizations had to take a hard look at all management levels and determine if their managers could model strong management practices. New performance goals were set that included management expectations.
- *Strong succession-planning process for leaders.* Organizations ensured that leadership team members had plenty of experience before being placed into major roles—members of local management were often not promoted to another level of management until they had been in place for 3–5 years. This allowed leadership to create consistency in messaging and a refined ability in managing performance, and it let upper management see a manager's true effectiveness by observing the impact of his or her decisions on the productivity of the unit being managed.
- *Meaningful progress conversations.*
    - Many organizations had never provided developmental conversations to their front-line staff, and the process had to be taught carefully. The most effective efforts taught the basics of progress conversations while allowing supervisors and managers to role-play the process and have a peer or trusted supervisor provide support if necessary.

- These organizations encouraged employees to be involved in outlining what work for the next year would provide them better expertise, skills, and overall development. This included helping employees think about their futures, whether that involved developing expertise in their current roles or developing opportunities in new roles.
- *Increased communication directly to front-line employees.* This included monthly forums, skip-level meetings, and walkabouts by the management team and location leader. Essentially, more ongoing dialogue gave leaders the opportunity to become familiar with the issues facing employees and alleviate any issues before they became grievances. Over time, employees began to see that management was on their side.

Conclusion

Organizations with union-member employees can create engaging work environments for their employees with the right infrastructure, organizational philosophy, and focus. As work environments continue to evolve, new challenges will also emerge—such as the current trend toward flexible work environments. Workplace flexibility is the most sought-after perk among American workers (Gallup, 2016). Trends toward flexible work hours and locations will likely enter into union and organization discussions, creating additional parameters for negotiation.

The union–employer dynamic is very complicated and varies considerably across industries, companies, unions, and union representatives. Our goal in writing this chapter was to outline the current state and share general best practices we've seen, knowing that these may seem very difficult to some or overly simplified to others depending on the dynamic a particular organization is facing. In the end, we couldn't identify any variables that replace hiring and developing great managers—those who consider the idiosyncrasies inherent to individual employees and situations and create solutions that are simultaneously in the best interests of both the employee and the organization.

References

Bryson, A., Cappellari, L., & Lucifora, C. (2004). Does union membership really reduce job satisfaction? *British Journal of Industrial Relations, 42*(3), 439–459.

Dinlersoz, E. M., & Greenwood, J. (2012). *The rise and fall of unions in the US*. NBER Working Paper 18079. Cambridge, MA: National Bureau of Economic Research.

Edmans, A. (2012). The link between job satisfaction and firm value, with implications for corporate social responsibility. *Academy of Management Perspectives, 26*(4), 1–19.

Freeman, R. B. (1978). *A fixed effect logit model of the impact of unionism on quits*. NBER Working Paper 280. Cambridge, MA: National Bureau of Economic Research.

Freeman, R. B., & Rogers, J. (2006). *What workers want*. Ithaca, NY: Cornell University Press.

Frey, C. B., & Osborne, M. A. (2017). The future of employment: How susceptible are jobs to computerisation? *Technological Forecasting & Social Change, 114*, 254–280.

Gallup. (2017a). *Gallup panel American workforce survey*. New York, NY: Gallup Press.

Gallup. (2016). *How millennials want to work and live*. Retrieved from http://www.gallup.com/workplace/238073/millennials-work-live.aspx

Gallup. (2017b). *State of the global workplace*. New York, NY: Gallup Press.

Getman, J., Goldberg, S., & Herman, J. B. (1976). *Union representation elections: Law and reality*. New York, NY: Russell Sage Foundation.

Hammer, T. H., & Avgar, A. (2005). The impact of unions on job satisfaction, organizational commitment, and turnover. *Journal of Labor Research, 26*(2), 241–266.

Harrison, D. A., Newman, D. A., & Roth, P. L. (2006). How important are job attitudes? Meta-analytic comparisons of integrative behavioral outcomes and time sequences. *Academy of Management Journal, 49*(2), 305–325.

Harter, J. K., Schmidt, F. L., Agrawal, S., Plowman, S., & Blue, A. (2016). *Q12 Meta-Analysis* (9th ed.). Gallup Technical Paper. Omaha, NE: Gallup Press.

Harter, J. K., Schmidt, F. L., Asplund, J. W., Killham, E. A., & Agrawal, S. (2010). Causal impact of employee work perceptions on the bottom line of organizations. *Perspectives on Psychological Science, 5*(4), 378–389.

Harter, J. K., Schmidt, F. L., & Hayes, T. L. (2002). Business-unit-level relationship between employee satisfaction, employee engagement, and business outcomes: A meta-analysis. *Journal of Applied Psychology, 87*(2), 268–279.

Judge, T. A., Thoresen, C. J., Bono, J. E., & Patton, G. K. (2001). The job satisfaction–job performance relationship: A qualitative and quantitative review. *Psychological Bulletin, 127*(3), 376–407.

Kochan, T. A., & Helfman, D. E. (1981). *The effects of collective bargaining on economic and behavioral job outcomes*. Working Paper 1181-81. Cambridge, MA: Massachusetts Institute of Technology.

Krekel, C., Ward, G., & de Neve, J. E. (2019). Employee wellbeing, productivity & firm performance: Evidence and case studies. In *Global happiness and well-being policy report* (pp. 73–94). New York, NY: United Nations Sustainable Development Solutions Network, Global Happiness Council.

Laroche, P. (2016). *A meta-analysis of the union–job satisfaction relationship*. British *Journal of Industrial Relations, 54*(4), 709–741.

Mackay, M. M., Allen, J. A., & Landis, R. S. (2017). Investigating the incremental validity of employee engagement in the prediction of employee effectiveness: A meta analytic path analysis. *Human Resource Management Review, 27*(1), 108–120.

Meng, R. (1990). The relationship between unions and job satisfaction. *Applied Economics, 22*(12), 1635–1648.

Miller, P. W. (1990). Trade unions and job satisfaction. *Australian Economic Papers, 29*(55), 226–248.

Pfeffer, J., & Davis-Blake, A. (1990). Unions and job satisfaction: An alternative view. *Work and Occupations, 17*(3), 259–283.

Renaud, S. (2002). Rethinking the union membership/job satisfaction relationship: Some empirical evidence in Canada. *International Journal of Manpower, 23*(2), 137–150.

Rothwell, J. (2016). *No recovery: An analysis of long-term U.S. productivity decline.* Washington, DC: Gallup, US Council on Competitiveness.

Saad, L. (2018, August 30). Labor union approval steady at 15-year high. Gallup. Retrieved from http://news.gallup.com/poll/241679/labor-union-approval-steady-year-high.aspx

Thompson, D. (2012, June 7). Who killed American unions? *The Atlantic.* Retrieved from https://www.theatlantic.com/business/archive/2012/06/who-killed-american-unions/258239/

US Bureau of Labor Statistics. (2018). Union members summary. Retrieved from http://www.bls.gov/news.release/union2.nr0.htm

Whitman, D. S., Van Rooy, D. L., & Viswesvaran, C. (2010). Satisfaction, citizenship behaviors, and performance in work units: A meta-analysis of collective construct relations. *Personnel Psychology, 63*(1), 41–81.

Wong, A. (2019, January 22). America's teachers are furious. *The Atlantic.* Retrieved from www.theatlantic.com/educaiton/archive/2019/01/teachers-are-launching-a-rebellion

Zalesny, M. D. (1985). Comparison of economic and noneconomic factors in predicting faculty vote preference in a union representation election. *Journal of Applied Psychology, 70*(2), 243–256.

SECTION 4

THE STATUS QUO AND
THE CONTINUING EVOLUTION
OF SURVEY RESEARCH

26

Current and Future Trends in Employee Survey Practice

A View from Employee Survey Practitioners

Christopher T. Rotolo, Christina R. Fleck, and Brittnie Shepherd

Employee survey research is one of the most popular topics among industrial–organizational psychologists (Church, Kuyumcu, & Rotolo, 2016; Kraut, 1996). For decades, researchers and practitioners have focused on a common survey–feedback–action-planning framework (e.g., Kraut, 2006; Levenson, 2014; Nadler, 1977) that has served as the basis for organizational best practices. Over the past several years, however, we have seen an influx of experimentation with this tried-and-tested framework. For example, organizations and survey vendors alike are experimenting with "new" content, administration frequency, alternative modalities, different sampling strategies, digital reporting methods, and action-planning tools. As current and former PepsiCo employees responsible for the organization's employee survey program, we were interested in whether our anecdotal perceptions were an indication of a broader trend as we revisited our own survey strategy. The purpose of this chapter is to review the results of a benchmarking study we conducted to understand the state of practice in organizations with regard to employee surveys.

Background

As noted by other authors throughout this book, the needs of the business over the last decade seemed to have challenged well-established survey best practices. Organizations increasingly need to anticipate and react to their environments in order to grow their business. Not surprisingly, business leaders increasingly need to make rapid, evidence-based decisions in chaotic

Christopher T. Rotolo, Christina R. Fleck, and Brittnie Shepherd, *Current and Future Trends in Employee Survey Practice*
In: *Employee Surveys and Sensing*. Edited by: William H. Macey and Alexis A. Fink, Oxford University Press (2020).
© Society for Industrial and Organizational Psychology.
DOI: 10.1093/oso/9780190939717.003.0026

situations. Functions such as marketing and sales for years have leveraged big data and artificial intelligence to help make rapid decisions to inform consumer insights and market strategies and respond to competitive threats. Only recently have big data entered the Human Resources (HR) function, particularly in areas such as recruiting, hiring, and workforce planning (Rotolo & Church, 2015).

Survey research has also evolved. Advances in all aspects of the survey cycle, from design and deployment to reporting and analytics, have lowered the barriers to conducting employee surveys previously restricted to specialized consultancies or large organizations with in-house expertise. Coupled with the needs of business leaders for more timely and relevant data, these advances have organizations rethinking their traditional survey approach (CEB Corporate Leadership Council, 2016; Deloitte, 2017).

In fact, one might argue that the field is encountering a second survey revolution. The first was a refocusing of survey content toward the concept of employee engagement, which began as a management theory concept in the 1990s and became common practice in the 2000s. Although consensus around the concept and its measurement has progressed significantly (e.g., Macey, Schneider, Barbera, & Young, 2009), engagement remains the topic of lively discussion among academics and practitioners. For example, according to the Society for Industrial and Organizational Psychology's (SIOP's) conference program Explorer (2008–2018), the annual SIOP conference had 16 sessions in 2008 with the term *engagement* in the title. In 2018, there were 38 sessions with the same.

This second survey revolution is less about the "what" and more about the "how" and "whom." Within the past decade, we have seen organizations experimenting with a new suite of tools to assess employee beliefs, opinions, and even mood at any given time, including on-the-spot polling, mood surveys, frequent pulsing, online discussion forums, and social analytics. All of these efforts seem to be in the spirit of providing leaders with a broader array of listening devices to provide better insights (not just information) about their employee sentiment and to provide these insights in as near real time as possible. Some have called this *continuous listening*.

Despite these recent trends described by vendors trade magazines, and conference proceedings (e.g., Benjamin, 2016), very little has been published describing the prevalence of these practices in organizations (much less the impact of these practices in the peer-reviewed literature).

Study Purpose

The purpose of this research was to understand the current and future/planned states of employee surveys within organizations from the perspective of employee survey practitioners. A survey was administered for 3.5 weeks in the late part of 2017 then again for 2 weeks in early 2018. It is hard to know the shelf life of these findings and the pace of some of the emerging trends that we see in these data (short of replicating this study in a few years, which we plan to do). That said, at the time of this writing, it has been a full 13 years since the last SIOP Professional Practice Series on the topic (Kraut, 2006). Using these two snapshots in time can help us understand how much the state of the practice has (or hasn't) shifted.

Survey Method and Sample

Both convenience and snowball sampling approaches were used to solicit respondents from companies of various sizes and industries. Invitations were requested from membership of local talent-management professional organizations and well-established employee survey consortia as well as posted on an online professional talent-management network webpage. Respondents were encouraged to pass the survey invitation to their survey practitioner colleagues in other organizations. Although our sample provisioning was rather loose, we were very strict on who could participate in the survey. To be eligible, respondents were required to be involved in the design, implementation, and/or analysis of employee surveys within their organization. In addition, only one employee survey practitioner per company was permitted to complete the survey on behalf of the organization. Thus, in the results reported here, each respondent represents a single organization. Although we did not attempt to capture a representative sample across industries, we believe we were successful in targeting large, typically multinational organizations with well-established employee survey programs.

A total of 57 survey practitioners responded to the survey. This completion rate is comparable to the number of responses in other similar studies (e.g., Church, Rotolo, Ginther, & Levine, 2015). Table 26.1 provides a detailed breakdown of the participating organizations' characteristics. Although the survey was anonymous, participants were offered the option to provide their e-mail address to receive a copy of the report summary.

Table 26.1 Organizational Characteristics of Survey Respondents

	n	%
Type of organization		
Public company	34	59.6
Privately held	13	5.3
Nonprofit	6	10.5
Government agency	3	22.8
Partnership	1	1.8
Number of employees		
11–50	0	0.0
51–200	3	5.3
201–500	4	7.0
501–1,000	0	0.0
1,001–5,000	8	14.0
5,001–10,000	5	8.8
10,000–100,000	25	43.9
100,000+	12	21.1
Global (presence outside the United States)		
Yes	33	57.9
No	24	42.1
Annual revenue		
<999 Million	6	14.0
1–20 Billion	14	32.6
20–39 Billion	10	23.3
40–59 Billion	5	11.6
60–79 Billion	2	4.7
80–99 Billion	4	9.3
100+ Billion	2	4.7
Industry		
Accommodation and food service	1	1.8
Agriculture, forestry, fishing, and hunting	1	1.8
Arts, entertainment, and recreation	2	3.6
Finance and insurance	8	14.3
Government	3	5.4
Health care and social assistance	5	8.9
Information	5	8.9
Manufacturing	12	21.4
Mining, quarrying, and oil and gas extraction	1	1.8

Table 26.1 Continued

	n	%
Other services (except public administration)	4	7.1
Professional, scientific, and technical services	3	5.4
Retail trade	8	14.3
Transportation and warehousing	2	3.6
Utilities	1	1.8
Fortune		
Fortune 50	11	19.3
Fortune 100	8	14.0
Fortune 500	19	33.3

Survey Structure

The survey consisted of 78 items across three broad topic areas:

1. The organization's survey research team including the education and background of the individuals on the team, structure of the team, and other responsibilities of the team.
2. Current and anticipated/future characteristics of employee survey programs in the company, including the organization's current survey practices and program characteristics, from administration to action-planning practices. We also asked respondents to detail their anticipated programs and practices in the future (e.g., 3–5 years from now). It should be noted, however, that due to the structure of the questionnaire, we were not able to ask about future practices for all survey types and stages.
3. Attitudes regarding the organization's current employee surveys. This final section of the survey focused what the respondent viewed as effective versus less effective survey practices within the organization.

About the Survey Results

There are a couple of caveats about the data that we should highlight before the results are presented. One is regarding the reporting of response frequencies—in particular, which unit of measure to use when calculating frequency of responses. The clearest option would be to report findings as a percentage of the number of companies responding. However, each company conducts several different types of surveys, and each survey type varies by several characteristics. Therefore, we decided to report results by survey type rather than by company.

Relatedly, another caveat is how a survey type was defined in this research. We know from experience that there is wide variance across companies relative to naming and content. Two companies can call their surveys the same name but have entirely different content and, conversely, can have similar surveys with different names. Thus, simply asking respondents to list the surveys they conduct is not informative. To address this, we asked respondents to list what types of surveys they conduct within their organizations. We provided them with a definition of *survey type* as being "distinct in purpose and/or content and may have many different names, even if they measure similar content in similar ways." We kept the responses open-ended to allow for variations across companies. To the extent possible, we content-coded the survey names to help in reporting (e.g., "All Employee" and "Census"); however, we were careful not to make assumptions about the content based solely on the survey name. For each survey type, we asked the respondent a variety of questions about the content (e.g., diagnostic, focused), cadence, etc. Although this aided in understanding the characteristics of different types of surveys, we could not control for the fact that similar content could be included across survey types. Thus, when reporting our results, we recognize that the survey types may not be completely distinct.

Key Themes and Insights

In this section we present the key themes and insights we found in the data. Where possible, we compare and contrast the current practice to anticipated future practices (3–5 years from now). Our results, taken together, indicate that organizational surveys are moving toward the "continuous listening" trajectory. However, organizations appear to be evolving more slowly than what the popular press would have us believe.

Surveys Will Remain a Key Part of an Organization's Listening Strategy

On average, 3.6 ($N = 57$; standard deviation [SD] = 1.6) different survey types are conducted in organizations currently (Table 26.2). When asked to anticipate how many types they would conduct in the future, respondents indicated that they expect to conduct about 4.0 survey types (n = 50; SD = 1.7), suggesting that the overall number of survey types may not change much in the future. Of the survey types reported, engagement/culture ($n = 56$), exit ($n = 18$), new hire-onboarding ($n = 18$), and pulse ($n = 15$) surveys are most common (excluding "other"). Again, as mentioned in the caveats, there may be overlap in content between some of these survey types (e.g., engagement, census, pulse). Although we didn't ask what other listening devices might be used to capture employee sentiment, the fact that respondent organizations indicated that they anticipate deploying about the same number of survey types in the future as they do now tells us that the practice is not going away any time soon.

Table 26.2 Count of Survey Types Across Participating Organizations

Survey Name	Frequency
Other	40
Engagement-culture	56
New hire-onboarding	18
Exit	18
Pulse	15
Ad hoc	10
Program-training evaluation	9
Business	8
Customer	8
Recruitment	5
Multirater	5
Leadership-manager	5
Learning and development	3
Candidate	3
Total	203

Engagement Surveys Remain the Predominant Survey Type

Our study showed that engagement/culture surveys were by far the most frequently cited survey type across organizations. The implication is that *engagement* as a concept remains strong and will continue to be a key focus for organizations for the next several years at least.

Of the 203 current survey types reported across all 57 respondent organizations (i.e., the sum of the survey types across respondent organizations), we obtained cadence information on 163 of them. Engagement/culture surveys are typically conducted annually or biennially. Quarterly surveys are most often pulse, ad hoc, or other types of surveys. Weekly and monthly surveys typically include surveys related to the employee life cycle (e.g., new hire, exit) or program/training evaluation. Daily surveys also include life-cycle surveys in addition to customer-related surveys such as customer satisfaction and customer loyalty (see Table 26.3).

Table 26.3 Survey Type by Survey Cadence

Survey Type	Daily	Weekly	Monthly	Quarterly	Annually	Biennially	Total
Ad hoc	2	1	1	4	0	0	8
Business	0	2	2	2	1	1	8
Candidate	2	1	0	0	0	0	3
Engagement-culture	1	0	6	3	29	11	50
Customer	4	0	1	0	1	0	6
Exit	10	1	3	0	0	0	14
Leadership-manager	0	0	0	1	1	2	4
Learning and development	1	0	1	0	0	0	2
Multirater	1	0	0	2	0	1	4
New hire-onboarding	6	4	4	1	0	0	15
Other	3	4	5	8	5	5	28
Program-training evaluation	0	4	0	1	0	0	5
Pulse	0	2	1	5	2	2	12
Recruitment	2	0	2	0	0	0	4
Total	32	19	24	27	39	22	163

In terms of the history of the survey programs, organizations reported that the longest-running surveys in their organizations are biennial (μ = 14.3 years; SD = 12.2; range = 2–50 years) and annual (μ = 10.5 years; SD = 10.6; range = 0–50). Quarterly and monthly surveys have been running in organizations for an average of 6 years (quarterly μ = 5.7; SD = 10.8; range = 0–40 years; monthly μ = 5.8; SD = 6; range = 0–23). Weekly and daily surveys have been running for about 5 years on average (weekly μ = 4.9; SD = 3.9; range = 1–10; daily μ = 5.5; SD = 10.3; range = 1–50). Thus, the more frequent the survey cadence, the less time it has been running in the organization. This at least somewhat supports the notion that "continuous listening" using more frequent surveys is a relatively new practice in organizations.

Organizations Are (Slowly) Moving Toward More Frequent Surveying

With much of the recent buzz around "continuous listening" and more frequent surveying, we were interested to learn how respondent organizations' survey cadences, sampling plans, and response rates might be changing. Of the 227 survey types expected in the future, 148 reported survey cadences (see Table 26.4). Organizations expect that quarterly surveys will be most prevalent and expect to reduce their annual surveys. The fact that the increase in quarterly (or more frequent) surveys didn't equal the anticipated

Table 26.4 Survey Cadence of Current and Future Survey Practices

Cadence	Current Practice		Future Practice (3+ Years)	
	N	%	N	%
Biennial	22	10.8	17	7.5
Annual	39	19.2	22	9.7
Quarterly	27	13.3	36	15.8
Monthly	24	11.8	17	7.5
Weekly	19	9.4	17	7.5
Daily	32	15.7	23	10.1

Note. Percentages are based on the total number of surveys reported across all respondent organizations as the denominator (current N = 203, future N = 227).

drop in annual and biennial surveys suggests that organizations might be doing less surveying overall. This shift suggests that quarterly surveys may take the place of annual surveys in some organizations or that they may be conducted in addition to a more traditional but less frequent annual survey. Either way, it is clear that a shift in survey cadence is underway.

In terms of sampling and response rates (Table 26.5), our results show, unsurprisingly, that organizations tend to invite the largest bulk of their total population for annual surveys, followed by biennial surveys. Weekly surveys have the smallest percentage of their population included, most likely because these surveys often contain more focused content such as program evaluations and exit surveys. Also unsurprisingly, the more frequent the survey, the lower the response rate (with the exception of daily surveys being slightly higher than weekly). This is most likely due to the increased effort around communications and the enthusiasm that accompany annual and biennial surveys.

Respondents indicated that professional and front-line employees are invited to their surveys most often, closely followed by executives (see Table 26.6). Targeted samples tailored to a specific population were used 37.9% of the time. When asked what the population mix would look like in the future, respondents indicated a very similar pattern (e.g., professional and front-line employees most frequently); however, they indicated that all groups would be invited to fewer surveys. Additionally, tailored samples will be utilized more for daily through quarterly surveys, while other groups (e.g., executives, nonexecutive professionals, and front line) are more likely to be tapped monthly to biennially.

Table 26.5 Sampling and Response Rate by Survey Cadence

	Sampling (% Population Invited)			Response Rate (% Sample Responded)		
Survey Cadence	n	μ	SD	n	μ	SD
Daily	23	75.0	36.5	19	44.8	22.6
Weekly	13	65.0	39.9	13	40.8	22.0
Monthly	17	43.1	43.5	18	54.1	22.8
Quarterly	23	73.9	37.5	21	58.0	22.6
Annually	34	90.3	24.8	34	75.4	13.4
Biennially	18	76.2	31.9	18	76.9	12.7

Note. Percentages are calculated based on the average across all respondent organizations. SD = standard deviation.

Table 26.6 Survey Population for Current and Future Survey Practices

Population	Current Practice		Future Practice (3+ Years)	
	N	%	N	%
Executive	86	42.4	84	37.0
Professional	98	48.3	97	42.7
Front line	90	44.3	94	41.4
Tailored sample	77	37.9	69	30.4

Note. Percentages are based on the total number of surveys reported across all respondent organizations as the denominator (current $N = 203$, future $N = 227$).

Survey Content Is Moving Toward More Abbreviated Diagnostic Content

Respondent organizations were asked about the content included their surveys, which was outlined as broad diagnostic, abbreviated diagnostic, mood/sentiment, focused topic, or a business-specific topic. Respondents described their current surveys as including focused content as well as broad diagnostic content most frequently, and they expected this pattern to hold in the future. That said, although broad diagnostic surveys will remain the predominant content type in the future, respondents indicated that such content would decline in the future. This is most likely a function of the planned decrease in annual and biennial surveys, which tend to focus on broad diagnostic content. At the same time, abbreviated diagnostic content is anticipated to increase slightly in the future (see Table 26.7).

Table 26.7 Survey Content for Current and Future Survey Practices

Survey Content	**Current Practice**		**Future Practice (3+ Years)**	
	N	%	N	%
Broad diagnostic	63	31.0	59	25.9
Abbreviated diagnostic	31	15.3	40	17.6
Mood-related	43	21.2	47	20.7
Focused	81	39.9	74	32.6
Business-specific	36	17.7	39	17.2

Note. Percentages are based on the total number of surveys reported across all respondent organizations as the denominator (current $N = 203$, future $N = 227$).

Confidentiality of Employee Responses Will Be Increasingly Held by Internal Teams

Survey researchers are frequently confronted with assuring that respondents can answer the survey honestly and without fear of reprisal. To help ensure this, surveys are usually conducted either anonymously (i.e., responses cannot be attributed back to the individual who provided them) or confidentially (i.e., responses can be attributed to an individual, but the ability to do so is held within the research team—either by the external survey consultancy or by the internal research team). According to the present research (Table 26.8), organizations are anticipating that the privacy of survey responses will be mainly held with the organization's internal team and less by external vendors. Conducting anonymous surveys is anticipated to decrease as well. This signifies a desire for organizations to do more with the data (e.g., via linkage analysis), although it's unknown at this time whether such a practice has any systematic impact on employee response rates.

Looking by survey cadence, daily surveys were most likely to be anonymous as opposed to confidential ($n = 9$), while monthly and weekly surveys were almost exclusively kept confidential by an internal team ($n = 19$ and 13, respectively). Quarterly, annual, and biennial surveys were evenly split across the two types of confidentiality (internal $n = 9$, 17, and 9; external $n = 9$, 15, and 6, respectively); but all three were slightly more likely to be kept confidential internally. In the future, respondents indicated that annual and biennial surveys will continue to be evenly split across the two types of confidentiality (internal $n = 10$ and 9; external $n = 8$ and 6, respectively), although both annual and biennial surveys will be more likely to be kept confidential internally.

Table 26.8 Survey Privacy for Current and Future Survey Practices

Privacy	Current Practice		Future Practice (3+ Years)	
	N	%	N	%
Confidential (internal)	90	44.3	95	41.9
Confidential (external)	34	16.7	28	12.3
Anonymous	26	12.8	16	7.0
Fully identified	6	2.9	9	3.9

Note. Percentages are based on the total number of surveys reported across all respondent organizations as the denominator (current $N = 203$, future $N = 227$).

Given the trends we saw in terms of survey confidentiality shifting more to internal research teams, we were interested in the nature and role of external consultancies. Forty-six organizations reported using an outside vendor to support their survey work (86.2%). Of those who indicated the number of vendors they work with, 27 (47.4%) work with one vendor, 12 (21.1%) work with two vendors, and 4 (6.9%) work with three or more vendors. Vendor support is used mostly for survey administration (74% of respondents) and reporting (63% of respondents). Other, less frequent vendor support tasks include survey analyses (42%), survey communications (26%), and survey action-planning (30%). The length of time companies have worked with vendors ranges from 1 to 22 years, with a mean of 3.4 years. Thus, it is evident that organizations still rely heavily on vendor support to conduct their survey research, although such support seems to be limited to administration and reporting, leaving the more strategic work to internal teams.

Respondents Will Increasingly Use Their Own Personal Devices to Take Surveys

As represented in Table 26.9, respondents were asked to report the percentage of their employee population currently taking surveys across different administration methods as well as how this may change in the future. As expected, most employees currently take surveys using a company-provided laptop, followed by a kiosk. About 11% take surveys using personal devices

Table 26.9 Current and Anticipated Percentage of Invited Participants for Survey Administration by Method

	Current	Future (3+ years)
Paper	7%	2%
Kiosk (station at work)	19%	11%
Personal mobile device/tablet	4%	12%
Personal laptop	7%	10%
Company-provided mobile device/tablet	10%	12%
Company-provided laptop	49%	35%
Other	7%	8%

and laptops. Organizations report that call centers/interactive voice response (i.e., employee provides responses over telephone) are not used at all and that paper is infrequently used. In the future, respondent organizations anticipate that employees will continue to take surveys using a company-provided laptop or device, followed by personal devices and laptops. Interestingly, it appears that personal devices (i.e., laptops, mobile devices, and tablets) will grow in prevalence in the future. This may be due to expectations of more frequent, abbreviated content coupled with the prevalence of smartphones and social media and a growing comfort in sharing information through personal devices. That said, we wonder if this trend might lessen the important message that is sent when an organization provides the time and resources to gather employee feedback (e.g., when front-line employees are given the survey to complete on company time and devices).

Survey Results Will Increasingly Be Distributed Through Dashboards and Infographics

One of the recurring challenges for survey practitioners is not only to deploy survey results that are understandable, useful, and insightful but to do so in a timely way. The time it takes between closing the survey and publishing the results has traditionally been a bottleneck for organizations and is largely a function of the complexity of the survey (e.g., if the survey can be taken in multiple languages, open-ended comments typically need to be translated for reporting and analysis), how the survey is deployed (e.g., if paper surveys are used, added time is needed to clean and scan the paper forms), and how reports are generated and deployed (e.g., pregenerated PDFs or dashboards). We asked respondents to indicate the report format they currently use and what changes they anticipate in the future.

As Figure 26.1 shows, organizations anticipate moving away from reporting in PowerPoint, Excel, and PDF formats toward dynamic dashboards. This is not to say that PowerPoint etc. won't be used, but their expected reduction is dramatic. Dashboarding and infographics are the only types of reporting that respondents indicate will increase in the future.

In terms of reporting delivery, it typically takes from a week to a month to deliver reports after survey administration closes. The majority (44%) of organizations who answered the question reported a 2- to 3-week period before reports are released. However, many organizations report that

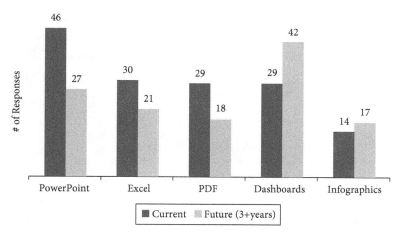

Figure 26.1. Comparison of current and anticipated reporting formats.
Note. Multiple selections were allowed; therefore, one company could be represented more than once.

the timing of survey results varies. See results in Figure 26.2. Interestingly, only 2% of respondents reported that results are available instantly. As organizations move toward dashboards and scorecards, it will be interesting to see whether they will opt to share results instantly or follow the reporting timelines as reflected in our data.

Relatedly, many organizations follow a cascading approach when delivering results. Out of those that responded, 34 organizations (68.0%) have a

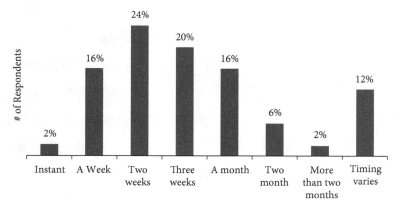

Figure 26.2. Reported time between survey administration and report release.

cascading approach, while 16 organizations (32.0%) deliver results to all af-
filiated parties at the same time. Most respondents described their process
as top-down where their team provides the results first to the chief executive
officer and the chief HR officer, then to their teams, and so on, eventually
landing with managers.

Challenges Will Remain

The present study gave us a good sense of the current practice of survey
research in organizations, as well as a glimpse into how these programs
might change in the future. However, how do the owners of these programs
(i.e., the respondents) feel about the state of their practice today? To understand this, respondents were asked to indicate their satisfaction with
different elements of their program (Figure 26.3). Overall, respondents are
most satisfied with their survey length/time to complete (77% favorable),
survey administration (76% favorable), and survey content (72% favorable).

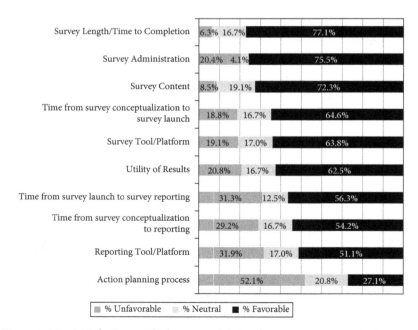

Figure 26.3. Satisfaction with the current state of survey components at
respondent organization.

Respondents are moderately satisfied with the time between conceptualization of the survey and survey launch (65%), the survey tool/platform (64%), and the utility of the survey results (63%). On the other hand, respondents are most unfavorable toward the time between survey launch and reporting (31% unfavorable) and the overall time required between conceptualization and reporting (29%). Most importantly, over half of the respondents are unfavorable toward the action-planning resulting from their surveys (52% unfavorable).

These findings reflect some recurrent struggles in the field of employee surveys. Much of the published literature has been dedicated to the topic of taking action from surveys (e.g., Church & Waclawski 2001; Kraut, 2006), primarily because taking action from surveys is much more difficult than conducting one. In fact, research by Church and Oliver (2006) as well as several follow-up studies (e.g., Church et al., 2012) has shown that engagement can be more significantly impacted if results are shared with employees but no actions taken than if results are not shared in the first place. It is not surprising then that the program owners surveyed are least satisfied with their organization's ability to quickly report survey results and readily leverage the data to inform change. Thus, it would seem that technological advances might enable us to "continuously listen" to employees, but such advances can only move the field so far. It appears that getting the right insights into the right hands and then getting leaders to use these insights will remain our focus for the foreseeable future.

References

Benjamin, B. (2016, August 15). Listen to your employees, not just your customers. *Harvard Business Review*. Retrieved from https://hbr.org/2016/08/listen-to-your-employees-not-just-your-customers

CEB Corporate Leadership Council. (2016). *The future of engagement: Trends and innovations in measuring employee engagement*. (Executive Briefing No. CLC4992116PRO). Arlington, VA: Author.

Church, A. H., Golay, L. M., Rotolo, C. T., Tuller, M. D., Shull, A. C., & Desrosiers, E. I. (2012). Without effort there can be no change: Re-examining the impact of survey feedback and action planning on employee attitudes. *Research in Organizational Change and Development, 20*, 223–264.

Church, A. H., Kuyumcu, D., & Rotolo, C. T. (2016). Survey feedback: Driving change through organizational surveys. *Oxford Bibliographies in Management*. Retrieved from http://www.oxfordbibliographies.com/view/document/obo-9780199846740/obo-9780199846740-0089.xml

Church, A. H., & Oliver, D. H. (2006). The importance of taking action, not just sharing survey feedback. In A. Kraut (Ed.), *Getting action from organizational surveys: New concepts, technologies and applications* (pp. 102–130). San Francisco, CA: Jossey-Bass.

Church, A. H., Rotolo, C. T., Ginther, N. M., & Levine, R. (2015). How are top companies designing and managing their high-potential programs? A follow-up talent management benchmark study. *Consulting Psychology Journal, 67,* 17–47.

Church, A. H., & Waclawski, J. (2001). *Designing and using organizational surveys: A seven step approach.* San Francisco, CA: Jossey-Bass.

Deloitte. (2017). Rewriting the rules for the digital age. *Deloitte Global Human Capital Trends.* Retrieved from https://www2.deloitte.com/us/en/pages/human-capital/articles/introduction-human-capital-trends.html

Kraut, A. I. (2006). *Getting action from organizational surveys: New concepts, technologies, and applications.* San Francisco, CA: Jossey-Bass.

Kraut, A. I. (Ed.). (1996). *Organizational surveys: Tools for assessment and change* (Vol. 3). San Francisco, CA: Pfeiffer.

Levenson, A. (2014). *Employee surveys that work: Improving design, use, and organizational impact.* San Francisco, CA: Berrett-Koehler.

Macey, W. H., Schneider, B., Barbera, K. M., & Young, S. A. (2009). *Employee engagement: Tools for analysis, practice, and competitive advantage.* Oxford, England: John Wiley & Sons.

Nadler, D. A. (1977). *Feedback and organization development: using databased methods.* Boston, MA: Addison-Wesley Longman.

Rotolo, C. T., & Church, A. H. (2015). Big data recommendations for industrial–organizational psychology: Are we in whoville? *Industrial and Organizational Psychology, 8,* 515–520.

Society for Industrial and Organizational Psychology. (2008–2018). SIOP Program Explorer 2008–2018. Retrieved from https://tiny.cc/SIOPprogram

27

Employee Surveys Move into the Future

A Tale of Evolution, Revolution, and Speed Bumps

Allen I. Kraut

Employee surveys are powerful tools for assessment and change. In this chapter, we will review how they have developed over recent decades, how they are likely to evolve in the coming years, and what is needed for surveys to be meaningful in the future.

We can think of changes in the survey world as being driven by two overlapping forces: *evolution*, in the form of improved survey practice, and *revolution*, through electronic technology. Along the way, these forces have created *speed bumps* for survey practitioners and their clients—these are the challenges and problems caused by the evolutionary and revolutionary forces and the environment in which they operate. To appreciate all this, we need a brief review of employee survey history.

What Is the Purpose?

Organizations do employee surveys for a variety of purposes—sometimes more than one at the same time—over a spectrum ranging from assessment to change (Kraut, 1996). Here is a quick look at the purposes we can see in practice.

- *Pinpoint areas of concern.* An overall assessment, like a person's annual medical checkup, is often the motivation when doing a survey for the first time and can set the tone for future efforts.
- *Observe long-term trends.* "Repeat surveys" are also primarily assessments of changes on various issues and may trigger specific actions.

Allen I. Kraut, *Employee Surveys Move into the Future* In: *Employee Surveys and Sensing.* Edited by: William H. Macey and Alexis A. Fink, Oxford University Press (2020). © Society for Industrial and Organizational Psychology.
DOI: 10.1093/oso/9780190939717.003.0027

- *Monitor program impact.* This gauges the reaction to organizational shifts on issues like benefit plans, flextime, product changes, training, and staffing.
- *Provide input for future decisions.* Gathering employee preferences on issues like training, telecommuting, and family–work life issues to make better-informed decisions.
- *Add a communication channel.* In large organizations, surveys are a way for executive management to learn about issues they may not otherwise see.
- *Do organizational behavior research.* Many surveys examine topics like employee attrition, stress, team effectiveness, and superior work efforts, to improve organizational success; results may also be reported in professional journals.
- *Provide symbolic communication.* By asking questions and then acting on the answers, surveys can signify a responsive, caring, and dynamic climate. (Ignoring the data or taking no action, of course, also sends a message.)
- *Drive organizational change.* Questions about customer satisfaction, product quality, or diversity and inclusion raise employees' awareness and can help to change organizational behavior. In some cases, surveys explicitly measure shifts that management has tried to produce.

Any of these purposes might be linked to the organization's strategic goals. When a survey is seen as related to a valued business purpose, it will garner more support and interest. This is confirmed in the experiences and writings of several survey practitioners (see Chapter 2; also Johnson, 2018; Wiley, 2010).

What Do Surveys Look at?

The focus of surveys has evolved since the 1930s. When they were getting their start in American industry, the emphasis of surveys was on worker "morale" (Higgs & Ashworth, 1996). Keeping morale high was thought to prevent unionization. During the 1950s and 1960s the emphasis was on employee satisfaction, apparently linking this to employee productivity.

In the 1970s and 1980s, more attention was put on the link of employee attitudes to turnover, absenteeism, and stress. In the 1990s, interest shifted to include a variety of other topics, like quality of work life, balance of work and family life, product quality, and even perceived customer satisfaction.

In the 2000s, the most common focus seems to be on "employee engagement." This topic has been examined in an earlier chapter (see Chapter 6), but it is worth noting here that the appeal of engagement seems to resemble much of the early interest in employee satisfaction and productivity. It continues the search for the always-desirable employees who are positively motivated, happy in their work, and highly productive. Many observers wonder if the concept of employee engagement is simply an old wine in a new bottle.

The Evolution: Better Survey Practice

The practice of organizational surveys has gradually and consistently improved over the years. At the same time, the use of surveys has become entrenched around the world. The vast majority of companies doing surveys are large and global firms. Wiley (2010) polled 14 large-economy nations and found that surveys are widely used in most of them. (For more on current survey usage, see Chapter 26.)

It is useful to consider these improvements in two major overlapping sets: survey administration and organization development.

Survey Administration

Administration is concerned with developing good surveys, conducting them, and analyzing and reporting the results. Several chapters in this book touch on these topics, but it will be worthwhile to point out some significant developments over the years.

Growth and Advantages of Consortia

One of the most important long-term developments has been the growth of survey consortia. Meeting once or twice a year, they have led the way in sharing best practices and trying to improve the conduct of members' survey efforts. The pioneer and best known of these is the Mayflower Group (Johnson, 1996). As described on its website (http://www.mayflowergroup.

org), it is comprised of more than 40 large companies, often with global reach. Another consortium is the Information Technology Survey Group. Their website (http://www.itsg.org) lists two dozen prominent high-tech companies.

A key function of these consortia is to create and share industry norms for survey items. All are required to ask a set of core items, and they then share their results to create norms. They do so confidentially, via a vendor, without identifying individual firms. (See Chapter 11 for an in-depth review of benchmark data issues.)

The US federal government has also created a bank of employee survey data norms, with results for each of the major departments and agencies (see www.opm.gov/policy-data-oversight/data-analysis-documentation/employee-surveys). The federal databank also includes a "private industry" norm group. Many of the items used are the same or similar to those used by Mayflower Group firms. (In fact, these items are so broadly used by companies, and consultants, that they may constitute a de facto baseline set of items for measuring the facets of organizational and job satisfaction.)

Equally important functions of consortia are the sharing of "tricks of the trade." Topics as mundane as ways to evaluate and display norm data, how to create and distribute survey announcement letters, and processes to report survey results to management are discussed at their meetings. Along with the usefulness of personal networking, these benefits have contributed to the long-term survival and value of membership in these consortia. These groups are responsible for much of the continued improvement in organizational surveys.

Questions Shift to Performance

A noticeable change has been a trend away from items that ask about employees' "satisfaction" with a topic and toward items that ask about "agreement" with a topic statement. For example, a popular item among Mayflower Group companies just a few decades ago on the topic of training was "How satisfied are you with the training you received for your present job?" (Answers from "Very Satisfied" to "Very Dissatisfied.") Compare that to the item that replaced it: "I have received the training I need to do a quality job." (Answers from "Strongly Agree" to "Strongly Disagree.")

The implication of the switch? We are not so much interested in your satisfaction as in your performance! Managers are sometimes at a loss as to how they can increase "satisfaction" and may ignore unfavorable responses. It is much harder to avoid dealing with employees who say they don't have what they need to do a good job. The wording of the new question underlines to employees that management cares about their doing a good job, and it makes it harder for managers not to pay attention to poor responses. Shifts in wording are unobtrusive indicators of shifting priorities; in this case, a bigger emphasis on performance than on satisfaction.

A related shift is to use respondents as observer-participants and reporters of their work situation and not just their own "satisfaction." Thus, more questions ask about employee views of issues like other team members working well together, managers respecting diversity and seeking staff inputs, and whether other workgroup members understand and try to satisfy customers. (See Chapter 8 for some good examples of this approach.) Whether worded as evaluations ranging from "poor" to "excellent" or as "agree–disagree" items, the responses describe key behaviors without calling them "satisfaction." However, when the findings are reported, they are often relabeled as "favorable" or not.

Over time, there have been some other notable shifts in practice. Generally, we see shorter surveys, much faster feedback and reports to managers at all levels, and the use of online tools for action-planning and action-reporting. (See Chapter 21 for examples.) With many more global surveys being done, there have been advances in translating items to other languages, developing country and international data norms, and adjusting to data privacy laws (as outlined on Chapter 24). The chance for international studies has also resulted in major new understandings of national work cultures. For example, see the classic studies of Hofstede (2001) and the recent integration by Ronen and Shenkar (2017).

Conceptual Models

A significant step forward has been the greater use of conceptual models, linking survey responses to other important outcomes. A landmark study in the *Harvard Business Review* (Rucci, Kirn, & Quinn, 1998) led the way. It showed that increases in positive employee attitudes in Sears stores were followed by better customer attitudes 3 months later and then by greater financial results in the following quarter.

This study generated more efforts to link employee feelings to business outcomes. Wiley has published several studies (Wiley, 1996; Wiley & Campbell, 2006) showing that such links exist, and Chapter 17 covers this topic. We will shortly come back to other work in this vein, done under the rubric of linking "engagement "to business outcomes.

These conceptual models help researchers and organization executives too. They show the links that may be useful levers for action, help practitioners to select and write appropriate items, suggest which variables may be strong—or testable—"drivers" of valued outcomes, and help explain survey findings to executive management.

Organization Development—Essential to Good Practice

The second major component of survey practice is how the survey results are used. A useful umbrella term is *organization development* (OD). (*Organizational change* is often part of this process.) Although definitions of OD differ, all varieties would have a survey practitioner start by "contracting" with the client to specify the purpose and expectations for the entire survey process, which includes data collection, analysis, diagnosis, and reporting and the design of appropriate actions or interventions that respond to the findings. Survey professionals must have OD skills for a survey to have meaningful and positive outcomes.

One of my most important lessons over the years is that a survey is not an event but is really a process. Administering a questionnaire is just one piece. Different parts of the survey process take place over time, usually many months, from first thinking about doing a survey to reaping the benefits of changes that are driven by the findings. Successful practitioners will "begin with the end in mind."

Effective practitioners also have the skills to prepare an organization to collaborate in the various steps of a survey, to think through the survey results, and then to respond in a meaningful way. For example, some practitioners will ask the organization being surveyed to form an "advisory group" made up of high-level representatives from different areas in the firm, to give counsel about steps in the process, and to pave the way for dealing with the survey findings.

Only a small fraction of survey professionals have been well educated in OD. Most learn by doing, and others look to good role models and helpful writings. There are some excellent books available, like Block's classic *Flawless Consulting* (2011) and Schein's primer on *Process Consultation Revisited* (1998). Fortunately, many fine practitioners have shared their experiences in Society for Industrial and Organizational Psychology workshops and other books (e.g., see Waclawski & Church, 2002, and Chapter 22 in this book).

Top executives' support is critical but not automatic. David Nadler (1996) has written eloquently about the chief executive officer's (CEO's) fears and concerns when doing a survey. While senior management may welcome the data to help them to make needed changes, they still worry about basic issues like "Why do it?" and "What will we measure and who will see the data?" They also need to understand their own role, what they will say and do. Nadler lays out such issues with useful replies by the survey practitioner. Empathetic and wise coaching skills are most helpful to be effective at this.

Presentation of Results

The presentation of results, to facilitate a genuine interest and understanding, is also vital for successful survey practice. In facing such a task, we might imagine trying to put a survey's findings into a *New York Times* news story and ask, "What should the headline be? How can I frame the gist of our findings in 10 to 15 words?" In the same vein, what charts will best show the findings? In Chapter 20, Johnson gives excellent guidance. Also, see Sinar's advice in Chapter 19.

Survey researchers often use correlations as a way to summarize results, but this can minimize real-life impacts (Rosenthal & Rosnow, 1984). For example, take a "modest" correlation, $r = .30$, between a predictor like engagement and an outcome like performance. A bar chart will show that among people in the top half of engagement scores, 65% would perform at an above average level compared to only 35% of those in the bottom half. In most organizations, that 30% gap is a huge difference.

The Importance of Action

Just a few decades ago, it was considered a big deal to give employees some survey data feedback, via a printed article or especially in a meeting. In truth, many managers are uncomfortable about conducting feedback meetings. These fears may motivate them to avoid meetings altogether or to over-rely on statistics, like "key driver analyses," believing that they rule out the need to actually talk to survey respondents. Managers would be best served if they saw the survey as a platform for meaningful dialogue with their employees and did not expect survey results alone to give them all the "answers."

In recent years, research has made it clear that taking action, and not just giving feedback, is the "secret sauce" for organizational improvement and for employees to see value in surveys (Church & Oliver, 2006). The data show that, as far as employees are concerned, it is better not to do a survey at all than to do it and not take action. No wonder that some firms have developed training for managers to run better feedback and action-planning meetings (Hinrichs, 1996). My experience in this area is that "less is more"; managers are best advised to focus on just one or two areas to take meaningful and visible action. Of course, the roles of the managers and their staffs will differ in cultures where they are not expected to take part in suggesting or directing actions.

Inaction happens in government as well as in private industry. An example is described in the *Washington Post* after a terrible set of survey results at the federal government's Transportation Security Agency. The agency then hired a consultant to look at the data, but the resulting study was put in a drawer. This process was then repeated three more times, costing more than $2 million, without any action being taken (Markon, 2015).

Researchers soon recognize that in most organizations survey results have a "political" quality. Executives may prefer to hear and talk about good results and bury poor ones, as in the following examples:

- In one of my engagements at a large bank, the CEO was pleased to see strong upticks in the ratings of top management since he was appointed. He thanked me and arranged for his board of directors to see the presentation.
- In a large university where annual employee surveys tracked reactions to a new suite of software programs, the findings were shown to top administrators. After, the fourth survey showed sharp declines and

increasing resistance, the sponsoring executives said, more or less, "Thanks, we'll take it from here." I was not invited to show the findings that year.

The Revolution: Impact of Technology

Considering the speed with which computers have overtaken our lives in general, and surveys in particular, this technology's impact deserves to be called revolutionary. Significant improvements in computer architecture and software have dramatically lowered cost and raised convenience in administering surveys and analyzing results.

More, Easier Surveys

Over the last few decades, survey administration has shifted swiftly from paper-and-pencil methods to the use of the Internet and company intranets to distribute surveys and collect data. Findings now can be tallied and reported in a matter of hours or days rather than weeks to months and at far lower cost.

Online surveys have other advantages as well. Survey content can be tailored up to the last moment before sending questionnaires to respondents. "Write-ins," the answers to open-ended questions, come back already digitized with no need to transcribe them or be concerned about handwriting. Questions can be "branched," and follow-up items offered only after there are problematic replies on an earlier question. Overall, computerized surveys have created huge benefits in cost, speed, and flexibility.

Due to ease and lower costs, we also see more variety in the types of surveys being done. There has been a proliferation of sample surveys, "pulse" surveys, and continuous listening paradigms such as those seen in "life-cycle" surveys (see Chapters 3–5).

Identified Surveys

With digitization, surveys typically are sent to a respondent's unique address so that each person is personally identified. This opens up new and extraordinary research possibilities. With identified surveys, we can connect to human resources (HR) information systems and be assured of accurate demographic data and, more importantly, links to other data. These can include job performance, turnover, salary, promotions, and even prior years' survey responses. This could lead to a golden age of meaningful research. However, as Saari and Scherbaum discuss in Chapter 24, identified surveys also raise many questions about confidentiality, ethics, and privacy (also see Chapter 15).

Computerization has made it far easier for laypeople to do surveys. In part, this is due to new tools to construct and administer surveys. Survey Monkey, for example, is just one of dozens of easy-to-use, do-it-yourself survey platforms. These tools also bring some big downsides. They make surveys look easy to do, neglecting the mechanics of good question writing, questionnaire construction, and follow-up. In fact, effective surveys are not easy to do.

There is also a widespread employee perception of oversurveying by multiple sources. In some firms, any group with the idea to do a survey will try it and do so repeatedly. Besides HR, this could include marketing, service, product groups, etc. As a result, there has been a growing tendency of employees to ignore or resist survey invitations and to produce lower response rates that imperil a survey's validity. Occasionally, a firm will require these groups to coordinate their survey efforts.

The Era of Big Data

Computer advances have brought us to the era of big data, allowing faster and more rigorous and sophisticated collection and analysis of survey data. Programs like IBM's Watson permit analysts to consider a huge range of variables and look for relationships that may not even have been considered before.

The statistical techniques being offered to make the most of big data are many and quite sophisticated. In focusing anew on the prediction of criteria like turnover or employability, these methods go beyond the linear assumptions of multiple regression and structural equation modeling or multilevel modeling.

Discussions of so-called big data methods and artificial intelligence (AI) often overlap. Sometimes the terms are used interchangeably. Big data tend to stress data collection and inputs, as well as their analyses. AI emphasizes the more sophisticated analysis and interpretation of this information and the self-learning and improvement of the computing methods. An astute observer (Lee, 2018) notes the paradox of what we may expect from these extraordinary advances: "it will feel both completely ordinary and totally revolutionary."

Speed Bumps (and Other Challenges) on the Way to the Future

The electronic collection of surveys, allowing individuals to be identified with their answers, is usually accompanied by promises of confidentiality (even if true anonymity is not possible). So far, data privacy and ethical handling of such information seem to be taken for granted. But I would regard identified surveys to be potential time bombs that may explode in any organization.

There is enough concern about this in the European Union that the General Data Protection Regulation (GDPR) went into effect in 2018. The GDPR has strict new standards for the collection and distribution of data, including survey data, and is certain to impact employee survey practices. The GDPR will impact all European surveys and, especially for global firms, will influence US practices too. A detailed description of this speed bump is found in Chapter 24.

Methodology Does Matter, Really

Sometimes, the speed bumps we encounter are of our own making because our methods are faulty or inappropriate. Certainly, we've learned that methodology does matter. Here are two examples of subtle but important methodological problems that should be more widely recognized.

- Comparing results from different surveys requires a look at where the items were positioned. Research shows that answers to an item will be different if the item is placed earlier than if it is placed later in the questionnaire (Kraut, Wolfson, & Rothenberg, 1975). As a survey goes on, respondents get fatigued and are less likely to use the extreme responses and instead drift to the modal response. As many reports show the results as percent favorable or unfavorable, this can make a significant difference. In a study using two questionnaires at the same time with matched samples, an item asking about "overall satisfaction" was 5 percentage points more favorable when the item was in the back of the questionnaire than when it was in the front. An item on "pay versus duties" became 10 percentage points less favorable. Consistent positioning of survey items across surveys is vital.

- Participation rates in the survey population need to be checked. In one firm, a survey showed an overall increase of 5 percentage points "favorable" since the prior survey. But when the total firm was split into management and non-management (unionized), there was only a 2 percentage point increase for each group. A difficult union strike a few months earlier had caused sharply reduced survey participation by unionized employees, so the more favorable management employees got a much higher weighting in the later survey's totals. In cases like this, proper weighting is needed to get an accurate set of results.

There are many other areas of survey practice that require methodological expertise, and we can see that many of the chapters in this book show areas where practitioners have accumulated and are sharing much wisdom. For example,

- Proper wording of survey items (Chapter 12)
- Sampling of the survey population, to serve different needs (Chapter 3)
- Alternatives and adjuncts to written questionnaires, such as interviews and focus groups (Chapter 7)
- Use of text analytics to make the most of write-in comments (Chapter 13)
- Assessing relationships among variables. One of my personal favorites is the development of relative weights analysis, which allows us to judge how strongly several simultaneous variables are related to an outcome measure. (Chapter 16)

Industrial–organizational (I-O) psychologists are well trained in research methodology but not usually in survey methods per se. Most practitioners learn a lot about survey issues on the job. Practitioners can continue to grow their expertise by reading and education. I-O colleagues have written worthwhile primers, like Church and Waclawski's (1998) account of a seven-step process, and detailed treatises such as *Employee Surveys in Management* (Borg & Mastrangelo, 2008). Also, university-based workshops, degrees, and online courses in survey methodology are available at the University of Maryland and the University of Michigan.

It is worth noting that a majority of studies in our top professional journals have gathered their data using survey questionnaires. So good survey methodology is basic to better science as well as practice. The "revolution" in survey technology can only make this more important.

Employee Engagement (and Scientist-Practitioner Heroes)

The focus on engagement surveys in recent years puts a bright light on the interaction between science and practice. In the long term, a fuzziness of the "engagement" concept may be the biggest speed bump to good survey practice. While survey vendors appeal to clients with the idea of employee engagement, some serious problems exist. Most contemporary employee surveys seem to use *engagement* as an umbrella term, and in various guises it is measured by items that tap all or some of the aspects of job satisfaction, organizational commitment, and work behavior. Practically, this may make little difference. One large consultant, based on extensive analysis of client survey data, says frankly, "there is little difference between the use of [overall] satisfaction alone and its combination with other questions into an 'engagement index.' . . . The correlation is 0.91!" (Sirota & Klein, 2014, p. 80).

To some degree, of course, the correlation among these closely overlapping concepts is a measurement tautology. In fact, at least two other major studies find that "engagement" adds very little prediction value above traditional work attitude measures alone (Harrison, Newman, & Roth, 2006; Mackay, Allen, & Landis, 2017).

Meanwhile, some professionals are doing extraordinary research to explore and test the promises of "engagement." These scientist-practitioners, experienced and capable in both science and practice, are especially admirable. Schneider and Macey and their colleagues have long grappled with and sometimes modified conceptualizations of "engagement" (see Macey

& Schneider, 2008; Macey, Schneider, Barbera, & Young, 2009; also see Chapter 6 on this topic).

- They have also shown that engagement is linked to business success. Using identical items in 65 companies for engagement feelings and engagement behaviors, they found positive links to return on assets and profitability (Schneider, Macey, Barbera, & Martin, 2009).
- In a parallel study, they found that employees' customer-focused engagement behaviors, across 44 companies, were correlated at a significant level ($r = .45$) with customers' reports in the American Customer Satisfaction Index. In a recent study with similar findings, they make a case that workforce engagement is preceded or "driven" by conditions such as work attributes, supervisory practices, and organizational practices (Schneider, Yost, Kropp, Kind, & Lam, 2017).
- Meta-analyses by Judge, Thoresen, Bono, and Patton (2001) show that work attitudes are correlated with individual-level performance at $r = .30$, rising to $r = .52$ in high-complexity jobs.
- Harter and Schmidt's work with more than 82,000 business/work units shows that employee attitudes are positively related ($r = .42$) to unit-level business outcomes like profits, sales, customer ratings, and turnover (Harter, Schmidt, Agrawal, Plowman, & Blue, 2016). Their longitudinal studies support the causality of job attitudes and work perceptions on business outcomes (Harter, Schmidt, Asplund, Killham, & Agrawal, 2010).

Harter et al. (2016) argue that their Q^{12} measure of employee engagement taps the antecedent conditions that create engagement. They cite conditions like clear goals, resources, and performance feedback. Harter believes that employee engagement is "best characterized as a global job attitude construct that best predicts global performance" (personal communication, 2019). Along with the linkage research discussed under Conceptual Models above, this scientific evidence is piling up to show that job attitudes indeed do reflect the conditions that lead to better organizational outcomes.

Genuine progress in this field depends on a deeper understanding of the "conditions"—such as goal clarity, training, resources, and supervisor behavior—that impact performance. It will require hard work, and courage too, to move beyond today's commercially attractive but amorphous notions of "employee engagement."

The "DELTA" Forces Impacting Surveys

The successful survey practitioner is a bit like a successful surfboarder in needing to adapt to the environment—not to get too far ahead of the "wave" and thus lose energy or to lag behind and be crushed by it. Aside from the "survey" world itself, many things that require survey practitioner sensitivity have changed in the last few decades and will continue to shift. As our environments change, we need to consider what and how we measure. Being attentive can minimize unwanted "speed bumps."

We can mention a few examples of such changes, using the DELTA mnemonic (Kraut & Korman, 1999).

- *Demographics.* The workforces we survey have become older, more female, and ethnically diverse.
- *Economics.* In the United States, more workers are in service industries, while manufacturing has shrunk; and globalization is growing.
- *Legal.* Civil rights laws have had major impacts, and new laws on privacy create huge impacts on surveys.
- *Technological.* Computerization changes how work gets done, upgrading the value of information technology skills and making telecommuting more popular.
- *Attitudinal.* The old psychological contract between workers and companies has changed. Workers want work–life balance and flexibility.

And the Future?

One can imagine that future employee surveys will change in dramatic fashion. Consider the possibility that AI might use employees' e-mails and comments on social media to predict their attitudes. The power of AI is already on track to do this (Lee, 2018). Facebook has used people's social media words and phrases to predict their personality dimensions (Sullivan, 2014). Some employee surveys could disappear completely, to be replaced by ongoing "sensing" of employees' e-mails and social media. For example, the 2017 Cambridge Analytica scandal showed how social media data (from Facebook in that case) could be used to reveal attitudes toward particular subjects, like presidential candidates. Chapter 14 also suggests that this could be done.

In Conclusion

It does not seem fantastical to imagine such spectacular possibilities, as just mentioned. However, the current style of employee surveys should endure for many years. In the near term at least, I believe that the prospects are quite good for survey researchers to continue to increase employee well-being and organizational performance and to contribute to better appreciation of organizational behavior. Understanding the topics in this book, survey practitioners can move forward with a sense of history, a sense of purpose, and—not infrequently—a sense of humor!

Acknowledgment

Jim Harter's help in noting some key studies is greatly appreciated.

References

Block, P. (2011). *Flawless consulting: A guide to getting your expertise used*. San Francisco, CA: Pfeiffer.

Borg, I., & Mastrangelo, P. M. (2008). *Employee surveys in management: Theories, tools, and practical applications*. Cambridge, MA: Hogrefe & Huber.

Church, A. H., & Oliver, D. H. (2006). The importance of taking action, not just sharing survey feedback. In A. I. Kraut (Ed.), *Getting action from organizational surveys* (pp. 102–130). San Francisco, CA: Jossey-Bass.

Church, A. H., & Waclawski, J. (1998). *Designing and using organizational surveys: A seven-step process*. San Francisco, CA: Jossey-Bass.

Harrison, D. A., Newman, D. A., & Roth, P. L. (2006). How important are the job attitudes? Meta-analytic comparisons of integrative behavioral outcomes and time sequences. *Academy of Management Journal, 49*, 305–325.

Harter, J. K., Schmidt, F. L., Agrawal, S., Plowman, S. K., & Blue, A. (2016). *The relationship between engagement at work and organizational outcomes, 2016 Q^{12^*} meta-analysis* (9th ed.). Iowa City, IA: Gallup.

Harter, J. K., Schmidt, F. L., Asplund, J. W., Killham, E. A., & Agrawal, S. (2010). Causal impact of employee work perceptions on the bottom line of organizations. *Perspectives on Psychological Science, 5*(4), 378–389.

Higgs, A. C., & Ashworth, S. D. (1996). Organizational surveys: Tools for assessment and research. In A. I. Kraut (Ed.), *Organizational surveys: Tools for assessment and change* (pp. 19–40). San Francisco, CA: Jossey-Bass.

Hinrichs, J. R. (1996). Feedback, action planning, and follow-through. In A. I. Kraut (Ed.), *Organizational surveys: Tools for assessment and change* (pp. 255–280). San Francisco, CA: Jossey-Bass.

Hofstede, G. H. (2001). *Culture's consequences: Comparing values, behaviors, institutions and organizations across nations* (2nd Ed.). Thousand Oaks, CA: Sage.

Johnson, R. H. (1996). Life in the consortium: The Mayflower Group. In A. I. Kraut (Ed.), *Organizational surveys: Tools for assessment and change* (pp. 285–309). San Francisco, CA: Jossey-Bass.

Johnson, S. R. (2018). *Engaging the workplace: Using surveys to spark change.* Alexandria, VA: ATD Press.

Judge, T. A., Thoresen, C. J., Bono, J. E., & Patton, G. K. (2001). The job satisfaction–job performance relationship: A qualitative and quantitative review. *Psychological Bulletin, 127*(3), 376–407.

Kraut, A. I. (1996). Planning and conducting the survey: Keeping strategic purpose in mind. In A. I. Kraut (Ed.), *Organizational surveys: Tools for assessment and change* (pp. 149–176). San Francisco, CA: Jossey-Bass.

Kraut, A. I., & Korman, A. K. (1999). The "DELTA forces" causing change in human resource management. In A. I. Kraut & A. K. Korman (Eds.), *Evolving practices in human resource management: Responses to a changing world of work* (pp. 3–22). San Francisco, CA: Jossey-Bass.

Kraut, A. I., Wolfson, A. D., & Rothenberg, A. (1975). Some effects of position on opinion survey items. *Journal of Applied Psychology, 60*(6), 774–776.

Lee, K.-F. (2018). *AI superpowers: China, Silicon Valley, and the new world order.* Boston, MA: Houghton Mifflin Harcourt.

Macey, W. H., & Schneider, B. (2008). The meaning of employee engagement. *Industrial and Organizational Psychology, 1*, 3–30.

Macey, W. H., Schneider, B., Barbera, K. M., & Young, S. A. (2009). *Employee engagement: Tools for analysis, practice, and competitive advantage.* New York, NY: Wiley Blackwell.

Mackay, M. M., Allen, J. A., & Landis, R. S. (2017). Investigating the incremental validity of employee engagement in the prediction of employee effectiveness: A meta-analytic path analysis. *Human Resource Management Review, 27*, 108–120.

Markon, J. (2015, February 20). DHS tackles endless morale problems with seemingly endless studies. *Washington Post.*

Nadler, D. A. (1996). Setting expectations and reporting results: Conversations with top management. In A. I. Kraut (Ed.), *Organizational surveys: Tools for assessment and change* (pp. 177–203). San Francisco, CA: Jossey-Bass.

Ronen, S., & Shenkar, O. (2017). *Navigating global business: A cultural compass.* Cambridge, England: Cambridge University Press.

Rosenthal, R., & Rosnow, R. L. (1984). On binomial effect-size display. In *Essentials of behavioral research* (pp. 318–322). New York: McGraw-Hill.

Rucci, A. J., Kirn, S. P., & Quinn, R. T. (1998, January–February). The employee-customer–profit chain at Sears. *Harvard Business Review, 76*(1-2), 82–97. https://hbr.org/1998/01/the-employee-customer-profit-chain-at-sears

Schein, E. H. (1998). *Process consultation revisited: Building the helping relationship.* Boston, MA: Addison-Wesley.

Schneider, B., Macey, W. H., Barbera, K. M., & Martin, N. (2009). Driving customer satisfaction and financial success through employee engagement. *People and Strategy, 32*(2), 22–27.

Schneider, B., Yost, A. B., Kropp, A., Kind, C., & Lam, H. (2017). Workforce engagement: What it is, what drives it, and why it matters for organizational performance. *Journal of Organizational Behavior, 39*(4), 462–480.

Sirota, D., & Klein, D. A. (2014). *The enthusiastic employee* (2nd ed.). Upper Saddle River, NJ: Pearson.

Sullivan, G. (2014, June 16). Creepy Facebook personality test could be dream for advertisers, nightmare for privacy. *Washington Post*. Retrieved from https://www.washingtonpost.com/news/morning-mix/wp/2014/06/16/creepy-facebook-personality-test-is-a-dream-for-advertisers-nightmare-for-privacy/?noredirect=on&utm_term=.4b32a1a0cae2

Waclawski, J., & Church, A. H. (2002). *Organization development: A data-driven approach to organizational change*. San Francisco, CA: Jossey-Bass.

Wiley, J. W. (1996). Linking survey results to customer satisfaction and business performance. In A. I. Kraut (Ed.), *Organizational surveys: Tools for assessment and change* (pp. 330–359). San Francisco, CA: Jossey-Bass.

Wiley, J. W. (2010). *Strategic employee surveys: Evidence based guidelines for driving organizational success*. San Francisco, CA: Jossey-Bass.

Wiley, J. W., & Campbell, B. H. (2006). Using linkage research to drive high performance: A case study in organizational development. In A. I. Kraut (Ed.), *Getting action from organizational surveys: New concepts, methods and applications* (pp. 150–182). San Francisco, CA: Jossey-Bass.

Name Index

For the benefit of digital users, indexed terms that span two pages (e.g., 52–53) may, on occasion, appear on only one of those pages.

Abbasi, A., 210–11
Abdul-Nasiru, I., 403
Abdulsalam, D., 12–13
Adair, D., 138–39
Adis, C. S., 97–98
Adler, A. B., 290, 291, 301
Adler, S., 2, 360
Afflerbach, S., 202
Agarwal, D., 220–21
Agbényiga, D., 144
Agrawal, S., 124–25, 233n3, 409, 411–12, 456
Agut, S., 130, 274
Akinola, M., 382
Al-Kassab, J., 307–8
Albrecht, S., 139
Alge, B. J., 90
Ali-Löytty, S., 138–39
Allen, D. G., 251–52, 280
Allen, J. A., 409, 455
Allen, N. J., 89
Allison, R. B., 193
Altintzoglou, T., 202
Angle, H., 273–74
Antón, A., 393–94
Antonakis, J., 383
Arad, R., 55
Arena, M., 222
Ariely, D., 382
Armstrong, R. L., 194
Arnould, E., 168
Arthur, W., 129
Ashkanasy, N., 137–38
Ashworth, S. D., 24, 375, 394, 444
Asplund, J. W., 124–25, 409, 456
Assimakopoulos, D., 220–21

Astrove, S. L., 158
Avgar, A., 407, 409–10
Avolio, B. J., 92, 94
Azanza, G., 139
Azen, R., 258–59, 262–63, 265

Bach, B., 320
Bagozzi, R. P., 380
Bailey, C., 383–84
Bainbridge, C. M., 319
Bajdo, L., 144
Baker, R., 307
Bakker, A. B., 87, 88, 90, 92, 93, 124–25, 400
Bales, R. F., 203
Baluch, A. M., 53–54, 274
Bamforth, K., 136
Banks, G. C., 211
Baraldi, A. N., 244
Barbera, K. M., 31, 426, 455–56
Barends, E. G., 385
Bariso, J., 342
Barnard, Y. F., 198
Barnett, G., 50–51, 56
Bartlett, C. J., 121
Bartunek, J. M., 130–31
Bashshur, M. R., 246–47
Bass, B. M., 92, 94
Bates, D. M., 290
Baumeister, R. F., 96–97
Baysinger, M., 257, 258–59
Beagrie, S., 38
Beatty, A. S., 250
Beckhard, R., 359
Behrend, T. S., 6, 175–76
Belias, D., 139
Benjamin, B., 426

Benkhoff, B., 274
Bercini, D., 104–5
Bergman, M. E., 129
Berry, J., 104
Bersin, J., 2, 13–14, 38, 220–21, 312–13
Bertini, E., 307–8, 319
Beus, J. M., 129
Biga, A., 399
Billsberry, J., 158
Bitter, C., 205
Black, J., 262, 342–43, 393, 394, 399
Blau, P. M., 97–98
Blei, D. M., 205, 212
Bliese, P. D., 12–13, 126, 289, 290, 291, 294,
    296, 299–300, 301, 302
Block, P., 449
Blue, A., 411–12, 456
Bolino, M. C., 383
Bommer, W. H., 97–98
Bonaccio, S., 103
Bono, J. E., 274, 384, 409, 456
Booth, R. J., 203
Bopp, F., 213–14
Borg, I., 42–44, 51n1, 454–55
Borkin, D., 319
Borkin, M. A., 319
Borovina Josko, J. M., 307
Boudreau, J., 402–3
Bowen, D. E., 130, 273
Bowling, A., 394
Boxwell, R. J., 171
Boyce, A., 142, 145
Boyd, R. L., 203
Bracken, D. W., 374
Bradley, J. C., 129
Branigan, C., 382
Bravo, J., 97–98
Brayfield, A. H., 273
Bresciani, S., 307–8
Bridgman, T., 382
Brimhall, K., 140
Bring, J., 255
Brislin, R. W., 196–97
Brooks, S. M., 3, 9–10, 11, 81, 172, 176, 179
Brouer, R. C., 97–98
Brown, K. G., 382
Brown, S. P., 274
Brummel, B. J., 257, 258–59

Bryant, P. C., 280
Bryk, A., 290
Bryson, A., 409–10
Buchanan, J. A., 202
Budescu, D. V., 256, 258–59, 265, 268
Buffardi, L. C., 97–98
Burch, M., 213–14
Burke, M. J., 129, 246–47
Burke, W. W., 283–84, 341, 359, 364,
    375, 376–77
Burrell, G., 376–77
Buxton, V. A., 129, 130, 273, 375
Bylinskii, Z., 319

Cable, D. M., 155, 160, 384
Caldwell, D. F., 137, 142, 146, 155, 160, 384
Caleo, S., 41–42
Callegaro, M., 307
Cameron, K., 137, 144
Campana, K. L., 202
Campbell, B. H., 274, 448
Campbell, D. T., 116–17
Campbell, J. P., 122
Cantor, N., 383
Cappellari, L., 409–10
Caputo, A. W., 10, 11, 17, 274
Carboni, I., 222
Carley, K., 203–4
Carpendale, S., 320
Carr, L. S., 24, 273–74, 375
Carr, S., 403
Carr, Schmidt, 121
Cartwright, S., 137–38
Cascio, W. F., 281–82
Casey, M. A., 108, 120
Catania, J. A., 196
Cavedon, L., 400
Chakrabarti, M., 4, 16–17, 221, 222
Chamberlain, A., 223
Chamorro-Premuzic, T., 31
Chan, D., 125, 196–97, 247, 289
Chang, S., 53–54, 274
Chatham, C. L., 202
Chatman, J. A., 137, 142, 146, 155, 160, 384
Chave, E. J., 375
Chen, F., 339
Chen, G., 302
Chilisa, B., 376

Chitwood, D. D., 196
Chiu, M., 38
Choi, J. N., 274
Christian, M. S., 86, 89–91, 93–95, 129
Church, A. H., 2, 3, 14, 16, 242, 341,
    357–58, 359, 360, 362, 364, 366, 367,
    375, 391, 394, 425–26, 427, 441, 449,
    450, 454–55
Clark, M. A., 251
Clark, R., 325
Clarke, S., 129
Clements, N., 319
Cliff, N., 193
Coates, T. J., 196
Cohen, A., 246–47
Cohen, J., 116
Colihan, J., 39, 41–42, 43–44, 357–58
Collins, J., 137, 180
Colquitt, A. L., 2, 360
Colquitt, J. A., 97–98
Conlon, D. E., 97–98
Contopoulos-Ioannidis, D., 246–47
Cooke, R., 137, 142, 144
Cooper, C., 137–38
Coovert, M., 398, 401
Cortina, J., 391, 392
Coruzzi, C. A., 359
Crawford, E. R., 88, 93
Creary, S. J., 362
Crockett, W. H., 273
Cronley, C., 139
Cropanzano, R., 97–98
Cross, R., 220–21, 222
Cucina, J. M., 12, 13, 16, 105, 130–31,
    259–62, 268
Cummings, L. L., 273
Cummings, S., 382
Cunningham, G., 139–40
Curtin, P., 13, 105, 130–31, 259–62, 268

Dalal, R. S., 257, 258–59
Dalessio, A. T., 38
Darlington, R. B., 255
Darrow, J. B., 6
Daum, D. L., 9–10, 250, 257, 259–60
Davenport, T. H., 1, 16–17
Davies, G., 154
Davis-Blake, A., 409–10

Davis, B. J., 202
Davis, C. K., 202
Davis, J. H., 97–98
Dawis, R. V., 261
de Neve, J. E., 409
de-Lara, P., 139
Deal, T., 137
Dean, A., 130
DeBar, B., 176, 179
Deci, E. L., 96–97
Del Duco, S., 11, 17
Delany, T., 391
Delfabbro, P., 139
DelVecchio, W. F., 383–84
Demerouti, E., 92, 93
Demétrio, C. G. B., 292
Den Hartog, D. N., 377
Denison, D., 12–13, 135, 137–38, 141,
    142, 145
Denny, E., 120
Denton, M. A., 202
Derfuss, K., 53–54, 274
DeShon, R., 10
Desrosiers, E. I., 367, 441
Dhar, M., 210–11
Dickson, M. W., 12–13, 137, 144, 377
Diener, E., 381
Dinlersoz, E. M., 408
Dion, D., 168
Dixon, G. W., 333–34
Doerr, B., 384
Donlon, J. P., 32
Dorfman, P. W., 137, 144
Dorio, J., 393
Dorsey, D., 398, 401
Doveh, E., 246–47
Dreibelbis, R., 398, 401
Duan, L., 140
Ducey, A., 391
Dulebohn, J. H., 97–98
Dunnette, M. D., 122
Dutta, S., 5, 10–11, 12, 114, 161, 341
Dye, D., 374

Earley, C., 137–38
Earp, J., 393–94
Easterby-Smith, M., 103
Ebert, D. S., 306–7

Edmans, A., 407
Edmondson, A., 378
Edwards, J. R., 155, 160
Efron, B., 265
Ehrhart, M. G., 126, 142
Eisenberger, R., 97–98
Eldridge, L. D., 46, 174
Elizondo, D. A., 205
Eller, T., 53–54, 274
Enders, C. K., 244
Epitropaki, O., 384
Eppler, M. J., 307–8
Erez, M., 55
Erickson, T. J., 9, 156
Ertl, T., 213–14
Euwema, M. C., 87
Evangelou, E., 246–47

Farren, C., 76
Fayeka, H., 400
Feinzig, S., 255, 259–60, 267, 268
Feldman Barrett, L., 382
Feldt, T., 140
Fenlason, I. J., 105
Fenlason, K. J., 3, 11, 31, 32, 391, 395
Fermin, J., 357
Ferreira, J. E., 307
Ferris, G. R., 97–98
Fink, A. A., 4–5, 50–51, 56, 391, 392
Finnegan, R. P., 280
Firth, D., 292
Fisher, C. D., 381–82
Fisher, G. G., 189–90
Fiske, D. W., 116–17
Fleck, C. R., 2, 255, 262, 263–64, 268
Fleishman, E. A., 126–27
Fogel, J., 394
Follmer, E. H., 158
Ford, D.-S., 121
Ford, M. T., 97–98
Foster, G., 2, 360
Francis, M. E., 203
Fredrickson, B. L., 382
Freeman, R. B., 409–10, 411
Freerks, K., 394
French, W., 340
Frey, C. B., 408

Friedmann, P. D., 251
Froelich, J., 394, 395
Frost, P., 137
Fuller, W. L., 246–47

Gagné, M., 96–97
Garrad, L., 2, 259–60, 265, 268
Garton, E., 228–29
Garwood, K. C., 319
Garza, A. S., 86, 89–91, 93–95
Gast, I. F., 13, 105, 130–31, 259–62, 268
Gaucher, E., 144
Gaurav, L., 220–21
Gavin, M. B., 294–95
George, J. M., 383
Gerbasi, A., 220–21
Gerhardt, M. W., 384
Gerolamo, M., 140
Getman, J., 407
Gibbons, A. M., 189–90
Gibby, R., 391
Gibson, D. R., 196
Giles, S., 341
Gillespie, M., 135, 142, 145
Gilson, R. L., 88
Gino, F., 382
Ginther, N. M., 427
Glaser, B. G., 203
Glerum, D. R., 383–84
Glibkowski, B. C., 97–98
Gloss, A., 403
Goetsch, D. L., 281–82
Golay, L. M., 367, 441
Gold, R. Z., 265
Goldberg, S., 407
Golden-Biddle, K., 103
Gong, Y., 53–54, 274
González-Romá, V., 88, 90, 122, 128, 129, 246–47
Gotfryd, A., 224
Gouldner, A. W., 97–98
Graeff, T., 394
Grant, A., 306
Gratton, L., 9, 156
Gray, P., 220–21
Greenberg, J., 97–98
Greenwood, J., 408

Griffeth, R. W., 78
Grimme, T. M., 202
Grobman, G., 377
Grotto, A. R., 274
Guenole, N., 391
Guest, G., 120
Guillaume, Y., 384
Guion, R. M., 121, 122–24, 130
Gundry, L. K., 76
Gupta, V., 137, 144
Guy, R. F., 194
Guzzo, R., 393

Hackman, J. R., 89, 92, 93, 385
Halbesleben, J. R., 383
Hall, D. T., 121
Hammer, T. H., 407, 409–10
Hanges, J., 144
Hanges, P. J., 137, 144
Hansen, S. D., 156
Harmon, S., 394
Harms, P. D., 155–56
Harris, J., 1, 16–17
Harris, M. J., 176, 179
Harris, R. T., 359
Harrison, D. A., 89–90, 124, 409, 455
Hart, D., 41–42
Harter, J. K., 11, 15, 53–54, 88, 124–25,
    181, 274, 409, 411–12, 456
Harter, L. M., 88
Harvey, J., 383
Hassan, A., 210–11
Hayes, T. L., 53–54, 88, 274
Hayles, K., 376–77
Heerwegh, D., 394
Heimerl, F., 213–14
Helfman, D. E., 409–10
Hendricks, J. L., 290, 291, 294, 301
Hendrickson, V., 172, 177
Hensher, D. A., 162, 165
Herleman, H., 391
Herman, A., 393
Herman, J. B., 407
Hernández, A., 246–47
Hernandez, I., 229–30, 399
Herscovitch, L., 89–91, 97–98, 261
Herzberg, F., 93

Heskett, J. L., 53–54, 137, 273–74
Hess, E. D., 385
Hessler, R., 394
Higgs, A. C., 24, 273–74, 375, 444
Highhouse, S., 154, 160
Hinkin, T. R., 288
Hinrichs, J. R., 338–39, 340, 450
Hoeffner, J., 320
Hoffman, P. J., 210–11, 255
Hofmann, D. A., 290, 291, 294–95, 301
Hofstede, G., 137, 143, 144, 447
Hogan, J., 280
Hogan, R., 280
Hogreve, J., 53–54, 274
Holland, E., 383
Holland, J. L., 261
Hollenbeck, J. R., 90
Hom, P. W., 78
Hong, Y., 140
Hooijberg, R., 141, 145
Hopstaken, J., 400
Horn, H., 222
House, R. J., 126, 137, 144, 383
Howardson, G., 6
Howes, J., 255, 259–60, 267, 268
Hsiao, H., 140
Hu, J., 140
Huang, Q., 307
Hudson, L. A., 377
Hughes, E., 255, 268
Huhtala, M., 140
Hui, C. H., 196–97
Hulin, C. L., 89–91, 123–24, 272, 274
Humphrey, S. E., 92, 93–94
Huntington, R., 97–98
Hutchison, S., 97–98
Hyland, P. K., 2, 10, 11, 17, 259–60, 265,
    268, 274, 374, 393, 394, 399

Iaffaldano, M. T., 273
Idris, M., 139
Ignatow, G., 210
Ilies, R., 383, 384
Ingels, D., 7, 12, 15, 186
Ioannidis, J., 246–47
Iseke, A., 53–54, 274
Isola, P., 319

Jacko, J. A., 310
Jackson, K. M., 203–4
Jackson, P., 359
Jackson, T. A., 94–95
Jacoby, S. M., 374, 375
Jacques, E., 136
Jaeger, M., 138–39
James, L. R., 122–23, 125–26
Javidan, M., 137, 144
Jean, V., 255, 262, 263–64, 268
Jensen, J. M., 6
Jeon, G., 229–30, 399
Jiang, K., 140
Jiang, Y., 211
Jimenez-Jimenez, D., 140
Johannesson, R., 123–24
Johnson, C. L., 31, 32
Johnson, E. C., 98–99
Johnson, J. W., 13, 15–16, 255, 256–57, 260, 264, 265–66, 267–68, 273–74
Johnson, K., 251
Johnson, R. H., 174, 187, 358–59, 445–46
Johnson, S. R., 3, 14, 16–17, 179, 379–80, 444
Jolton, J. A., 3, 50–51, 56, 59, 393
Jones, A. P., 122–23, 125–26
Jones, C., 319
Jones, L. V., 193
Jones, T. O., 273–74
Jordan, M. I., 205
Joseph, D. L., 89–91, 383–84
Judd, S., 306
Judge, T. A., 94–95, 160, 272, 274, 384, 409, 456
Junnonen, J., 138–39
Juster, F. T., 196

Kahn, R. L., 121, 135, 362, 376–77
Kahn, W. A., 88
Kahneman, D., 381–82
Kaiser, R. B., 31, 280
Kamen, A. M., 179
Kammeyer-Mueller, J. D., 272, 274
Kang, Y., 310
Kaplan, A., 378
Kaplan, J., 374
Kaplan, S., 10
Kappes, H. B., 383

Katz, D., 121, 135, 362, 376–77
Kaur, J., 4–5
Kavvoura, F., 246–47
Kawulich, B. B., 376
Keen, L., 38
Keeton, K. E., 7, 12, 15, 191–92
Keller, S., 141, 145
Kendall, L. M., 31–32, 90, 123–24
Kennedy, A., 137
Kern, M., 306–7
Kernbach, S., 307–8
Killham, E. A., 124–25, 409, 456
Kim, A., 140
Kim, E., 63–64
Kim, N. W., 319
Kim, Y., 139
Kind, C., 86, 130, 142, 456
King, E., 391, 392
Kirk, A., 313
Kirn, S. P., 392, 447–48
Klein, A., 144
Klein, C., 3, 255, 259–60, 267, 268, 393
Klein, D. A., 455
Klein, H. J., 90
Klein, K. J., 126, 289
Klein, N., 223
Kochan, T. A., 409–10
Koetsier, J., 400
Kompier, M., 400
Korman, A. K., 457
Kotrba, L., 135, 137, 145
Kotter, J. P., 137
Kouri, J., 246–47
Koustelios, A., 139
Kozlowski, S. W. J., 126, 289
Kratochwill, E., 144
Kraut, A. I., xi, 1, 2–3, 12, 56, 181, 272, 359, 391, 425, 427, 441, 443, 457
Krekel, C., 409
Kristof-Brown, A. L., 98–99, 158
Kropp, A., 86, 130, 142, 456
Krueger, A. B., 381–82
Krueger, R. A., 107, 108, 120
Kruger, J., 381
Kuhn, M., 251
Kumar, A., 205, 206
Kurtessis, J., 97–98
Kuyumcu, D., 359, 425

Ladd, R. T., 257
Lafferty, C., 142
Lafferty, J. D., 212
LaFollette, W. R., 124
Lam, H., 86, 130, 142, 456
Lam, S. K., 274
Landers, R. N., 175–76
Landis, R. S., 409, 455
Lane, N., 141, 145
Lange, S., 213–14
Laroche, P., 410
Latham, G. P., 55
Law, K. S., 53–54, 274
Lawler, E. E., 122, 273
Lawrence, P. R., 136
Le, H., 383
Leary, M. R., 96–97
LeBreton, J. M., 126, 255, 256, 257, 258–
    59, 262–63, 266, 267–68, 307
Lecha, M., 400
Lee, A., 384
Lee, J. Y., 380–81
Lee, K.-F., 452–53, 457
Lee, M., 139
Lee, T. W., 78
Lee, W. C., 130, 340
Lefkowitz, J., 394–95, 403
Lehman, J. A., 333–34
Leif, C., 141, 145
Leiter, M. P., 124–25
Lemon, S. C., 251
LePine, J. A., 88, 93
Leung, Y., 400
Levenson, A., 249, 425
Levine, R., 427
Lewin, K., 359
Lewis, R. L., 179
Liao, H., 140
Liberopoulos, G., 246–47
Liden, R. C., 97–98
Lievens, F., 154, 160
Likert, R., 136, 376
Lincoln, J. R., 294–95
Lindeman, R. H., 265
Litwin, G. H., 364
Liu, S., 140
Liu, Y., 211
Lizano, E., 140

Locke, E. A., 55, 89
Locke, K., 103
Lofquist, L. H., 261
Lohmann, S., 213–14
Long, D., 245–46
Looker, E. D., 202
Loosveldt, G., 394
Lorsch, J. W., 136
Louis, M., 137
Louviere, J. J., 162, 165
Lovato, C., 255, 259–60, 267, 268
Loveman, G. W., 273–74
Lowery, M. R., 176, 179
Lowman, G. H., 155–56
Lowman, R., 403
Lucifora, C., 409–10
Lundberg, C., 137
Lundby, K. M., 264
Luong, A., 394
Luria, G., 127–28
Lutz, K. A., 334
Lutz, R. J., 334

Macey, W. H., 8–9, 31, 46, 86–87, 88, 89,
    126, 130, 142, 174, 219, 250,
    257, 259–60, 274, 340, 360,
    426, 455–56
Mack, N., 120
Mackay, M. M., 409, 455
MacKenzie, S. B., 380–81
MacQueen, K. M., 120
Madden, A., 383–84
Maglio, S., 383
Malik, A., 306–7
Maltarich, M. A., 290, 291, 294, 301
Mandell, L. M., 49–50
Manivannan, A., 307–8
Mann, F. C., 375, 376
Mansfield, R., 123–24
Manzey, D., 191–92
Margiloff, A., 359
Marin, L., 154
Marinescu, I., 223
Markon, J., 450
Marrs, S., 340
Marshall, C., 116–17
Martin, D., 391
Martin, J., 137, 398, 401

Martin, N. R., 13, 105, 130–31, 259–62, 268, 384, 456
Maslow, A. H., 96–97
Massman, A., 399
Mastrangelo, P. M., 3–4, 42–44, 50–51, 51n1, 56, 454–55
Mathieu, M. J., 302
Matthews, R. A., 189–90
Matthijs, K., 394
Mauno, S., 140
Mausner, B., 93
Maxwell, S. E., 265
May, D. R., 88
Mayer, D., 383
Mayer, R. C., 97–98, 325, 333–34
Mayo, E., 103
McCabe, G. P., 265–66
McCance, A., 399
McClelland, D., 144, 203
McCune, E. A., 4, 12, 16–17, 176, 179
McDowell, T., 222
McFarland, L., 399
McGregor, D., 136
McLain, D., 11, 15
McManus, S., 378
Meade, A. W., 246–47
Mendes, W. B., 382
Meng, R., 409–10
Merenda, P. F., 265
Meyer, J. P., 5–6, 8–9, 89–91, 94–95, 96, 97–98, 251–52, 261
Mihalcea, R., 210
Miller, P. W., 409–10
Minchington, B., 153
Miori, V., 319
Mitchell, M. S., 97–98
Mitchell, T. R., 78
Mitchelson, J. K., 377
Mohr, D. C., 154
Molero, F., 139
Moore, D. S., 265–66
Moore, J. C., 196, 308
Moore, L., 137
Mor Barak, M., 140
Morgan, B. S., 24
Morgan, D. L., 107
Morgan, G., 376–77
Morgeson, F. P., 92, 93–94

Moriano, J., 139
Morris, D., 394
Mosley, R., 157
Mowday, R. T., 89, 90
Moye, M., 6
Muchinsky, P. M., 273
Mullins, M., 12–13
Murdock, C., 261

Nachreiner, F., 92, 93
Nadler, D. A., 365–66, 375, 425, 449
Nagle, B., 119
Nahrgang, J. D., 92, 93–94
Namenwirth, J. Z., 203
Namey, E., 120
Naranjo-Valencia, J., 140
Neale, W., 137
Neely, A., 307–8
Nehmad, E., 394
Neuman, W. L., 377
Neumann, E., 191–92
Newman, D. A., 89–91, 124, 229–30, 399, 409, 455
Ng, A. Y., 205
Ng, K. Y., 97–98
Ng, V., 306–7
Nielsen, F. A., 210
Nielsen, K., 140
Nieminen, L., 137, 142, 145
Norem, J. K., 383
Norman, D. A., 282–83
Norvell, M., 194
Nøstvold, B., 202
Nov, O., 307–8, 319

O'Malley, A., 6
O'Reilly, C. A., 137, 142, 146, 155, 160, 384
O'Rourke, E., 5, 10–11, 12, 114, 161, 306
Ock, J., 263
Oerlemans, W., 90
Oestereich, T., 403
Oettingen, G., 383
Oh, I. S., 383
Oldham, G. R., 89, 92, 93
Oliva, A., 319
Oliver, D. H., 367, 441, 450

Ones, D. S., 31
Organ, D. W., 273, 274
Orme, B. K., 165
Osborne, M. A., 408
Ostroff, C., 122, 128
Oswald, F. L., 263, 393
Ouchi, W. G., 137
Ouertani, Z. M., 307–8
Ozanne, J. L., 377

Page, A., 222
Pandey, A. V., 307–8, 319
Paolillo, A., 139–40
Parfyonova, N. M., 5–6, 251–52
Park, N., 382
Parker, A., 222
Parkington, J. J., 129, 130, 273, 375
Paro, P., 140
Parrigon, S., 307
Pascale, R., 283
Pasini, M., 139–40
Patsopoulos, N., 246–47
Patton, G. K., 274, 409, 456
Patton, M. Q., 376
Paul, A., 205, 206
Paul, K. B., 2, 3, 11, 31, 32, 360, 374
Paul, M. C., 128, 130, 137
Payne, R. L., 122–24
Payne, S. C., 129
Payne, S. L., 202
Pedhauzer, E. J., 245, 288
Peiró, J. M., 129, 130, 274
Pennebaker, J. W., 203
Perry, J., 273–74
Peters, T. J., 137, 180
Peterson, C., 382
Peterson, M., 137–38, 143
Pfeffer, J., 409–10
Pfister, H., 319, 320
Piccolo, R. F., 94–95
Piening, E. P., 53–54, 274
Pilch, I., 138–39
Pinheiro, J. C., 290
Plowman, S. K., 411–12, 456
Ployhart, R. E., 196–97, 247, 257, 399
Podsakoff, N. P., 380–81
Podsakoff, P. M., 380–81
Pokela, J., 120

Polonetsky, J., 393
Poole, M. S., 376–77
Porras, J., 137
Porter, C. O. L. H., 97–98
Porter, L. W., 89, 90, 273
Porter, M., 24
Porter, S. R., 56
Pratt, M. G., 103
Pressman, A., 374
Price, B. A., 255, 262, 263–64, 268
Price, C., 141, 145
Prien, E., 391, 394
Prusak, L., 220–21
Pugh, D. S., 122–23
Putka, D. J., 250, 263, 393

Quick, J. C., 228–29
Quinn, R. T., 137, 144, 392, 447–48

Raab, C., 130
Rakowski, W., 251
Rall, K., 319
Raudenbush, S., 290
Ray, R., 374
Reeder, M. C., 250
Reeves, D. W., 10, 11, 17, 259–60, 265, 268
Reichers, A., 143
Reichman, W., 403
Renaud, S., 409–10
Resick, C., 144
Rhee, M., 140
Rich, B. L., 88, 93
Riche, N. H., 320
Ridout, M. S., 292
Riis, J., 381
Ritchie, S., 135
Rivers, D. C., 246–47
Rizzo, J. R., 126
Robbins, S. B., 383
Roberts, B. W., 155–56, 383–84
Roberts, C. W., 203
Rogelberg, S. G., 42–43
Rogers, J., 409–10, 411
Rohrbaugh, J., 137, 144
Ronen, S., 447
Rosenthal, R., 449
Rosnow, R. L., 449

Ross, R. L., 211
Rossman, G. B., 116–17
Roth, P. L., 89–90, 243–44, 409, 455
Rothwell, J., 408
Rotolo, C. T., 2, 255, 262, 263–64, 268, 359, 360, 362, 367, 391, 394, 425–26, 427, 441
Rounds, J., 261
Rousseau, D. M., 76, 97–98, 137, 144, 156, 385
Rowh, M., 38
Roy, J., 251
Royston, P., 104–5
Rubin, D. B., 243–44
Rubino, C., 191–92
Rucci, A. J., 392, 447–48
Ruiz-Quintanilla, S., 137
Ruiz, S., 154
Rutigliano, P., 393, 394, 399
Ryan, A. M., 142, 145, 196–97, 247
Ryan, K., 274
Ryan, R. M., 96–97
Rynes, S. L., 130–31

Saad, L., 408
Saari, L. M., 6, 240–41, 274, 359, 391, 392, 395, 451–52
Sackmann, S., 137–38, 142
Saks, A. M., 88, 90, 142
Salanova, M., 88, 90, 130, 274
Salge, T. O., 53–54, 274
Saltzman, J. M., 3, 9–10, 11, 81
Salvaggio, A. N., 129
Sanchez, J., 12–13
Sandberg, J. A. C., 198
Sanders, M., 391
Sanz-Valle, R., 140
Sashkin, M., 391, 394
Sasser, W. E., 53–54, 273–74
Satterthwaite, M. L., 307–8, 319
Schaufeli, W. B., 88, 90, 92, 93
Schein, E. H., 449
Scherbaum, C. A., 6, 240–41, 262, 391, 392, 395, 451–52
Scherer, K., 400
Schiemann, W. A., 24
Schiuma, G., 307–8

Schkade, D. A., 381–82
Schlesinger, L. A., 53–54, 273–74
Schmelkin, L. P., 245, 288
Schmidt, A., 135
Schmidt, F. L., 53–54, 88, 124–25, 181, 274, 409, 411–12, 456
Schmitt, N., 196–97
Schneider, B., 1, 8–9, 11, 15–16, 17, 24, 31, 32, 86–87, 88, 89, 98, 121, 122, 124, 125–26, 128, 129, 130, 137, 140–41, 142, 143, 219, 261, 273–74, 340, 360, 375, 426, 455–56
Schoorman, F. D., 97–98
Schwab, D. P., 273
Schwartz, J., 220–21
Schwarz, N., 381–82
Scollon, C. N., 381
Scott, K., 176, 179
Semedo, C., 274
Senter, J. L., 126
Shah, P., 320
Shamdasani, P. N., 120
Shapiro, J., 1, 16–17
Shea, L., 120
Shenkar, O., 447
Shepherd, W., 9–10, 168, 273–74
Shull, A. C., 2, 360, 362, 367, 441
Silva, S., 139–40
Simonton, D. K., 383
Sims, H. P., 124
Sims, J., 222
Sims, K., 138
Sinar, E. F., 14, 306–7, 317–18
Sirota, D., 455
Skinner, J. L., 179
Slade, L. A., 196–97, 247
Slaughter, J. E., 86, 89–91, 93–95, 154
Smart, M., 223
Smerek, R., 135
Smith-Crowe, K., 246–47
Smith, J. P., 196
Smith, P. C., 31–32, 90, 123–24
Smither, J. W., 2, 360
Smoak, V. J., 255, 262, 263–64, 268
Snyder, R. A., 124
Snyderman, B. B., 93
Sogn-Grundvåg, G., 202

Sone, I., 202
Soo Yi, J., 310
Sowa, D., 97–98
Sparrowe, R. T., 97–98
Spector, P. E., 197
Spitzmüller, C., 191–92
Spitzmüller, M., 7, 12, 15, 191–92
Stanley, D. J., 89–91, 97–98, 261
Stanley, L. J., 5–6, 251–52
Stasko, J. Y., 310
Steblea, J., 120
Steers, R., 89, 90
Sternin, J., 283
Sternin, M., 283
Stewart, D. W., 120
Stewart, K. A., 97–98
Stinson, L. L., 196
Stoll, J., 9–10
Stone, A. A., 381–82
Stone, P. J., 203
Strauss, A. L., 203
Sturman, M. C., 130
Su, R., 261
Subirats, M., 129
Sucklow-Zimberg, K., 105, 391, 395
Sullivan, G., 457
Sung, S. Y., 274
Sunkavalli, S., 319
Sunstein, C. R., 345–46
Surface, E., 391, 394
Surowiecki, J., 227
Sutcliffe, K. M., 385
Sutton, M. T., 191–92
Svensson, C., 31
Swait, J. D., 162, 165
Swedberg, C., 224
Sweeney, P. J., 382
Synovec, R., 255, 259–60, 267, 268

Talbot, D. L., 158
Tate, R., 56, 59
Tatsioni, A., 246–47
Tay, L., 306–7
Taylor, C. W., 126–27
Tene, O., 393
Tenin, R., 224
Teräväinen, V., 138–39

Terzi, A., 139
Tetrick, L. E., 10, 228–29
Thaler, R. H., 345–46
Thibodeaux, W., 341–42
Thomas, D. A., 362
Thomas, D. R., 255, 268
Thomas, G., 384
Thompson, D., 408
Thompson, L., 391, 394
Thoresen, C. J., 274, 409, 456
Thurstone, L. L., 193, 375
Ting-Ding, J., 139
To, M. L., 381–82
Tolvanen, A., 140
Tomprou, M., 156
Tonidandel, S., 257, 258–59, 262–63, 266,
    391, 392
Topolnytsky, L., 89–91, 97–98, 261
Tornow, W. W., 273
Tourangeau, R., 196, 394
Traxel, N., 262–63
Triandis, H. C., 144, 196–97
Trist, E., 136
Trochim, W. M. K., 203–4
Tugade, M. M., 382
Tuller, M. D., 362, 367, 441
Turska, E., 138–39

Uhl-Bien, M., 222

Van De Ven, A. H., 376–77
van der Linden, D., 400
van Emmeri, H., 87
Van Maanen, J., 137
Van Quaquebeke, N., 16–17
Van Rooy, D. L., 41–42, 409
van Someren, M. W., 198
van Woerkom, M., 90
Vanhove, T., 394
Vardaman, J. M., 280
Viswesvaran, C., 409
Viteles, M. S., 338
Vo, A. A., 319
Vogel, D. R., 333–34
Voldnes, G., 202
Volini, E., 220–21
Von Bertalanffy, L., 376–77

von Treuer, K., 139
Vroom, V. R., 273

Waber, B., 6, 385, 393, 394–95, 400–1
Waclawski, J., 3, 14, 16, 39, 41–42, 43–44, 242,
    357–58, 359, 366, 375, 441, 449, 454–55
Wallace, J. C., 129
Walmsley, P. T., 13, 105, 130–31,
    259–62, 268
Wang, J., 211
Wang, W., 383–84
Wang, X. H., 94–95
Wang, Y., 211
Wanous, J. P., 156
Ward, G., 409
Waterman, R. H., 137, 180
Way, S. A., 130
Wayne, S. J., 97–98
Weber, R. P., 114–15, 120
Weick, K. E., 122, 142–43, 385
Weiner, S. P., 4–5, 7, 14, 38, 50–51, 56, 262,
    391, 393
Weiss, H. M., 272, 274
Weitzer, W. H., 56
Welniak, E., 196
Wenzel, R., 16–17
Wesslen, R. S., 211
Wesson, M. J., 90, 97–98
West, M., 122, 128
Westfall, J., 250
Westrick, P., 383
Whitcomb, M. E., 56
White, S. S., 128, 130, 137
Whitman, D. S., 41–42, 409
Wicher, E., 12–13
Wiebe, J., 210–11
Wiener, N., 376–77
Wigert, B., 233n3
Wilderom, C., 137–38
Wiley, J. W., 24, 273–74, 340, 392, 444,
    445, 448

Williams, N., 119
Willis, G. B., 104–5
Wilson, T., 210–11
Wiltse, D., 38
Wirtz, D., 381
Witkowski, D., 222
Wong, A., 409
Woo, S. E., 251–52
Woo, V. A., 259–60, 265, 268
Wood, D., 155–56
Woodsong, C., 120
Woznyj, H. M., 211

Xin, K. R., 53–54, 274
Xu, W., 211

Yagil, D., 130
Yan, T., 196, 394
Yang, Y., 205, 307
Yarkoni, T., 250
Yeh, C. S., 319
Yi, Y., 380
Yost, A., 86, 130, 142, 456
Yost, A. B., 6
Young, H. R., 383–84
Young, J., 393–94
Young, S. A., 31, 130, 340, 426, 455–56
Yu, G., 138–39

Zalesny, M. D., 407
Zeitz, G., 294–95
Zerella, S., 139
Zhang, H., 255, 259–60, 267, 268
Zhang, J., 306–7
Zhao, H., 97–98
Zickar, M. J., 154
Zielinski, D., 351
Zillman, C., 227–28
Zimmerman, R. D., 98–99
Zohar, D., 127–28, 129
Zumbo, B. D., 255, 268

Subject Index

Tables and figures are indicated by *t* and *f* following the page number

For the benefit of digital users, indexed terms that span two pages (e.g., 52–53) may, on occasion, appear on only one of those pages.

accept/decline survey, 72, 74*t*
action-driving design, 58*f*, 58
action-planning *vs.* action-taking, AI and, 339
action pulsing surveys, 62
action-taking challenges, in AI, 340
action-tracking design, 58*f*, 58
adaptability framework, 137
additional report requests, 248–49
ad hoc surveys, 62–63
affective commitment, 89–91, 94–95.
    See also engagement surveys
AFINN, 210
aggregation. *See* ICC (1) values
AI. *See* artificial intelligence
allocation exercises, 162–64, 164*f*, 166*t*
alluvial diagrams, 313–14, 314*f*
always-on polling, 63–64
analytics
    advanced modeling, 401–2
    ANOVA techniques, 276–77
    emotive, 400
    key drivers (*See* key driver analysis)
    linkage analyses (*See* linkage analyses)
    person-centric, 5–6, 9–10
    predictive, 250–51, 255
    text (*See* text analytics)
    text analysis tools, 182
annotating techniques, 320
ANOVA techniques, 276–77, 290
APA ethical guidelines, 396–97
artificial intelligence
    AI-augmented solutions, 342–50, 352–53
    applications of, 4–5, 425–26, 452–53, 457
    background, 338–39
    benefits of, 351–53

big data and, 341 (*See also* big data)
defined, 339
forward-thinking practices, 342–50
limitations/considerations, 350–51
manager coaching, 345–46
managers as facilitators, 342, 350
network performance, 341–42
NLP, 344–45, 351 (*See also* natural language processing (NLP))
open-ended questions, 204*f*, 204–5
organizational change, 349–50
organizational learning, 349
in organization development, 7
organization-wide action, 346–47
platform defined, 339
predictive models, 348–49
real-time changes/connectivity, 341
results analyses/interpretation, 343–45
stakeholder education, 351
survey results integration, 347–48
teams, 341–42, 350
terminology, 339
assimilation survey, 72, 74*t*
attraction–selection–attrition theory (ASA), 261
attrition/boomerang survey, 72, 74*t*

bag-of-words model, 212, 212*t*
behavioral engagement, 87*f*, 87, 97–98
Belmont Report, 396
benchmarking
    background, 12
    compromises, 184
    consortia, 174–75
    context provision, 183–84
    continuous listening programs, 182

benchmarking (*cont.*)
  data analysis comparisons, 247–48
  data protection, 178
  defined, 171
  demographic reporting, 178–79
  external, data evaluation, 176–80
  external, data sources, 172–76
  generalizability, 176–77
  geography in, 177
  internal *vs.* external, 171–72
  item comparability, 177–78
  leveraging, 183
  methodological considerations, 179–80
  normative data/databases, 171,
    176–77, 178
  panels/crowdsourcing, 175–76
  points of reference in, 177
  role/utility of, 180–81
  single-item measures, 181
  studies/white papers, 173
  survey best-practice sharing, 171
  survey content, 181–82
  survey vendor, 173–74
  text analysis tools, 182
best practices
  action, importance of, 450–51
  benchmarking, 171
  big data, 452–53
  conceptual models, 447–48
  data visualization, 319
  DELTA impacts, 457
  employee engagement, 455–56
  federal norms databank, 446
  methodology, 453–55
  organization development (*See*
    organization development (OD))
  performance, shifts to, 446–47
  privacy/transparency, 402–3, 453
  results, presentation of, 449, 450–51
  survey administration, 445–48
  survey consortia, 445–46
  technology impact, 451–53
big data
  applications of, 425–26, 452–53
  artificial intelligence and, 341
  best practices, 452–53
  data visualization, 306–7
  executive presentations, 324

  lifecycle surveys, 69, 83
  linkage analyses, 284
  privacy/transparency, 392, 402–3
biometrics, 223–25
bootstrapping, 265
bubble lines, 318–19, 318*t*
bubble plots, 314*f*, 314–15
bump charts, 316*f*, 316–17

careless respondent identification, 243
case studies
  accident reduction, 281–82
  employee survey research, 375–78
  leader personality/effectiveness, 281
  organization development (OD),
    368–71, 370*f*
  pulse surveys, 368–71, 370*f*
  surveys for change, 368–71, 370*f*
census–sample alternating pattern, 41–42
census surveys
  census-based pulse, 60–61
  described, 59–60
  sampling *vs.*, 40–41
change. *See* surveys for change
choice architecture, 345–46
choropleth maps, 317*f*, 317
circle packing, 315*f*, 315–16
classification/regression trees (CARTs), 251
climate surveys
  analysis levels, 125–26, 132n3
  background, 121–22
  as description, 123–25
  focus in, 126–29, 132n2
  functionalism, 123
  gestalt in, 122, 123, 128
  items, 127–29
  job satisfaction, 123–25, 130–31
  as perception, 122–23
  strength construct, 129
  validity, 129–31
closing questions, in focus groups, 109
cluster maps, 213–14
cluster modeling, 168
competing values model, 137
composition process, 289
Comprehensive R Archive Network
  (CRAN), 244
ConcentriCloud, 213–14

concept mapping, 203–4
conceptual models, 447–48
concierge services, 345–46
confidence intervals, 265–66
confidence survey, 72, 74*t*
confidential/anonymous surveys, 239–41
confidentiality. *See* privacy/transparency
conjoint analysis, 164*f*, 164–65, 166*t*
consortia, 445–46
constructs. *See* specific constructs
content analysis, history of, 203–4
continuous listening
    accountability, 57
    applications/data usage, 41–42
    background, 53–54
    benchmarking programs, 182
    defined, 54, 426
    design of, 55, 57–66, 58*f*
    development of, 3–4
    experience/feedback/connectivity, 55
    information, providing, 55
    leader- /manager-created, 56–57
    leadership involvement/ownership, 55
    opportunities/risks, 55–57
    sample size, 45
    survey fatigue, 56
    tracking, 54
    tracking *vs.* action/change focus, 56
contrasting techniques, 320
corporate culture. *See* culture
correlated topic models (CTMs),
    212–13, 213*f*
correlation/regression techniques, 276–77
cross-cultural equivalence, 196–97
crowdsourcing/panels, 175–76, 227–28
culture. *See also* employee listening systems
    facets of, 140
    Hofstede's model, 143
    national culture differences model, 137
    Organizational Culture Assessment
        Instrument (OCAI), 138–39, 144–45
    Organizational Culture Inventory
        (OCI), 142, 144
    organizational culture model
        (Hofstede), 143
    Organizational Culture Profile, 146
    Organizational Culture Survey
        (Denison), 145

current practice. *See* employee survey
    research case study

daily diaries, 381–82
dashboards, 438
data analysis. *See also* analytics; key driver
    analysis; text analytics
    additional report requests, 248–49
    administration method, 242
    advanced modeling, 401–2
    ANOVA techniques, 276–77
    careless respondent identification, 243
    cleaning, 243–45
    confidential/anonymous surveys, 239–41
    factors/dimensions, 245
    history/norms/benchmark
        comparisons, 247–48
    item design, 242
    means, 245–46
    minimum *n* rules, 248
    missing data, 243–45
    model-building, 249–52
    multicollinearity, 250, 255
    organizational hierarchy, 241–42
    percent responding, 245–46
    person-centered approaches, 251–52
    predictive analytics, 250–51, 255
    privacy/transparency, 248–49
    reporting elements, 245–49
    statistical significance reporting, 249
    structure, 239–42
    variability, 246–47
data-based feedback model, 2,
    283–84, 365–66
data mining evolution, 4–6
data protection regulations, 397–99
data visualization
    audience, 308–9
    background, 306
    big data, 306–7
    data sources, 312–13
    design principles, 311–12, 311*t*
    evidence-based best practices, 319
    foundational techniques, 320
    geospatial, 317*f*, 317, 317*t*
    group comparisons, 313–14, 313*t*
    hierarchical/part-to-whole, 315*f*,
        315–16, 315*t*

data visualization (*cont.*)
  interactivity, 310–11
  legibility, 309
  modality, 309–11
  over-time, 316*f*, 316–17, 316*t*
  potential for research, 306–7
  print *vs.* slide-based presentations, 310
  proficiency/objectives, 307–8
  text, 318–19, 318*t*
  tools, 321
  type matched to purpose, 313–18,
    313*t*, 314*f*
  variable connections/relationships,
    314–15, 314*t*
Day Reconstruction Method, 381–82
deep-dive pulse surveys, 61–62
DELTA impacts, 457
design. *See* survey design
Doctors Without Borders, 230
dominance analysis (DA), 256–57
dot maps, 317*f*, 317
dynamic dashboards, 438

ELSs. *See* employee listening systems
e-mail metadata, 220–21, 233n2
emotive analytics, 400
employee burnout, 233n3
employee engagement. *See* engagement
    surveys
employee engagement constructs, 8–9
employee experience constructs, 9
employee-focused feedback systems, 4–5
employee health/well-being data, 228–29
employee lifecycle constructs, 9–10
employee listening systems. *See also*
    linkage analyses; *specific frameworks
    or models by name*
  analysis units, 140
  attitudes/behaviors influence, 139
  background, 135–36
  culture (*See* culture)
  diversity/inclusion, 139–40
  history of, 136–38
  job satisfaction, 139
  meaning making, 142–43
  Microsoft, 221–22
  mixed, 232–33
  organizational type, 138–39

  outcome drivers, 142
  people mobilization, 148
  performance, 148
  personal interactions, 140–41
  prescriptive *vs.* descriptive
    approaches, 141–42
  progress tracking, 147
  qualitative *vs.* quantitative methods,
    141, 147
  real time/long term, 147–48
employee opinion survey, 72, 74*t*, 78*f*,
    78–79, 81
employee preferences
  allocation exercises, 162–64, 164*f*, 166*t*
  attributes, satisfaction
    assessment, 168–69
  candidates/general labor
    market, 159–60
  conjoint analysis, 162, 164*f*, 164–65, 166*t*
  defined, 153
  direct preference measurement,
    162–65, 166*t*
  employees, critical to retain, 159
  employees, customer-facing, 159
  employees, experiencing major
    changes, 158
  employer branding, 153
  EVP, 153, 154–55, 156–57
  executive leadership, 157–58
  focus groups, 161
  individual fitness judgments, 155–56
  interviews, 161
  job satisfaction, 154
  measurement rationale, 154–57
  measures, choice of, 160
  measures, tool selection, 160–69
  new hires, 158
  normative, 155–56
  open-ended survey questions, 161
  organizational resources usage, 157
  personas, 168
  profiles, 168
  publicly available data sources, 161
  ranking exercises, 162, 163*f*, 166*t*
  revealed choices, 169
  segmentation, 168
  signature experience, 156
  stakeholders, 157–60

talent/business strategy
relationship, 156–57
value congruence, 155
employee sensing. *See also* surveys/sensing
actual behaviors focus, 222
background, 219–20, 233n1
biometrics/sociometrics, 223–25
blue-collar work applicability, 224–25
classification, 220*f*
content bias, 223
course correction, 224
data privacy, 222–23 (*See also* privacy/
transparency)
employee health/well-being data, 228–29
external data sources, 220*f*, 220
external employee reviews,
229–30, 231–32
Hawthorne effect, 225
internal communication portals, 221–23
internal data sources, 220*f*, 220
job portals, 230–32
listening architecture, mixed
systems, 232–33
network data, 220–21, 222–23, 233n2
passive data sources, 220*f*, 220
performance management data, 225–26
publicly available data, 230–32
service request data, 225–26
structured qualitative input, 227–28
technology investments, 223
technology precision, 225
work history/skills/capabilities,
230, 231–32
employee sentiment/sentiment analytics
constructs, 10–11
employee survey research
analyis/interpretation errors, 382–85
bias/causality, 380–81
contextual factors overemphasis, 383–84
cross-sectional design limitations, 379–80
defined, 375
evaluating/remembering self, 381
limitations of, 377–78
methodological/analytical
mistakes, 378–85
more is better assumption, 382–83
principles, 375–77
program development, 385–86

results-change assumption, 384
theoretical foundations, 375–78
variance reduction, 381
employee survey research case study
administration methods, 437–38, 437*t*
background, 425–26
confidentiality, 436–37, 436*t*
engagement surveys as predominant,
432–33, 432*t*
method/sample, 427, 428*t*
program satisfaction, 440*f*, 440–41
purpose of, 427
results, caveats, 429–30
structure, 429
survey cadence, 433–34
survey content as diagnostic, 435, 435*t*
survey distribution, 438–40, 439*f*
survey frequency, 433*t*, 434*t*
surveys as key strategy, 431, 431*t*
employee termination surveys, 77–80, 78*f*
employee turnover attitudinal antecedents
case study, 280
employee value proposition (EVP), 9–10
engagement. *See* engagement surveys
engagement surveys
background, 8–9
best practices, 455–56
defining/measuring, 88–91
design of, 99
dissemination, 100
elements of, 87*f*, 87
guiding principles, 87*f*, 87
interventions, designing, 95–99, 100
JCM, 93–94
key drivers, measuring, 92–95, 99
leadership, 94–95
need satisfaction, 96–97
person–environment fit, 98–99
rationale, 91, 99
recommendations, 99–100
social exchange, 97–98
ethics. *See* privacy/transparency
executive presentations
advocacy, 336
audience, 332–33
background, 324–25
big data, 324
data visualization, 308–9

executive presentations (*cont.*)
  delivering, 334–36
  employee preferences, 157–58
  format selection, 332–34
  objective, clarifying, 325–26
  in person *vs.* virtual, 333
  pictures *vs.* prose, 333–34
  presentation *vs.* workshop, 334
  static *vs.* dynamic, 334
  story creation, 326–32
  surveys/sensing presentations, 14
  time allotment, 333
exit survey/interview, 72, 74*t*, 79–80
external consultants, 335–36
external employee reviews, 229–30, 231–32

federal norms databank, 446
focus groups
  analyses, combining, 116–17
  assistants, 111–12
  closing questions, 109
  conducting, 113–14
  content analysis, 114–15, 120
  design of, 106–18
  employee preferences, 161
  facilitator guide preparation, 109–10
  facilitators, 110–12
  findings, reporting, 117–18
  history of, 104
  location selection/scheduling, 112
  note takers, 110–12
  opening questions, 108
  participants, inviting, 113
  planning, 106–7
  post-survey administration/analysis, 105
  procedure establishment, 107–12, 109*t*
  as qualitative research, 103–4
  quantitative analysis, 115–16
  question development, 107–9, 111*t*
  recordings, 112
  resources, 119–20
  sampling strategies, 106–7
  survey development, 104–5
  virtual, conducting, 113–14
formal design, 58*f*, 58
formality in design, 58*f*, 58–59
full-range model/leadership styles,
  92, 94–95

Gallup Q^{12}, 15, 124–25, 412, 416, 456
Gallup Workplace Audit, 88
General Data Protection Regulation
  (GDPR), 240–41, 397–99, 453
General Inquirer, 203
geospatial visualization, 317*f*, 317, 317*t*
Gilbane Building Company, 224
global service climate, 128–29
GLOBE project, 137, 144
group comparison visualizations,
  313–14, 313*t*
group level analysis. *See* multilevel analysis

hierarchical/part-to-whole visualization,
  315*f*, 315–16, 315*t*
high performance model, 274
Hofstede's model of organizational
  culture, 143
horizon charts, 316*f*, 316–17
HRIS data files, 239–40
Human Synergistics, 142, 144

IBM, 227–28
ICC (1) values. *See* multilevel analysis
idea jams, 66
identified surveys, 392, 395, 451–52
informal design, 58*f*, 58–59
Information Technology Survey Group
  (ITSG), 12, 174
integrated survey model, 364*f*, 364–65
intention-to-quit item, 78*f*, 78–79, 79*f*, 80*t*
internal communication portals, 221–23
internal HR leaders, 335
internal survey team members, 335
interpretivism, 377
introductory questions, 108–9
item response theory, 247
items. *See* survey items

JD-R model, 93
job characteristics model (JCM), 92, 93–94
job demands–resources (JD-R) model, 92, 93
job portals, 230–32

key/core questions, 109
key driver analysis
  background, 254–55
  capitalization on chance, 260

case study, 257–59, 258*t*
causality, assuming, 267
criticism of, 259–62
distributional properties, 262–63
dominance analysis, 256–57
engagement surveys (*See* engagement
    surveys)
importance weights, 267–68
intention-to-quit, 78*f*, 78–79, 79*f*, 80*t*
item content, 263–64
job satisfaction, 255–56 (*See also* job
    satisfaction)
latent factor structure, 261
libraries, 13
linkage analyses, 142, 268 (*See also*
    linkage analyses)
measurement error, 266
methods, 255–57
multivariate RWA, 258–59
perceived organizational support, 97–98
random item selection *vs.,* 260
relative weight analysis (RWA), 256–57
retention, 79*f*, 80, 80*t*
sample size, 265
scales *vs.* items, 264
significance tests, 265–66
situational specificity, 261–62
standard deviations impacts, 259–60
standard errors, 265–66
temporal specificity, 261–62
variable types, 262–64

labor unions
background, 407
communication with front-line
    employees, 419
continuous feedback, 415
engagement, increasing, 417–19
engagement, union *vs.* nonunion
    employees, 415–16, 416*f*
engagement data, providing, 418
involvement in, 408–9
job attitudes of members, 409–13, 413*t*
leader succession-planning
    process, 418
manager hiring/promotion, 418
organizational tone setting, 417
progress conversations, 418–19

public sentiment, 408–9
supervisors/managers selection, 417
supervisor training, 417–18
surveying, challenges to, 413–14
survey participation rates,
    ensuring, 413–14
workforce management
    challenges, 414–17
work tasks stipulations, 415
latent class modeling, 168
latent Dirichlet allocation (LDA),
    211–12, 212*t*
latent semantic analysis (LSA), 209
leadership. *See* executive presentations
lexicons, 210
libertarian paternalism, 345–46
lifecycle surveys
background, 68–69
design, 84–85
employee turnover, 77–80, 78*f*
implementation challenges, 82–84
individual experience *vs.* organizational
    performance, 69–71
program planning, 69–73
tool *vs.* objective, 70, 71–72
types of, 72, 74*t* (*See also specific surveys
    by name*)
utilization of, 73–81
Likert-type scales, 7–195
line charts, 316*f*, 316–17
Linguistic Inquiry and Word Count
    program (LIWC), 203
linkage analyses
big data, 284
case studies, 279–82
data sources, 275
efficacy of, 340
employee turnover attitudinal
    antecedents case study, 280
findings, presentation to decision
    makers, 282–83
history of, 272–74
importance of, 284
key drivers, 142, 268
null/nontheoretical findings, 279
organizational action, 282–84
organizational members
    involvement, 283–84

linkage analyses (*cont.*)
  outliers/positive deviants/
    exceptions, 283
  predictive validity, 191–92
  process, 274–77
  response scales, 194
  restriction of range, 278–79
  statistical power, 278
  techniques, 276–77
  time-lag issues, 277–78
  trends in, 392
  units of analysis, 275–76
LinkedIn v HiQ Labs, 233n4
listening architecture, mixed
  systems, 232–33
listwise deletion, 244
loss of data, 243–44

machine learning. *See* natural language
  processing (NLP)
manager coaching, AI and, 345–46
manager-driven polling, 64–65
managers as facilitators, 342, 350
mass-customized survey model,
  364*f*, 364–65
maximum likelihood estimation
  (MLE), 244
Mayflower consortium, 12, 174, 358–59,
  360, 445–46
Médecins Sans Frontières (Doctors
  Without Borders), 230
Microsoft, 221–22
Microsoft Excel, 321
mind maps, 213–14
minimum *n* rules, 248
missing data, 243–45
model-building, 249–52
multilevel analysis
  background, 288–90
  between-group differentiation,
    291–95, 293*f*
  constructs/values relationship, 300–1
  described, 290–91
  individual psychometrics and,
    301–2, 302*t*
  low, interpreting, 295–97
  referents, broad *vs.* focused, 297–98
  R statistical code, 304–5

sample description, 297–302
SPSS syntax, 305
stability of, 299–300, 299*t*
multilevel measurement. *See* ICC (1) values
multiple imputation (MI), 244

national culture differences model, 137
natural language processing (NLP)
  artificial intelligence, 344–45, 351
  bag-of-words model, 212
  CTMs, 212–13, 213*f*
  definitions, 207*t*
  described, 204*f*, 204–5
  internal capability *vs.* external
    vendors, 214–15
  latent Dirichlet allocation (LDA),
    211–12, 212*t*
  latent semantic analysis, 209
  machine learning, 4–6, 9–10, 202, 204*f*,
    204–5, 207, 215, 276–77, 348, 349,
    391, 392, 401–2
  principal components analysis, 209
  resources, 215–16
  sentiment analysis, 10–11, 210–11
  techniques, 206–13, 207*t*
  text classification algorithms, 210–13
  Tf-idf, 208–9
  topic modeling, 211
  word relatedness, 208–9
  word2vec, 209
Natural Language Toolkit (NLTK), 216
network data, 220–21, 222–23, 233n2
new hire surveys. *See* onboarding/new
  hire survey
New Product Vitality Index (NPVI), 34–35
NLP. *See* natural language
  processing (NLP)
normative data in employee
  preferences, 155–56
nudge theory, 345–46

omnibus surveys, 63
onboarding/new hire survey, 72, 73–77,
  74*t*, 75*f*
online surveys, 451
open-ended questions
  artificial intelligence, 204*f*, 204–5
  background, 202

CTMs, 212–13, 213*f*
data analysis, 242
employee preferences, 161
internal capability *vs.* external
    vendors, 214–15
latent Dirichlet allocation (LDA),
    211–12, 212*t*
latent semantic analysis, 209
natural language processing (*See* natural
    language processing (NLP))
sentiment analysis, 210–11
text analytics (*See* text analytics)
text data visualization, 213–14
Tf-idf, 208–9
topic modeling, 211
word relatedness, 208–9
word2vec, 209
organizational change, AI and, 349–50
organizational climate. *See* climate surveys
Organizational Culture Assessment
    Instrument (OCAI), 138–39, 144–45
Organizational Culture Inventory (OCI),
    142, 144
Organizational Culture Profile, 146
Organizational Culture Survey
    (Denison), 145
Organizational Health Index
    (OHI), 145–46
organizational learning, AI and, 349
organizational network analysis
    (ONA), 220–21
organizational sensing, 191–92
organizational strategy constructs, 11
organization development (OD).
    See also surveys for change
    artificial intelligence in, 7
    best practices, 448–51
    case study, 368–71, 370*f*
    decline of, 357–58
    diminishing effect/observational
        change, 366–68, 367*f*
    elements of, 366
    evolution of, 359
    level of operation, 365–66
    social systems perspective, 362–63
    survey implementation, 13
    360 feedback for, 364
OrgVitality, 72–73

orienting techniques, 320
over-time visualization, 316*f*, 316–17, 316*t*

pairwise deletion, 244
panels/crowdsourcing, 175–76
parallel coordinates, 314*f*, 314–15
perceived organizational support, 97–98
performance management data, 225–26
person-centric analytics, 5–6, 9–10
Polyglot, 216
predictive analytics, 250–51, 255
predictive validity
    artificial intelligence, 348–49
    linkage analyses, 191–92
    survey items, 7–192, 199
prehire survey, 72, 74*t*
principal components analysis (PCA), 209
privacy/transparency
    advanced analytics modeling, 401–2
    APA ethical guidelines, 396–97
    Belmont Report, 396
    best practices, 453
    big data, 392, 402–3
    confidential/anonymous surveys data
        analysis, 239–41
    data analysis, 248–49
    data breaches, 393
    data-collection methods, 399–401
    data integration/storage, 401
    data protection in benchmarking, 178
    data protection regulations, 397–99
    decision-guiding principles, 394–99
    employee misconduct, 393
    employee perceptions/data quality, 393–94
    employee sensing data, 222–23
    identified surveys, 392, 395, 451–52
    information access, 393
    levels of concern, 394, 397–99
    recommendations/best practices, 402–3
    risks to, 393
    sensitive items, 196
    survey participation rates,
        ensuring, 413–14
    in surveys/sensing generally, 6
    technology in, 391–93, 399–402
    trends case study, 436–37, 436*t*
    trends in, 392–93
    trust issues, 394

publicly available data sources, 161
pulse surveys
  action pulsing, 62
  ad hoc, 62–63
  always-on polling, 63–64
  background, 53–54
  case study, 368–71, 370*f*
  census-based, 60–61
  data visualization, 312–13
  deep-dive, 61–62
  design (*See* survey design)
  limitations of, 3–4, 357–58, 366
  manager-driven polling, 64–65
  mixed methods, 65–66
  tracking, 54

Ramco Systems, 221
ranking exercises, 162, 163*f*, 166*t*
RawGraphs, 321
RcmdrPlugin.temis, 215
reaction measures, 66
relative importance, 256
relative weights analysis (RWA),
  256–57, 276–77
response rate/response rate bias, 243–44
results, ownership of, 14
results, ownership of in AI, 14
retention drivers, 79*f*, 80, 80*t*
retirement preparation survey, 72, 74*t*
RFID technology, 223–24
R programming language, 205–6, 210,
  215, 244

sampling strategies
  appropriate population
    determination, 11
  bias in, 48–49
  cluster sampling, 48–49, 51n3
  concepts in, 42–43
  error in, 3–4, 42–44, 51n1
  focus groups, 106–7
  methods, 48–49, 51n3
  prescribed minimum sample size, 43–
    46, 45*t*, 51n1, 51n2
  sample sizes/statistical rigor, 46–47, 47*t*
  weighting, 49–50, 51n4
scatterplots, 314*f*, 314–15
segmentation, 168

self-determination theory, 96–97
sensing. *See* employee sensing
sensor technologies, 400
sentiment analysis, 10–11, 210–11
sequencing techniques, 320
service–profit chain, 273–74
service request data, 225–26
single-item measures, 181
singular value decomposition, 209
SKDA. *See* key driver analysis
slopegraphs, 313–14, 314*f*
social media in employee sensing, 221–22
sociometrics, 223–25
spaCY (Python), 216
stakeholder education, AI and, 351
Stanford CoreNLP, 216
state engagement surveys. *See* engagement
  surveys
statistical approaches. *See* data analysis
stemming/lemmatization, 206
stop word removal, 206
strategic climate. *See* climate surveys
strategic surveys
  analysis/intervention levels, 28
  appetite for truth assessment, 26
  approach/technique, 31–32
  background, 23–24
  business focus, 28–29
  complacency, 35
  concepts, definitions, 24–25
  creativity, 35–36
  history data, 27
  influence of, 34–35
  leadership as client, 33–34
  nature of, 26–33
  relevancy, 25–26
  as self-teaching tool, 30–31
  success/failure, 29–30
  tool selection, 32–33
stratified random sampling, 48–49, 51n3
stream graphs, 316*f*, 316–17
strength of constructs, 129
structural equation modeling
  (SEM), 276–77
structured qualitative input, 227–28
sunbursts, 315*f*, 315–16
supervised/unsupervised learning, 5–6
supplemental pulses, 41–42

suppressor variables, 268
survey design. *See also under specific*
     survey types
  applications/data usage, 43–46
  approach selection, 41–42
  construct validity, 15–16
  data analysis, 242
  data visualization principles,
     311–12, 311*t*
  integrated model, 364*f*, 364–65
  mass-customized model, 364*f*, 364–65
  motivations in, 11
  prescribed minimum sample size, 43–
     46, 45*t*, 51n1, 51n2
  pulse surveys, 38–40, 57–66, 58*f*
  recommendations, 50–51
  sample sizes/statistical rigor, 46–47, 47*t*
  sampling strategies (*See* sampling
     strategies)
  sampling *vs.* census, 40–41
  statistical significance, 45–46, 51n2
  weighting, 49–50, 51n4
survey items
  actionable, creation of, 5–190
  climate surveys (*See* climate surveys)
  content domains selection, 2–6
  cultural differences in
     interpretation, 196–97
  design of, 7, 195, 198
  difficulty levels, 191
  infinity sliders, 192–95
  pilot testing, 188–89, 198–99
  practice recommendations, 188–95
  predictive validity, 191–92, 199
  response scale format, 2
  response scales, 192–95
  sensitive items, 196
  simple *vs.* complex, 192
  summary of steps, 197–99
  surveys for change, 363–65, 364*f*
  total number determination, 189–90
survey key driver analysis (SKDA), 13,
     105, 254. *See also* key driver analysis
Survey Monkey, 452
survey results integration, AI and, 347–48
surveys for change. *See also* organization
     development (OD)
  background, 357

capability development, 371
case study, 368–71, 370*f*
characteristics of, 361–68
described, 360–61
diminishing effect/observational
     change, 366–68, 367*f*
evolution of, 358–61
integrated survey model, 364*f*, 364–65
item selection, 363–65, 364*f*
leadership alignment/sponsorship, 362–63
mass-customized survey model,
     364*f*, 364–65
purpose, clarity of, 361
purposes of, 360, 360*t*
results, communication/employee
     usage of, 365–68
social systems perspective, 362–63
transparency in, 365–66
surveys/sensing. *See also* employee sensing
  analysis level, 12–13
  appropriate population
     determination, 11
  benchmarking (*See* benchmarking)
  business case building, 17
  content focusing, 8–11
  data science in, 7–8
  data/technology evolution, 4–6
  data usage, 16–17
  executive presentations, 14
  findings/action-taking, 13–14
  focus of, 444–45
  meaning-making, 12–13
  methodology, evolution of, 2–6
  privacy/transparency, 6
  purpose of, 443–44
  qualitative data leveraging, 12
  real-time feedback, 13–14
  results, ownership of, 14

teams, AI and, 350
text analytics. *See also* natural language
     processing (NLP)
  data visualization, 213–14
  evolution, 203–4
  internal capability *vs.* external
     vendors, 214–15
  preprocessing techniques, 205–6
  tools, 182

TextBlob (Python), 216
text data visualization, 318–19, 318*t*
Tf-idf, 208–9
Thoresen, C. J., 456
3M
   analysis/intervention levels, 28
   appetite for truth assessment, 26
   approach/technique, 31–32
   background, 23–24
   business focus, 28–29
   concepts, definitions, 24–25
   creativity, 35–36
   history data, 27
   influence of, 34–35
   leadership as client, 33–34
   nature of, 26–33
   relevancy, 25–26
   success/failure, 29–30
   tool selection, 32–33
tidytext package (R), 210
tm (application), 215
tokenization, 205
topic modeling, 211
trait engagement, 87*f*, 87
transactional leaders, 94

transformational leaders, 94–95, 97, 98
transition questions, 109
tree maps, 315*f*, 315–16

unionization. *See* labor unions

validity of constructs, 15–16
variable connections/relationships
   visualization, 314–15, 314*t*
variance inflation factors (VIFs), 250
virtual focus groups, 66
visual correlation matrices, 314*f*, 314–15

well-being constructs, 10
white space elimination/lowercase
   conversion, 205–6
word clouds, 213–14, 318–19, 318*t*
word trees, 318–19, 318*t*
word2vec, 209
work engagement, 89–91, 94–95. *See also*
   engagement surveys
work history/skills/capabilities,
   230, 231–32
written comment analysis, 5. *See also*
   natural language processing (NLP)